C2 000000 8871
KU-673-707

BIRMINGHAM LIBRARY SERVICES
DISCARD

THE HISTORY OF WARWICKSHIRE COUNTY CRICKET CLUB

THE CHRISTOPHER HELM COUNTY CRICKET HISTORIES

Series Editors:
Peter Arnold and Peter Wynne-Thomas

DERBYSHIRE
John Shawcroft, with a personal view by Bob Taylor

GLAMORGAN
Andrew Hignell, with a personal view by Tony Lewis

GLOUCESTERSHIRE
David Green, with a personal view by B. D. Wells

HAMPSHIRE
Peter Wynne-Thomas, with a personal view by John Arlott

KENT
Dudley Moore, with a personal view by Derek Underwood

LANCASHIRE
Peter Wynne-Thomas, with a personal view by Brian Statham

MIDDLESEX
David Lemmon, with a personal view by Denis Compton

SURREY
David Lemmon, with a personal view by Peter May

WORCESTERSHIRE
David Lemmon, with a personal view by Basil D'Oliveira

YORKSHIRE
Anthony Woodhouse, with a personal view by Sir Leonard Hutton

THE HISTORY OF WARWICKSHIRE COUNTY CRICKET CLUB

Jack Bannister

With a personal view by
M.J.K. SMITH

CHRISTOPHER HELM
A & C Black · London

Christopher Helm (Publishers) Ltd, Imperial House,
21–25 North Street, Bromley, Kent BR1 1SD,
a subsidiary of A & C Black (Publishers) Ltd,
35 Bedford Row, London WC1R 4JH

ISBN 0-7470-0217-7

A CIP catalogue record for this book is available from the British Library

Black-and-white photographs © Ken Kelly

Typeset by Cotswold Typesetting Ltd, Gloucester
Printed and bound by Biddles Ltd, Guildford, Surrey

CONTENTS

A Personal View by M. J. K. Smith 1

1. The Club is Formed 9
2. The First Decade 15
3. Success in 1893 27
4. First-class Status and the County Championship 32
5. Into the Twentieth Century 42
6. The Arrival of Frank Foster 49
7. County Champions 54
8. After the Lord Mayor's Show 66
9. Starting All Over Again, 1919 71
10. Calthorpe Hands Over to Wyatt 81
11. The Wyatt Years 90
12. Wyatt Sacked as War Stops Play 99
13. Rebuilding Again 107
14. Dollery's Path to the Summit 124
15. Champions Forty Years On 134
16. The End of the Dollery Era 144
17. The Start of the Smith Years, 1957–1959 165
18. A Lord's Final 176
19. From One Smith to Another 190
20. Champions a Third Time 204
21. A Late 1970s Decline 222
22. The Willis Era, 1980–1984 234
23. From Strife to Peace, 1985–1989 252

Epilogue 276

Statistical Section 279

Bibliography 323

Acknowledgements 324

Index 325

A PERSONAL VIEW

M. J. K. Smith, O.B.E.

I JOINED THE CLUB after the University season of 1956, but had to qualify and so could not play in the Championship until 1957. A pair at Lord's in the MCC v Champion County match and a first-innings duck against Worcester made it an inauspicious start. However, I got away in the next innings and settled down.

The Championship side of 1951 was breaking up. The key men in the attack had been Tom Pritchard, Charlie Grove, Eric Hollies and Ray Weeks. Only Ray and Eric remained for one more season. Justice could never be done to Eric on paper. Few could relate so easily to spectators and be such a pleasure to play with and against. It is trite to say he was a credit to the game, but he certainly broke the mould since we are unlikely to witness anyone get over 2,000 wickets in the future. I have two regrets over Eric – first, that I had only one season playing with him, and second, a regret that I know he shared, that he didn't have the opportunity to play limited-overs cricket. I remember watching a Sunday League match with him when he said how much he would have fancied having a go. His fielding would have produced some choice remarks, but there is no way he wouldn't have handled it with the ball.

Dick Spooner and Bert Wolton finished in 1959, Fred Gardner and Alan Townsend a year later. Dick would have been a leading performer in any age, and was one of a number of post-war keepers who have suffered in competing with Godfrey Evans, Alan Knott and Bob Taylor. In this time few keepers have scored more hundreds than Dick – the current keeper, Geoff Humpage, is one. Left-handed, he had a few shots of his own invention to frustrate the bowler, and batting anywhere from opener down he was a very complete player. Bert Wolton and Alan Townsend, both very clean strikers of the ball, will probably be remembered more for their outstanding fielding, Bert in the deep and Alan at slip, where he stood throughout his career and was rated the best in the country. A side without a good slip goes nowhere, and Alan's ability there was a major factor in the Championship success. He also had a well-deserved reputation for having a 'golden' arm to break a stand while all other bowlers were struggling.

Fred Gardner attracted the caricaturists who emphasised his slow scoring and dry subtle wit. He was another with whom it was a particular pleasure to play. Far worse players than he have played for England, and given the present concentrations on pace and the short stuff his strengths would have been more widely appreciated now. A 'comfortable' frame went well with a rock-solid technique. He would withdraw the bat all day and let the ball hit him rather than play a false shot. More than one over-rated quickie blew himself out and wasted a new ball trying to intimidate him. He had an enviable philosophy that 'that little ball can't hurt you' and the next one was inevitably treated on its merits. If the ball was flying around there was no better man to have on your side than Fred.

At the other end, Norman Horner, half his size and keen to score off every ball, was a good foil. Good friends make good opening partners. Norman, a greyhound between the wickets, would have run Fred's legs off him if he had been allowed, but frustration never crept in as Fred played the senior partner and advised Norman there would be easier runs after tea if he didn't go and exhaust them both beforehand. I have no hesitation in bracketing Norman with the very top cover fielders, particularly in saving the quick single. Anyone pushing for one through extra cover was taking on someone very quick over 10–15 yards in Norman, and one very quick to have a shy at the bowler's wicket.

The County had the reputation of producing fast bowlers, probably based on the success of Tom Pritchard, who until Brian Statham and Fred Trueman came along, was consistently the only genuine fast bowler in the country. Youngsters like Jack Bannister and Roly Thompson were able to be brought into a good attack. A fair number of batsmen got out to these younger men after being pressurised by the greater experience of the other bowlers. But once the old guard retired it was a different matter, and the lack of real pace was a problem until David Brown arrived. It was therefore very annoying that we managed to miss David White, a local lad who had played with the Colts and Aston Unity, and who was allowed to join Hampshire for whom he took 1,000 wickets with real pace. When that sort of thing occurs it is a real horror story – he would have made all the difference in the world to us in the 1960s. Jack Bannister took over 1,000 wickets and Roly Thompson 500, but neither had real pace. Roly probably shortened his career by trying to bowl too fast. Ray Carter, on the other hand, cut his pace down and became a dual-use performer with off-cutters, particularly useful on wet wickets. But there comes the day when you just have to be able to blast someone out to make that vital breakthrough which can mean the Championship or another trophy.

I appreciate all the reasons for the full covering of wickets, but over my career, both as a batsman and captain, I rate the most interesting cricket I played as that played on rain-affected wickets. That the run-ups were also uncovered meant major problems for the fast men, since there was no guarantee that on delivery the front foot would not slip. Thus they might injure themselves, or give too many runs away through being wayward in what was likely to be a slow-scoring innings. Dry footholds could have made them unplayable. Without the pacemen the batsman always had a chance. But he had to develop a sound defence in order to cope and I thought it very good training to develop a sound technique overall. However, not all wet wickets misbehaved, and it wasn't all milk and honey for the bowlers. A wet ball just skidded through, besides being difficult to hold, particularly for the spinners. Sometimes it was just like a bar of soap. Wet footholds kicked up and had to be avoided by dropping behind them or to the side, and the seam might fill with mud and so not bite. So they had to adapt. Some developed the cutter bowled across the seam. I don't see anyone doing this these days. Length was vital. Anything slightly erratic was punished. The short ball sat up and with a clutch of close fielders usually went for four, earning the bowler plenty of black looks from catchers who had to duck and dive. The bowler was then tempted to overpitch to compensate, which of course the batsman was waiting for. Runs were generally hard won, totals small, so the bowlers had to bowl tight and everyone knew it. I have heard many a bowler say that to learn to perform on rain-affected wickets was the most difficult part of his apprenticeship. If he bowled as well as he should then he would probably win the game, but the margin in his favour could be pretty tight. He had to attack and there was a lot of pressure on him.

I found this the most interesting situation in which to captain a side. There could be a small total to defend; conditions would be in your favour, but a couple of poor overs to a poorly set field and the balance could be turned. It was the poker game. Was the batsman going to try to 'play' and accumulate, so the extra catcher could come in, or would he chance his arm so that the man should be on the boundary. Jack Bannister and Tom Cartwright were superb bowlers under these conditions. The battle was on, they never gave an inch. Fielding close, I rated this the best contest.

Tom Cartwright first played as a 16-year-old, opening the innings with his great friend and mentor Fred Gardner. He saw his future as an opening batsman, and at one stage preferred to stay in the seconds and go in first rather than to go down the order in the Championship side. A fine fielder anywhere, he was an outstanding prospect, but hardly rated as a bowler. He was capped as a batsman and when he started to bowl in the first team I don't think anyone really fancied him as a first-change bowler. Eyes were opened when in a Second Eleven Championship play-off against Yorkshire he was put on by Tom Dollery to change the openers round and took seven for 19 in the innings.

His First Eleven analysis for the season was two for 180. Next season, 1958, he scored 900 runs and took 18 wickets bowling medium-pace inswingers, and then the following season he developed into a leading bowler, but still moving the ball in. Then came the breakthrough, when he developed the one to go the other way. He further refined his method to cut out the swing in order to concentrate entirely on moving the ball off the seam. In this method, along with Derek Shackleton of Hampshire, he became the leading performer, not only in the country, but the world. Both these bowlers posed special problems for the batsman. Neither had any real pace, so that many of the close catches went fairly gently to hand and a high percentage were caught. Tom regularly bowled without anyone outside the inner ring – two slips and three saving one on the offside, a backward short leg, sometimes two, a forward short leg and the others saving one on the legside with the keeper standing up. This required pinpoint accuracy not only in length and line, but also in hand action, so that the ball landed consistently on the seam. Only in this case was there any chance of any deviation.

The opening attack was strengthened by the appearance of Ossie Wheatley, and it was a loss when he left to join Glamorgan; not only because he had a career record of 1,000 wickets, but that he was a swinger of the ball (away) while the others concentrated on movement off the seam. This loss did not appear too expensive when Albert Wright came through, certainly with the most natural ability of any of the young seamers in my time. He was leading wicket taker in 1962, but sadly also left for South Wales.

No spinner had taken Eric Hollies' place until Basil Bridge came up from the Colts – another of Derief Taylor's boys. He took 85 wickets in 1959, then had a mixed year before in 1961 he had 121 victims and was the first spinner in the country to take 100 wickets. After a close season operation he 'lost it'. Rudi Webster was a fine performer, taking 80 wickets in little over half a season in 1963, but his medical studies precluded a full-time career. Then came David Brown, basically straight into First Eleven contention from school, and the start of an outstanding career. However, the loss of Albert Wright and Basil Bridge in a matter of two seasons was really devastating. I was never more certain of two bowlers who would take 1,000 wickets for us, and their absence meant a lack of depth in the attack, even though at the time we had three 1,000-wicket men in Bannister, Cartwright and Brown. Put David White with that group (all local men) and bring in Bob Barber with his leg-breaks, and that would have been an attack which surely would have been winning things.

After Basil Bridge, Lance Gibbs was the next spinner to take 100 wickets, and then Dilip Doshi and Norman Gifford, all brought in from outside the County. I find it very interesting that in all the Club's history it has never produced a local slow left-arm bowler to reach cap status, and yet traditionally this type was the lynch-pin of any side. Agreed Eric Hollies, from Staffordshire, did the job for 25 years, but it is a surprising statistic. Geoff Hill took 50 wickets in half a season after leaving the RAF, and then Ron Miller looked the part until limited by a nasty finger injury, although he was from the north-east.

Alongside Tom Cartwright, the outstanding young batsman was Jim Stewart, who established himself in the vital position of number 3. He scored 2,000 runs in 1962 and his outstanding striking, particularly of off-spinners, took him to 12th man for England and an A team tour to New Zealand, along with Bob Barber. He was also selected for a final Welsh rugby trial. He missed it through injury and his replacement was capped. Has anyone come closer to a cap than that and missed out? His 17 sixes and two hundreds in the Lancashire match at Blackpool was a remarkable exhibition of straight hitting. At the time a world record for sixes. There were few off-spinners who took him on with equanimity. Billy Ibadulla went immediately into the side on qualification. He was always in the game. He started bowling off-cutters, then seamers and even had a part season with leg-breaks. Opening the innings in 1962 he scored 2,000 runs and was a fearless forward short leg. So often his type are called bits and pieces cricketers, but really they are the linkmen who bind the specialists together. Ray Hitchcock did a sterling job, usually batting at number 7, the last of the accredited batsmen, so that often he had to look after the man at the other end, while trying to score against the clock. Anyone who could be persuaded to play back to his leg-breaks was usually lbw. His best batting came after he took to spectacles, while John Jameson's came after he took his off, although I'm not sure what you should read into that.

There seemed a steady supply of outstanding local players to join the staff: Dennis Amiss, signed at 15, John Jameson, with strong local connections although he was born in India, Alan Smith, John Whitehouse and Neal Abberley, who went on an under-25 tour to Pakistan very early in his career only to sustain an injury and end his tour in the first game. While the others were affected to varying degrees, only Neal could really say his opportunities were greatly reduced by the introduction of overseas players in the late 1960s. Top overseas players became major influences in every county. Lance Gibbs was the first and his experience was interesting. The leading Test spinner at the time he was not the overnight success expected. A very big spinner of the ball, he bowled from wide of the crease and made it bounce, so he always wanted a slip. County players padded him off to distraction and he didn't like bowling round. However, he realised he had to do this, and once he had sorted it out he became the complete bowler. But it did take quite a time and it illustrates the danger of expecting too much too early from a younger spinner.

Throughout my career, it was generally reckoned much harder to get wickets than runs at Edgbaston. Thus to win anything we always reckoned we had to speculate; to set attainable declarations and be prepared to chase to the end ourselves. In 1971 at the Oval this worked against us when Alan Smith set Surrey a target on a good wicket which they achieved fairly easily. Had we closed the game down presumably we would have won the Championship, since we finished equal on points with Surrey. But that had to be the right way to play it and next season Alan Smith's reward for positive leadership was the Championship. Although in the Championship year Norman McVicker was the chief wicket-taker, over the two seasons Lance Gibbs took 50 wickets more than anyone else. Bob Willis was qualified only from mid-season and then coming in fresh was a major asset, as with David Brown we now had pace from both ends, which was not so common in those days.

After the Championship win we really needed the squad system. Apart from inevitable injuries, Bob Willis was soon to establish himself in the England side and Kanhai, Kallicharran, Gibbs and Deryck Murray toured with the West Indies. It was a time of change again. Norman McVicker left for Leicestershire, which left Bill Blenkiron with more responsibility. Steve Rouse, quickish left-arm, who in my opinion would have been a key bowler over the next five or ten years, was forced out through injury before his time, and too much was expected too quickly from Steve Perryman. Eddie Hemmings came through in front of two other young spinners, Peter Lewington and Warwick Tidy. It was the County's loss that he later chose to join Nottinghamshire. Having said that, it now looks an expensive error that a greater effort was not made to keep him.

In view of what happens now it is very surprising that we never went for an overseas pace bowler. But only since the success of the West Indies pace battery has it been accepted that the genuinely fast bowler, in addition to the fact that he is bowling first and is therefore best placed to make the quick breakthrough, has also the most versatile method of attack. Extreme pace will take wickets on its own account and doesn't need a green wicket to be effective. A slow wicket probably limits a spinner more than it does the quick man. If the surface 'goes' and it turns, it usually seams too. To suggest that a good slow bowler may still get wickets with flight when the wicket is green is really for the birds, because by the time he has done it, compared to a good quality seam attack, he had usually given so many runs away that the result is affected.

Rohan Kanhai came in 1968, the year Tom Cartwright completed 10,000 runs and 1,000 wickets – the first Warwickshire player to do this. I have no hesitation in nominating Rohan as the best batsman ever to play for the County. No one could miss his 'presence' at the wicket, the stance perfectly natural and relaxed, and no bowler could ever be confident of containing him. In 1970 at Gravesend, on a wicket which was a birthday present for Derek Underwood, he hit his first ball for six over long on and went on to make 107 out of 204. Later at Courtaulds he made 187 out of 295. Incredibly, here the last four wickets put on 126 of which he made 124, all the time shielding his partners from the strike. It was almost the innings of a lifetime – but Rohan tended to play one or two of these per season.

Like Rohan, Alvin Kallicharran came from Port Mourant in Guyana. I would place him and Dennis Amiss 2 and 3 in the batting merit order. Put them in which order you like – I would not like to separate them. I shall always remember Alvin in the World Cup getting a ball from Dennis Lillee on his hip which he flicked for six, ten rows back in the stand. In the Gillette Cup at Taunton Joel Garner was taken apart, and I can't remember anyone else doing that to Joel in his prime. Dennis Amiss scored a hundred hundreds and was up with the greats – enough said really. He was a model for any youngster, and a note of caution for any Committee, in that he was 23 before scoring his first hundred in the Championship. John Jameson opened with Dennis and as he will tell you was a great help to him. John's idea was to put bat to ball. He was very strong off the back foot, which is usually an indication of a very good player. He scored so quickly that Dennis was never under pressure to have to force the pace and so could relax and let the runs come. The young Imran Khan fancied having a go at John in the Pakistan game and in four overs 61 runs were scored, 57 to Jameson – spectacular striking particularly in the opening overs of a match. A batting order starting with Amiss, Jameson, Kanhai and Kallicharran would have graced any Test team.

Two interesting statistics about John Jameson are that in the West Indies in 1974, batting number 3 in the second Test, he hit his first ball for six – a top-edge hook over third man off Keith Boyce bowling round the wicket. Less spectacularly, he is the only man to be run out in three consecutive Test innings, although he does mention he didn't do much of the calling!

The strength of the contingent of overseas players made it difficult for young batsmen to break through. John Whitehouse did it, scoring 173 on his debut against Oxford University and becoming 'Young Cricketer of the Year'. But with hindsight we should really have strengthened the bowling more rather than the batting. It seems amazing now that Dennis Lillee, Jeff Thomson, Wes Hall and Charlie Griffith never appeared in county cricket in their prime.

Now that wickets are fully covered it is difficult to envisage a side winning the Championship without some genuine pace. Without this, on good wickets, the opposing bottom order can hold out long enough to save games which just have to be won to finish top. David Brown did a tremendous job during the 1960s, but we should have brought in more support for him.

Season 1963 saw the introduction of the Gillette Cup and Bob Barber's arrival from Lancashire. He was already a Test player, but his move coincided with a change of outlook with the bat, and from an accumulator of runs he became a striker from the first ball, and quickly established himself as an opener for England.

Many were the theories on how to play the Gillette. For our first match at Northampton we had decided to bat first – no rush – and hopefully have wickets in hand for a last 10-over charge. Fine, but everyone panicked with the bat and Northampton had nothing to do other than to sit back and wait for the game to be handed to them.

Next year everything went perfectly and in the early rounds we averaged 300 runs per innings, winning comfortably. Then at Lord's we made the mistake of winning the toss. An earlier start, plus the fact that it was six weeks later in the season, meant difficult conditions to bat in before lunch, as has been shown in many a final since. Ian Thomson bowled us out comfortably. Sussex, had they won the toss, would also have batted first, in which case I have no reason to believe the result would not have been reversed.

The dangers of batting first at Lord's were to catch us in a later final against Lancashire. This time the wicket started damp and its perils were very obvious. We lost the toss – and the match – and later a Special General Meeting was held on our 'poor' performance. I had retired by then, but if ever a game was won by the toss it was this one. In 1971 we had a similar problem in a semi-final at Canterbury against Kent. On the first day we bowled with a wet ball, while the following day they had a dry one to bowl against us.

In 1965 we looked like getting to Lord's again, but in the semi-final against Yorkshire at Edgbaston, needing only 178 to win, we lost by 20 runs. There were five run-outs and I holed out to mid-on off a gentle full toss which had slipped from Don Wilson's hand. It was a long time before we could see anything funny in this comedy of errors. Even our keenest supporter thought we had a death-wish. However, in 1966 we triumphed against Worcestershire – who had won the toss and batted. Tom Cartwright took three of the first four wickets for 16 runs off 12 overs and Worcestershire never recovered – the top scorer was Norman Gifford with 38 – after lunch. Bob Barber won the Man of the Match award with 66. There was a slight tremble, but with 21 wanted and a crisis there for the making, Alan Smith went in and scored them all.

It is interesting to look back at the Gillette matches over the first four years, we having played more matches than anyone. Billy Ibadulla had the most wickets with 28; David Brown was next with 19 and he was the meanest at runs per over. Jack Bannister and Tom Cartwright had 17 and 15 wickets. The probable reason for the surprising wicket totals was that so often we batted first and took a stranglehold on the match, so that Billy would be bowled out more regularly than the rest, with the opponents having to go for him, and he took full advantage.

Our second win in the Gillette was altogether more knife-edge. Tom Cartwright was injured. Earlier when Jack Bannister had broken down in a match Alan Smith had taken off his pads and bowled. Now it was decided that Dennis Amiss would bowl and he managed the full 12 overs. The Sussex total of 215 (Alan Oakman 31) was looking too many until Alan Smith went in. Scoring two to one with Dennis Amiss playing anchorman he won the Man of the Match award with 39 not out. In three finals he had not been dismissed. He was very dangerous through the offside given any room. This was Don Bates' usual line of attack and he was expensive in the latter overs. Only when the game was 'lost' was John Snow brought back, but it was too late and stereotype captaincy was punished.

One more final was reached in 1972. We scored 234 which, as it turned out, was to be the highest losing score of a side batting first. Clive Lloyd hit a superb 126, arguably the finest innings in a one-day final, and Lancashire deservedly won.

The Gillette we took to. We never really threatened in the Benson and Hedges or the John Player League, and I can think of no reason why. Limited-overs cricket has provided tremendous excitement. The strangest story I recall came from after my retirement, when Bob Willis masterminded a very close semi-final victory at Headingley. Chatting to some members afterwards in the car park, I found one who had left the game early because he felt the excitement was too much for his heart pacemaker. It got a bit like that on the field on occasions.

CHAPTER ONE

THE CLUB IS FORMED

'IT IS ALMOST SAFE TO ASSUME that if there had been no Mr Ansell in Birmingham, there would be no Warwickshire County Cricket Club at the present time.' That tribute to the work of William Ansell in 1892 was penned in *Birmingham Faces and Places* in 1892 about a man who was born at Westcott, Surrey, on 25 February 1849 and, but for parental opposition, would have played for Surrey Colts.

Instead he took up teaching and found his way at the age of 25 to Old Park School, Wednesbury, where he played for the local club and also became honorary secretary of an association of clubs spread around Warwickshire, Worcestershire and Staffordshire.

The birth of the Warwickshire County Cricket Club was a stumbling, makeshift affair, with only one man possessed of the vision necessary to bring together the various factions which had organised cricket in a haphazard way throughout the first eight decades of the 19th century.

That man was William Ansell who, on Saturday, 8 April 1882, knocked a few heads together at a meeting held at the Queen's Hotel, Coventry, and helped formulate a constitution for the Warwickshire County Cricket Club. This meeting followed an informal one held the previous month in Leamington, when Ansell was joined by David Buchanan, M. P. Lucas, the Rev G. Cuffe and Col W. Swynfen Jervis. These five men decided formally to start a Warwickshire County cricket team.

Ansell and Col Jervis were appointed joint honorary secretaries, and were instructed to circularise various clubs in the county asking for their co-operation in the historic venture. Ansell's Birmingham and District Cricket Association, of which he had been secretary since he settled in Birmingham several years earlier, would have four representatives, Col Jervis's Warwickshire Gentlemen CC (he was their secretary) three, Coventry two and Rugby one. The circular seeking members asked for an initial £10 donation for life membership, and an annual subscription of one guinea which would allow free admission to matches played by the County team.

The first president was Lord Willoughby de Broke, and so Ansell's dream to centre cricket in the county on Birmingham came true. He firmly believed that if Warwickshire was ever to make its way in the cricketing world, a headquarters in Birmingham which, incidentally, was still a town, was essential.

After the historic second meeting in Coventry, Ansell wrote: 'Thus the amalgamation of the county element and the democratic Birmingham association was completed and the Club started on its new career.'

Before chronicling the first matches of the new County Club, it is interesting to go back in time to the first recorded cricket in Warwickshire, on Monday, 15 July 1751 at Holte Bridgman's Cricket Ground, at the Apollo at Aston.

The announcement of the match between 'Eleven of the Gentlemen of the Holte Bridgman's Club and Eleven of the Gentlemen of Mr Thomas's Bellamy's Club, the most of three innings, for Twenty-two Guineas' included the fact that admission would be two pence. How many people paid, and what they saw, is not on record. But a match at Warwick in 1833 between the home club and the Birmingham Union Cricket Club, played for £20 a side, led to such a violent disagreement that the game was not finished, and the matter had to be resolved at the Warwickshire Assizes, when Lord Denmar nonsuited the Birmingham team, who were the plaintiffs.

A happier match on 7 and 8 August 1843 at Coventry was the first recorded Warwickshire match against Leicestershire, although the county name had been taken 17 years earlier by the Wellesbourne Club in South Warwickshire.

They changed their name to Warwickshire County Cricket Club in November 1863, but what was mainly an amateur side catered little for other parts of the county, and they gracefully dissolved in 1883, when Ansell's initiative was successful.

A club which featured prominently at the time, and is still in the forefront of midlands club cricket, was Leamington, founded around 1848. Such was the enthusiasm for cricket in the area that the following year they engaged two of the best-known professionals in the country, George Parr of Nottinghamshire and John Wisden of Sussex.

The famous pair became sole proprietors of a ground, part of which is now Victoria Park. After levelling the area they successfully resisted any temptation to false modesty, by naming it 'Parr and Wisden's Ground'. They successfully promoted games between the South and the North, and brought to Leamington all the leading cricketers of the period, including Fuller Pilch, Alfred Mynn, William Lillywhite and William Clarke, the Nottinghamshire lob bowler.

Age was no barrier in those times, with Clarke 51 and Pilch 46. The following year, Lillywhite played for the MCC at 58 and took five for 80 off 275 balls.

In 1852 the I Zingari Club met Warwickshire at Leamington, the home side winning easily after scoring 145 and 172, while the distinguished opposition could muster only 84 and 69. Another

William Ansell, one of the founders of Warwickshire CCC, and Hon Secretary from 1882 to 1902.

prestigious contest took place in August 1856 between Fifteen Gentlemen and the Players, for whom Parr, Wisden and one Julius Caesar played. Despite Wisden taking 15 for 113 in the match, numerical superiority triumphed, with Mr A. Payne taking 13 for 95.

The success of the Leamington Club prompted the cricketers of Birmingham to stir themselves, and the newly named Aston United Club laid a ground in Aston Park in order to host a North v South match in September 1861. Even the science of modern groundsmanship might find it difficult to produce a playable pitch within a few months, and it was small wonder that the best professionals in the country played on a pitch described by a local reporter as 'terribly rough and quite unfit for cricket'. The four-innings match aggregate was only 373, the South's 86 and 122 being good enough to triumph by 43 runs. The match was made memorable by the selection during the luncheon interval on the second day of the first England team to tour Australia.

Despite the sponsored offer by a firm of caterers, Spiers and Pond, to underwrite all expenses and guarantee each player £150 and a return first-class passage, eight players declined the trip. Not the least remarkable feature of the saga was that the selected personnel were decided upon in under an hour.

Aston Park was used in September 1871, though this was the Lower Ground about 200 yards further along Trinity Road. A benefit match there for Mat Wyre and Hiram Slack marked the first appearance in the area of W. G. Grace who, at the age of 23, was still 'slim of build'. Slim or not, he scored only 8 – and that in the season when he became the first batsman ever to score 2,000 first-class runs in a season. His final aggregate of 2,739 at an average of 78.25 included ten hundreds, two of which were 'doubles'.

Before that momentous appearance, a match at Rugby School in September 1863 between the Gentlemen and Players of Warwickshire was notable for the appearance of David Buchanan – later to be one of the 'famous five' founders of the Warwickshire County Cricket Club and its first captain.

Buchanan began his distinguished cricket career as a fast left-arm bowler, but in the 1860s changed so effectively to bowling slow spinners that he went on to claim 87 wickets for the Gentlemen against the Players in ten games at Lord's and The Oval betweeen 1868 and 1874. He took ten wickets in the 1863 match for Gentlemen of Warwickshire and with the Rugby School Coach, A. Diver, going one better, the professionals were well beaten.

The following year, the Wellesbourne Club, having changed its name to the Warwickshire County Cricket Club, opened a ground opposite Warwick Racecourse instead of taking the club to Leamington, which would have been a more popular choice. The club's first president was the Earl of Warwick, with J. M. Mordaunt and K. Greenway as the first honorary secretary and treasurer respectively.

The team was mainly drawn from the amateur ranks in the south-east of the county, with Buchanan consistently reaping harvests of wickets, two of his main support bowlers coming from the clergy.

The first captain of Warwickshire CCC, David Buchanan. He was captain from 1882 to 1883 and was also the Club's first Chairman, from 1882 to 1885. He founded the Club, with William Ansell.

They were Canon F. R. Evans, Rector of Bedworth, the uncle of George Eliot the novelist, and the Rev Osbert Mordaunt, who was subsequently to combine the Rectorship of Hampton Lucy with the duties of licensee of the local pub. The ability to tread such a spiritual tightrope might have come from the same source as the cunning of his successful lob bowling, which was considered by some experts to be at least the equal of that of Simpson Hayward and Walter Humphreys.

As the new county club played more games, *Wisden* began to chronicle them in its second edition in 1865. 'A club referred to as the Gentlemen of Warwickshire' played among other counties that season, Hampshire, one of whose two matches provided Buchanan with 14 wickets at Warwick, and Beaumont Featherstone with the first hundred scored for the club. Strangely enough, this was at the

Oval, because the Warwickshire Gentlemen could not persuade a side of sufficient strength to travel into Hampshire.

The so-called county side made its debut at Lord's in July 1867, but the weather unkindly spoiled the match. For several years the fixture list was variable in content, with the number of games dwindling on occasions to very few.

The first teams from Australia were now appearing in England, and in 1878 a 12-strong party arrived at Bournbrook following an astonishing performance at Lord's, where they humbled a powerful MCC side captained by W. G. Grace, dismissing them for 33 and 19. The Birmingham host club, Pickwick, had already chosen 18 players but, influenced by the result at Lord's, unilaterally increased their strength by four for an unfinished match which produced some amazing bowling analyses.

The Australians were put in to bat on a wet pitch and squeezed 105 against an attack which could dot 21 fielders around the ground. The Rev Mordaunt emerged from either pulpit or bar to return figures of 23-20-3-4 (four-ball overs). Despite F. R. Spofforth taking 11 for 60, the 22 local batsmen earned a lead of 18 before Australia reached 106 for six, rain ending play prematurely on the third day. Undaunted, the Australians returned to Birmingham in 1880 and, with their task numerically eased by a Birmingham and District side turning out only 18, won by an innings and nine runs.

It was in this year that Ansell's dissatisfaction with the lack of progress made in developing cricket in the Birmingham area led to him lobbying the secretary of the Warwickshire Gentleman's Cricket Club, Col Swynfen Jervis, on behalf of his own active Birmingham Association. He represented 36 clubs, and complained that the county was being represented by scratch sides which rarely took into account the playing strengths in the cities and urban districts. As far as he was concerned. Birmingham – with its population of over 400,000 – was being unjustly ignored and, as he told Jervis: 'If Warwickshire was ever to occupy a leading position in the cricket world, Birmingham's co-operation was necessary.'

Jervis accepted the chance to join forces, and so the two historic meetings in Leamington and Coventry in March and April of 1882 were convened. The second one was presided over by David Buchanan, and also present were amateur fast bowler Hugh Rotherham, Edward Clements, a Birmingham lawyer, A. H. Albut, Jervis and Ansell.

Rotherham also had the distinction of originating the term 'bogey' at golf, so in addition to destroying the reputation of many leading batsmen in his own time he has inflicted everlasting mental scars on golfers the world over ever since.

CHAPTER TWO

THE FIRST DECADE

THE REALISATION OF THE ANSELL DREAM follows a few early season matches, including one at the Aston Lower Grounds – 50 yards from the Villa Park of today – against Eighteen Colts of Warwickshire, in which rain affected the pleasures of 100 spectators for three hours. The numerical handicap was again too much, with the County Eleven managing 61 for nine after bowling out the Eighteen for 95.

The first official match against county opposition took place at Lichfield against Staffordshire on 17 July 1882. The two-day contest was drawn, with rain badly affecting the second day, as it did in the return fixture at Coventry on 21 and 22 August when, unaccountably, Hugh Rotherham chose to play for Uppingham Rovers and Colonel Jervis took over the captaincy. Despite J. E. Williams taking seven for 75 off the equivalent of 52 six-ball overs, Staffordshire reached 284, and they enforced the follow-on after dismissing Warwickshire for 77. Rain saved the home side, and despite an earlier away win against Worcestershire, thanks to deadly bowling by Buchanan aand Rotherham, it was a disappointed Ansell who reflected on the first depressing season, which produced income of £25 16s 3d and expenditure of £25 7s 0d.

It must have been especially galling to Ansell when a United All England XI, led by W. G. Grace, came to Roebuck Lane in West Bromwich and thrashed Twenty-two of Salters Cricket Club and District at the August Bank Holiday in front of a large crowd which enjoyed lovely weather. W. G. and his brother, E. M. Grace, excelled, scoring 111 between them out of 215, and taking no fewer than 31 wickets as the home side were bundled out for 98 and 118. By the end of the month, Spofforth's 14 wickets for 90 at the Oval presaged the famous newspaper obituary notice of the 'death of English cricket', and the beginning of the little urn and the Ashes.

Ansell soldiered on, organising five matches for 1883, of which two were won, two lost and one drawn, with MCC, Cheshire and Staffordshire providing the opposition. David Buchanan took over the captaincy from Col Jervis to add to his duties as chairman and joint secretary. Buchanan was now 54, and although the committee drew up a list of 20 players at the start of the season, from which it was planned to choose the eleven (almost like modern England selectors), the final number of those chosen was greater by six. They included the Club president, as well as Henry James 'Nack' Pallett, an opening bowler from the Aston Unity Club who was to share the attack with John Shilton for over ten years.

Ansell realised after the first two seasons that, with a subscription list amounting to 70 guineas, a ground in Birmingham was essential if more members and spectators were to be attracted. The only viable ground in Birmingham, at Aston, was unsuitable because of a pitch which gave Spofforth fourteen for 37 for the Australians against an All England XI in which, although the tourists required just 33 to win, at one stage the result was uncertain with them toiling at 28 for six.

Ansell persuaded the then Mayor of Birmingham, Sir Thomas Martineau, to give official support to the efforts to obtain a permanent ground in the town, but he had to steer a procedural amendment through a public meeting at the Regent Hotel, Leamington on 19 January 1884, before he obtained the consensus view he wanted – that 'it was desirable to establish a central county ground'.

A committee was appointed to make inquiries and report within two months, and they urged a subsequent public meeting on 8 March in Leamington to support the idea of a permanent county ground in Birmingham, before which home county matches should be played where most gate money could be taken. The Rugby faction supported Ansell and the committee, but the Leamington-Warwick section did not. They argued that as that area provided four-fifths of the subscriptions, the words 'at Birmingham' should be deleted.

Ansell would not be denied by such parochial and illogical views, and when the three home games at Coventry and Rugby in 1884 produced only £11 3s 6d, his hand was strengthened. The game against Hertfordshire at Coventry was notable for the feat of Buchanan and Rotherham, who bowled unchanged throughout the match, taking all 20 wickets for 90.

Buchanan had then been bowling slow for 20 years, after switching from the fast method which had served him so well for the previous 18 years. The change had been sudden and dramatic, coming in a match between Rugby and Manchester at Old Trafford on 11 and 12 July 1864. The home side were made to follow on, but a stubborn second-wicket partnership looked like saving the match when Buchanan – despite having already taken eight of the first eleven wickets to fall – suddenly decided to toss the ball up from a short run-up. Although he took only two more wickets and the match was drawn, he was never to bowl fast again. His ten games for the Gentlemen against the Players from 1868 to 1874 gave him 87 wickets at 14.89, and in those games he took five or more wickets in an innings nine times, and ten or more wickets in a match five times. In four matches against the Oxford and Cambridge University sides in 1870 and 1871 he took 33 wickets, with 14 undergraduates bowled and ten stumped. His batting was less productive, yielding him 14 runs for the Gentlemen in a similar number of innings against the Players.

The search for a permanent home for the County Club was extensive, taking in existing grounds at Camp Hill and Aston, but a £20,000 asking price in the first instance, and the unsatisfactory pitch at the Aston Lower Ground, ruled both out. The Mayor, Sir Thomas Martineau, favoured the YMCA ground on the corner of Eastern Road and Bristol Road, but there were doubts about the drainage.

Ansell wanted the Wycliffe Ground in Pershore Road, but the landlord, Lord Calthorpe, declined, and offered instead an area of 'rough grazing land' in Edgbaston. A committee inspection of the site in June 1885 approved what they saw and decided to 'secure the land upon a lease of 21 years for use as a cricket ground'.

Preliminary costing of draining and fencing the 12-acre area convinced the committee that two steps must be taken. A 'Cricket Ground Company' should be formed to raise the necessary capital, and then sub-let the ground to the Club, and the Mayor was asked to call a public meeting to help raise the money. This meeting took place at the Council House on 16 July 1885, and although a Calthorpe covenant precluded any of his ground being let for purposes at which money should be taken, negotiations were satisfactorily concluded which the Mayor considered to be equitable. The rent was £5 an acre – £60 per annum for 21 years – and the overall cost of drainage, fencing, furniture and the erection of a pavilion amounted to £1,250.

On 11 August 1885 the new company was formed, and so the Warwickshire Cricket Ground Company Limited was registered, with an authorised 300 shares at £10 each, with Lord Willoughby, G. H. Cartland and William Ansell appointed, firstly as lessees, then as directors, together with David Buchanan, R. Williams, C. G. Beale, E. O. Smith and the Mayor.

While this historic acquisition was taking place, the team enjoyed its best season, despite calling on 36 players for seven matches. Runs were in short supply, although H. C. Maul scored the first hundred for the Club against Hertfordshire at St Albans, but the arrival of Yorkshireman John Shilton provided such a sharp cutting edge to the attack – his 48 wickets cost 8 runs each – that only one team scored more than 150 against them.

The ambitions of Ansell grew thick and fast. In the Annual Report of 1885 he wrote that as Warwickshire had lifted themselves from bottom to top of the second-class counties; 'if this form is maintained, its rank as a first-class county is only a question of time'.

That final step was to take nine years, but of more immediate concern was getting the new ground ready for the 1886 season. The professional from Elstree School, Wellingborough, Frank Breedon, was appointed groundsman and caretaker at a salary of £100 a year, plus an accommodation allowance of five shillings a week, which would be paid until the new pavilion was ready. Out of his salary he had to find and pay his own help, which would clearly be necessary if he were to carry out his wide-ranging duties, which included responsibility for all pitches, maintenance of the ground including the toilets, preparation of committee lunches as necessary (sub-contracted to his wife), and the organisation of his duties so that he would be able to bowl as required.

The new County Club already had its now-famous emblem of the Bear and Ragged Staff which, although not heraldic, quickly became established as a motif of historical, as well as nostalgic, significance. The first mention of the Bear in the Club records appears in the spring of 1885, when the curtain finally fell on David Buchanan's magnificent career.

On 26 May 1885, at the age of 55, he took seven for 23 against Leicestershire, and decided that enough was enough. The Club was now on the verge of realising the dream that he and Ansell, among others, had worked so hard to achieve during the previous 20 years.

The new ground was ready for its first match on 7 June 1886, and Ansell's forecast that the Birmingham public would support cricket was proved right when 3,000 people watched the inaugural two-day match against, fittingly, the MCC.

G. H. Cartland, who the previous year had followed Buchanan as chairman and who went on to hold the office for 46 years, captained Warwickshire, and scored the first half-century on the ground. His 55 out of a second-innings total of 109 enabled his side to draw the match. MCC, needing 127 to win, were 70 for three when stumps were drawn to enable them to catch a train.

George Cartland, Chairman of Warwickshire 1885–1931. He played for the Club in its early days and scored the first 50 on the Edgbaston ground.

Warwickshire's membership increased by 651 during that momentous season, which also included a game on 9 and 10 August against the Australians. Rain washed out one day, but some 6,000 people still turned up to watch another low-scoring game in which, thanks to Shilton's eight for 55 in the match, Australia totalled only 107 and 35 for three while the home side managed 70. The top scorer was H. W. Bainbridge, whose debut was to presage a 15-year span as captain. Subsequently he was chairman of the Club from 1931 until the outbreak of the Second World War. He had played for Surrey before coming to Edgbaston, and among his sporting achievements was an appearance in the FA Cup final in 1883 for the Old Etonians against Blackburn Olympic.

The Australians returned to Edgbaston in September to play against an England XI captained by W. G. Grace. Scores of 185 and 56 for two by Australia and 208 by England indicated that the pitch was satisfactory. The England side included Ludford Docker, who joined Warwickshire after playing for Derbyshire, and was to become president from 1915 to 1930.

The 1887 *Wisden* recorded the first season thus:

> Of the counties which are not reckoned first-class, not one has brighter prospects than Warwickshire, cricket in the county having received a great impetus through the opening of the new ground at Edgbaston, Birmingham. In 1886, Warwickshire played in all eleven matches, winning four, losing three and leaving four unfinished. In bowling the county is particularly strong, including as it does Shilton, Pallett, Mr C. W. Rock, Mr Whitby and Mr H. Rotherham.

Rotherham was a schoolboy prodigy rare in successfully reproducing his skills in higher levels of cricket. At Uppingham School he devastated opposition including 13 wickets in a match with Haileybury, including eight for 12 in the second innings, 16 for 53 against the Incogniti, and 14 wickets in the match against MCC, when he clean bowled eleven of his victims. In 1879 in schools cricket he took 98 wickets at 4.38 each, before he played such a brief, but important role as a bowler and captain at Edgbaston until the end of the 1886 season.

The two professionals, Pallett and Shilton, in the opinion of R. V. Ryder, 'bowled Warwickshire out of second-class cricket into first-class cricket', although of their aggregate of 1,693 wickets, only 352 were first-class after Warwickshire's admission to senior status in 1894. Pallett was just under medium pace, and spun the ball both ways with a remarkable combination of penetration and accuracy, while Shilton was a faster bowler who relied on pace rather than spin.

The 1887 annual meeting was a happy one, with Lord Willoughby de Broke able to declare a surplus of £188 and a membership increase from 51 in 1885 to 782. Gate receipts totalled £869 and W. G. Grace was fulsome in his praise of what he thought could be 'one of the best grounds in the country'. Barely half of the 12 acres was used for cricket, and so other sports, including tennis, bowls, football, lacrosse, and even baseball, were played on the remainder.

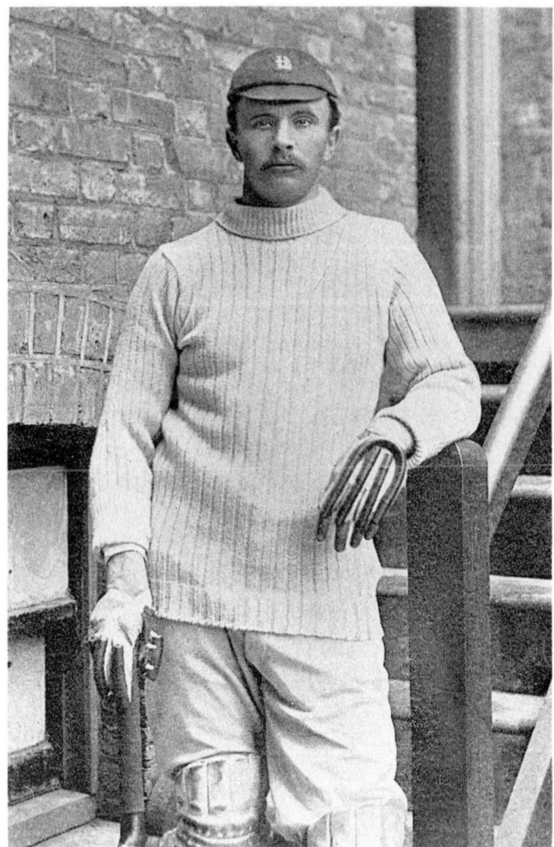

H. W. Bainbridge played for Warwickshire from 1886 to 1902, after playing for Surrey from 1883 until 1885. He captained the Club from 1887 to 1901, and was Hon Secretary from 1903 to 1940 and Chairman from 1931 to 1939.

The 1887 season provided the first games against Yorkshire, and in one of these Warwickshire were ignobly dismissed twice in the same day between 11.54 am and 4.15 pm. However, an encouraging win against Somerset at Edgbaston prompted *Wisden* to comment that the win 'was perhaps the most directly encouraging thing for the game in Warwickshire that has ever occurred', and the overall climate at Edgbaston so encouraged the indefatigable William Ansell that he further strengthened his efforts to get Warwickshire elevated to first-class status. He was one of the guiding lights behind the formation of the County Cricket Council, which represented the second-class clubs.

A. F. A. 'Dick' Lilley, who played for the Club from 1888 to 1911; he also played 35 times for England.

The fixture list of 1887 also included a prized home match against Nottinghamshire, who won a dour struggle in which 186 out of the 370 four-ball overs were maidens. Pallett claimed six wickets, and Docker's batting earned him an invitation to tour Australia under Arthur Shrewsbury.

The 1887 season overall, however, was a disappointment, with only four out of 12 matches won, and all too often the better amateurs did not turn out. Hugh Rotherham failed to make a single appearance.

In 1888 Warwickshire finished third in the table of second-class counties, winning three of their eight games and losing only one, with Pallett in particularly destructive form against Leicestershire with twelve for 65. Fred Collishaw's 145 in the same game was the first hundred scored for the Club by a professional. Against Somerset, Pallett went one better, or rather three better, with 15 wickets for 46 off 43 four-ball overs, and against MCC he took nine for 35 while Shilton was shoring up the other end with figures of 22-20-3-1.

The season marked the first regular appearance of Bainbridge and Lilley, two of the most distinguished cricketers to play for Warwickshire in the 19th century and, in the case of Lilley, through the first decade of the 20th.

Although Nottinghamshire and Surrey did not grant fixtures, the final record of four wins and only two defeats in eleven matches was a good one, including a fine performance at Halifax when Warwickshire had much the better of a drawn match against Yorkshire, in which the home side were 66 ahead with two wickets left when the rains came. Frustratingly enough, the return match was similarly affected by rain when again Warwickshire held the upper hand.

The poor weather reduced the season's gate receipts to £432, as a result of which the chairman met Mr Howard Lloyd of Lloyd's Bank to discuss the overdraft of £453. All sorts of economies were proposed, including the replacement of groundsman Breedon by another at the reduced rate of 25s a week plus allowances including a lad who would help for 30 weeks at 5s a week. A juggling of the 'horse power' resources and the withdrawal of lunches for the professionals produced an overall saving of £47 – cheese-paring of the worst kind. The committee even considered sacking Shilton by moving him to the Lord's staff, but the chance to save something over £100 was thankfully turned down after second thoughts.

At least one of the economies proved successful, with the new groundsmen, John Bates from Werneth not only producing some of the best batting pitches in the country, but also a son, Len, who was born in the groundsman's flat on the ground, and went on to grace the Warwickshire team between the two World Wars.

The 1889 fixture list was the largest yet – 16 matches including six against first-class opposition – and with the financial crisis eased by various donations, the committee offered talent money of £1 extra per match against Gloucestershire, Yorkshire, Lancashire and Leicestershire, but only 10s for games against lesser opposition.

The side won half of its games to finish top of the table of second-class counties, and also beat both Yorkshire and Gloucestershire. The win at Bristol in late May was one of great merit, and marked the inauguration of the new county ground at Ashley Down.

H. C. Maul won the toss and decided to bat, but the total of 146 was reached only through a determined rearguard action by Lilley. Disappointing as that score was, it was good enough to earn a lead of 33, thanks to some superlative fielding and wicket-keeping, and then a Shilton half century set the home side, including W. G. and E. M. Grace, 194 to win.

Shilton and Pallett repeated their first-innings form to such good effect that they shared 17 of the 20 wickets to fall, and Warwickshire won a famous victory by 68 runs. It started a successful season which would have been even better but for misguided selection policies, particularly against Staffordshire and Yorkshire.

At Sheffield, the side actually travelled without, among others, Bainbridge, Docker and Pallett, and furthermore they actually went by train on the morning of the match. Both matches were lost in humiliating fashion – the margins were nine wickets and an innings and 54 runs respectively – and so upset were the Yorkshire authorities at what they interpreted as lack of respect for the fixture that there was a real chance that future matches would not be automatically granted.

The return match at Edgbaston fortunately redressed the balance, with four stumpings and three catches by Lilley helping another 17-wicket haul by Shilton and Pallett to defeat the northerners, who at one stage in their first innings were 36 for eight. The two professional bowlers actually took 103 of the 139 wickets taken by Warwickshire bowlers in county matches, Shilton taking 100 in all matches, and Pallett 91. The financial position was much better, with gate receipts topping £1,000 for the first time, and with an increase of £119 from subscriptions and a reduction of £221 in working expenses, the Club's first official Year Book was able to announce a surplus of £120.

Ansell badly needed the impetus of playing success to sustain his committee's strenuous push for first-class status, but the 1890 season was a disappointing setback, with Warwickshire dropping to sixth place among the eight clubs comprising the second-class championship.

Curiously, the Club's record against the first-class counties was better, with Yorkshire defeated twice, although this time it was the White Rose County who fielded sides considerably below full strength, being without Lord Hawke, Peel, Ulyett and Hunter in the home match at Halifax, and the first three of that quartet in the match at Edgbaston. But the batting for most of the season was appalling, with totals of 27 and 29 against Somerset and Lancashire the low points. Against Australia, after Pallett's seven for 38 dismissed the tourists for 89, the home batsmen capitulated for 38 and managed only 13 more in their second innings. Docker's 100 in 81 minutes brought the only competition win against Leicestershire, and a team record of 11 totals of under 100 runs from 29 completed innings tells its own story. Only Docker averaged over 20, and but for the Herculean efforts of Shilton and Pallett (now also assistant secretary), who took 231 of the 280 wickets to fall to Warwickshire bowlers, the season would have been a disaster.

Ansell had never wavered in his determination to make his Club first-class, and the previous December he persuaded the Cricket Council to adopt a proposal to form a sub-committee to 'classify counties and to provide means of promotion from one class to another'. Furthermore, he was a member of that body, and so it was not too surprising that their recommendation to the Cricket Council was that each year 'the two weakest first-class counties should play the two strongest second-class counties for right of place'.

The word 'two' was halved, which clearly was unacceptable to the second-class counties, who briefed Ansell to raise the matter again in December 1890. This meeting was in Ansell's words 'stormy', and came to a 'startling conclusion' according to *Wisden*, which seems an accurate description of events after the Warwickshire proposal to increase the first-class counties by up to four, was defeated by 11 votes to four. The chairman, Mr M. J. Ellison of Yorkshire, cast his vote for an amendment that the Council should adjourn sine die – i.e. a slamming of the door to Ansell, Warwickshire and the other naturally ambitious counties.

What Ansell needed most of all was a successful 1891 season, but things could not have turned out worse. In another wet summer, Warwickshire won two matches out of 17, and finished bottom of the second-class county table, now reduced to seven because of the promotion to first-class status of Somerset. The batting was again unreliable, with totals of 31 against Cheshire, 57 against Durham and 54 against Surrey just three of 14 totals of under 100 in 28 completed innings. All seven matches against first-class opposition were lost, although Bainbridge emphasised that contributory factors were poor pitches, together with the enforced absence for long periods of Richards, Law and Lilley.

The committee's attempts to increase the Edgbaston playing strength owed more to determination than propriety, with Walter Quaife of Sussex being interviewed and offered terms as early as January, despite the fact that he was a contracted player for the southern county. On 13 July the Sussex Club announced the instant dismissal of Walter Quaife because a 'clandestine agreement to qualify for Warwickshire had been discovered'.

There are two sides to every such controversy, but it is significant that on 3 February the Warwickshire committee *defeated* by 14 votes to two a resolution that 'the honorary secretary be instructed to inform Sussex committee of the acceptance of Quaife's offer, but at the same time to intimate that this committee is willing to cancel the agreement if Quaife makes an arrangement with Sussex and wishes this agreement cancelled within one month of this date'. Whatever the rights and wrongs, by the end of July Walter Quaife and his younger brother, Willie, were sacked by Sussex and warned off the ground, and so Warwickshire obtained the services of one man who was to play for them until 1901 and another who played until 1928.

The committee also came under fire, this time from their own membership, for the standard of fielding in the 1892 season which, allied to the batting weakness, nullified the efforts of Pallett and Shilton, who this time took 173 wickets between them. As a result, they engaged for the following season the services as coach for the first four weeks of the season of Arthur Shrewsbury, then 36, and a *Wisden* 'Cricketer of the Year' two years earlier.

Lilley, now restored to full health after missing the last seven matches of 1891, was particularly appreciative of Shrewsbury's approach, and gives the leading professional batsman of his time full credit for the big improvement in his own technique.

Shrewsbury's views on some of the players who came under his guidance were perceptively shrewd, particularly concerning Syd Santall, who had already been offered a contract the previous November. Shrewsbury's view of the young bowler was: 'Should he improve as I anticipate he will, he should make one of the best bowlers in the country.'

There was surprising criticism of the need to employ Shrewsbury, particularly from Bainbridge, who apparently attached little importance to practice, other than for two weeks or so before the start of a season. Also, Shrewsbury decided to travel daily between Nottingham and Birmingham, and so as soon as his afternoon duties were completed at 5 pm, he would hurry away to catch his train. Perhaps it was the players' reaction to his inability to stay for a chat which prompted his view that although several of the players he coached were keen to learn, he was 'much struck by the seeming indifference to practice among both young and old players'.

The 1892 season brought a spectacular turnabout in Warwickshire's fortunes, with seven wins out of 14 matches, even though they did not beat any of the first-class counties. Surrey crushed them at the Oval, with George Lohmann taking six for 54 and six for 17 in a second-innings debacle of 23, and they also lost twice to Lancashire and once to the powerful Nottinghamshire. Nevertheless, the batting improved with hundreds for Bainbridge and Lilley, while the wicket-keeper and Ludford Docker played in the North *v* South match in June. Staffordshire were defeated twice, despite Bainbridge being twice run out for a pair, and Durham were also comfortably beaten twice as Warwickshire chased their second title. A controversial away defeat by Leicestershire on an illegally watered pitch was followed by another poor performance at Stockport against Cheshire, but Lilley's maiden hundred and ten for 133 from Shilton against Essex put Warwickshire on top of the table to clinch the title.

The improved playing record did little for the Club's finances, and the crisis which developed before the start of the season resulted in William Ansell seeking a vote of confidence from the committee. Treasurer David Buchanan had presented a balance sheet which showed debts and an overdraft amounting to £1,425, and so Ansell's re-election as honorary secretary was expected to tide the Club over until improved finances could allow for a paid officer.

Ludford Docker wanted a paid secretary as soon as possible, which is why Ansell wanted an assurance that his re-election did not depend upon Docker's resolution to this effect being passed. Docker naturally denied that he was criticising Ansell, although his statement that Warwickshire were unpopular with other counties was hardly a statement of approval. Bainbridge supported Docker, and even offered the slanted compliment that should Ansell wish to retire, he would do so full of honour.

Ansell was made of sterner stuff than to bow to such comment, and with typical forthrightness he said that whatever he had done had been from an unwavering sense of duty. He followed this with a letter in which he said that he had a duty to the membership which overrode other considerations. He won the day, albeit at the cost of resignations from the Docker brothers, Ludford and Dudley. Dudley cited business reasons, but Ludford said he disapproved of the committee's policy, and his resignation was accepted, although he was to return as president 23 years later.

The crisis was over, and so was the financial one, at the end of the 1892 season when the Club's need of £1,100 to meet current liabilities was met by a public appeal which realised £1,167 before the start of the 1893 season.

CHAPTER THREE

SUCCESS IN 1893

FOLLOWING THE SOMEWHAT MIXED SUCCESS of Arthur Shrewsbury's coaching in April 1892, Ansell replaced the Nottinghamshire man with a younger colleague – William Attewell who, at the age of 31, had already played the last of his ten Tests against Australia and had been named a Cricketer of the Year by *Wisden* the previous year. His fee of £20 for three weeks' work represented a saving of £30 from the payment made to Shrewsbury, which was a considerable item now that the cost of staging a county match was £50 a day.

With the batting strengthened by the qualification of Walter Quaife and Edwin Diver, Warwickshire's season was successful, with the second-class championship title shared with Derbyshire after a campaign in which Bainbridge's side, remarkably, did not draw a single game. They won seven of their eight games, the only defeat coming against Hampshire. Both Quaife and Diver scored over 750 runs and averaged 31, and with the rare luxury of support from the batting department, the efforts of Pallett, Shilton and Whitehead crowned what was to be Warwickshire's last season as a second-class county with a share of the title.

Whitehead's mixture of spin and medium pace bowling provided the ideal support for Pallett and Shilton who, all too frequently in previous years, had been forced to carry the bowling between them. So well did the trio perform that they claimed 203 out of the 217 wickets obtained by the side, with Whitehead's eight for 49 helping his side beat Yorkshire by nine wickets, and this after he had shared a priceless last-wicket stand with Pallett of 73. The same two bowlers destroyed Cheshire in a day, with Pallett taking eleven for 46 and Whitehead nine for 38, and although Surrey beat them twice, with Lilley scoring a brilliant 124 at a run a minute in the first match at the Oval (in which Tom Hayward made his debut) the side continued to brush aside the minor counties.

The match against Durham – a non-championship game – gave Willie Quaife his debut at the age of 21 and, as he did in his final game for Warwickshire 35 years later, he scored an unbeaten hundred. Brother Walter also reached three figures and such was Warwickshire's dominance that they lost only three wickets in the match. A win in the last away match against Leicestershire was essential, and the result could hardly have been closer, with Warwickshire triumphing by a single run after bowling the home side out for 155.

Ansell, now 44, was prompted by the resignation due to ill-health of

Stephen James Whitehead, who played for Warwickshire from 1889 to 1900. With Pallett and Shilton, he helped Warwickshire to attain first-class status.

the honorary treasurer, Frederic Messiter, to write to the committee repeating his view that the time was ripe for paid administrators to be appointed, particularly as he was beginning to feel the strain of the demands made on his time.

Before any decision was taken, he and Bainbridge were sent to Lord's to attend a meeting convened to consider a momentous proposal from Yorkshire which could open the door at which Warwickshire and Ansell had been knocking so consistently in previous years. The proposal was that, for the purpose of classification, there should be no distinction between counties which played a minimum of six other counties home and away.

The game's authorities nearly 100 years ago were no more willing to grasp such a contentious nettle as their modern counterparts today, and a series of meetings that winter ensured that the same nine clubs – Gloucestershire, Kent, Lancashire, Middlesex, Nottinghamshire, Somerset, Surrey, Sussex and Yorkshire – which comprised the 'Leading Counties' in 1893, would not be increased until 1895.

That year was to be the first in which the term 'County Championship' was first used by *Wisden*, but what of the status of the five applicants from the second-class counties: Warwickshire, Derbyshire, Essex, Leicestershire and Hampshire?

The succession of meetings in the winter of 1893–94 finally agreed on a proposal which produced the historic decision on 1 May 1894 that:

> The matches played by Derbyshire, Essex, Leicestershire and Warwickshire against those counties styled first-class, and also against one another, and against the MCC shall be regarded as first-class matches, and the records of the players engaged in these matches shall be included in the list of first-class averages.

Hampshire were given the same blessing the following year.

Ansell's delight at the realisation of his dream was expressed rather reservedly in a subsequent written statement that 'although it was a simple matter of justice, the many years it took to bring about reflects the conservatism of the game and the ineptitude of its governing body'. *Plus ça change . . .*

For Warwickshire to attain first-class status in such a short space of time was a remarkable tribute to the energies and drive of Ansell. Just ten years earlier, Warwickshire cricket was rudderless. The fixtures and gate receipts could nearly be itemised on one hand; they had no ground and selection was decided on availability, rather than talent. Furthermore, while other midland counties like Derbyshire, Leicestershire and Nottinghamshire were given fixtures against Australia, Warwickshire had to make do with a representative team and play on the infamous Aston Lower Ground on which on one occasion, 36 wickets fell in one day.

Only a real visionary could have planned such a transformation, but to establish a new County Club safely housed in its own ground, all within ten years, was nothing short of miraculous. The bureaucratic administrative opposition was implacable to begin with, and Ansell and his committee not only had to break down those barriers, they also had to nurse and nourish a playing strength which would not buckle when the call came.

Their success in this vital department can best be judged by an examination of the cricketing sources outside Warwickshire that were tapped to enable the Club to compete so successfully in the 1890s. Bainbridge and Diver came from Surrey, the latter already having become the first cricketer to play for the Gentlemen and the Players, before he resumed a teaching career and disappeared from cricket for several years. Smethwick-born Docker came after playing briefly for Derbyshire, Shilton from Yorkshire, Whitehead from Middlesex, Santall from Northamptonshire and the Quaifes from Sussex, their move secured under circumstances of considerable acrimony. In fact, only five of the 13 players who played for Warwickshire in 1894 qualified for the Club residentially.

Of the 'outsiders', Ansell believed that Jack Shilton had 'done, perhaps more than any other, something for Warwickshire cricket'. He was a rich character, the archetypal professional of his time. He was engaged in 1885 as 'head ground bowler', whose duties in that capacity involved bowling from 4 pm until dusk, with a break of 30 minutes. Compared with his colleagues of that season, his pay was considered good – £3 10s for 22 summer weeks and £1 10s for the rest of the

The Edgbaston ground in 1899, taken looking towards the pavilion.

year, with the proviso this latter amount would be reduced if he obtained other employment. An additional £1 was paid to him for every match won, and Jack who was 24 when he signed, already had considerable professional experience with the Northumberland and Durham Club, as well as the Aigburth Club in Liverpool.

His self-confidence – some critics called it cockiness – frequently brought him into conflict with the Club authorities, notably Ansell, whose subsequent glowing tribute was thus prized all the more by Shilton. He played in every Warwickshire match for ten years, but his closing year was a sad one in 1895. Aged 33 he insisted on playing in his own benefit match against Yorkshire – the first benefit awarded by Warwickshire – although suffering from bronchitis and asthma, and it was to be his last match.

He was an undischarged bankrupt, and actually had to be released from prison for 'being in debt' in mid-June to play in the match. His affairs were not unravelled until the following February, when he was sent a cheque for £500 – at least double the amount due to him which reflects well on the committee's sympathetic appraisal of Shilton's service before his life was overtaken by financial problems. In a last effort to restore his failing health, the Yorkshireman visited Cape Town – albeit vainly, because he died in 1899, five days short of his 38th birthday.

CHAPTER FOUR

FIRST CLASS STATUS AND THE COUNTY CHAMPIONSHIP

WARWICKSHIRE'S OFFICIAL ENTRY to first-class cricket could hardly have been more spectacular, with a trio of conclusive wins. Nottinghamshire at Trent Bridge were beaten by six wickets, Surrey at the Oval by seven wickets, and there was a home victory by eight wickets against Kent.

That splendid first fortnight of the 1894 season was the springboard for a remarkable playing record which included only two defeats from 15 first-class matches – easily the most ambitious fixture list so far in the Club's brief history. In addition, only one was lost of seven other games, and *Wisden* commented that their success 'set all the cricket world talking'.

The Almanack went on to pay tribute to consistent batting and the bowling of Pallett, Shilton and Whitehead, which was 'always smart and accurate, and at times most destructive'.

Among the batsman, Ludford Docker averaged 37.20, to make him the leading amateur batsman in English cricket, and six other batsmen averaged over 20, while Pallett's 79 wickets at 11.69 earned him sixth place in the national averages. In all matches he took 99 wickets at 13.19, with Whitehead hardly less effective with 91 wickets at 15.86.

Whitehead was basically a leg spinner, born in Enfield, Middlesex, who developed his cricket with Kings Heath, and he, more than anyone else, was responsible for the electric start to the season, with 33 wickets in three of the first four wins.

His ten wickets at Trent Bridge complemented the first first-class hundred scored for Warwickshire – a splendid 139 by Ernest Hill, who steered his side to a match-winning score of 351, after coming in to bat with the first four wickets down for 83.

The follow-on was enforced successfully, and it was a triumphant team which played just as well at the Oval to give Surrey their only taste of defeat in a season which brought them their fourth title win out of five in the first six seasons of the County Championship. Surrey fielded six England players – Abel, the two Reads, Walter and Maurice, Lockwood, Brockwell and Richardson, as well as Hayward, who was to win 35 caps, but Whitehead swept through them to reward his captain's enterprising decision to open the bowling with him by taking eight for 39.

Willie Quaife's 92 gave Warwickshire a decisive first-innings lead of 144, and such was the ease of the victory that it is difficult to

Warwickshire CCC in 1894.
Standing (l to r): J. Whitehead, E. J. Driver, H. Pallett, A. A. Lilley, Walter Quaife, Alf Law, W. G. Quaife.
Seated: J. Shilton, H. W. Bainbridge (capt.), Ludford Docker, W. Ansell (Secretary).

understand the carping comment in *Wisden* that: 'It would of course be absurd to pretend the better side won, but it is quite true that on this particular occasion the Warwickshire eleven showed far finer cricket than their rivals.' It is difficult to reconcile those two opposite views with the balanced opinions normally expressed in 'the Bible'.

Sydney Santall made his debut, his five wickets for 51 in the second innings heralding one of the longest and most successful careers in the County's history. In the 20 years to the outbreak of the First World War, the Northamptonshire all-rounder took 1,207 wickets – only Eric Hollies has ever taken more – and he scored 6,490 runs, before, as coach, he went on to complete 47 years' service at Edgbaston. Born in 1873, the ubiquitous Santall fulfilled many roles, in addition to playing and coaching, because he also acted as talent scout, historian, statistician and ground superintendent. In 1911 he published the first History of the Warwickshire Club, seven years after producing two threepenny paperbacks: 'Ten years of First Class Cricket in England', and 'Warwickshire as a First County, 1894–1903.'

Kent might have finished fourth in the Championship, but they

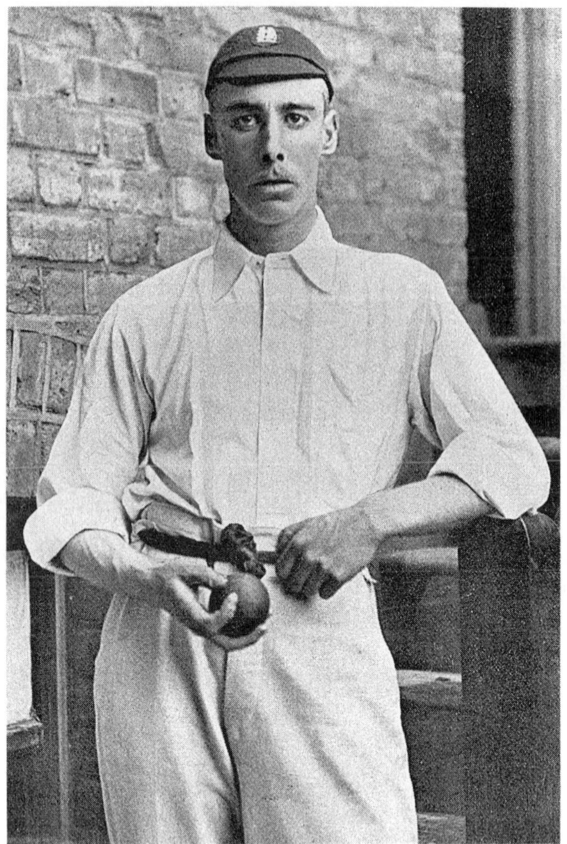

Sydney Santall.

were no match for Pallett's 13 wickets for 78, including seven for 13 in 12 five-ball overs in the first innings. There were only seven scoring strokes off him, and 9,000 supporters created the best atmosphere seen at Edgbaston, with Bainbridge likening the cheers at the game to those heard 'at a football match at Perry Barr'.

The gate receipts were a record £377, and the good form continued with only heavy rain preventing a second win against Nottinghamshire and also a seemingly certain victory over Essex, who later were not to be played between 1905 and 1929.

After ten matches, the Club was the only unbeaten side in the country, with a more kindly *Wisden* offering that 'their success was achieved in a most genuine manner by thoroughly good all-round cricket'.

The unbeaten record had earlier nearly gone at Leicester, where

Bainbridge decided to play, even though his business duties prevented his attendance at Grace Road until after lunch. A collapse meant he rushed in to bat at number 11, but his partnership of 71 with Whitehead saved the innings, and gave his bowlers enough runs for them to squeeze a win.

On the then current basis of calculating final positions in the County Championship – the simple one of a point for a win and one deducted for a defeat, with draws disregarded – Warwickshire, had they been included, would have run Surrey close for the title in what was, apart from fifth position in 1901, their best season until they won the title in 1911.

The 1895 season was the first official one in the Championship, and the first in which Warwickshire took part, and a record of six wins and six defeats from 20 matches gave them a final position of sixth in the list of 14 clubs (Worcestershire, Northamptonshire and Glamorgan were the counties missing from the present complement).

Groundsman John Bates began to produce the good batting pitches which were to be a feature of Edgbaston for the next 90 years, and it was not surprising that the first seven games of the season produced four high-scoring draws, including the first game of the season against Essex, in which, 1,013 runs were scored for the loss of 25 wickets. *Wisden* commented that 'on such a perfect wicket, it is hardly surprising to find the public somewhat lukewarm in their interest'. Ever since cricket began, the problem of striking a satisfactory balance between bat and ball has rarely been solved, and it does seem that the English climate precludes the quality of groundsmanship found more often abroad.

Even though Santall bowled steadily, the loss of form and fitness of Shilton, together with the better batting pitches, left the County short of penetration in the attack, manfully though Pallett in particular performed. Much depended upon him after a loss of form by Whitehead, so serious that the spinner took only five wickets in the first four matches. In the games against Essex, Derbyshire, Surrey, Yorkshire and Surrey, Pallett bowled the equivalent of 229 six-ball overs and took 19 wickets for 503 runs.

By mid-June, Warwickshire were still without a win, but Whitehead returned to form with eight wickets in the first innings against Lancashire at Liverpool, and Santall's five for 36 in the second innings, brought the County's first-ever win against the red rose county. This started a run of four wins in five matches and took the side to fourth in the Championship table. Hampshire provided two more wins to round off a first Championship season that was adequate, yet disappointing after the spectacular rise to first-class status.

Off the field, the historic decision was taken to engage a paid assistant secretary. There was a false start of one year when Mr H. A. Newey nosed out five other candidates, including one R. V. Ryder, but then Ryder, a 23-year-old from Wetherby, began a 50-year administrative career which was to include the first Test match ever to be staged at Edgbaston in 1902 and Warwickshire's first Championship nine years later.

Ansell was re-elected honorary secretary, but he considered his work virtually finished, and the power he had used so effectively to establish Warwickshire's first-class status gradually passed to Ryder.

Ansell, Ryder and Deakins sounds like a doughty soccer half-back line. No other county club has been blessed with three such distinguished and single-minded administrators. They spanned nearly 100 years with a devotion to the cause of Warwickshire cricket which is unsurpassed anywhere in the history of the game.

The 1896 season was the Club's least successful of the decade. They never recovered from the infliction by Yorkshire of what is still the highest total recorded in the County Championship: 887. The visiting captain, Lord Hawke, made little attempt to win the game, his batsmen batting throughout the first two days until 6.20 pm. The rules of the time curiously precluded a declaration until the third day, and the suggestion that the Yorkshire batsmen could have been instructed to sacrifice their wickets forgets the hard-headed approach by cricketers of that county which placed them apart from all others for at least the first 70 years of the 20th century, by which time they had won the last of their 30 titles.

For instance, a study of the scorebook for that historic match reveals that their number 7, Bobby Peel, finished with an unbeaten 210, and not only were his last 13 scoring strokes all singles, but at least nine of them were taken at the beginning of an over. Hawke, batting at number 9, scored 166, the fourth hundred of the innings, and if the Warwickshire attack thought they were off the rack when Pallett bowled him, George Hirst came in to score 85 out of 136 added for the ninth wicket with Peel. The home bowlers got through 274.3 five-ball overs, of which Pallett bowled 75.3 to take four for 184 in what was, by common consent, as fine a sustained performance as even he ever turned in for Warwickshire. Incidentally, an over rate of no more than 120 per day hardly suggests that the tactic of a fielding captain slowing things down as a defensive ploy was unknown in those days. Coincidentally, it was to be a Yorkshire captain, Brian Close, whose actions in that context in 1967 were responsible for the introduction of the modern legislation which ensures that a minimum of 20 overs are bowled from the start of the last scheduled hour of the final day of a game. Bainbridge completed an unusual double, having fielded throughout the previous highest recorded total in first-class cricket – 843 by the Australians three years earlier at Portsmouth against the Past and Present team of Oxford and Cambridge.

Quaife's 92 ensured a draw, but not even he reached 1,000 runs in the season, and although Lilley's spendid form behind the stumps earned him the first of his 22 home appearances for England against Australia, the decline in his batting together with, as *Wisden* put it, bowling 'which was too much of the same character and lacking pace' meant that the side inevitably struggled throughout the summer.

The Australians beat Warwickshire by an innings and 60 runs, but consolation to the young Ryder came from record gate receipts of £2,601 provided by a paying public of over 10,000, which was among the largest crowds Ryder had seen at Edgbaston.

Ryder's salary was increased to £125 a year once he agreed to sign a three-year agreement, and other notable happenings of the year included a dispute between the Committee and Syd Barnes concerning his expenses in the only match he played that season, away against Essex at Leyton.

An on-field dispute occurred between W. G. Grace and Bainbridge at Bristol when, after the Warwickshire captain had been promised the loan of a twelfth man by W. G. and therefore abandoned his plans to bring one down from Birmingham, the worthy Doctor rather unworthily reneged on his word and Bainbridge had to make do with a local fielder whose unsuitability had prompted the original negotiations. The Warwickshire victory by five wickets did not lessen Bainbridge's indignation at what, even for Grace, was an unsporting act.

Warwickshire's final match at Edgbaston against Derbyshire gave Tom Fishwick his debut. The 20-year-old from Stone, who played for Wellingborough School, scored an impressive 55 to start a 14-season career in which he went on to score 8,644 runs at 26.28, including 12 hundreds. *Wisden* did not overlook his debut: 'Distinctly the best batting on the side. Mr Fishwick is likely to be heard of again.'

The search for talent went on, with fast bowler Frank Field from Pershore, and Sep Kinneir, a young batsman from Wiltshire, taken on the staff, but it was more with hope than expectation that the Edgbaston authorities approached the 1897 season.

The summer was glorious, and so, for the batsmen, were the home pitches. No fewer than eight of the side averaged over 22, but with the bowling no more penetrative, the first six matches failed to produce a win, and the first three at Edgbaston were all drawn.

Even the skills of Pallett were blunted, although in his benefit match against Lancashire his frustration at bowling 63 five-ball overs to take three wickets for 144 was eased somewhat by receipts of £500. The match lasted the full three days, thanks to separate hundreds by Johnny

Frank Field, who took 982 wickets for Warwickshire in 256 games.

Tyldesley, the seventh batsman to achieve that feat. Field made his debut in the match, and so started a career which was to embrace 23 years and 982 wickets at 23.41 each, the last of which he took in 1920 at the age of 45. He developed into an outstanding fast bowler after overcoming several injuries in his early days, and would have been even more effective had he enjoyed the sort of support that only came when he was in his mid-30s, with the arrival of Frank Foster in 1908, and Harry Howell five years later.

With only a home win against Leicestershire in the first ten games, Warwickshire's high percentage of drawn games enabled them to take advantage of the scoring system, which awarded a point for a win and deducted a point for a defeat. Only five sides in the table finished 'in the black'. A second win against Leicestershire and a magnificent win at Edgbaston against Gloucestershire enabled Warwickshire to finish with a score of minus one, which was good enough to earn seventh place.

At Leicester, Pallett's seven for 67 off 30.4 overs was his last performance of note, and Bainbridge countered a spectacular 126 in 90 minutes from Gilbert Jessop with 101 of his own, which won a narrow, exciting victory by two wickets with 15 minutes to spare.

The following season yielded one victory fewer, which meant a drop of two places in the table, but although the 1898 season was a wet one, Willie Quaife enjoyed a wonderful summer, heading the national averages with figures of 1,219 runs from 20 completed innings at an average of 60.95. In mid-July, he had a run of six consecutive unbeaten innings, in which he scored 60 against Derbyshire, 117 against Hampshire, 157 and 24 against Yorkshire and 52 and 61 against Essex. He was, however, already under fire for the length of some of his innings, and the following year's *Wisden* pulled no punches: 'More than once in his anxiety to keep up his end and secure a not-out innings, he prejudiced his side's prospects of success . . . a little unselfishness would have been more sportsmanlike.'

Strong words, but ones which were to be repeated more than once during Quaife's long career. Perhaps had Bainbridge not been forced to miss the rest of the season after injuring a wrist against Lancashire in June, Quaife might have played differently. The replacement captain, A. C. S. Glover, also had trouble with brother Walter, who was accused of 'insolence' against Gloucestershire at Cheltenham. There was even talk of dismissing the elder Quaife, but a full apology from him resolved the matter.

Wilfred Rhodes had been offered the chance to qualify for the County, but despite the all-rounder's acceptance, a minute from a committee meeting on 4 October 1897 said that 'it was decided on account of heavy expenses already incurred in connection with next year's groundstaff, an engagement would not be offered to W. Rhodes, of Huddersfield'. Which explains why the Yorkshireman's subsequent 4,187 first-class wickets and 39,802 runs stayed at home.

Santall was the mainstay of the attack, but the fact that his aggregate of 68 wickets was more than twice that of any other bowler pinpointed yet again the side's main weakness.

Among the batsmen, the 27-year-old Kinneir made rapid progress to average over 40, and the Wiltshire-born left-hander played until the First World War, scoring 15,040 runs at 32.62, including 25 hundreds. *Wisden* classified him as 'one of the finest batsmen who played for Warwickshire', and despite his being 40 when he scored 158 and 53 not out for the Players, his ability received belated recognition by the England selectors, who chose him to go with Pelham Warner's side to

Australia in 1911–12. He was named a *Wisden* 'Cricketer of the Year' in 1912. After playing his last match in 1914 at the age of 43, he died from natural causes 14 years later, when motorcycling home after a game of golf.

Although Ryder and Quaife were to play such important roles in the next three decades at Edgbaston, both were involved in hard bargaining before the 1899 season. Ryder used an offer to share a business partnership to obtain a four-year agreement with annual £25 increments, but Quaife was marginally less successful. He informed the committee that although he was in receipt of a ten-year contract with an unnamed county which offered to pay him £200 per year, he would stay for a five-year agreement at £3 per week. Was he bluffing or not? The committee did not know and, because they had no way of finding out, decided by 12 votes to five to accede to the 'request'. An unexpected and surprised benefactor was Lilley, because in the interests of parity, the committee extended the same offer to the wicket-keeper, and so in the end, everyone was happy . . . more or less anyway.

The 1899 season was a crowded one. Modern touring teams would blanch at the itinerary undertaken by Joe Darling's Australian party of 14 players, who played for 95 out of 96 weekdays between 18 May and 6 September. No time was allowed between the end of a county match and the start of a Test. Counties could arrange however many fixtures they wished, which is why in comparison with Yorkshire's 28 Championship matches, Warwickshire played 20, and newly promoted Worcestershire just 12. Some counties, notably Yorkshire, even eschewed the tea interval, with Lord Hawke allowing only five minutes for refreshments on the field. In the Nottingham Test there was no tea interval, which inspired one Birmingham critic to suggest that 'Mr Bainbridge might follow the same example'. No comments are available from the umpires of that period, but of course it is still written into the modern playing conditions that, subject to mutual agreement by both captains, a tea interval can be dispensed with under Law 16.

By the end of June, the two midlands neighbours, Warwickshire and Worcestershire, were the only sides without a win, but Warwickshire broke the ice by beating Leicestershire, with both Quaifes and Kinneir scoring hundreds. The next match was the return local derby at Worcester – the first match being abandoned because of rain – and a grim stuggle ended with Warwickshire winning with 30 minutes to spare. Quaife became involved with the crowd, who barracked him so loudly when he batted that he held up play to spin his sun-hat around the handle of his bat. The home captain had to act as peacemaker to end an incident in which the *Birmingham Post* defended

Quaife because the behaviour of the crowd 'was in distinctly bad taste'.

An unusual decisive edge to the next four matches produced wins against Kent and Hampshire, and defeats by Gloucestershire and Kent, and so a season which began so badly ended with the side in seventh place in the table.

Glover was in trouble in the home fixture with Gloucestershire, throwing the ball into the crowd and unwittingly hitting two spectators after he had been jeered following a clumsy mis-field in front of the covered stand. The deputy captain apologised at the end of the game, pleading in mitigation that he considered he was 'deeply insulted by a remark', and the matter was considered closed.

The Warwickshire committee accepted his explanation – but not that of Quaife, who in another spot of bother was reported by the Essex Club for deliberately flouting the rule of the Leyton Ground that only amateurs could use the centre pavilion gate, and professionals must use an entrance on the side. Never mind that the Essex crowd, who saw and understood the incident, cheered Quaife, or that the *Post* said 'Such incidents and unnecessary insistence on class distinctions between amateurs and professionals cannot be for the benefit of the game'. The Warwickshire committee's strong disapproval of Quaife's action, compared with the feeble way they glossed over Glover's much more serious misdemeanour, suggests that they did not share the *Post* correspondent's view.

Wisden chipped away again at Quaife: 'A little more vigour and a little less regard for his individual success would at times have been in the interests of the game.' The little batsman played in two Tests, but scores of 20, 8 and 13 were not good enough to retain his place. Lilley, however, did himself full justice with four appearances.

Fishwick and Field made steady progress, but Santall had a poor season due to illness. Charlesworth was given greater opportunities, but most significantly for the long-term prospects of the Club, the left-arm Lancastrian spinner Sam Hargreave had now qualified, and began a career which eventually brought him 851 wickets at 21.73 in 11 seasons. Frank Foster was later to refer to Hargreave as 'probably one of the best slow left-arm bowlers ever seen'.

CHAPTER FIVE

INTO THE TWENTIETH CENTURY

THE FIRST SIX YEARS OF THE 1900S saw Warwickshire finish either fifth, sixth or seventh in the County Championship, with the pattern of those seasons remarkably similar – a strength and depth in batting which was never matched in the bowling department, despite the rapid advance of Hargreave, who between 1901 and 1906 only once failed to take 100 wickets.

He thus achieved this feat five times for Warwickshire, who have had the feat performed for them remarkably rarely. Including the 14 times that Eric Hollies took 100 or more wickets for the Club, the three-figure total has been reached on only 59 occasions.

The new century began on a sad note, with the death at the age of 70 of David Buchanan. He was such a successful left-arm bowler – for 20 years as a slow bowler after a similar period previously bowling fast – that it is difficult to imagine that he would not have taken wickets against any opposition at any time in the history of the game. After being one of the Club's original founders, he captained the side briefly, before he served as honorary treasurer from 1884 to 1891.

Wisden's summary of Warwickshire's performance in 1900 was that while 'the batting was never stronger, the bowling was scarcely ever poorer'. Santall was ill with scarlet fever and missed most of the season, although Field eased that blow with a sustained effort throughout, which brought him 88 wickets.

It was a wet summer, with 11 of Warwickshire's 18 matches affected by rain. The inherent weakness of the points scoring system, which ignored drawn games in the County Championship, gave Bainbridge's side an undeserved final place of sixth. They won only three of their 18 games – the same number as Worcestershire and Leicestershire, who finished 12th and 14th respectively. Even more unfair was the fate of Middlesex and Gloucestershire, who each won nine of their 22 matches, but because they both lost seven games compared with Warwickshire's two they finished seventh and eighth. In fact, only Derbyshire (two) and Hampshire (none) registered fewer wins. The method of calculating the final order of merit was now based on the percentage of victories gained in matches decided. Sussex were even more fortunate than Warwickshire, gaining third place despite winning just four of their 24 games.

Willie Quaife headed the County averages for the fourth successive season, and finished ninth in the national averages. Kinneir was in

Warwickshire CCC in 1900.
Back row (l to r): S. P. Kinneir, Walter Quaife, C. Charlesworth, F. Field, E. J. Diver, S. Hargreave, W. G. Quaife.
Seated: A. A. Lilley, J. Devey, H. W. Bainbridge (capt.), T. S. Fishwick, F. Dickens.

eighth place, thanks to runs scored in other matches. Ernest Hill played the last innings of his brief career – 665 runs from 34 innings in seven seasons – and ended with 145 against the West Indies in a match which was denied first-class status.

The professional staff at Edgbaston numbered only eight, and an effort to enlarge it resulted in expenditure of over £1,000, which led the Club inexorably to the bank to obtain a secured overdraft of the same amount, in order to clear outstanding debts before the start of the 1901 season.

Quaife was chosen as one of the 'Five Cricketers of the Year' by *Wisden* after another successful season, but even that accolade was not conferred without the almost obligatory reference to the tempo of his batting: 'The only reproach that can be urged against him is that he keeps his average a little too much before his mind, and is apt to play a slow game when caution is the last thing needed by his side.'

Ansell claimed that the general slow play of the previous season was the reason behind some counties, including Warwickshire, reducing their fixtures. He told members that several clubs were in financial difficulties, and with fewer invitations extended to Warwickshire, the Club had to undertake a reduced fixture list of 16 matches – the least played by any of the counties.

Quaife, unusually, had topped the County bowling averages as well, his newly developed leg-breaks bringing 37 wickets at 22.51

each. Even more unusual was that his action was previously so suspect that he was on a list of bowlers drawn up by county captains, who agreed not to use those bowlers. Suspect or not, he went on to take 900 wickets in his long career, and it is to his credit that he was able to switch to spin so effectively.

The annual meeting was warned of impending subscription increases unless the 1901 season were a successful one, but the members' fears were quickly allayed by their players, who combined to record their most successful season since joining the County Championship – achieving fifth position for the first time in seven seasons.

Quaife and Kinneir averaged over 50, Quaife at one stage hitting four hundreds in five innings. With Charlesworth improving still further and Hargreave taking over 100 wickets in all first-class cricket, seven Championship matches were won, four lost, and five drawn. More important, six wins came at Edgbaston to generate the sort of support needed to boost Warwickshire's claims for a Test match, and although Frank Foster's dramatic entry into first-class cricket was still seven years away, the rest of what was to be the Championship side of 1911 were beginning to weld into a formidable attacking unit.

The South Africans were beaten – Warwickshire's first win against a first-class touring side – and Lilley's benefit match against Yorkshire was a financial success with receipts of £849 the highest yet for the County.

One of the most meritorious victories came in the return game against Lancashire, who had thrashed Warwickshire in the first game of a season. Quaife and Kinneir added 327 for the third wicket, with the little man unusually hitting out towards the end of his 177, while his left-handed partner remained unbeaten with 215. The total of 532 for four declared was permissible under the new declaration law, which was amended the previous year to allow a second-day closure, provided it took place after lunch.

A six-wicket burst from Field brought about a Lancashire collapse to 253 all out from the prosperous position of 184 for two, but with the fast bowler unable to bowl much more because of an attack of muscular rheumatism, the game looked liked drifting to a draw until the introduction of Quaife and his leg-breaks did the trick.

After another high-scoring match at Leyton there were hopes of beating the Champions, Yorkshire, but Warwickshire were caught on a drying pitch and seemed certain to follow on. A masterly defensive performance by Quaife, however, for once brought unreserved approval from the anxious crowd, even though the first 50 of his unbeaten 118 took three hours.

The game was saved, and the away game at Derby would have been won, thanks to another fine hundred from Quaife, but for rain washing out play when Warwickshire needed 38 to win. The chance of a rare win in Yorkshire was thrown away by fielding errors which were estimated to have cost 300 runs, but the side bounced back with a wonderful win against Surrey at Edgbaston.

At one stage, with Warwickshire 22 ahead with only five second-innings wickets left, a Surrey win seemed certain, but with Santall and Field adding 48, the visitors were finally set 125 to win. Even then, at 44 without loss at lunch, the home side had such little chance that most spectators went home, but Hargreave and Charlesworth engineered a breakthrough so successfully that the pendulum swung the Surrey score to 89 for eight. Santall was off the field, with Ryder the substitute, but the neat hand of the assistant secretary deserted him when he dropped the dangerous Lees, who had just cleared the pavilion with a massive six. Fortunately for everyone's peace of mind, Field took the last wicket to seal a win that the *Post* correspondent wrote was 'far and away the best performance for many seasons'.

Worcestershire were thrashed, thanks to Quaife taking 12 wickets for 127 in a match which was remarkable for the dismissal of the visiting wicket-keeper, T. Straw, for obstructing the field for the second time on the ground in three seasons. Straw is the only man to be given out twice for this offence in first-class cricket, and even more remarkably, his double transgression – against Glover in 1899 and Lilley in 1901 – comprises half the total of four recorded instances in the history of County Championship cricket up to the end of the 1989 season.

Warwickshire finished the season in style with an innings victory over Derbyshire, although the sloppy fielding which cost at least three more wins attracted further criticism. It was such a widespread malaise that one critic rather originally suggested that even dropped catches should bring about a batsman's dismissal. He said that would certainly reduce the number of drawn games.

At the end of the season, Walter Quaife applied for a benefit, but despite his nine years' service, and the circumstances surrounding his original engagement he was insensitively sacked, to end a 17-year first-class career, in which he twice played for the Players.

Despite its successful playing record, the Club recorded a loss of £100, and after somewhat unethically borrowing from Lilley's benefit funds in the winter, the committee decided they would have to increase the subscription. Attempts to unseat Lord Willoughby de Broke from the presidency he had held since 1881 were unsuccessful, although he died within the year while undertaking a cruise for the benefit of his health.

Quaife and Lilley toured Australia under the captaincy of Archie

MacLaren, and although both played in all five Tests, the side was outgunned, losing the series 4-1, with Lilley scoring 211 runs and Quaife only 184, with moderate averages of 23.44 and 20.44.

The 1902 season brought the first Test match ever staged at Edgbaston, to bring to fruition yet another of the many dreams of William Ansell which seemed unattainable when he initially shaped the faltering administrative side of cricket in the county of Warwickshire.

The decision to allocate a Test match against Australia to Edgbaston was made at Lord's on 1 February – shades of today's long-term planning, when such a decision would take at least three seasons to implement – and much activity had resulted in new stands being erected, as well as 3,000 seats being loaned from Aston Villa Football Club.

Ryder had masterminded the arrangements, which evolved from 36 general committee meetings held in the previous 12 months in anticipation of the late decision from Lord's. Provisions were made for a catering staff of 200 and, even more surprisingly, 90 pressmen. Only just over half that number of accredited cricket correspondents were housed at the last Test Match at Edgbaston against Australia in 1989, but such was the phenomenal interest aroused 87 years earlier that 60 gatemen and the same number of policemen were engaged.

Almost proudly, Ryder ran the whole show with no clerical staff, typewriter or even telephone, although the latter instrument might have prevented the near-riot which took place on the third day of the rain-ruined game.

The England selectors – newly constituted in 1899 – before which the respective ground authorities used to pick the team – had chosen a team of all the talents. Seldom can a captain have led such a team as MacLaren was given: C. B. Fry, K. S. Ranjitsinhji, F. S. Jackson, J. T. Tyldesley, G. H. Hirst, G. L. Jessop, L. C. Braund, W. H. Lockwood, W. Rhodes and A. A. Lilley. The three players omitted were Tom Hayward, J. R. Mason and C. B. Llewellyn.

Tyldesley's 138 in 260 minutes pulled the England innings round, and on the second day, after MacLaren had declared at 376 for nine, Yorkshire got to work, with Rhodes taking seven for 17 and Hirst three for 15. Australia were rushed out for 36 and, following on, were 8 without loss when, as happened in 1989, rain stopped play early, with several hours of rain, then and during the night, putting the ground under water.

At 11.30 am next day, it began to rain again, and the fateful decision was taken to release half the gatemen and policemen. Perversely, the sun shone, and with thousands of growingly impatient spectators outside the ground, the umpires advised that the gates could be opened at 3.45 pm, although the Club minute says 4.30 pm.

At the city end of the ground, only one turnstile was manned and the two policemen on duty were powerless to maintain order when the entrance was opened. Hoardings were smashed and many people were reported to be thrown to the ground in the scramble. Mercifully there were no serious injuries.

Play started at 5.15 pm, but although Rhodes took two more wickets to show what might have been but for the rain, Australia saved the game with little trouble.

Over 25,000 people officially attended the historic match, but after the Australians' share of the gate had been paid, the running expenses left a deficit of over £2,000 – and that was before claims began to come in from people for damage to clothing.

Warwickshire's playing season was again successful, their sixth position in the table a reward for the efforts of a team described by *Wisden* thus: 'They have seldom had a better eleven than in 1902. Nevertheless, the wet summer played havoc with the home programme – seven of the 11 fixtures were badly affected by rain – and it was thus not surprising that with an overall deficit of £3,000, a public appeal was launched.'

The response was magnificent, with Aston Villa and West Bromwich football clubs staging benefit matches, while in addition to proceeds from special performances staged by the Empire and Gaiety theatres, offices, factories and the city's 1,500 public houses were canvassed so successfully that in in four months £3,700 was raised, and the Club's finances were once again on the right side of the ledger.

Of even greater historical significance than the staging of Edgbaston's first test match was the decision by Ansell to resign at the age of 53. He had again been criticised for what some members saw as his personal responsibility for the reluctance of some county clubs to play Warwickshire. Ansell was adamant that their reasons were financial and not personal, and refused the offer of a vice-presidency because, as the chairman, George Cartland, said, he did not wish 'to be raised to the House of Lords'.

Ansell itemised in writing his reasons for wishing to step down, and they could be sub-divided thus: the routine ground matters on which he disagreed with Club policy, included the question of equipment, and the curtailment of the privileges of the public in the matter of pass-out checks. More significantly, he referred in the letter to his doubts about whether any honorary secretary were necessary: 'The office is purely a nominal one, carrying responsibility with little power.'

With Ryder eager to assume both responsibility and power, it made little sense for Ansell to stay, and so came to an end the career at Edgbaston of the man without whom it is unlikely there would ever have been a Warwickshire County Cricket Club – certainly not in the form it took under his driving guidance.

Happily, his retirement was fittingly marked with a dinner at the Old Royal Hotel in Temple Row, Birmingham, to which all past and present committee members were invited. Cartland gave Ansell the entire credit for starting the Club and then presented him with a combined secretaire and roll-topped desk, while Mrs Ansell received a gold and opal bracelet. Ansell's reply, made on the 28th anniversary of his wedding, included proud references to the Edgbaston ground and the team – both of which he said were poised to go forward to even better things.

Ansell's subsequent election to honorary life membership was a fitting gesture to a man who, more than anyone else, was responsible for bringing first-class cricket to Birmingham. The fact that he was only 53 when he retired says much for his foresight and visionary attributes in his younger days, particularly in the last quarter of the 19th century.

CHAPTER SIX

THE ARRIVAL OF FRANK FOSTER

LATE IN APRIL 1903, James Frederick Byrne was appointed County captain and exactly three weeks later the great Nottinghamshire batsman, Arthur Shrewsbury, shot himself at the age of 47 because he thought he had an incurable illness. The poignant link between the two happenings was forged 11 years earlier, when Shrewsbury was employed in April 1892 to coach the Warwickshire players before the start of the season. At the end of his month's engagement, he wrote appraisals of several youngsters, including this one: 'Mr J. F. Byrne should be a welcome member of the county team when he gets thoroughly into practice.'

Following that assessment, apart from 1897 when he scored 642 runs in 20 innings, Byrne played little until 1901, due to business commitments, including a period abroad. Like Peter Cranmer 35 years later, he was an England international at rugby, who brought the same sort of hustling, enthusiastic approach to his cricket activities as Cranmer would.

His first match produced an unexpected win at the Oval where a player who was not chosen for the match took 15 wickets for 75, enabling Warwickshire to beat Surrey by 105 runs, even though because of rain, the visitors had only 170 minutes in which to take ten wickets. The destructive bowler was Hargreave, who was originally not named because he was still completing his month-long voyage home from the tour of Australia and New Zealand, and when the match was due to start, the ship had still not reached Tilbury.

Heavy rain washed out the first day, and so, although travel-weary and short of practice, Hargreave played and masterminded the win in just over a day and a half. It was the start of a magnificent season for the slow left-arm bowler, who took 134 wickets in all first-class cricket at 14.02 each to earn him seventh place in the national averages and the tribute from *Wisden* that he was 'among the great bowlers of the year'.

Another wet summer denied likely victories at Old Trafford but again in the return match against Surrey Hargreave took 11 for 68 against his native Lancashire, and another 12 in the innings victory against Leicestershire took his side to the top of the table by 20 May. But a decision by Byrne to field first on a rain-affected pitch against Worcestershire was costly, and defeat was followed by three successive matches spoiled by rain, including one at Leyton where Hargreave had bowled unchanged again, for the fourth time in an innings that season, to take eight for 42 from 27.5 overs as Essex were routed for 78.

Byrne's faith in the partnership of Hargreave and Field was often carried stubbornly to excess – notably against Derbyshire, when a likely win receded when the two bowled 83 overs, even though wickets were not falling.

Also against Lancashire, the same bowlers delivered 72 overs compared with 32 by the rest of the attack, and the *Post* condemned Byrne for a 'reluctance to experiment'. Quaife scored only one hundred, but was consistent enough to average 36.18.

The year was one of change. In addition to the retirement of Ansell and the election of a new president, the fifth Earl of Warwick, Bainbridge became honorary secretary, despite the advice of Ansell that the office was redundant. Ryder was offered a new three-year contract with a special award of £25 for the work he had done the previous winter for the appeal fund, but he was still denied a telephone, because the committee felt that he should continue to transmit match results by telegram.

Quaife, Lilley and Moorhouse – a Yorkshire all-rounder – were given five-year contracts, Charlesworth and Field agreements of three years, while Santall was limited to one year. A young player who was to share an association with Edgbaston that was to last professionally for nearly 70 years was Ernest James Smith, an 18-year-old wicket-keeper from Bournville who, because of his readiness to fight any battles of his own or other 'under-dogs', was soon christened 'Tiger' by Lilley, after a boxer named 'Tiger' Smith fought for the British Championship.

Lilley became the first Warwickshire player to captain the Players in both matches against the Gentlemen at Lord's and the Oval, although the amateurs won both matches, thanks to B. J. T. Bosanquet and his googlies.

Warwickshire's reputation as a dull side still precluded fixtures against several clubs, including Kent, Middlesex, Nottinghamshire, Somerset and Sussex. When, additionally, Essex and Gloucestershire also refused to play in 1904, Warwickshire were faced with the real prospect of dropping out of the County Championship because they would be unable to play the required minimum number of games. Happily, Essex relented, but the Edgbaston authorities were on a knife-edge with 16 games, again the least of all the counties.

Warwickshire finished in seventh place in the table for the second of what was to be three successive identical final placings, but the season was overshadowed by tragedy. Whitehead, who last played in 1900, was awarded a joint benefit with another former stalwart from the 1880s and 1890s, Walter Richards. The allocated home match was against Essex, and Warwickshire won a high-scoring match in which Quaife scored an unbeaten 200.

Whitehead was taken ill during the game, and although he insisted on watching the final day's play, he was dead within 24 hours at the age of 41. A post-mortem revealed tuberculosis and a pleurisy of such long standing that it must have affected his last years as a player, when his form declined so rapidly.

Santall remembered him as 'the best of comrades and a credit to his profession', but the net receipts from the game of £205, especially as they had to be divided with Richards, who was now a first-class umpire, provided little compensation to Mrs Whitehead and her four children. The *Sports Argus* ran a trust fund for the children which realised £135, but Whitehead was another case of a man whose sporting career never brought him adequate financial recompense.

Field was only fit enough to play in four games, but his seven for 63 at Huddersfield and 11 for 119 in the match brought Warwickshire their first-ever win against Yorkshire in the County Championship, at Huddersfield, by six runs.

Despite a welcome fine summer in which Quaife averaged 63 thanks to a run of four hundreds in successive games, the Club's financial problems continued, with the public offering such meagre support that the annual report, itemising a loss of £659, said 'the fact is that there has been little or no growth in the patronage of the public during the last ten years. Unless this is forthcoming there is little prospect of the Club being able to pay its way'.

The following season of 1905, in which Northamptonshire were given first-class status, was no better for the Edgbaston authorities. The team did not win a match until the beginning of July, and altogether there were 13 draws out of a fixture list now happily extended to 22 games, thanks to Sussex, Somerset and Northamptonshire agreeing to play Warwickshire.

In the end, five victories came against Northamptonshire (twice), Essex, Derbyshire and Hampshire, who occupied four of the bottom five places in the table. The balance of the team was again lop-sided, with Quaife leading the batsmen to many large scores, made in a way and at a tempo that again prompted criticism that little thought was given by some individuals to the needs of the side.

Quaife scored six hundreds to top 2,000 runs at an average of 54.21 and finished third in the national averages, while Kinneir returned to form, Fishwick played several attractive innings and there was a promising start from Charles Baker, who was to score nearly 10,000 runs for Warwickshire.

Byrne's leadership again was suspect, notably in the home match against Lancashire, when he allowed his side's first innings to reach 518 for eight before he declared in mid-afternoon on the second day – and that after he and Kinneir had put on 333 for the first wicket on the first day. Kinneir scored 158 and Byrne 222. Another double hundred came from Quaife (255 not out) in a game at the Oval in which Warwickshire scored 676 for seven in reply to Surrey's 479.

Essex were beaten on 5 July, with Fishwick scoring 116 at nearly a run a minute. In August Fishwick scored 460 runs in eight completed innings.

An official complaint was received by the committee from a member about the slow play of Quaife and Kinneir, and *Wisden* said: 'A little more resolution to try and win, and a little less endeavour to avoid being beaten would, in our opinion, largely increase the local interest, and improve the financial position of the county club.' Chairman Cartland concurred with that view, and told the Annual General Meeting in 1905 that he wished to record the committee's general dissatisfaction with the team's record.

The team was beset with injuries at the start of the 1906 season, a dislocated elbow sustained by Field in the second match by far the most serious. He did not play again that summer, but Hargreave's 101 wickets papered over some pretty wide cracks in a side which, for once, was short of runs.

Perhaps because he was called upon to bowl much more, Quaife failed to reach 1,000 runs – a mark which was only passed by Devey, who achieved the rare feat of scoring a hundred in his own benefit match against Surrey, when he retired at the end of the 1907 season he had scored 6,615 runs at an average of 28.20 in a career which lasted 14 seasons. However, he is best remembered in Birmingham as the centre forward and captain of Aston Villa during the same period.

The Earl of Warwick was succeeded as president by Lord Calthorpe in a year which showed another loss – this time of £312, which resulted in an overall deficit for the year of £800. Different people offered different solutions, but Ryder adopted a more practical approach. He tramped the streets, knocking on doors to obtain new members, and actually enrolled 600 of them – an amazing personal performance which typified the hardheaded approach of a man who had the strength to carry the Club through its lean times.

The 1907 season began with Byrne resigning the captaincy, and then reconsidering his decision, although Fishwick finally took over at the end of May. Before then Worcestershire were defeated, thanks to a career best of 171 from Lilley, and after the change in captaincy Northamptonshire were easily beaten by 125 runs. Yet stormclouds were gathering on and off the field, with the poor financial outlook affecting morale.

Lilley and the Quaife brothers were in legal dispute, after a sporting goods business partnership failed to provide agreement on their respective marketing rights, and the matter was so serious that it had to be resolved at the Birmingham Assizes. The Judge found for the Quaifes, but the Warwickshire committee could hardly have been impressed, with the two senior players unable to play in the away matches against Lancashire and Yorkshire.

The normally equable Hargreave was next to become involved in acrimonious dispute – in his case it was with the Club, who strangely insisted that he play in a Club and Ground game at Old Hill, although he had already declined to play. The local press supported the player, but the committee first omitted him from the match against the South Africans, and then on 24 June – 16 days after his first refusal – made him play in another Club and Ground match.

It was an untidy season, with the side dropping to ninth place. Lilley missed several more games after injuring a finger in the first Test against South Africa, and deputy captain Fishwick had to do duty with the gloves. Devey's form declined, but Kinneir distinguished himself by carrying his bat twice in the away game against Leicestershire. He scored 70 out of 239 and 69 out of 166. At that time only three batsmen – Bainbridge, Quaife and Fishwick – had achieved the feat once for the County.

No batsman scored 1,000 runs, and only three hundreds were made, but Santall came to the rescue with his best season – 101 wickets at 16.62 each.

So gloomy was the general outlook at the end of the season that nobody could have foreseen the miracle that was just four years away. A miracle that was to be brought about through the genius of a cricketer who joined Warwickshire as a 19-year-old in 1908, and produced these startling match figures on his debut at Derby on 25 June 1908: 36.4 overs, 15 maidens, 52 runs, 6 wickets.

The genius was Frank Rowbotham Foster from Small Heath.

CHAPTER SEVEN

COUNTY CHAMPIONS

A CONTINUATION OF WARWICKSHIRE'S playing slump took them to 12th place in the table – their lowest position since 1896 when they were also 12th – with a drop of three places for the second consecutive year, proof of the players' inability to convert their undoubted skills into match-winning cricket.

Byrne was replaced as captain by A. C. S. Glover, who had first played for the Club in 1895, but any successful team needs a good attack, and not even the revival of the fortunes of Field and the debut of Foster could reverse a desperate start in which six of the first nine matches were lost, and none won.

Field, at long last injury-free, took 106 wickets at 20.66 apiece, but with Hargreave missing the second half of the season because of injury it needed something out of the ordinary to bring relief to a season that could not even provide that great servant, Santall, with a satisfactory benefit return. His 14 years' tireless service should have brought proper recompense, but a rain-ruined match against Yorkshire yielded pathetic receipts of £270, and even a big effort to increase that amount only resulted in the all-rounder receiving £400 – under half the amount received by Lilley seven years earlier.

There was one redeeming feature of the depressing season – the debut of Foster. It was story-book stuff for the 19-year-old, Small Heath all-rounder. He was given permission by his employers to play in five county games – the first of which was in the tenth game of the season at Derby. It was a pretty dispirited Warwickshire team he joined, but not only did Foster match Field's six wickets in the match, his efforts contributed to that first elusive win on 25 June.

An examination of Warwickshire's performance later in the season reveals a line in the scorebook that was a gleaming signpost for the start of the next decade – at Test as well as Club level. At the Oval, in Foster's second game, he had Tom Hayward stumped by 'Tiger' Smith, a fate to befall the Australian Clem Hill three years later at Adelaide. Foster was later to describe Smith as 'the very best leg taker I have ever seen', and although the modern player might think such praise too fulsome, they should remember that, together with other bowlers of his type of that period, Foster bowled his left-arm deliveries from *round* the wicket, which made him so much more difficult for a wicket-keeper to see, with his stock ball coming across the right-handed batsmen.

Even in the 1930s, the Nottinghamshire left-arm fast bowler, Bill Voce, operated from round the wicket, because of the different lbw

Frank Foster, the first player to do the double for Warwickshire. His brilliant career of just seven seasons produced 5436 runs and 587 wickets in 127 games.

law obtaining then, although since the Second World War all the leading Test bowlers of that type – Alan Davidson and Gary Sobers, for instance – invariably bowled over the wicket with the new ball. Foster bowled off a run-up of around ten yards only and, in order to accentuate his natural inswing to the right-hander, used the edge of the return crease as his stock point of delivery: a wicket-keeper's nightmare if the glove-man chose to stand up to the stumps.

Foster took 23 wickets in his five games, and gave clear indication of the talent that was to blaze a glorious trail to the title in 1911. The 36-year-old Glover was praised by *Wisden* for his captaincy, and Lilley – six years older – considered that the playing strength was such that the 1909 season could be anticipated with some relish. He still had five Tests to play in that year against Australia, but the rise of Smith behind the stumps was to prove irresistible, and Lilley's last years with the Club were as a batsman.

An interesting feature of the 1908 season was the introduction, for the first time, of Saturday starts. An initiative from the Leicestershire secretary, Mr Robson, resulted in Warwickshire taking part in the first County match to start on a Saturday – on 9 May at Leicester, and Ryder finally overcame the reservations of those amateurs who wanted their week-ends left free, to experiment with three Saturday starts at Edgbaston. The following year, five Warwickshire games started on Saturdays, and despite opposition from Yorkshire and Kent, a strong lobby among the other counties pushed a proposal through the Advisory County Cricket Committee that all matches from 1914 onwards should begin on Saturdays and Wednesdays. The First World War postponed the implementation of what was then still considered to be a daring experiment, until 1920.

The 1909 season was even worse for the Warwickshire team than the previous summer. Their final position of 12th for the second successive season prompted *Wisden* to write: 'We are forced to the conclusion that some of the crack players are not getting any younger.'

Only Quaife, now 37 years old, scored over 1,000 runs, and although Foster's total of wickets improved to 49 from 18 matches, the decline of the form of Field (45 Championship wickets), and the end of Hargreave's splendid, but all too short career, meant that winning opportunities were rare.

Not until the 12th match of the season, on 14 July, did Warwickshire triumph in an exciting finish against Sussex, thanks to a ninth-wicket partnership of 47 between Santall and Foster. Only two other games were won, and one of the heaviest defeats was against Worcestershire, who won at Edgbaston by an innings and 233 runs.

The side lost the toss 15 times, an unbalanced percentage that was still better than that achieved by the England captain, MacLaren, who lost all five tosses to the Australian captain, Montague Noble. Inevitably, such success with the coin enabled Australia to win the series 2-1 and retain the Ashes, but at least the Edgbaston Test match gave England their solitary success by ten wickets.

The Edgbaston Test also ensured that, although the Club receipts were the lowest in 1909 for 17 years, there was a surplus of £477. Around the country, the outlook for 1910 was little brighter, with Derbyshire perilously close to going out of existence.

Warwickshire's playing record went from bad to worse in 1910, despite the dramatic advance from Foster, who took 112 wickets in all matches, and no less an authority than Plum Warner said that had an England team been picked that summer, 'Foster would surely have been in it.'

Glover had given up the captaincy, with H. J. Goodwin, the son of the Club's treasurer, elected in his place. He was only 24, and it is hard to imagine a more difficult task for a youngster to persuade senior players to play at a tempo they found difficult to sustain, and although several amateurs were tried, the fact that six players took part in every match, and two more missed only one, shows what a hard nut to crack was a professional approach that badly needed a spark of inventiveness.

The attack did well, with Field and Santall profiting from the sheer class of Foster, and other markers put down for the Championship title that was now but a year way, included the best season to date of Charlesworth, who headed the averages and scored a wonderful 216 in even time against Derbyshire – easily the best innings played for the Club that season. His runs came in a high scoring match, out of 504 for seven, and in addition to six sixes, he hit 30 fours. Derbyshire were in trouble in their second innings until Warren (123) and Chapman (165) added 283 in 175 minutes for the ninth wicket, and over 80 years later, that is still the world record.

Goodwin led the side in only half the games, and although his dash and vigour occasioned praise, the lack of continuity at the top was too big a handicap for the side to overcome. Lilley played as a batsman, now that Smith – 13 years his junior – was clearly ready to take the gloves on a permanent basis. Not least of the new wicket-keeper's qualities was a self-confidence that carried him through times of adversity that would have lowered the morale of a less resilient man. Over 40 years later when Smith was Senior Coach at Edgbaston in the early 1950s, the young Bannister asked him how he used to react whenever he dropped a catch. Smith's reply was typical: 'I never ever dropped one' . . . pause of several seconds, before the punchline was delivered with a twinkling smile: 'Mind you, a hell of a lot fell out.'

The season was notable for two things. Foster's batting began to make an increasingly significant impact, and the system of points scoring in the County Championship was so unsatisfactory that it was altered for 1911 in a manner that was to be a crucial factor in Warwickshire's title win.

First things first, and the Warwickshire committee made a captaincy appointment in January 1911 which turned out to be a stroke of genius. Foster, only just 22, was given the job, just before Santall's first history of the Club gave Bainbridge the chance to put on record his dissatisfaction with the side's fielding *ever since they had enjoyed first-class status*. And that from the man who was not in favour of regular practice once the season had started – the view he put forward when Shrewsbury was engaged for a month in 1892.

The Annual General Meeting had to listen to a revealing, but depressing, account from Ryder of the financial structure of the modern game. The previous year's deficit was £434, compounded by a drop in subscriptions of over £300. The attractions of golf were advanced as one reason for the local apathy, and among the gnats strained after to improve the playing performance, was the suggestion at the meeting by Cartland that if the outfield was left uncut, batsmen would have to run their runs, and that would discourage 'stout and elderly gentlemen continuing so long in county cricket as they have done in the past'.

Presumably the said elderly professionals did not offer themselves new contracts each year, so any responsibility for the employment of cricketers who were too old must rest with the Club.

The season began with Warwickshire in disarray. Foster first accepted the captaincy, and then refused it because of an engagement which, so said the *Post*, 'altered his immediate plans'. Captain Cowan, a distinguished naval officer, who was to become treasurer after the Second World War, led the side in the first match of the season on 4, 5 and 6 May against Surrey, but bagged two of the ten ducks suffered by Warwickshire who, despite bowling out Surrey for 195, lost by an innings and 46 runs.

Seldom can the ultimate County Champions have started a season so disastrously – and that after finishing ahead of only Derbyshire and Somerset in the table the previous year. Foster senior apparently promptly told Frank that his Club obviously needed him and he had better answer the call. That one decision was to revolutionise Warwickshire cricket in the most dramatic fashion imaginable, with the young Foster bestriding English cricket like a colossus.

The new system of scoring, proposed by Somerset, at last tried to allow for drawn games – giving three points to the side leading on first innings, and one point to the other side. For winning a match, a side would now win five points, with matches in which there was no result on the first innings not counting.

Foster's first match in charge was at Old Trafford, and what a thrashing was handed to a side which finished fourth for three successive seasons, starting in 1910. Both sides were bowled out on the first day, with Warwickshire's 201 earning them an unexpected lead of 50, thanks to an inspired piece of captaincy from Foster, who was to show many times that summer that youth knows no fear.

Tyldesley, who had scored so heavily against Warwickshire in the past, came in early, and Foster immediately brought on Jack Parsons. The 20-year-old was to go on to score 16,737 runs in a first-class career which lasted – except for a four-year break from 1919 to 1923 because of regular army duties – until 1934 when he was then 43. He was also to take 55 wickets in those 22 seasons, but none could have been more valuable than his first – the mighty Tyldesley, whom he had caught down the leg side by Smith off his first ball 'loosener'.

An attacking 110 from Charlesworth, well supported by 91 from Quaife and 61 from Kinneir, meant that Lancashire needed 416 to win, and Foster juggled his attack so well that four of them shared the ten wickets to beat the home side by 117 runs. Warwickshire were on their way, and two more consecutive victories followed against Leicestershire and Sussex. The win at Edgbaston against Leicestershire was achieved thanks to some splendid second-innings batting from Kinneir (102), Lilley (90), and Charlesworth (51), which enabled Foster's side to score 266 to win, with the last 82 coming in an hour. And so to Coventry and Sussex. Another brilliant 116 in two hours from Charlesworth set up a win in which Foster played a substantial part with six wickets for 40 in the Sussex innings, and then the captain held the tail together in Warwickshire's second innings to clinch the third consecutive victory.

Defeat by Worcestershire put the side into ninth place in the table, and not even their most avid supporters could have forecast what was to come in July and August. At Worcester, Warwickshire's 213 earned them a first-innings lead of 12, but a splendid 155 from Pearson meant that the visitors had to score 300 to win on a pitch which was far more helpful to bowlers than those in previous years, when the local derbys provided an instant recipe for dull, high-scoring draws. Warwickshire lost by 116, and returned to Edgbaston to meet Yorkshire in a match which was also lost, despite a phenomenal all-round performance by Foster. Coming in with his side's innings on the verge of ruin at 61 for five, he smashed a brilliant 105 in 135 minutes to steer Warwickshire to 317, and then surpassed himself with the ball when Yorkshire were cruising to a substantial lead at 299 for three. He took the last seven wickets – clean bowling five – in 33 balls to finish with the first ever nine-wicket haul on the ground. His magnificent figures of 29.3-4-

118-9 subsequently earned him the presentation of the suitably mounted ball.

Yorkshire's lead was thus limited to 30, but an opening stand of 130 between Parsons and Kinneir was not supported and, needing 219 to win, Yorkshire got home by four wickets, despite another three wickets for Foster.

A trip to Blackwell in Derbyshire put the Club back on the victory trail. They won a low-scoring game, thanks to two more precocious gambles by the new captain. He promoted wicket-keeper Smith to open the second innings, and Smith's forthright 81 meant that Derbyshire needed 176 to win. At 131 for five they were well placed, when Foster brought on A. B. Crawford, a young pace bowler making his championship debut. His final career tally of wickets was to number only 13. No matter, the first two were vital. Needham and Root quickly went to the tyro, and Warwickshire won their fourth game of the season.

Their seesaw form continued at Gloucester in another low-scoring contest in which no batsman reached fifty. Field and Dennett each took 12 wickets in the game, with the Gloucestershire victory by three wickets probably turning on Foster's mistaken decision not to bowl Field until the home side was 100 for two because of the wet pitch. The fast bowler promptly took seven for 29 in 11.1 overs, but the damage was done – for the last time that season, because Foster, obviously a quick learner, opened the bowling with himself and Field in all of the remaining matches that summer except one.

At this stage, Warwickshire were in the bottom half of the table in tenth position, but with four wins and four defeats in the first nine games, the significant attacking approach of the new captain, together with the marvellous personal playing example he set, meant that the team was no longer one whose first thoughts were negative. Some titles are won by front runners, and most of the others are taken by sides who are in the top few positions throughout the season. Occasionally a side bursts out of the pack to race through and bring off a shock result, but seldom can a Club have come from so far back as did Warwickshire, with a marvellous run of nine wins from the last 12 games, with first-innings lead taken in the other three drawn matches.

They took 54 points out of a possible 60, beginning with a crushing win against Hampshire by an innings and 296, despite the absence of Foster who was playing in the second Test Trial at Lord's, after refusing to play in the first Trial because he thought he would be unavailable for the coming tour of Australia.

He took nine for 154 in the trial, with Phil Mead's selection balancing the demands on the Hampshire game. Byrne led the side, and Kinneir obliged with what was then the highest score for

Warwickshire – an unbeaten 268 scored in 430 minutes. Field, now striking top form, finished the match with a conclusive hat-trick in which he clean bowled all three victims.

Foster's return against Surrey was not marked by a win, but he scored a magnificent 200 in three hours, including three sixes, two fives and 21 fours. When he, Field and Santall reduced Surrey to 182 for nine, there were high hopes of a win against the Championship leaders, but after Hitch and Strudwick added 131 for the last wicket, Foster did not enforce the follow-on. Smith scored a second-innings hundred – one of 20 he scored for the Club – but Surrey did not attempt the stiff target of 396 in four hours, and so the game ended as one of only three games Warwickshire did not win before the end of the summer. Kinneir was chosen for the Players and won his place to Australia the following winter with a match aggregate of 201 for once out.

Foster and Field decimated Northamptonshire in a match in which Quaife scored both a hundred and a fifty (Foster scored a brilliant 98), and in the following game Kinneir's two separate hundreds at Chichester took full advantage of Foster's ninth successive win of the toss to bring the second of four consecutive wins.

Before the third success against Gloucestershire, Warwickshire had slipped into fifth place in the table, with Foster making it clear to his players for the first time that they could win the Championship. The Saturday start to the game was rewarded with a 12,000 crowd, and what an individual performance Foster turned on.

Gloucestershire scored 340 – a total which rarely leads to defeat – but a quick-fire 56 from Foster enabled him to declare unexpectedly before the end of the second day. His enterprise was rewarded with two quick wickets, and after he had completed a match haul of eight wickets on the final day, his 87 in 75 minutes won another great victory.

The next game inspired even better deeds from a young man who was now the talk of the cricketing world. On a difficult pitch at Harrogate he scored 60 and 101, and took seven wickets in a match which found the Yorkshire players, unusually, with little stomach for the battle on the last day when the ball flew all over the place. Field was the destroyer with seven wickets for 20, and the home side was bundled out before lunch for 58 to give Warwickshire a victory margin of 198. Naturally, the pitch was criticised – it being a newly-cut one before the match started. Rumours abounded that home supporters were going to doctor it overnight to lessen the erratic bounce, but an overnight guard prevented this – even though Frank Stephens, who later was to describe Foster's hundred as the best he ever saw, was certain that the pitch was illegally treated during the match.

The next two games against Hampshire and Worcestershire were drawn, with the game at Southampton bringing the curtain down in sad circumstances on the wonderful 17-year career of Lilley. Field was injured, and with the attack, for once, toiling, a frustrated Lilley – not for the first time – undermined his captain's authority by moving fielders and shouting instructions. To his credit, Foster – half Lilley's age – would have none of it and demanded that 'Dick be dropped' for the next game. His retirement was announced on 12 August, with his County career record of 632 victims and 12,813 runs, including 16 hundreds, evidence of a rare consistency that played no small part in Warwickshire's emergence from the shadows at the turn of the century.

The Bank Holiday home match against Worcestershire drew a huge crowd of 19,000, but with Field retiring with sunstroke after 13 overs, the visitors escaped with a draw in which Baker scored 101, Foster 85 and 62, and F. G. Stephens 50 and 96. With Kent winning two of their previous three games, when the round of matches started on 10 August they were firm favourites for the title.

The games involving the leaders altered the odds, with Lancashire beating Kent at Canterbury, and Warwickshire successful at Edgbaston against Derbyshire on a broken pitch on which Quaife scored an unbeaten 144 – an innings he described as one his best. Curious how the normally perfect batting pitches at Edgbaston had suddenly become 'sporting'. The more things change . . .

Foster wound up the match with six wickets for 37, which made the following game against Lancashire of even greater importance. Foster was again imperious, both as captain and with the bat – his 98, together with 80 from Kinneir and 67 from Quaife, helped his side to 422, and with Field in magnificent form, the crucial win was obtained. The fast bowler followed his five wickets for 78 in the first innings with a devastating seven for 12 (including six clean bowled), and underlined what feats he might have achieved had he not bowled for most of his career without adequate support.

So often plagued by injury and rheumatism, Field's efforts in the long, hot summer of 1911 also reflected how sympathetically he was handled by a captain who, as a new-ball bowler, was perhaps better able to understand the mind and body of his partner than earlier captains.

On 19 August, Warwickshire were third in the table, over two and a half points behind Kent, and with five points for an outright win, they needed the leaders to falter, even if their winning ways continued. Kent won two more games but, astonishingly, with the title all but won, they lost to Surrey by eight runs after needing only 102 to win. Middlesex, the second-placed side, failed to beat either Lancashire or

Nottinghamshire, and with Field and Foster sharing 16 wickets in a two-day win at Hinckley against Leicestershire, Warwickshire travelled to Northampton for the final fixture, knowing that although victory would seal the Championship title, a defeat or even a draw could open the door to Kent and Middlesex.

It later transpired, with Kent bringing off ten-wicket wins against Yorkshire and Essex, and Middlesex beating Hampshire and Surrey, that Foster had to lead his side to their 13th win, and the signs were not encouraging when he lost the toss on what seemed a good pitch.

Fittingly, Foster and Field were at their very best, dismissing the home side before lunch for 73, with the fast bowlers sharing nine wickets. Charlesworth hit a typically belligerent 130, and although Warwickshire were strongly placed with a lead of 208, rain prevented any play until 3 pm on Monday, and with the pitch now lifeless, it needed another superlative performance from Foster and Field to bring victory.

Foster's six wickets for 63 gave him match figures of 11 for 81, and Field finished with seven for 80 – enough to bring the Championship title to Edgbaston for the first time in 17 attempts by the narrowest of percentage margins – 74.00 compared with 73.84 by Kent.

The editor of *Wisden*, Mr Sydney Pardon, criticised the scoring system, but paid generous tribute to Foster and his players, and wrote that 'it was a good thing that the Championship should have gone to one of the outside counties'.

The argument about the merit of the scoring system is two-sided. Warwickshire won 13 games out of 20, compared with Kent's 17 games out of 26 and Middlesex's 14 out of 22, but had they played more games their title win might have been more conclusive. A valid criticism is that, following a dispute with Kent in 1899, Warwickshire had not played them since, and it is clearly unsatisfactory, for the leading two clubs in the Championship table not to have met.

Of Foster, *Wisden* wrote: 'Not since W. G. Grace in the early days of the Gloucestershire eleven, has so young a captain been such a match-winning force on a county side.'

The new captain's string of magnificent all-round performances brought him 1,383 Championship runs at 44.61, including three hundreds, and 116 wickets at 19.15. Seldom can a 'double' have meant so much to a side, although, as with Tom Dollery's Championship side 40 years later, every player made important contributions.

For instance, Kinneir scored five hundreds in his 1,418 at 44.31, to finish fifth in the national averages. In addition to the 1,298 runs and four hundreds from Charlesworth and the 1,108 from Quaife, who scored three hundreds, wicket-keeper Smith scored 807 runs.

Seventeen hundreds were scored, and with five batsmen averaging

Championship Dinner held at the Grand Hotel, Birmingham, on 21 September 1911.

over 35, the runs were there for Foster and Field to bowl against. Field was superb, and he enjoyed a slightly better season than his captain with 122 wickets at 19.48, with both opening bowlers sending down over 700 overs.

There was one match still to play – the Champion County against The Rest at the Oval, which took place two weeks and countless champagne celebrations later. Field came to the game a tired man, having taken 19 wickets in two games at the Scarborough Festival, including nine against the MCC team for Australia, which included Foster, Kinneir and Smith. The Rest fielded the strongest side available: R. H. Spooner, Hobbs, Mead, P. F. Warner, J. W. Hearne, C. B. Fry, Rhodes, Woolley, Hitch, Strudwick and Dean, and they bowled the Champions out for 129.

Warner's 244 led his side to a massive 631 for five, with Field and Foster managing one wicket for 336 between them off 82 overs, and the rout was completed when Warwickshire subsided in their second innings for 137, to lose by an innings and 365.

The 1911 Championship winning team.
Standing (l to r): W. C. Hands, E. J. Smith, J. H. Parsons, C. Charlesworth, S. P. Kinneir.
Seated: S. Santall, F. G. Stephens, F. R. Foster (capt.), G. W. Stephens, F. Field.
Seated on ground: W. G. Quaife, C. S. Baker.

No matter, it had been a memorable season, marked with many celebratory functions, culminating in a dinner at the Grand Hotel on 21 September, presided over by the Earl of Warwick, with George Cartland and a proud William Ansell also on the top table. Gilbert Jessop proposed the toast of the Warwickshire XI, and in addition to Foster, there were responses from Lilley, Quaife and Field.

A talent money fund had been set up, and £300 was available to the players and, happily, there was also a presentation to Lilley. Receipts for the season were £2,754 – a record for any season except when the Australians played at Edgbaston.

Not only the world of cricket paid tribute to Foster and Warwickshire. *Punch* carried a full-page cartoon, showing William Shakespeare grasping Foster's hand above a caption TWO GENTLEMEN OF WARWICKSHIRE. Mr F. R. Foster from II Henry IV 10: 'Tell Kent from me that she has lost it.' William Shakespeare from III Henry IV 6: 'Warwick thou art worthy.'

Indeed they were.

AFTER THE LORD MAYOR'S SHOW

FOSTER STARTED THE YEAR OF 1912 in splendid form in Australia with Douglas's team, and was little, if anything, behind the legendary Syd Barnes in effectiveness. Undoubtedly, as with every effective bowling partnership in the history of the game, one complements the other, and the resultant unrelenting pressure from both ends means that the batsman is invariably struggling.

In the five Tests, they took 66 of England's 95 wickets, with Barnes taking 34 and Foster 32. Foster considered his figures of 26-9-36-5 in the third Test at Adelaide among the best of his short career, and his batting also contributed towards England's 4-1 victory in the series which regained the Ashes for the first time since Warner's tour in 1903–04, four series previously. The Warwickshire man scored 226 runs in the series at 32.38, and his tour aggregate of 683 runs included consecutive innings in State games of 158 and 101.

'Tiger' Smith kept beautifully for the first three of his four Tests, with manager Warner particularly impressed with the keeper's work at Melbourne and Adelaide. The other Warwickshire representative, Kinneir, played his only Test at Sydney where he scored 22 and 30, but any disappointment was eased when, on his return home, he was named as a *Wisden* 'Cricketer of the Year' in recognition of the part he played in his Club's title win the previous year.

The committee still kept a tight hold on the financial reins, despite a deficit of £434 in 1910 having been turned into a surplus of £570. The original substantial reduction in Quaife's terms was subsequently amended in an offer of £125 per annum, but even that was substantially more than the monies earned by the rest of the staff – few of whom received £100 for their season's work.

What the committee, thankfully, did do, was to acknowledge the 24 years of skilful and loyal service from groundsman John Bates with a donation of £50 to the testimonial fund organised by the players. They were presumably grateful players, because after years of favouring the batsmen, he played his own part in the Championship win with a few pitches that were more helpful to bowlers than at any time in his stay at Edgbaston. Ryder was also the recipient of a presentation – a gold watch to mark the first 17 years of his dedicated service to the cause of Warwickshire cricket.

The side finished ninth in 1912, despite winning four consecutive matches in May, but the absence of Foster for the six Test matches in the Triangular Tournament made a big difference, although he still took 85 wickets. Field could hardly be expected to sustain his form in his 16th season, and he managed only 53 wickets. Smith also played in all six Tests, and was the only Club batsman to keep his form with 839 runs at 24.67, although after scoring only 47 runs in five innings in Australia, he did no better for England with 57 in eight innings. Quaife topped 1,000, but at an average of 37, while the average of Foster, Kinneir and Charlesworth dropped from 44, 44 and 39 to 17, 19, and 20 respectively.

The loss of the last three matches meant a bottom-half finish of ninth and the penultimate season before the First World War brought a further decline to 11th. The side actually won one more match, but they suffered more defeats to counterbalance that, and although four batsmen took advantage of the dry summer to reach 1,000 runs, Kinneir was not one of them. Ill-health meant he missed most of the season after scoring a fine unbeaten 152 at the Oval. The loss of five matches before the end of June indicated a general decline in batting and bowling departments.

Foster's 91 wickets cost 24.6 each, and with Field missing a number of games because of injuries, only the spectacular advance made by Percy Jeeves could be considered a plus. He delivered over 800 overs for his 106 wickets to head the averages, and also scored 765 useful runs at 20.13. A fast-medium bowler and natural hitter, he surely had a glittering career to enjoy had he been spared, but while on duty with the Royal Warwickshire Regiment on 22 July 1915 he was tragically killed at High Wood, Montauban, France. In only two seasons, he scored 1,193 runs and took 194 wickets at 20.20 each – form which drew from Warner a prediction that he looked certain to play for England.

Another Warwickshire player who was to serve with distinction was Parsons, and he progressed well with more than 1,000 runs at an average of 31. Quaife scored two separate hundreds at the Oval – the first time he had done this in his long career – and Charlesworth emulated him in the return game at Edgbaston.

Between these two high-scoring games, Warwickshire were bowled out for 63 against Middlesex, at the time the lowest score in the history of the Club. Fixtures with Kent had been resumed for the first time since 1899, and when Warwickshire's first innings total of 262 at Tonbridge earned them a lead of 130, with Foster taking six wickets for 62, a win seemed likely against the eventual Champions. But in just 62 deliveries, Warwickshire were dismissed for 16, with Woolley and Blythe both taking five for 8. Woolley then scored a brilliant unbeaten 76. It was the second appearance of Len Bates, whose unbeaten duck was one of five, and with wicket-keeper Huish getting three stumpings, all the blame could hardly be laid on the pitch.

P. G. WODEHOUSE
REMSENBURG
NEW YORK

Oct 26.1967

Dear Mr Ryder.

Yes, you are quite right.

It must have been in 1913 that I paid a visit to my parents in Cheltenham and went to see Warwickshire play Glos on the Cheltenham College ground. I suppose Jeeves's bowling must have impressed me, for I remembered him in 1916, when I was in New York and starting the Jeeves and Bertie saga, and it was just the name I wanted.

I have always thought till lately that he was playing for Gloucestershire that day. (I remember admiring his action very much)

Yours sincerely

P. G. Wodehouse

Percy Jeeves, whose name inspired the famous letter from P. G. Wodehouse.

The Club's finances were better, with membership now over 2,000 for the first time, and with another surplus of £600 Warwickshire were one of the few clubs to be in credit. In the winter of 1913–14, Smith went to South Africa as emergency replacement for D. C. Robinson of Gloucestershire but, travel then not being quite so speedy as nowadays, he spent six weeks on the high seas making the trip. 'Quite enjoyable really, with no manager or captain to keep an eye on me,' he said.

The surplus funds prompted an offer to buy the ground for £5,000, but the war postponed the completion of negotiations.

A worse blow was the resignation of Foster as captain following the death of his father although, as when he first accepted the position and then refused it, he was persuaded to change his mind, and marked his last season with 117 wickets at 18.24 each.

With Jeeves taking 85 (that earned him selection for the Players, together with Parsons), Field coming back strongly with 64, and new fast bowler Harry Howell taking 41, the Club rose four places in the final table to seventh.

Foster did the double, scoring 1,396, including the highest score ever achieved for the Club. His 305 at Dudley against Worcestershire came when he went in to bat at 197 for three, with his side already nine runs in the lead, and in a dazzling display of hitting, even by his standards, he scored his runs out of 448 added in the 260 minutes he spent at the crease. The first four fifties of his prodigious innings came in 60, 15, 80 and 30 minutes, while he went from 200 to 300 in a further 65 minutes. He did not hit a six, but managed 44 fours as well as a five and 14 threes. He finally declared at 645 for seven, perhaps settling a few past scores from matches in which the local rivalry often exceeded that of the ordinary derby.

Field finished the match off in blistering fashion, with one of the most astonishing analyses ever recorded. In 50 balls he took six wickets for 2. The only scoring stroke was, according to *Wisden*, a lucky two off his eighth delivery before he had taken a wicket. So he actually took six for 0 in 44 legal balls, to which he added five no-balls – one of which bowled M. K. Foster. A win by an innings and 321 was the highlight of a season which was overshadowed by the impending war. The committee met on 7 August to decide whether to abandon the rest of the programme, but thought little could be accomplished by such an act.

By not doing so they gave Foster and Jeeves the chance to sign off their tragically short careers with two wonderful personal performances in the last match of the season at Edgbaston. Jeeves dismissed Hayward and Ducat twice and Hobbs once in his match haul of seven for 88, while Foster took nine for 72. Little did the Edgbaston members know they would never see either young man again in first-class cricket.

Jeeves was killed in action two years later, while Foster, who joined the Royal Flying Corps in 1915, so badly injured a foot in a motorcycle accident that although he played a few games during the war, he knew that he could never stand up to the strain of first-class cricket again.

Foster came, conquered, and went in seven seasons – effectively five full ones – in which time he flashed across the cricketing horizon like a dazzling meteor. His 5,406 runs at 26.91 and 596 wickets at 20.44 showed him to be a genuine all-rounder, but he was much more than that. His presence lifted other players in a way that is supposed to be the post-war prerogative of Ian Botham, but some of Foster's deeds matched any ever achieved by anyone in the history of cricket.

He was only 25 when he played his last game, and it is doubtful if any young man has given so much pleasure to so many people in such a short span of time. Warner wrote: 'As a player, we shall seldom see his like again on the cricketing field', and even the cautious Ryder wrote that Foster wrote, for him, 'an exciting chapter in the book of English cricket'.

During the war, members were asked to pay their subscriptions to help keep the Club in existence, with £1,800 needed each year. Pallett died in the Erdington Infirmary in June 1915, and although Warwickshire's late entry into first-class cricket limited his number of wickets in that category to 296, he took another 662 at a time when he and Shilton did much to advance the name of the Warwickshire Club far beyond the boundaries of the county.

When W. G. Grace died on 23 October of the same year, *Wisden* published a list of the cricketers who had managed to hit his stumps, and it included Quaife and Santall (twice each), and Field. At the end of the year, 115 members had volunteered £1,105 in subscriptions, and Ryder further eased the financial problems by taking up work with, first Lloyds Bank, and then a local firm of accountants.

In the army, Parsons had worked his way up to sergeant and then captain, and he took part in what is generally agreed to be the last cavalry charge made by the British Army, at Beersheba.

Other Warwickshire casualties included Harold Bates, elder brother of Len, who had been on the Lord's ground staff and had also played a few times for Warwickshire, and Harold Goodwin, who captained the side the year before Foster took over.

When the war ended, the MCC, in a move which *Wisden* considered to be one of unseemly haste, decided that the County Championship would be resumed in 1919, with the point of real controversy the fact that all matches would be of two days duration only.

Warwickshire had more problems than most, certainly more than Worcestershire, who refused to compete, leaving the competition to the other 15 counties.

Although only four seasons had passed, gone were Foster, Jeeves, Bates, Goodwin, Langley, Kinneir, Santall and Parsons, who decided to pursue a military career, while Quaife was now 47, Smith 33, and Charlesworth and Field both 44.

So, of the regular side in 1914, only five returned: Quaife, Charlesworth, Smith, Field and Baker. What was to be done?

CHAPTER NINE

STARTING ALL OVER AGAIN, 1919

THE FIRST POST-WAR MEETING of the Warwickshire Committee was held in November 1918, with Ryder relieved to hear the realistic view expressed that the task of rebuilding the County side could not reasonably be expected to be completed in less than five years.

With such a small nucleus of professionals – and three of the five aged 40 or over – it was just a case of fulfilling the hybrid fixture list of 14 two-day games, and hoping to take the first stumbling step to respectability.

The problems facing the Club were more acute than those confronting any other county, and could fairly be likened to those of the first MCC sides to tour Australia under J. W. H. T. Douglas and Walter Hammond in 1920–21 and 1946–47, when eight Test matches were lost, and none won. Both sides, of necessity, included a high proportion of pre-war players.

It could be argued that the final position in the table of 15th – bottom for the first time in Warwickshire's history – proved that the Club would have been better advised to emulate Worcestershire, and drop out of the County Championship for that season. But a beginning had to be made somewhere, and even though only Derbyshire were beaten, with seven matches lost and six drawn, at least the 25 players selected that year enabled the committee quickly to assess which players had the best chance of developing a first-class career.

The senior professionals were joined by Len Bates and Harry Howell – 24 and 28 respectively – and the new captain, G. W. Stephens, could also call on the services of amateur batsmen like R. L. Holdsworth from Oxford, the Hon F. S. G. Calthorpe from Cambridge, and, from much further afield, the Australian Rev E. F. Waddy, who taught at Rugby School.

Not surprisingly, with the two-day competition offering fewer opportunities – and in Warwickshire's case, fewer matches – no Club batsman managed 1,000 runs, with Bates (823) and Quaife (818) the nearest, although Parsons topped 500 despite playing only intermittently because of his military duties.

The two-day competition was a failure, with the experiment 'doomed before half the season had run its course', according to *Wisden*. The public did not take kindly to the long hours, with play scheduled to finish at 7.30 pm.

The committee met frequently to try to shape a future in which the effect of their short-term decisions would have a big influence on the era between the two World Wars. Just about the shortest discussion on a major policy issue concerned the application from Frank Foster to be appointed 'team manager' at a salary of £1,000 per year – more than three times the money earned by the senior professionals. Whether it was the cheek of the financial request which prompted the instant rejection of Foster's request or the concept of a team manager is not known, but 60 years were to pass before David Brown was the choice of the committee to do the job Foster thought was necessary so long before.

The President, Ludford Docker, and Bainbridge both begged for a breakaway from the pre-war fixation, as they saw it, with choosing a team of predominently professional players, saying with some justification that a team of ten or eleven paid players could not fairly represent the cricket strength of the County. Maybe, but the professionals coud hardly be expected to agree, especially the senior caucus. Quaife, Baker and Smith were deputed by the rest of the staff to negotiate levels of salary which would reflect the substantial increase in costs of travel, hotels and equipment compared with 1914.

Match fees were agreed which gave the leading players £320 for the 1920 season, with Quaife receiving marginally less because, by then, he had been relieved of the irksome ground duties which, traditionally, had always been undertaken by paid players. Quaife was thus on his own in that respect and so, in another, was Parsons, whose idea of his value to the Club was rather different to that of the committee. He demanded the same money as the other players, which was reasonable, together with an additional retainer of £160 per year for six years and a guaranteed benefit of £900 in 1924, which patently was not. Understandably, the committee refused to accede to such demands, one of which – the contractual right to a benefit – was, if not illegal, certainly unethical, and so Parsons returned to his regiment in India, where he stayed until the 1923 season.

Ansell died at the age of 70, and later his successful single-handed efforts to bring first-class and then Test cricket to Birmingham were marked by the handsome stand at Edgbaston which now bears his name.

The most important decision for the committee concerned the captaincy which had been undertaken with great enthusiasm in 1919 by G. W. Stephens. His limited availability – when he retired in 1925 he had played only 203 first-class innings since his debut in 1907—meant that an appointment had to be made which would ensure vital continuity, and Calthorpe was the obvious choice.

Aged 27, he was a member of the Edgbaston family who owned

much land, including the county ground, in the district, and his cricketing credentials were of some quality. Following a successful schoolboy career at Repton, he went on to earn his Blue as a Freshman at Cambridge in 1912 and also played against Oxford in 1913, 1914 and 1919. He also played two games for Sussex in 1911 and 1912. It has been said that he might have been captain the previous season, had not the letter of invitation gone astray, although surely the Warwickshire Committee could have repeated the offer in the absence of a reply. He was also a scratch golfer, but such was the enjoyment from cricket he both received and generated among his players, there was no real doubt that he would make his career with the Warwickshire team.

A splendid all-round cricketer who scored 8,311 runs at 24.88 (ten hundreds), and took 513 wickets at 29.82 before he retired, he invariably attached more importance to a happy dressing-room and team spirit than to tactics, which explains why 'Tiger' Smith, who played under eight appointed Warwickshire captains, said that the period of the 1920s, with Calthorpe was easily the happiest of his career.

Yet only twice were Warwickshire to finish in the top ten of the County Championship under Calthorpe, such were the difficulties of building a side after the war. He had a splendid first season, taking 91 wickets at 23.20 each as well as scoring 872 runs, including his maiden Championship hundred against Gloucestershire.

His lively medium pace was the ideal foil for Howell, who made a huge advance with 132 wickets at a cost of only 17.50 each, but the lack of bowling support meant that Quaife was the next most successful bowler with 44 wickets. So despite such an effective new-ball attack, the side advanced only to twelfth in the table, albeit in a competition now 16-strong following the re-entry of Worcestershire.

Thanks to an amateur run-feast in the home local derby, in which Holdsworth made a career best 141, Stephens 111, Calthorpe 87, Smith 80, the Rev. E. F. Waddy 71 and C. A. Fiddian-Green 53, Warwickshire secured the biggest victory in the Club's history, winning by an innings and 340 runs.

On the debit side, they lost at the Oval by an innings and 239 runs, then the third heaviest defeat ever suffered, and still only the fifth.

Howell and Calthorpe opposed each other in the Gentlemen *v* Players game at the Oval, with the fast bowler dismissing his captain as one of his six wickets for 40, and with six more in the match at Lord's, Howell's choice for the tour of Australia that winter was a certainty.

Charlesworth's well-earned benefit brought him a record return of £1,050 – a figure which was not be surpassed until Hollies received £4,896 in 1948. Another financial announcement of even greater significance to members was the committee proposal to finalise the

Warwickshire in 1914, the season before the First World War.
Standing (l to r): C. S. Baker, C. Charlesworth, S. Santall, J. H. Parsons, F. Field, Percy Jeeves.
Seated: S. P. Kinneir, W. G. Quaife, F. R. Foster (capt.), E. B. Crockford, E. J. 'Tiger' Smith.
Of this team, only five players came back to play for Warwickshire after the war. They were W. G. Quaife, C. Charlesworth, 'Tiger' Smith, F. Field and C. S. Baker. Frank Foster had to retire after a motorcycle accident, Kinneir retired, Syd Santall became coach, Parsons stayed in the Indian Army and Percy Jeeves was killed in the war.

purchase of the freehold of the ground. The cost of £5,000 would be funded by mortgage debentures, and the money provided by the president and a few friends, with the Club paying six per cent interest to the ground company.

On a wider front, the financial position was satisfactory, with record crowds of 123,209 and an extra 612 members joining the other 1,472 in paying the increase of four shillings (20p) on the previous subscription level of one guinea (£1.05).

Charlesworth's final season in 1921 – after which he became coach to the Royal Naval College, Dartmouth, ended an association with Warwickshire which began in 1898, and 'Tiger' Smith for one, was a player who had much for which to thank the kindly Lancastrian, who brought an unfailing cheerfulness to the dressing room which helped the side through its more difficult times.

How sad that his end came 32 years later in the anonymity of a

Frederick Gough-Calthorpe, who captained Warwickshire and England.

Salvation Army Hostel in Huddersfield, although the former Yorkshire captain, F. E. Greenwood, helped ease the last few months slightly by passing on, at £1 per week, money made available by the Warwickshire committee. The suggestion that, in the absence of a benefit in 1953, more substantial funds might be raised, was incomprehensibly turned down by the committee, apparently on the grounds that it would set a dangerous precedent. After all, even if many more former players fell on hard times, what possible justification could there be for not making every effort to help the man in question?

The Salvation Army major, who only knew Charlesworth for a brief time, nevertheless paid him this perceptive tribute: 'He was quite a remarkable man. A fool to himself maybe, but he never did anyone any harm, and very often offered a helping hand. The world would be an infinitely better place if more men were like him and had his philosophy.'

His last season was a poor one for Warwickshire, with only Glamorgan's election to the County Championship preventing the Club finishing bottom. Even so, before the side finished bottom of the

17 clubs in 1981 and 1982, their 16th position in 1921 was to be the lowest in their history until 1958.

However, Calthorpe went close to the 'double' and Howell took 100 wickets in all matches, despite a foot injury keeping him out of ten games for Warwickshire, during which period the side actually lost seven successive matches.

The Australians were played twice, with Warwickshire managing a draw in the game in which Gregory and McDonald did not play. When the fearsome pair of fast bowlers did turn out in August, the tourists won by an innings and 61 runs, after scoring an adequate but by no means conclusive 312.

Calthorpe played two magnificent innings of 176 and 209 against Somerset and Hampshire, but the side's lack of depth in both batting and bowling strengths inevitably was still too marked to prevent them being consigned to the cellar of the Championship.

Quaife ended the season in dispute, because of an unauthorised report in the *Birmingham Post* which said that, at the age of 49, he was contemplating retirement. When called before the committee, he gave as his reason that although his son, Bernard, had been promised six matches, he had only played in four, and anyway he was dissatisfied with the treatment of certain professionals by the committee. The elder statesman refused to withdraw his complaints, and although the outcome is not on record, the fact that he continued to play for another seven seasons suggests that the Club recognised the folly of losing his services, even at such an advanced stage in his career. From the Club's point of view, the fact that his son's 81 innings in seven seasons yielded 1,096 runs at an average of 14.81, shows that their reluctance to honour the original six-match commitment was, at least, understandable.

The 1922 season has a special place in the Club's history. Not because of any improvement in the final position in the Championship – won by Yorkshire for the first of four successive seasons – but more for the manner of two defeats sustained against Hampshire, and two more by Yorkshire, with three of the losses coming in June.

Pride of place – at least in the history of the Hampshire Club – must go to Warwickshire's home fixture against the county on 14, 15 and 16 June. *Wisden* still carries the historic performance of Tennyson's side as being the only side in the history of cricket to win after scoring their lowest score in history and being made to follow on. Of the 26 recorded instances of a side being bowled out for under 20 in first-class cricket, anywhere in the world, eleven have been in county cricket. Of the nineteen occasions it has happened in England, all but one were before that fateful mid-June match in 1922 when Hampshire were dismissed by Howell (4.5-2-7-6) and Calthorpe (4-3-4-4) in 53 deliveries for 15 runs. There were eight ducks, with Phil Mead, coming in at number 4, top scorer with an undefeated six runs, the next highest score being four by Tennyson, with four byes and a single to W. R. Shirley completing the total of 15.

All this happened after Warwickshire were put in to bat on a rain-affected pitch, and reached 223, thanks to 84 from Reg Santall, son of Sydney, and 70 by Calthorpe.

The Hampshire innings began at 4pm and ended forty minutes later, and but for 'Tiger' Smith conceding four leg-side byes, and Tennyson's runs coming from a missed chance, a world record would have been established which would still obtain today. Mead insisted that the pitch was not to blame, and all Smith would say was that he had never seen Howell bowl so fast.

H. L. V. Day, bowled by Calthorpe at number 3, said that the home captain swung the ball prodigiously, but however well both he and Howell bowled, the conclusion must be that the total of 15 came from one of those inexplicable sequences of events which occasionally happen to a side. Despite Calthorpe, with generosity that was not just misplaced but unwise, not opening the bowling with Howell in the follow-on, Hampshire were seemingly booked for defeat at 186 for six when George Brown played an innings which made history. He batted for four and a half hours for 172, sharing partnerships of 85 with Shirley and 177 with wicket-keeper Livesy, whose unbeaten 110 was his maiden hundred.

The bowling analyses of the Warwickshire attack were startlingly different, with Howell and Calthorpe taking five wickets for 253 from 96 overs, and Quaife bowling 49 of the other 75 overs to take three for 154. The Hampshire total of 521 left the home side needing 314 to win, but Kennedy and Newman shared nine wickets to complete a recovery which made grown men in the match unsure whether to laugh or cry.

Each side of that match, Yorkshire crushed the team twice, with the return match at Huddersfield bringing the third heaviest defeat at that time in the Club's history – an innings and 271 after Percy Holmes had scored his second double hundred of the month against a Warwickshire attack weakened by the absence, because of injury, of Calthorpe and Howell.

At Southampton, Hampshire won by an innings and 178, and the surprise was that, despite those four morale-shattering defeats, Warwickshire still improved from 16th to 12th in the table.

Quaife scored over 1,000 runs and, at the age of 50, took that number of wickets, to provide a much-needed improvement of support for Howell. Howell took over 100 wickets again, and Calthorpe's 972 runs and 72 wickets underlined once again his fine all-round talents.

Quaife had the unusual experience at Derby in June of playing in the same side as his son, Bernard, against another father and son pairing of W. and R. Bestwick, with the Quaifes at one stage batting against the two Bestwicks in a match which Warwickshire won by an innings, thanks to Howell twice routing the home side for 130 and 122.

Amateur seam bowler Norman Partridge, a schoolboy prodigy from Malvern, who never quite fulfilled his promise, made his mark with 55 wickets at under 20 apiece – he was to finish a career which lasted until 1937 with 347 wickets at 22.76 each.

A decent side was slowly taking shape, and the committee decided that the return of Parsons, if he could be persuaded to return from the Army and India, would help considerably towards that end.

Negotiations were undertaken by post, resulting in Parsons playing under a match-fee arrangement for the last few weeks of the 1923 season. Then the hard bargaining started which resulted in the Captain becoming a civilian and resuming his professional career for six years, before he joined the Church and the amateur ranks.

The most astonishing feature of the committee's dealings with Parsons was their agreement to guarantee him a benefit of £750 in 1926. Although the famous test case of Reid *v* Seymour was still to be fought by the Inland Revenue in the High Court, there is little doubt that the contractual award of a benefit by Warwickshire would have made both Club and player an easier target which, presumably, would have dealt a death blow to the tax-free element of the benefit system, which still survives well over 60 years later.

The season of 1923 also brought to Edgbaston the then 22-year-old Robert Elliott Storey Wyatt from Surrey, and although his first season only produced 658 runs at 16.04 and 35 wickets at 31 each, the *Birmingham Post* forecast 'a highly successful career for one of the most promising all-round players discovered in Warwickshire for a long time'. His final career figures for the Club of 21,687 runs at 41.54 (including 51 hundreds), and 652 wickets at 32.82 proved what a shrewd forecast that was by George Egdell, although, because little of what Wyatt accomplished was ever spectacular, the impact of the side's next captain was not significant for several seasons.

The year belonged to Howell. He took 152 wickets from 'only' 1,067 overs – twice the number bowled by anyone else – and in the third of six successive seasons that he took over 100 wickets, he became the first bowler to take all ten wickets in an innings for the Club. His figures against Yorkshire of 25.1-5-51-10 could not stave off defeat in a match which did not start until 4.30 pm because of rain but, once again, they underlined the Herculean efforts put in by Howell after the war. He took 747 of his 899 wickets from 1920 to 1925. Before his historic 'all-ten', he had twice taken eight wickets in an innings (in

1921 and 1922), and still to come were nine wicket hauls against Somerset and Hampshire in 1924 and 1925, as well as another eight-wicket performance at Leicester in 1925. In that golden year for him of 1923, he took 12 wickets against Surrey and Kent – sides that finished fourth and fifth in the table respectively.

The batting was disappointing, despite the late entry of Parsons, who produced 302 runs from nine innings and an average of 33.55 – sufficient to top the Club averages. Only Quaife reached the 1,000-run mark.

The wet summer halved gate receipts and so, despite predictable opposition from a membership which has always adopted the turkey philosophy of not voting for an early Christmas, subscriptions were raised to £1 11s 6d (£1.57) and, for the first time, discussions took place about the question of maximising the use of pavilion facilities during the winter months.

The following season featured another remarkable match at Edgbaston – the third Test of the summer against South Africa. England were put in to bat and with Sutcliffe, in his debut game, scoring 64 out of a first-wicket partnership with Hobbs of 136, they scored a commanding 438 before Gilligan and Tate bowled out the tourists for 30 in 75 deliveries. Gilligan's six for 7 paved the way for a match return of eleven for 90, which is the best ever achieved by an England captain, and Tate followed his four for 12 with four for 103 to clinch a victory by an innings and 18 runs.

The match was a financial disaster, giving the Club a proportionate share of the receipts of £662, compared with £763 in 1902, and £886 seven years later. That, together with a wet summer in which there were five blank Saturdays and no play at all in the home match against Nottinghamshire, meant an unheard-of deficit of £3,175, and another public appeal was necessary to redress the depressing balance.

The side still managed, for the first time since the war, to win more matches than it lost, and again the major credit belonged to Howell, who took 122 wickets at 16 each, with only Wyatt giving him reasonable support with 61 wickets at 21.44 each.

Howell devastated Somerset at Taunton with 14 for 71, and no Warwickshire benefit has ever been more deserved. He finally received £804, and to crown another magnificent season, he played in a Test trial, both games for the Players, and England in the final rain-ruined Test at the Oval. He went to Australia with Gilligan's party the following winter, but with Tate doing so well he did not play in a Test match, and it is an historical travesty that one of the greatest fast bowlers in the history of Championship cricket should have ended with just seven wickets from five England appearances.

Only Parsons topped 1,000 runs, and although Calthorpe headed the batting averages, the decline in his bowling meant that the captain took only 24 wickets.

On the administrative side, Ryder completed 30 years' service at Edgbaston and was rewarded with an ex-gratia payment of £50 and the decision by the committee to fund, for their secretary, a £1,000 life insurance policy.

Having risen from 16th to ninth in three seasons, thanks largely to Howell, could Warwickshire's improvement be maintained in 1925?

CALTHORPE HANDS OVER TO WYATT

WARWICKSHIRE'S FINAL POSITION of eighth in 1925 was, except for one place better in 1914, their highest in ten seasons since the title win in 1911, thanks to a remarkable improvement in the side's batting.

Smith and Parsons established a regular opening partnership that brought them an aggregate of nearly 3,000 runs, and with such a solid foundation, Quaife and Bates both topped 1,000 runs, with Santall only a few runs short of the four-figure total. Wyatt was still regarded by Calthorpe as a genuine all-rounder, although his accurate medium-pace method was short of penetration. As a result, he scored only 729 runs – an aggregate which was disappointing for a player of his undoubted ability, although he scored a maiden hundred against Worcestershire at Dudley.

The summer of 1925 was a dry one, and although the Club got off to a bad start, losing six of their first seven games by the middle of June, they pulled themselves together following the return of Howell, who had missed much of May with illness, and won seven of the next 17 games, losing five with five matches drawn.

The first of two defeats by Kent was at Edgbaston and, although the order of innings was different compared with the debacle in 1922 against Hampshire, the fortunes of the match swung nearly as violently. After Warwickshire were put out for 137, Howell (four for 24), and Calthorpe (six for 17) rushed Kent out in 70 minutes for 42, with Woolley's 10 the only score in double figures. Warwickshire added 246 to their lead of 95. A certain win? Not quite, because Woolley and Hardinge hit hundreds, and Kent cruised home by seven wickets.

In the match at Tonbridge, Warwickshire only narrowly escaped an innings defeat, despite Kent losing seven first innings wickets for 19, thanks to a young fast bowler, who began his career in local Parks cricket, R. Cooke, taking four wickets in five balls, including the hat-trick. As happens all too often in cricket, his career began and ended in a few weeks, with his final figures of 16 wickets for 507 at 31.68 each from 209 overs, indicating a lack of penetration that made his burst at Tonbridge look suspiciously like a fluke.

The Club managed, for once, to get on to the right end of the see-saw in a home match against Sussex, whose powerful attack, consisting of Tate, Gilligan, Bowley, Wensley and Cox, could not prevent Smith (139 not out), Parsons (124), and Calthorpe (109 not

SUSSEX, June 27, 29, 30, 1925 Spectators not allowed on Playing Area

SCORE CARD WARWICKSHIRE • COUNTY • CRICKET CLUB

Play 1st day 12 other days 11 15 Lunch 1.30-2 15 Stumps drawn 6 45, Third day 5.30
An extra half-hour may be allowed on the third day on the demand of Capt of either side

SUSSEX	1st Innings.		2nd Innings.	
1 Bowley	b Howell	14	c Howell b Partridge	133
2 Parks	c Smith b Partridge	18	b Calthorpe	9
3 Cornford	c Parsons b Partridge	3	INNINGS DECLARED	
4 Cook	c Calthorpe b Quaife	20	b Howell	0
5 A. J. Holmes	c and b Quaife	38	not out	100
6 Cox	c Bates b Partridge	95	b Croom	18
7 Langridge	c Parsons b Howell	4	c Smith b Howell	8
8 A. H. H. Gilligan	b Howell	5	b Quaife	7
9 Capt. L. C. R. Isherwood	run out	18	b Howell	53
10 Wensley	not out	7	not out	17
11 Stannard	c Partridge b Quaife	7	c Smith b Quaife	10
	Extras	14		15
	Total	243	Total	370

1 wkt for 23 2-35 3-40 4-70 5-133 6-161 7-177 8-235 9-238 10-243

1 wkt for 28 2-138 3-140 4-232 5-267 6-293 7-312 8-328 9-... 10 ..

Bowling Analysis	O	M	R	W	Nb	Wd	O	M	R	W	Nb	Wd
Calthorpe	8	2	24	–	–		15	2	66	1	...	...
Howell	27	8	62	3	...	–	22	4	60	3	...	...
Partridge	27	7	64	3	...	–	19-2	3	67	1	...	...
Quaife W G.	13-4	2	41	3	..		18	2	57	2		...
Santall	7	1	12		...	–	9	...	36	...	...	...
Wyatt	13	2	26	–	...		17	1	62	–	...	..
Croom	..					–	1	...	7	1		

WARWICKSHIRE.	1st Innings		2nd Innings.	
5 Smith	c Cox b Parks	3	not out	139
8 Parsons	c Cornford b Wensley	38	c Cook b Cox	124
6 Croom	b Cox	8		
7 Quaife W. G.	c Cornford b Wensley	18		
2 G W Stephens	c and b Bowley	0		
1 Hn. F. S. G. Calthorpe Cpt.	c Cook b Bowley	25	not out	109
3 R. E. S. Wyatt	c Gilligan b Langridge	55		
10 Santall	c Langridge b Bowley	20		
9 Bates	b Bowley	16		
4 N E. Partridge	not out	29		
11 Howell	b Wensley	1		
Umpires: Burrows & Brown; Scorers: Austin & Isaacs	Extras	9		20
	Total	222	Total	392

1 wkt for 11 2-30 3-67 4-70 5-70 6-102 7-143 8-184 9-199 10-222

1 wkt for 176 2- 3-... 4-... 5- 6- 7-... 8-... 9- 10 ...

Bowling Analysis	O	M.	R.	W	Nb.	Wd.	O.	M.	R.	W.	Nb	Wd.
Wensley	34-5	10	67	3	–	–						
Parks	8	2	12	1	...	...	...	–	...	–	–	...
Bowley	34	8	99	4	...	...	...	–	...	...	...	...
Cox	18	7	32	1	...	...	...	...	...	...	...	...
Gilligan	1	–	3		...		...	...	–	–	–	...
Langridge	1	1	...	1			...	...	...	...	...	...

A. REDMAN, Head Groundsman, Outfitter to Warwickshire County Cricket Club.
Sole right of sale on ground of Cricket Requisites. Good selection on view main entrance.

Printed & Published by A. G. Barclay, 18, Clarence Avenue, Handsworth, Birmingham.

See the name "Cadbury" on every piece of Chocolate

Warwickshire v Sussex at Edgbaston, 30 June 1925. The complete scorecard shows that all three Warwickshire batsmen in the second innings scored a century. They were 'Tiger' Smith, with 139 not out, Jack Parsons, with 124 not out, and Freddie Calthorpe, with 109 not out. Warwickshire won by nine wickets.

out) scoring the 392 runs they were set to win – with 45 minutes to spare and, astonishingly, only losing the wicket of Parsons.

Parsons blazed the way, with his runs coming out of an opening stand of 176, but even that innings was dwarfed by a valiant, but unavailing, innings from Santall in a match at Dewsbury which Warwickshire lost by an innings and 56. After Sutcliffe had scored a double hundred, Santall scattered Weddington, Macaulay, Rhodes and Kilner to all parts in 100 minutes, during which his unbeaten 119 included seven sixes and eight fours.

The son of the Club's former all-rounder and coach Santall was a cricketer whose flamboyant style reflected an extrovert character and temperament which never allowed him to make the most of his talent. His debut in 1919 made him the youngest Warwickshire cricketer ever at the age of 16 years and 23 days, and his total of 496 games for the Club has only been exceeded by Quaife (665), and Amiss (547). His final career figures of 17,518 runs at an average of 24.84, and 280 wickets at 43.52 each were too moderate for comfort, revealing a self-destructive characteristic that refused to allow a commensurate fulfilment of his ability.

The fine summer drew 113,020 spectators – nearly double the number of the previous year – and there was a welcome profit of £1,636 to bank before 'Australian year', which usually gave the poorer clubs a quadriennial chance to balance their books.

At the end of the season, Howell informed the Club that he could not carry on because of the enormous physical strain which, at the age of 35, he felt unable to endure for even one more year. He went into the Birmingham League with Aston Unity, but played a handful of games in the next three seasons before his last game in 1928 – four years before his tragically early death through illness at the age of 41.

His record of an average of 4.92 wickets a match (975 from 198 games) is a better strike rate than any other Warwickshire bowler in history – even that of Frank Foster, whose 596 wickets from 127 games gave him an average of 4.69. No wonder *Wisden* commented: 'Unless some bowler of real skill is discovered, the prospects of Warwickshire disposing of their opponents at a reasonable cost next summer appear slight.'

This was cruelly prophetic, with 17 of the Club's 28 games in 1926 drawn, and only two victories, despite the heroic efforts of Quaife, without whose 78 wickets at 25.89 from 754.1 overs the final position of 12th would surely have been much worse. At the age of 54, his 786 overs were more than he had ever bowled in a season before, and although Wyatt had his best season with the ball (86 wickets), and a new fast bowler, J. H. Mayer, started a career which was to last until

1939 with 34 wickets, the departure of Howell meant that the attack was really of a powder-puff variety.

With the side seldom engineering a winning opportunity, the batsmen could concentrate on batting for its own sake, and Parsons, Wyatt, Kilner, Bates and Quaife exceeded 1,000 runs, with Quaife achieving this for the 20th time for Warwickshire and the 24th and final time in all matches.

Calthorpe missed 13 matches, and his deputy, Partridge, moved Wyatt up to open the innings, and after a hundred against Derbyshire in May, the Club's next regular captain rightly stayed up the order – a long overdue move. In all matches he missed the double by eight wickets, with appearances for the Gentlemen starting a run of 14 consecutive seasons in which he played in the traditional fixture until the war started in 1939.

Calthorpe's return was only notable for the loss of 13 consecutive tosses, and the only highlights of a depressing season were individual ones. Bates hit 187 against Derbyshire, and at Worcester Kilner scored his first hundred for the Club in an opening stand with Wyatt of 221.

Smith, now 40, established a new record in first-class cricket – since surpassed by Australian Wally Grout and Essex's David East – by becoming the first wicket-keeper to claim seven victims in an innings (three stumpings and four catches) against Derbyshire at Edgbaston.

Parsons received £881 from his dubiously awarded benefit – and that in the year that Kent were preparing their taxation test case for Seymour against the Inland Revenue. Had the Revenue known of the arrangement between Parsons and the committee, there can be little doubt that the structure of the game as we now know it must have undergone a radical change.

The Club president, Ludford Docker, told the Annual Meeting that dull batting was becoming more prevalent, but it is difficult to see how his radical proposal to widen the lbw law to include deliveries pitched outside the leg stump would reverse this trend. The proposal has since surfaced from time to time, but has been rightly rejected because the beneficiary would not be the leg-spinner, but rather the round-arm slinger of stultifying medium pace delivered from round the wicket.

A new groundsman, Ted Leyland – the father of Yorkshire's famous Maurice – was appointed before the start of the 1927 season, which was to be so wet that, in the middle of the season, there was an unbroken sequence of 15 drawn games. Six other matches were also drawn, but with Parsons hitting five hundreds and averaging 52, and Wyatt averaging 51.38 and Bates 40.58, the side was able to move up a place in the Championship table to 11th.

Quaife received £917 from his second benefit, and whatever the criticisms he faced from within, and outside, the Club for slow scoring, his prolific career figures speak for themselves. Against a Glamorgan side which had risen to eighth place the previous year after inaugural finishes since 1921 of bottom place (twice), 16th (twice) and 13th, Quaife batted for the equivalent of a full day for an unbeaten 155, after Parsons had hit his career-best score of 225. Parsons, the would-be cleric, was a tremendous driver of the ball and he reached his first hundred out of only 145. An equally fine 136 from him at Hull improbably ended a run for Yorkshire of 70 first-class games without defeat.

Bates became the fourth Club batsman – Kinneir, Quaife and Charlesworth were the others – to score two separate hundreds in a match, achieving this rare feat against Kent at Coventry, and the son of the former groundsman also scored a notable 11 runs in the final game of the season at Portsmouth – he was the only batsman to reach double figures in an innings collapse of 36, brought about by Kennedy with final figures of 10-7-8-7.

Since the First World War, the committee's inability to build a side with a long-term future was evidenced by the continued presence on the staff of Quaife and Smith – born in 1872 and 1886 respectively – and although young professional batsmen had made limited progress, the side lacked a dynamic all-rounder who could add a much needed attacking flair to both batting and bowling departments.

Calthorpe's bowling fell away after a fine start in the early 1920s, and the main use of Wyatt's medium pace was as a support bowler, while the batting which was always likely to be his greater strength was held back by Calthorpe's surprising reluctance to promote his eventual successor to a higher position in the order.

The winter months between the 1927 and 1928 seasons inexplicably provided another instance of a dispute between Club and a long-serving player, which has bedevilled county cricket throughout the ages, with no club immune from a charge of insensitivity from players who believe that their services have been either badly used, or terminated prematurely – or even both. Whether the Warwickshire committee or Quaife was in the right is immaterial. The committee minuted a statement from the player that, after hearing their views about future plans for the playing staff, he 'intimated his intention to retire as from the end of 1927'. In other words, he had retired. Conclusive? 'No', wrote Quaife. 'It seems to me unfair that neither the public nor myself should have any notification before last season closed. My desire was, and still is, to play at least some part of next season and for the public to have due notice of the date of my last match.'

The committee refused to change their mind, which led to an unseemly Annual Meeting at which to their discredit, the committee allowed the deputy chairman, J. P. Heaton, to put forward the absurd theory that, as Quaife had not been on the playing staff for some years, the question of his dismissal did not arise. That technical no-ball was hit out of sight by George Ward, the proposer of a motion 'that the services of W. G. Quaife be retained for the season 1928'. He asked why, if Quaife was not on the staff, he had been asked to resign?

The issue was a classical instance of whether the player had to jump because he was pushed so hard, but the rights and wrongs of such arguments which, sadly, are repeated far too often around the 17 counties, are less important than the age-old need for county committees to bring to cricket the same sort of man-management which its members employ more successfully in the businesses which allow the time for their honorary duties on county committees. The outcome was that Quaife was allowed to choose his retirement match, and he picked the match on 4, 6 and 7 August against Derbyshire, although he knew that that would be his only appearance that summer. At the age of 56, he couldn't end his career as he started it, with a hundred . . . could he?

The scorebook shows that 260 minutes after taking guard, he walked off with 115, one more than Parsons, in Warwickshire's highest score of the season, 564 for seven declared. For good measure, he bowled 40 overs in the match and took two wickets to round off a career which *Wisden* said was 'memorable'. The Almanack itemised his 36,012 first-class runs – 33,862 for Warwickshire, for whom he scored all of his 71 hundreds, and took 900 of his 931 first-class wickets. *Wisden* paid tribute to his skill and stylish method – a view with which Ryder concurred. He had already written in 1925:

> Some there were who were inclined to cavil at the rate of his run-getting. How many times has he saved Warwickshire, now turning aside imminent defeat, now making victory possible by his dominance? His footwork is an object to any cricketer, and he possesses all the strokes the game has evolved. His undoubted greatness rests most surely on his many wonderful achievements when conditions have favoured the bowler and runs have been difficult to get.

Comparisons between cricketers of different eras are rarely valid, so let it be sufficient to place the little master in his own time. The best statistical tribute I can find is that when he retired, only W. G. Grace, Tom Hayward, John Tyldesley and David Denton had retired with more runs, although batsmen like Woolley, Hendren, Mead and Rhodes, among others, were well on the way to aggregates which were subsequently higher.

Furthermore, his feat of reaching 1,000 runs in a season 24 times had been exceeded only by W. G. Grace, who did it 28 times. On only three occasions since 1896 did he fail to score 1,000, and the *Birmingham Post*'s George Egdell called him 'one of the Masters of the Art of Cricket'.

The end of Quaife marked the real beginning of Wyatt as a major batsman. He became the first player to score 2,000 runs for the Club – his 2,075 runs in 1928 included six hundreds and came at the magnificent average of 61.03. The previous winter, he had toured South Africa under R. T. Stanyforth, playing in all five Tests, and the experience and knowledge he gained were important factors in the marked advance by one of the greatest students of cricket the game has ever known.

Parsons hit five more of his eventual total of 35 hundreds, and scored 1,341 runs, with the feat of Croom, Kilner, Smith and Bates in also passing 1,000 helping to mask the inadequacies of an attack which was without Mayer for part of the season, and also lacked the usual bowling commitment from Wyatt.

No fewer than 19 games were drawn, but the previous season's modest 11th place was maintained in what was to be the last season when the Championship was decided on a percentage basis. The new

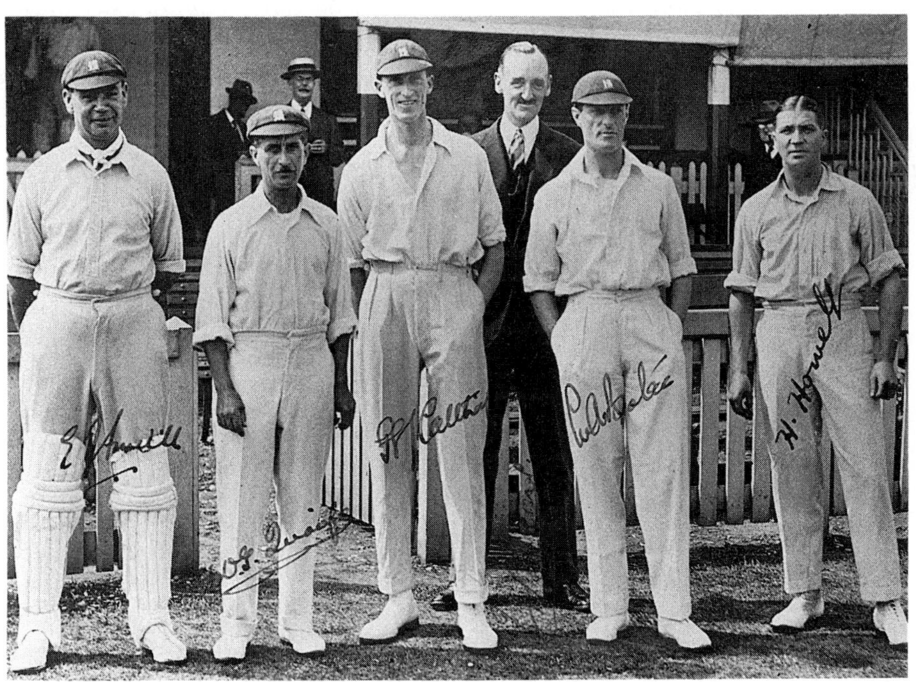

Six Warwickshire stalwarts who held Warwickshire together through most of the 1920s: E. J. 'Tiger' Smith, W. G. Quaife, Hon F. S. G. Calthorpe, J. H. Parsons, L. A. Bates and H. Howell.

scoring system meant that every county played 28 games – the first time every club had played the same number of games – with the eight points available for each game shared in any match on which no first-innings decision was reached.

Other much more momentous changes included the enlargement of the stumps by both an inch in height and width, as well as an astonishing lbw amendment which decreed that a batsman be out if the ball satisfied other provisions, even if he had hit it. It was called 'the snick rule', and even more astonishing to this author over 50 years later was that when I tackled cricketers who played through the several years of the snick rule, none of them could easily remember it – not even the late Bill Bowes of Yorkshire, whose career was then well under way.

As for Warwickshire, Calthorpe's last year as captain saw the side drop to 14th place, with only Wyatt among the batsmen maintaining the consistency of the previous season. He scored 2,630 runs in all cricket, but failed by just 60 to score 2,000 for his Club.

Parsons had now been ordained, and of course his more intermittent appearances were now made as an amateur, and with the form of Bates declining, it was only a welcome resurgence in the fortunes of the bowlers which prevented a season of real disaster. Mayer returned the best seasonal figures of his honest, toiling career, with 126 wickets in all games at 22.36 each, and with amateur fast bowler Derek Foster underlining his immense promise with 52 wickets and the newly qualified George Paine taking 57, the attack performed better than at any time since Howell's last full year in 1925.

Foster, at 22, was a real find who returned the startling figures of 11.5-7-11-6 at Cardiff, and the Welsh county provided Warwickshire with the fifth biggest victory in their history at Edgbaston, when the Club won by an innings and 247 runs. Foster did the hat-trick against Hampshire at Edgbaston in an impressive season which earned his selection for the Gentlemen at the Oval, alongside Wyatt and the former professional, Parsons.

Wyatt scored 150 in the crushing win against Glamorgan, and quickly followed with 161 against Surrey and 125 against Middlesex, and his first hundred for England came at Old Trafford against South Africa. Of his seven hundreds for Warwickshire, four were unbeaten, and he reached three figures in both fixtures against Worcestershire. Smith, Santall and Croom scored two hundreds each, with Kilner making 121 against Surrey.

Gate receipts fell by £1,408, and if the modern treasurer bemoans the growing number of counter-attractions, he is singing an old song, because in 1929, the rapidly growing popularity of greyhound racing and speedway was cited as a major difficulty facing cricket.

Calthorpe resigned the captaincy at the end of the season, but surprisingly, Wyatt was offered the post only after Partridge declined it because of an inability to play regularly.

During the winter, Lilley and Hargreave died at the ages of 62 and 53 respectively.

CHAPTER ELEVEN

THE WYATT YEARS

WYATT'S FIRST SEASON as captain in 1930 might have brought about a big change in approach at the top, but it was not translated into results, with the Club dropping a place in the final table to 15th, due to an all too familiar lack of penetration in the attack.

Mayer had a second successive successful season with 108 wickets at 20.34 but, apart from Paine, who took 75 wickets in the wet summer, no other bowler managed 50 wickets. Had Foster been able to play more than four times, the story might have been different, his 18 wickets including a blistering spell against Surrey in which he took seven for 42.

Only two of the 28 games were won – both in the first eight fixtures of the season, at which time the side was unbeaten. Even though the batsmen earned their money, with six of them exceeding 1,000 runs, nine of the last 20 matches were lost to give the Club the unenviable record in the period from 1926 to 1930 of winning only 15 out of 140 Championship matches played, with 41 defeats and 84 draws.

Better times were ahead, but not until the bowling and fielding improved. The new captain scored four hundreds and Smith, in his final season, scored three, with Bates, Parsons and Santall getting two each.

Even Wyatt's match aggregate of 215 out of his side's two-innings total of 488 could not prevent Kent, at Edgbaston, completing a conclusive double, with one match won by an innings and the other by nine wickets, thanks to the remarkable analyses of 'Tich' Freeman. The most prolific wicket-taking leg-break bowler in the history of cricket had an astonishing two-match aggregate of 25 wickets for 303, with Warwickshire scoring only 797 in the four innings.

Wyatt's continued good form, together with Chapman's failure to halt the first Bradman march through the record-books, brought the Warwickshire captain the leadership of his country in his first appearance in the five-match series in the final game at the Oval. The change in captaincy made no difference with England, despite scoring 405 in their first innings, thanks to 161 from Sutcliffe and a dogged 64 from Wyatt, losing by an innings and 39 runs.

Like Howell before him, Mayer had had enough of carrying a new-ball attack more or less singlehanded, although his disenchantment had come sooner – after just five seasons. He secured an agreement with the Accrington Club which cost Warwickshire £300 in compensation to get their fast bowler back, as well as a two-year agreement at a guaranteed minimum of £350 per year, and a benefit in 1933. Thankfully, there was no mention of a guaranteed minimum return from the benefit, which explains the disappointing final figure of £509, compared with £792 which Bates received in 1930. Had the committee repeated its unwise gesture with Parsons of guaranteeing a certain sum, Mayer must have received a sum of approximately double the amount.

So Mayer was saved for the 1931 season, but Smith was not. Despite his three hundreds and continued good form, it was decided – not unreasonably – that at 45 the time had come to look to the future, and so he was offered match money, instead of a basic full-time contract. As usual nothing if not forthright, Smith was having none of that and asked the Committee to nominate him for the first-class list of umpires – thus beginning another chapter in the life of a man whose association with first-class cricket was eventually to span eight decades. Smith went on to stand in seven Tests. At that time, only Quaife and Santall senior had played in more games for the County than the 444 logged by as tough a character as has ever played first-class cricket. His 800 victims for Warwickshire is still a Club record, although it is conceivable that Humpage could overtake him, and it is a tribute to his determination and fitness that 18 of his 20 first-class hundreds came after the age of 35.

The three chief offices of the Club changed hands within twelve months, with Sir Charles Hyde, H. W. Bainbridge and Dr Harold Thwaite replacing Ludford Docker, George Cartland and Cecil Wheeler, as president, chairman and treasurer.

In the winter of 1930–31, Wyatt was approached by the chairman and treasurer with the astonishing proposal to make G. D. Kemp-Welch, a Cambridge Blue, captain on the patently flimsy grounds that Wyatt appeared to be more interested in playing for England than Warwickshire. Such a suggestion was insulting and wrong, with Wyatt having already disagreed with the England selectors' suggestion before the Oval Test that he should miss each of the county matches immediately prior to, and after, the Test. Wyatt suspected that Ryder was behind the bizarre meeting, because he already believed that Ryder was 'much too inclined to interfere with the running of the county eleven', and was thus looking for a captain who would be easier for him to deal with than the independent Wyatt.

The rest of the committee knew nothing of the meeting, and anyway, the reason behind it was not tested in 1931 when Wyatt, having scored only 205 runs in the five Tests in South Africa the previous winter, did not play in any of the three Test matches against New Zealand.

A marked improvement in the performances of the bowlers helped the side to rise six places to ninth in the table, which was now calculated on a different basis, with 15 points for a win and five for first innings lead, with three going to the other side.

Paine, only 23, had a terrific season with his 127 wickets in all matches at 19.20 each, starting a run of five successive seasons in which he took more than 100 in a season, and actually in that period took 651 of the 962 wickets he secured before the end of his career. Mayer's output in the Championship dropped to 75 wickets, but with Wyatt getting 56 and Foster taking 47 from 20 games, the side developed all-round strength, instead of just being a good batting team.

Croom had a golden summer with six hundreds and Parsons, curiously appointed deputy captain despite his limited availability, finished fifth in the overall averages, with four hundreds helping him to an average of 56.29.

In a wet May, Warwickshire were destroyed at Headingley by Hedley Verity with the first of his 'all-ten' performances. He dismissed Smith's successor as wicket-keeper, Jack Smart, Foster, Tate and Paine in one over to finish with figures of 18.4-6-36-10, with Warwickshire all out for 72. In the return match, Percy Holmes hit his fourth double hundred against the Club, but a steady improvement meant that although the first three matches of the season were lost, only one more match was lost, and such was the impact made by the revitalised side that five players were selected for the Gentlemen *v* Players game at the Oval and three for the second match at Lord's. Wyatt, Foster and Kemp-Welch were the chosen amateurs, with Croom and Mayer playing for the Players in the first fixture.

The new treasurer, Thwaite, reported the lowest gate receipts since 1924, and was instrumental in establishing a special development fund in order to meet the needs of an enlarged playing staff and the start of ground improvements which were the first tottering steps towards Edgbaston regaining its status as a Test match ground over a quarter of a century later.

Thwaite pulled few punches at the annual meeting before the 1932 season began, itemising a loss from the previous year of £2,000, and his research showed that in the previous 37 years as a first-class county, aggregate profits amounted to £9,895, compared with losses sustained of £12,631 – with the redress only made possible because of special public appeals of £9,000.

Among youngsters considered for engagement were Eric Hollies and H. E. 'Tom' Dollery, whose careers were to run, more or less in parallel either side of the Second World War, and who, between them, wrote two of the most distinguished chapters in the history of Warwickshire cricket.

Older by two years, Hollies was taken on but, inexplicably Dollery was not, although his engagement was only to be delayed for a season. Because Hollies was born over the border in Staffordshire, he was billeted in Pershore Road in order to qualify, and made a surprise debut in the first of his four 1932 games in late June against Sussex. A South African born leg-spinner, Harold Jarrett, was originally chosen for the match, but Hollies, having just completed a couple of hours' work in preparing the pitch and the ground for the match, was suddenly summoned by Ryder to say that he was playing.

Jarrett was a terrific spinner of the ball, but like spin bowlers before, and after, him his best form was usually reserved for the nets, as is evidenced by his final total of wickets for Warwickshire of 47 at 34.14 each from 14 games. Jarrett played one game for Glamorgan in 1938, and his son, Keith, played rugby with distinction for Wales in the 1960s, and also played a few times for Glamorgan.

The 20-year-old Hollies took one wicket for 150 from 27 overs in a massive Sussex total of 511 for seven, and other salutary experiences he suffered that season included being thrashed for 57 off six overs against Gloucestershire, with Walter Hammond handing out most of the punishment. He was, however, always ready to seek advice, and talks with his father, and the captain of his former Birmingham League club, Old Hill – Bert Homer – persuaded Hollies that he needed to bowl quicker, and he soon adopted this method against quick-footed batsmen with increasing success.

The playing record in a wet summer was reflected in a second successive final placing of ninth, with five wins and five losses, plus eight wins and ten losses on first innings in drawn games. This was despite not having won a match by the middle of June. Wyatt scored most runs – 1,347 – although four other batsmen passed 1,000. The bowling was over-reliant on Paine, whose increased workload of 1,103 overs in all cricket brought him nine more wickets (136), at the reduced cost of 18.93.

Although Warwickshire lost the first match of the season at Lord's, their first-innings score of 69 was still good enough for a precious first-innings lead, thanks to Paine, who marked his return to the ground where he spent his early days with figures of 13.1-6-14-7. Yet another defeat by Kent, this time at Folkestone, was brought about by Freeman, whose match return of 17 wickets for 92 was then the ninth best analysis ever recorded, with the little leg-spinner already in fifth place with his 17 for 67 against Sussex at Hove ten years earlier.

Leslie Deakins, now in his fifth year at Edgbaston, had his salary increased to £156 a year, roughly a fifth of the money earned by Ryder, and it is interesting to note that the career threads of three men – Deakins, Hollies and Dollery – who were to influence

Warwickshire cricket so heavily after the war, were now about to be interwoven.

Wyatt's meticulous approach to the captaincy was now bringing a slow, but welcome, seasonal improvement, with the 1933 Championship table – headed by Yorkshire for the third successive season – showing Warwickshire in seventh position, thanks to a dry summer in which the bowlers showed improved form to support a set of batsmen who, led by Wyatt and Kilner, produced some startling feats. Kilner's aggregate of 2,114 in all Warwickshire matches was then a Club record, and among his six hundreds of the 20 scored that season, the one that gave him greatest pleasure was his 197 in the home fixture against Yorkshire. It was the eleventh of his 23 hundreds for Warwickshire, and the only one the ex-Tyke made against his own.

Wyatt scored five hundreds, but the most exciting batting came from Santall, with the highlight of his erratic career coming at Northampton. He became the sixth Warwickshire player to score a hundred before lunch – Diver, Fishwick twice, 'Tiger' Smith, Bainbridge and Glover, were the others – but his 173 was comfortably a world record. His 50 came in 45 minutes, 100 35 minutes later, his 150 took another half an hour, and in the remaining ten minutes before the bewildered Northamptonshire bowlers went to lunch, he hit 23. His final score of 201 was a career-best, and he hit four sixes and 24 fours.

Mayer's benefit match was a personal and financial disappointment for one of the most whole-hearted triers ever to play for the Club, with one wicket, an injury and £500 his return for eight years' hard work, with six more to come. County cricket can be an unfair game, with the wrong type of player sometimes on the receiving end of its cruel blows – so it was with Mayer who carried an arthritic knee into retirement after 1939 as his most lasting memento of a long and loyal career.

Wyatt played in two Test matches against the West Indies in 1933, and during his absence, for the first time in 20 years, the side was led by a professional – Bates. Even though he was now 37, he still continued the habit he developed early in his career of looking at least sixty degrees, and sometimes more, away from the photographer's lens, as anyone who studies the Warwickshire team photographs can verify for themselves. The first time it happened was probably accidental, but not afterwards.

The most encouraging feature of the season was the rapid progress made by Hollies, whose 79 wickets complemented perfectly the steady bowling of Paine, which brought him 123 wickets, albeit at a higher cost of 24.47 each from the much higher number of overs bowled in all matches of 1350.1. That workload remains the third highest ever by a

R. E. S. 'Bob' Wyatt tossing the coin, with his left hand because of a thumb injury to his right. Looking on is the Australian captain, Woodfull, during the 1934 season.

Warwickshire bowler, with Hollies bowling 1,470 and 1,393.2 in 1946 and 1951.

A loss of £2,259 for the season was reduced by a special appeal from the president which raised £1,735, but after Thwaite revealed that the projected annual income of £8,000 would not meet the anticipated running costs of £10,000, cuts had to be made. The staff was reduced by three and, even more short-sightedly, the Club withdrew from the Minor Counties, thus denying their younger players the best available grounding school for their developing skills.

Warwickshire's application for a Test match in 1935 against South Africa was rejected in favour of Trent Bridge, and an apparent change of mind by senior committee officials concerning the immediate and long-term future of Wyatt, resulted in a ten-year endowment policy being funded for him, with a maturity value of £1,000.

Wyatt's fifth year as captain in 1934 was easily the most successful, with the side's ten wins lifting them to fourth place in the table – then the second highest position in the Club's history. How much this was due to Wyatt's influence is arguable, because his return to the England captaincy for the first four test matches against Australia, together with a broken thumb, limited his Championship appearances to 12.

The deputy captaincy was shared between Bates, Parsons, Partridge and Kemp-Welch, who played only once, but scored an unbeaten 123 against Glamorgan at Swansea. Jack Buckingham took over behind the stumps at the age of 31, and the Yorkshireman went on to enjoy a short, but successful career up to the war as another in the line of Warwickshire wicketkeeper-batsmen. Peter Cranmer, then only 19, made his debut and with an innings of 113 in the home fixture against Northamptonshire, prompted the annual report to refer to him as: 'A new glory, whose prodigious hitting and activity in the field endeared him to the hearts of the regular habitues of the Edgbaston ground.'

Paine had his best season, taking 155 wickets from 1,269.5 overs at an average of 16.94 each to head the national averages. He took 12 wickets in a match three times, including eight for 43 against Worcestershire at Edgbaston, and eight for 62 at Scarborough against Yorkshire. Solid support was given by Mayer, with 88 wickets, and Hollies, whose 84 wickets earned his selection with his senior spinning partner in the party to tour West Indies under Wyatt the following winter.

Dollery made his debut (nought and one) in the match at Scarborough in which Warwickshire earned one of their narrowest wins in a low-scoring game, which was eventually won by a captain's innings from Parsons, the parson. Paine's eight wickets helped dismiss the home side for 101, but that still earned them a lead of 56, with only Buckingham reaching double figures in a pathetic total of 45. Paine,

Hollies and Mayer shared the wickets, but a target of 216 looked impossible until Parsons, in a typically attacking innings of 94 out of 121, so rattled the previous year's Champions that when Mayer hit the winning boundary, with a relieved Hollies looking on at the other end, Macauley jumped on his cap in rage, and the Yorkshire players walked off without a word.

Paine successfully used his best-ever season as a negotiating lever to obtain a four-year agreement with a benefit in 1938, but his insistence that he be given the Bank Holiday match against Derbyshire was only acceded to with great reluctance. The committee were also not impressed when his other demand was for a minimum guaranteed sum of £1,000.

In the West Indies, Hollies headed the Test averages with ten wickets at 21.7 each, and Paine was also successful with 17 wickets at 27.47. Hollies told the author after the war how impressed he was with the way he was looked after by Wyatt – citing the instance when, after an early net session in which Hammond set out to smash every ball Hollies bowled straight back at him, Wyatt took his young leg-spinner out of the net and told him he never need bowl at Hammond again on the tour.

The tour ended with England losing the series 2-1, and Wyatt having his jaw fractured in four places by Martindale. That was in March, but back in England, before the end of May the Warwickshire captain had hit unbeaten hundreds against Surrey at the Oval and in the home fixture against Gloucestershire.

Before the start of the 1935 season, chairman Bainbridge reminded the members that the Club was still in financial difficulties, with Thwaite underlining the point by comparing Lancashire's income in 1934 of £9,250 with that of Warwickshire, which had never topped £5,000. Whatever the problems, it did not prevent a well-merited testimonial fund being launched for Ryder, with the secretary's final receipts of £1,608 more than double those of the official beneficiary, Santall, who received only £712. That return was a niggardly one, especially as – perhaps coincidentally, perhaps not – the three hundreds he scored in 1935 meant that ten of his final total of 21 hundreds had come in the three-year period immediately after he first knew of the award of his benefit.

Wyatt enjoyed a better season overall than the previous year – 2,019 runs compared with 1,776 – although his England captaincy was marked with another defeat – this time to South Africa, who won the only match decided of the five-match series. This meant an unenviable record for the Warwickshire man of losing successive series to Australia, West Indies and South Africa, with Wyatt captaining England in ten of those games.

After an early challenge for the title in 1935 could not be sustained, the side fell back to eighth position, although their former reputation for dull cricket had seemingly gone, according to *Wisden*: 'Often their lack of restraint brought disaster, only the soundness of Wyatt preventing a complete collapse.'

Paine took over a hundred wickets – 110 in all – for the fifth and final time, but the most encouraging features of the season were the continued progress made by Hollies and the arrival in the side as a regular batsman of Dollery. He passed 1,000 runs and followed his maiden hundred against Glamorgan with another against Gloucestershire – both at Edgbaston. Already good judges marked him down as one of the most promising batsmen in county cricket, and with Hollies taking 127 wickets at 18.91 each, the two men who were to become such great stalwarts of the Club were on their way. Hollies was chosen for the third Test match, but had to withdraw when, in the match preceding the Test at Swansea, a colleague mistook the bedroom of Hollies for his own, and inadvertently caused the leg-spinner to suffer a badly ricked neck, by flopping down on what, in the dark, he thought was an empty bed.

At the end of season, Bates, then 40, decided to retire, and sadly for a man who was born on the ground and made his debut in 1913, when he walked through the Edgbaston gates, he was never to return. An attractive batsman, whose 19,326 runs included 21 hundreds, his average of 27.92 is surprisingly modest, especially as he batted throughout his career on the good pitches originally laid by his father. Any specialist batsman would consider a career average of 30 as a minimum, and it is surprising to note that among batsmen who scored more than 10,000 first-class runs for the Club but did not achieve this mark are Charlesworth, Horner, Ord, Santall and Ibadulla, although the Pakistani was more of an all-rounder. Apparently Hendren once said to Bates: 'Len, you have too many strokes', but some batsmen are unable to maximise the returns from their ability, and the records show that Bates was one of those.

The year ended with an accumulated deficit of £3,025, but another astutely devised appeal from Sir Charles Hyde not only wiped that out but gave the Club a surplus of £2,500 to carry into 1936.

CHAPTER TWELVE

WYATT SACKED AS WAR STOPS PLAY

THE FOUR SEASONS LEADING to the start of the Second World War comprised a period of trouble off the field, and poor results on it, that brought about a change of Club captain and chairman, and gave the side successive final positions in the Championship table of 13th, 11th, 13th and 11th.

The problems started in the 1936 season with the away match against Gloucestershire, where Warwickshire were thrashed by an innings and 117 runs on a pitch which quickly disintegrated after the home side had scored a patient 453 for eight declared. It was not the defeat, but the manner of it, which precipitated an astonishing written criticism to Wyatt of his 'responsibility' for the result. The facts are that, after following on 284 behind, Wyatt decided that the match could be saved only by unrelenting defence, which explains why he batted for 135 minutes for 25, and the normally dashing young Dollery spent 90 minutes for seven. The surface of the pitch was now broken, and any forcing stroke off such a master off-spinner as Tom Goddard was fatal, which explains why Wyatt decided that, in the interests of salvaging pride and self-respect from the defeat, his players must avoid risks and sell themselves dearly. Although Wyatt later thought that Ryder may have been behind the offending letter he received, chairman Bainbridge signed it, and thus must take full responsibility for its contents. Wyatt said: 'The committee seemed to put our failure down to my management of the team both on and off the field, apparently ignoring the fact that under my captaincy Warwickshire had risen from nearly bottom in the table to the highest they had been since before the 1914 war. The committee said I hadn't given enough encouragement to the younger players.'

On that point alone, the views of Hollies are pertinent:

> He was ready to help any young player who was keen and eager and willing to help himself, but he had no time for the easy-going, lackadaisical type of player.
>
> I consider myself fortunate that when I was trying to win a place in county cricket, Wyatt was captain. Of the four captains I played under, Wyatt was without doubt the finest. He knew the strengths and weaknesses of every batsman, and I have seen him place the field for an incoming batsman almost before he reached the wicket. He simply lived cricket.

Furthermore, when Wyatt was relieved of the captaincy at the end of the 1937 season, Hollies' father wrote a letter of thanks to him for the way he had helped his son. 'I am sure your advice and help has been the chief cause of any success he has achieved in the cricket world', he wrote.

Wyatt's request to the chairman to discuss the letter was not only refused, he was further insulted by being told that he should devote more time to the success of the team rather than of his own personal performances. During his six seasons as captain before the 1936 season, Wyatt's four tours and 29 of his final total of 40 appearances for England clearly reduced his involvement with his players, but the views of Hollies and his father give a much rounder picture of the Club captain's contributions to the cause of Warwickshire cricket than do those of the committee.

The matter was not to come to a head until the end of the next season, and meanwhile Wyatt in 1936 suffered the longest period of poor form he had ever known, although he still hit three hundreds for the Club and topped the averages. Dollery was the only other player to reach 1,000 runs, Croom's failure to reach the mark being his first since 1927.

Croom's 18-season career spanned most of the period between the two wars. His benefit match against Sussex was ruined by rain and final receipts of £679 sadly provided a model professional with the second lowest Warwickshire benefit since that of Kinneir in 1914, the lowest belonging to Mayer.

Croom batted through an innings for the fourth time – only Fred Gardner equalled that feat – in George Geary's benefit match at Hinckley, in a match in which 39 wickets fell for 423, and the home side sneaked in by one wicket. Croom's unbeaten 69 out of his side's first innings of 133 ranks among his best innings, but even he was powerless to prevent the beneficiary turning the match with second innings figures of 13.3–8–7–7.

Mayer and Hollies carried the bowling with 84 and 79 wickets respectively in the lengthy absence because of illness of Paine, who took only 30 wickets. The accounts showed a loss of £2,000, and the president trumpeted another plea for brighter cricket at the Annual Meeting: 'Today people like jazz, not funeral dirges. I do not blame them if they stop away from dull cricket. The display of the Warwickshire team at Bristol last season was a blot on cricket. That sort of thing must stop. The selection committee, the captain and the players must bear that in mind.'

Wyatt was still in Australia with England but, had he been present, even his equanimity would have been tested by the contrast between that studied comment and the hearty vote of thanks then accorded him for his services as captain. Not only that but a recommendation from the executive committee that he be re-elected captain was approved. It seems that the committee must have been divided on an issue which was further to split the Club and its membership within a few months.

Ironically, the 1937 season was one of Wyatt's best, providing him with a record eight hundreds for Warwickshire – equalled by Kanhai in 1972 – in an overall aggregate of 2,625 at an average of 53.27, which earned him sixth place in the national list. He scored two double hundreds, including an unbeaten 201, in Kilner's benefit match against Derbyshire, with Warwickshire's much criticised first-innings total of 523 for eight declared – the closure did not come until 3pm on the second day, with only seven runs coming in the last 45 minutes of the innings – in vivid contrast to the 28 for which they were dismissed in the return game. In this, Bill Copson, who missed the first game, bowled so fast and straight that his final figures were 8.2–2–11–8, with five wickets falling in six deliveries, including four in four. The latter feat has since been accomplished in county cricket in one innings only, by Fred Ridgway of Kent against Derbyshire in 1951 and Pat Pocock for Surrey against Sussex at Hove in 1971. The four Warwickshire players to be dismissed in successive deliveries were Dollery, Mayer, Fantham and Hollies, with the latter later revealing that, such was the panic in the dressing-room that batsmen who were struggling to get their pads on were conducting conversations like:

'You go in.'

'I've already been in.'

'Well, you go in.'

'I've been in as well.'

Dollery scored four hundreds to earn a place for the North against the South, as well as for MCC, and runs were so plentiful, particularly at Edgbaston, that after a high scoring game against Sussex which produced six hundreds, the committee decided that the next home match would be played on a pitch which did not have the same amount of rolling or general preparation.

Revelling in the unusually helpful conditions, Mayer was able, for once on his home ground, to attack, and the fact that he returned the best match figures of his career, shows what he might have achieved had he been able to bowl on pitches which were better suited to his undoubted skill. He took seven for 46 and six for 24, to bring a win by an innings and 32, despite Warwickshire scoring only 222. The victory was one of six gained in Wyatt's last season as captain, but the knives were now considered sharp enough, and at the end of the season, the announcement was made that the committee wanted a different captain for 1938.

Wyatt still felt that the hand of Ryder was involved: 'He and I for a long time had not seen eye to eye about the running of the County XI.

I thought he wanted to influence, if not make, decisions which properly belonged to the captain of the side.'

To be fair to the secretary, his record shows that he always did what he believed to be best for the Club, and few long-serving secretaries avoid a charge of exceeding their authority, because of the need to make day-to-day decisions without always being willing or able to refer to senior officers.

Wyatt was told by Bainbridge and Thwaite that the match against Lancashire had not been won because he delayed the declaration until he reached 200, and more long-term criticism, that the side had got into a rut under his leadership. An unnamed playing colleague apparently opined that: 'Had he been more unselfish he would have been the best captain ever,' and it is a fact that his ratio of one 'not out' in every six innings he played for the Club is the highest of anyone. Even Quaife, who suffered similar criticism, had a marginally higher average with two 'not outs' every 13 innings. Mike Smith, for instance, who batted 114 more times for Warwickshire than did Wyatt, had six fewer not-outs, but whatever the verdict, it cannot be denied that the change of captaincy was not handled well.

In October, the executive recommended to the general committee that Peter Cranmer be appointed for the 1938 season, but this was only agreed after a procedural wrangle which split the proposal into two parts, with the separation of the appointment of Cranmer carried by 16 votes to three. The *Birmingham Post* reserved comment pending a full explanation at the next general meeting. The paper acknowledged that while he 'was not a lucky captain, he was by far the best all-round amateur England has produced since the war'.

Over 300 members heard Sir Charles Hyde explain in March 1938 that 'it is a great responsibility to drop our pilot, but the ship has been sailing in troubled waters for some time'. Wyatt had distanced himself from a proposal from the floor calling for the decision to be rescinded, and although the committee could have refused a vote on that issue on procedural grounds, the threat of their resignation if the proposal succeeded was, like that made by Alec Hastilow in 1953 over the Grove affair, good enough to win the day. The meeting closed with a vote of thanks to Wyatt which, while not perhaps meaningless, was hardly one he would have valued overmuch.

So the 21-year-old Cranmer was appointed captain, two months after he had led his country against Wales at rugby, and he soon found that his predecessor was ready and willing to help him in any way he could. But not without the odd drop of acid, as Cranmer recalled after his first match in 1938 at Lord's against Middlesex. Mayer had to return to Birmingham because of the illness of his daughter, and the home side was well over 100 without losing a wicket. because Wyatt,

Peter Cranmer, who played 166 games for Warwickshire between 1934 and 1954.

still one of the nimblest fielders in the side, had been fielding at cover and fine leg, Cranmer asked him what he should do as they went back on the field after an interval. 'How do I know? I can't see from deep fine-leg,' answered Wyatt.

Cranmer said: 'I made sure he fielded at slip for the rest of the season, and he was of enormous help to me.'

The same number of games – six – were won, with the same number lost, and ten draws put the side down two places to 13th.

Kilner had gone after a 14-season career which brought him 16,075 runs at an average of 31.89, and Cranmer's decision to promote Santall to open the innings was unsuccessful. So, with Croom only just reaching 1,000 and Dollery 1,272, the considerable advance by the new captain from 576 runs to 932 was welcome to the committee in every sense.

Of the six matches won, four came from a run of five games in June, including a win at Derby that featured a remarkable partnership for the sixth wicket between Dollery and Buckingham of 220. They came together at 39 for five with Copson again on the rampage, and the game nearly won and lost. Dollery later revealed how Buckingham won an important psychological trick when he came in to bat with a typical show of cockiness which, at times, bordered on the insufferable and was guaranteed to penetrate the thickest of opposition skins.

Copson was known to dislike any disparaging remarks about the colour of his red hair, so imagine the effect when, as Buckingham passed Dollery, he said – loudly enough for the bowler to hear: 'Don't worry about "Ginger". I'll deal with him and if you see to the rest of 'em, we'll soon get the runs.'

Never mind the enraged Copson, whose bowling became faster but more erratic, Dollery was sufficiently stirred by the ebullience of his partner to play what he always said was his best-ever innings of 134 not out, and with 'the Duke' scoring his maiden hundred (124), a famous victory was won.

The return match was Paine's benefit, but his hoped-for minimum return of £1,000 fell short by £124. As well as the visitors winning by an innings and 28 runs, the beneficiary got a 'pair' – rare in times when a single to get off the mark was a time-honoured custom. He also took only one wicket for 102 off 25 overs. It was almost the end of the road for Paine, because after refusing a contract for 1939, which was too heavily weighted with match monies for his liking, he only played one more match – in 1947 – before going into the Birmingham League. In his distinguished career of ten seasons he took 962 wickets at an average of 22.73. Before he qualified for Warwickshire, he had played five games for Middlesex as an 18-year-old, and he was still only 30 when his full-time professional career ended.

Before the 1939 season began, Bainbridge stepped down from the chair because of ill-health, and Thwaite succeeded him, while another change resulted in the resignation from the committee of A. C. Griffiths, who had been Wyatt's chief supporter the previous year. He resigned because of his disenchantment with the cricket committee's manner of handling the engagement and selection of players, as well as the coaching methods used.

With the war looming ever nearer, the season was played in an unreal atmosphere, but at least Club supporters could cherish in the dark days ahead the performances of Dollery and Hollies which, but for four defeats in August, would have lifted the side to a higher place in the table than 11th. The side won seven games, lost eight and drew nine, with the best win of the season, against Derbyshire, made possible by a magnificent 177 by Dollery when his side was in serious trouble. He headed the averages with 42.56, scoring three more hundreds in a Championship aggregate of 1,362 which was his best yet, and one good enough to earn his selection for the tour of India, which was naturally later called off because of the war.

Hollies was the only bowler to take 100 wickets, his 117 wickets in all games at 22.09 being the third time in a successive run of ten years each side of the war in which he was to exceed three figures. He became the sixth Warwickshire bowler to take nine wickets in an innings – taking the last seven for 29 out of his nine for 93 in the win at Edgbaston against Glamorgan. Mayer's last season brought him 84 wickets, and a new medium-pacer, Charlie Grove, hinted at what was to come with 34 wickets in his first season.

The West Indies sailed home early because of the impending war, and Warwickshire's season dissolved at Lord's where they played their last match, after which the team went their various ways, some never to play again.

As for Dollery and Hollies, they parted at Birmingham station on that evening in late August, and did not see each other again until April 1946.

For the second time in 25 years, the Club had to decide how best to deal with an open-ended situation, in which they needed to balance the long-term hoped-for resumption of county cricket with the harsh financial realities brought about by no guaranteed income to offset permanent overheads. An appeal was made to members to continue their subscriptions, and over £700 was received by the end of the year from that source. Compared with the First World War much more cricket was played, and although Dollery and Cranmer were in the Army, and Wyatt was to join the RAF, a strong County team played at Worcester in 1940, with Wyatt, Hill, Santall, Ord, Buckingham, Paine, Hollies and Grove all turning out.

Ryder operated on half pay, but soon found alternative work, and Thwaite ran the Club together with Deakins until the call-up of the latter into the Navy. Somehow things ticked over – albeit on a haphazard basis.

Midway through 1942, the Minister of Labour, Ernest Bevin, wrote to the Lord Mayor of Birmingham, among other civic heads, asking for daylight entertainment to be provided for factory workers, with the result that Alderman Tiptaft had the foresight to delegate the job to Lieut-Col 'Rusty' Scorer from Moseley, who had played a handful of games for the Club after the end of the previous war. He was already running the Queensberry All-Services Club in Hurst Street, Birmingham, and was in the Home Guard as well as operating his own business, but that did not deter one of the most enthusiastic all-round sportsmen Birmingham has ever produced.

His first sight of the Edgbaston ground was a depressing one, with, in his own words: 'the grass 18 inches high and four-foot thistles covering the seats on the banks. The small scorebox near the pavilion had been bombed, and the desolate scene nearly convinced me that it was impossible to stage a festival of cricket in six weeks.' But Scorer's well-known ingenuity and determination produced a mower from the *Birmingham Post*, help from the Parks Department, and even petrol coupons from unknown sources.

The Warwickshire Club let him have the ground free of charge and so, provided he could attract the players, the dream of Scorer to stage wartime matches was close to realisation. He achieved it in tremendous style, with players like Wyatt, Parks, the Langridge brothers and Gimblett turning out, and the crowds being entertained still further by the band of the 30th Warwickshire Home Guard. Around £450 was contributed to the Lord Mayor's War Relief Fund, and the activity encouraged the Club to engage Fred Pope as groundsman, with the cricket week now likely to be repeated.

Sir Charles Hyde died and was replaced as president by Thwaite, who had thus done duty in the three main offices in four years, and who was able to announce a surplus of £357 to the annual meeting.

In 1943, Scorer's matches attracted 20,000 cricket-starved spectators, and this time £1,300 was raised for charity. Understandably, it was then decided that the Festival Week should become a permanent feature, and in 1944 the results were even more spectacular, with 42,000 watching a week that bubbled with attractive cricket and names of the past and future like Keith Miller, Learie Constantine, 'Bertie' Clarke, Frank Woolley, Herbert Sutcliffe, Walter Hammond and Reg Simpson. Simpson's run of 41, 69, 16, 79, 99, 86, 21, 47 and 71 prompted P. F. Warner to write: 'I think he is by far the most promising of the young batsmen, and I guess he will be playing for England one day.' He was right.

The Lee Brothers, 'Stewie' Dempster and Dennis Brookes were others to turn out, as did Leslie Compton and New Zealand Test wicket-keeper, K. C. James, together with locals like Hollies, Grove and Goodway. Cricket survived its Second World War, with Scorer's contribution a major factor to the ability of the Warwickshire County Cricket Club to be in a much better position than otherwise would have been the case when the opportunity came to resume normal service.

CHAPTER THIRTEEN

REBUILDING AGAIN

THE FOURTH AND FINAL series of festival matches provided the perfect transitional period from war to peace. Not only was Adolf Hitler to depart the international scene but Edgbaston, already without Ryder for the first time since 1895, was to bid farewell to Wyatt.

A regular player in the festival weeks, he scored 58 on the final Sunday for the RAF against Scorer's Festival XI to help wind up a gloriously uninhibited four-year programme which, as well as giving untold pleasure to 140,000 spectators, also raised £10,000 for wartime good causes.

Birmingham was the only city in the country which held an annual festival in wartime, and their foresight prompted the somewhat optimistic view in *Wisden*, that the crowds proved that the city had a keen public for the game. Ironically it was the apathy of the same public, once the post-war euphoria had evaporated in the mid-1950s, that was to make more difficult the re-establishment of Edgbaston on the Test match ground rota.

Scorer, whose brainchild proved such an outstanding success, ended his final broadcast on the festivals with these words: 'And so my wartime festivals come to an end – for me happy memories of wonderful sportsmen, great cricket and happy crowds bringing money for those who need it. I give you a toast – to Cricket.'

Scorer's astute and humorous use of the microphone during his four festivals was a revelation. His enlightened approach broke through the barriers which had previously prevented any worthwhile empathy between authority and public, and the considerable advance in modern public relations owes much to a man whose innovative ideas were well ahead of his time. His self-styled 'crazy natters' to an enthralled public ranged from explanatory comments between overs and at the fall of a wicket, to tongue-in-cheek remarks like: 'This is to announce that Mr R. E. S. Wyatt will sign no more autographs this week because of remarks scrawled in the dust on his car.'

Deakins was still in the Navy when he was appointed as successor to Ryder, and although his initial plans for the complete reconstruction of his beloved Edgbaston were drawn up on Royal Navy notepaper in 1943, efforts to secure his release from the service were unsuccessful until October 1945. On the penultimate day of that month he attended his first committee meeting as a secretary in his own right, and so began a reign spanning four decades which was to turn Edgbaston into a Test match venue which now is unrivalled for spectator facilities, as well as faultless administration and hospitality.

Leslie Thomas Deakins, Warwickshire Secretary from 1945 to 1976.

Deakins brought with him Sydney Harkness, a naval colleague who had shared many a dog watch at Scapa Flow, and a man from the north-east of England who clearly was a willing disciple to the Deakins dream.

Those first scribbled notes had developed into a 40-page treatise which, although it was to be modified many times, never lost sight of its three fundamental aims: comfortable seating, a good view uncluttered by pillars, and every possible spectator facility.

Many have been the groans in recent years at the constant reminders over the public address system for spectators to refrain from treading on the sacred grass, and although the Club's attitude is more relaxed now than in the first 30 years after the Second World War, it is worth chronicling the early thoughts of Deakins which were quickly to crystallise into such a rigid ground rule:

'In 1921 at the age of 12 I was taken by a teacher, together with five

> other boys, to see my first match at Edgbaston, which was against the Warwick Armstrong touring Australians. Long before play started I can recall being enthralled by the wonderful expanse of beautiful turf and captivated by the thought of earning the right, one day, to walk on it.
>
> It never occurred to me that it was anything other than sacrilege that such a hallowed area, rich in cricket history, should be desecrated by the feet of the multitude. The ground represented a particular heaven you earned, if you were good enough, the right to enter. If you were not good enough, then you must admire, and indeed consider yourself privileged to do so, from afar.

Many people have never agreed with that view, but they cannot question the sincerity of the reasons given by a man who never lost his initial starry-eyed love for the game that was to enrich his life from that first match in 1921, until he died in 1989.

The first committee served by Deakins was the object of much local criticism from local journalists M. F. K. Fraser in the *Birmingham Evening Despatch* and Claude Westell in the *Birmingham Evening Mail*, as well as some members who even resigned in protest at what they felt to be a lack of interest by the committee in the festival idea. Wyatt wrote to Scorer saying: 'I can assure you that those who matter at Lord's thoroughly approved of your festival.'

The committee decided to shelve the matter until the 1946 fixtures had been determined – a far cry from the computerised procedure nowadays which arranges a skeleton fixture list well over 12 months in advance. Subsequently, the passing of time showed that the Scorer-type festival concept could have happened only in wartime. When the clouds are at their darkest, any shaft of light is welcome.

The Club's annual report of 1945 was a slim 25-page booklet – the first to bear the co-signature of 'L. T. Deakins, Secretary.' Colin Langley, as Club chairman, shared the credit for a publication which was quickly to expand into the best and most comprehensive in county cricket. It acknowledged the absence of any worthwhile improvement on the ground between the two wars and that 'the present premises, largely wooden in construction, were inadequate, quite out of date, and constantly absorbing an undue proportion of the Club's annual income to retain them in a serviceable condition'.

An appeal fund launched to aid the reconstruction had already yielded £10,871 13s 7d, but the president, Dr Thwaite, told the annual meeting that post-war planning would be divided into two parts – capital outlay on premises and an income adequate to meet reasonable expenditure. He announced that twin aims would be to increase the ground capacity to 20,000 at a cost of £200,000, possibly to be spread over the next 20 years.

The reconstruction plans were far-reaching. They provided for a double-deck stand which would seat 2,400 under cover and 4,400 in the open on the popular side. There would also be buffet bars, luncheon room, kitchen, dressing rooms and toilets, as well as a second double-deck stand to seat 1,200, another luncheon room, small gymnasium, squash courts, a new house for the groundsman and a cricket shop. A new members' pavilion was planned, including accommodation for the secretary and committee. Further terracing with open seating and a third double-deck stand would give total accommodation of 21,000, with roughly one-third under cover.

The precise cost was forecast to be £201,150, which included the cost of purchasing six acres of ground between the existing west boundary and Pershore Road. The report paid a generous tribute to Mr Frank Wager, the club's architect, 'for the professional skill, time and care which he has devoted to the really excellent plans forming the basis of the reconstruction scheme. Further thanks are due to him for his endeavours to renovate the existing premises to make them serve for the time being'.

The first post-war change to affect the members was an upward review of subscriptions which saw the ordinary ticket increase from £1 10s 0d (£1.50) to £2 2s 0d, (£2.10) with other categories increased to £1 5s 0d (£1.25) for country members, £1 1s 0d (£1.05) for ladies' tickets, and 10s 6d (52p) for boys under 15.

The playing programme for 1946 incorporated one major change from the last one played in 1939, when only 12 of the 17 counties were played. The fixtures sub-committee at Lord's decided that each county would meet every other county at least once, while no county would be absent from any other's home ground more than once in every four years. The six counties whom Warwickshire would meet only once in 1946 were Glamorgan, Hampshire and Somerset at home, and Gloucestershire, Middlesex and Surrey away. Clubs were also allowed to choose four counties who would become permanent opponents to be met home and away each season. Warwickshire chose Worcestershire, Derbyshire, Leicestershire and Lancashire.

The home games against Hampshire and Lancashire were allocated to the Courtaulds ground in Coventry, but the Mitchells and Butlers ground was not considered to have recovered sufficiently from its war-time ravages to stage a game. Lip service was paid to the war-time festival concept by designating the August Bank Holiday fixture against Derbyshire plus the following one against India as a 'Festival Week'.

The new system would give each county 26 games and eliminate the unfair necessity for percentages to assess positions in the Championship.

The big headache was the availability of players, and the committee started on its mammoth task of reassembling a County side by appointing Peter Cranmer as captain.

The only professionals he could call on were Dollery and Hollies, who had not set eyes on each other during the war, together with Ord and Ken Taylor, who over 30 years later was to become cricket manager at Trent Bridge. Grove was still in the army, and the MCC decided that Tom Pritchard would have to qualify for 12 months before he could play. 'Tiger' Smith was coach and Alec Hastilow agreed to captain the 2nd XI for the season.

Only a man of Cranmer's resilience and breezy outlook on life could have come to terms so well with his task. The war, which affected so many playing careers, had brought to a premature end those of Buckingham, Santall, Mayer and Croom, and only by using the services of local club cricketers could the Club fulfil its demanding fixture list. Before the campaign began, Cranmer thought he could count on the services of such distinguished amateurs as Wyatt, New Zealand Test batsman C. S. Dempster, who had decided to leave Leicestershire for business reasons, Cyril Goodway, Dick Sale and John Thompson.

Twelve of the 31 players who played for Warwickshire in 1946.
Standing (l to r): Eric Hollies, Bill Fantham, Tom Dollery, 'Tiger' Smith (coach), M. Barker, Ken Taylor, Norman Shortland, Jimmy Ord.
Seated: R. Mead-Briggs, C. S. Dempster, Peter Cranmer (capt.) Cyril Goodway, Charles Adderley.

Wyatt became the first piece of the jigsaw to fall away, despite the fact that he has always maintained that he intended to continue playing for Warwickshire after the war. The committee is on record as wanting him to play but, as Wyatt put it, 'relations were never particularly harmonious'. He had moved house to Worcestershire at the beginning of the war, and because of 'the general atmosphere and attitude adopted towards me by certain members of the committee', he decided he would play out his career at New Road. As late as 18 April 1946, only days before the scheduled restart of country cricket after the enforced break of seven years, the Edgbaston committee minuted their decision to inform Lord's that Wyatt was still wanted by Warwickshire, and therefore they could not sign his registration form for Worcestershire. Wyatt met the executive committee, and once it was plain he was determined to go, Alec Hastilow, who acted as chairman in the absence of Colin Langley, reluctantly agreed to draw up a joint statement release to the press:

> Mr R. E. S. Wyatt, at his own request, met the executive committee at the Club today and intimated that he did not wish to accept the invitation already given to him to play for Warwickshire, and desired registration under Rule 10(1) to play for Worcestershire. The committee, although they very much regretted his decision, did not wish to stand in the way of so able a cricketer remaining in the county game, and informed him that they would not oppose his decision. The final decision, of course, would rest with the MCC.

On the verge of his 45th birthday therefore, Wyatt was finally granted his registration, although not before he had felt obliged to remind the committee that although they might prevent him playing for Worcestershire, he would still be free to play for Surrey, the county of his birth. Furthermore, if he did go to Surrey he would consider it necessary to give publicly his reasons for leaving Warwickshire. Good sense however, prevailed with the final parting an amiable one, although there followed an inordinate delay before he was granted life membership 30 years later. In his career Wyatt scored 21,687 of his final first-class total of 39,405 runs for Warwickshire, including 51 of his 85 hundreds. He also took 652 wickets in his 17 seasons at Edgbaston.

Wyatt was to go on to captain Worcestershire at the age of 50 and in his last county match he hit the winning six against Somerset. His last first-class match was in 1956 for Douglas Jardine's side against Oxford University, and the then 23-year-old M. J. K. Smith will need no reminding that he provided one of his predecessors as Warwickshire captain with his last wicket in first-class cricket, secured at the age of 56.

With the decks cleared and the war-time clouds having finally rolled away, the scene was set for Cranmer and his ever-changing side to answer the umpire's long-awaited call of 'Play.'

Warwickshire's 1946 record of seven wins, 14 defeats and only five drawn games out of the 26 played, earned them 14th position in the Championship table. Only once – in 1930 – had they finished lower since 1921, but the *Birmingham Post*'s description of the team's performance as 'disappointing' was challenged with some justification by the Club's honorary treasurer, Captain C. F. R. Cowan, DSO, RN. As he said, to win seven matches with such thin resources was more than could have reasonably been expected, and reflected great credit on Cranmer's ability to lead by example.

The average number of club cricketers chosen for each match was six, as borne out by the 31 players who turned out to help lift aloft once more the proud flag of first-class county cricket. No fewer than 11 of them had three innings or fewer, with eight of the amateurs sharing 504 overs which yielded 30 wickets at an average cost of 50 each.

All this was while Hollies bowled 1,433 overs in the Championship to take 175 wickets at 15.16 each. That is an average of 50 overs a match, but remembering that Warwickshire batted twice more often than they bowled twice in a match, his average number of overs per innings was much higher than 25. His wicket total was a record haul for the County, and like Dollery and Mike Smith in subsequent years, Cranmer had good reason to be grateful for the consistent reliability of one of the greatest slow bowlers the game has seen. Hollies might have bowled out of the back of his hand, but he was more than a leg-break bowler. his line and length never faltered, even under the most difficult conditions, and he could always be trusted to do a good job, even on well-grassed pitches when other spinners in the game would not get a turn.

Dollery was a similar pillar of strength with the bat, scoring a wonderful 1,901 runs in all games at an average of 43.20 – all the more meritorious in a season in which pitches were understandably less than perfect after seven years of neglect, and of course he was the only constant factor in an ever-changing batting order.

Dempster played only five innings, and although the left-handed Sale topped the averages, his 538 runs came from only 11 completed innings, while John Thompson, from whom much was expected, could manage only three innings.

Cranmer deserved his 1,071 runs and, more than any other cricketer in living memory, never once did other than put the interests of his side first and foremost. Goodway kept wicket well, and his never-failing cheerfulness played its part in maintaining a happy dressing-room spirit which rarely flagged despite several crushing defeats.

The highlight of the season was the unique performance of Hollies in taking all ten wickets in the first innings of the home fixture against Nottinghamshire, unassisted by any fielder, with seven clean bowled and three lbw victims completing magnificent figures of 20.4–4–49–10. He became the second Warwickshire bowler to accomplish the rare 'all-ten' feat – Howell did it also, at Edgbaston, 23 years earlier – and made St Swithins day in 1946 the most memorable of his career.

Any long-term selection policy was impossible, particularly when the Club had two or more consecutive away matches. The amateurs flitted on and off stage, at least one being such a mystery that, other than the fact he turned up with a complete new set of cricket clothing, the captain was no wiser after his two matches about his ability. Let Hollies tell the tale: 'He turned up at the first of two away matches, and the skipper was a bit embarrassed to ask him whether he batted or bowled. He asked me to go and watch him in the nets, but I had to confess that I was no wiser.' (The immortal quote of Hollies to his skipper was 'well he cor bowl, and he cor bat'.) The poor man, whose anonymity shall be preserved, scored two runs from three innings and bowled two overs for nine runs, before he departed the county scene with his particular cricketing strengths still unrevealed.

Stories abound of incidents and comments in that first post-war season, with two of the best concerning Goodway and the Kings Heath opening bowler, the late Charles Adderley. Both stories come from the match against Gloucestershire at Bristol. Goodway had been pressed into service as an emergency opener, and somewhat haughtily brushed aside a photographer at the pavilion gate who had set up his tripod to snap the opening batsmen as they went out to open the innings.

The cameraman had the last word when Goodway was out in the first over, and as he made to return through the pavilion gate, found to his embarrassment that insufficient time had elapsed to dismantle the tripod, and the wrong sort of photograph was promptly taken.

When Warwickshire fielded, Adderley was given the new ball to bowl at the belligerent Charlie Barnett. He asked Hollies, to his horror, to stand at silly mid-off in the sort of field setting that his military medium-bowling style used with outstanding success in club cricket. The first two deliveries were smashed one on each side of an apprehensive Hollies to the extra cover boundary, before an understanding Barnett winked and whispered: 'If you stand still, I won't hit you.'

Dollery made 59 in the rain-ruined Test trial at Lord's. Hollies also played, and it is a mystery why neither was selected for Hammond's side to tour Australia that winter.

The real bright spot of the season was the bowling of Pritchard against the Indian tourists in the only match in which he was allowed to play. On a rain-softened pudding of a pitch, he whipped out Hazare, Makad and Mohammed without conceding a run, and sustained a magnificent hostility throughout the visitors' final total of 375 for nine declared, to finish with the outstanding analysis of 46–19–54–4. In 'Tiger' Smith's words, the New Zealander 'ran in like a human whipcord'. His lithe, excitingly furious action whetted the Edgbaston crowd's appetite for the comming years, and the cheerful 29-year-old New Zealander would not disappoint them.

Warwickshire managed to balance their books with a profit of over £5,000, including £807 compensation from the Auxiliary Fire Service for damage done during their war-time occupation of the ground, and the land and buildings were valued at £11,400.

The Club's application to rejoin the Minor Counties was refused because of their failure to obtain qualifying fixtures, so they gave notice of entering the competition in 1948.

Despite the wet summer, over 2,500,000 spectators watched county cricket, the home matches against Derbyshire and India producing over £3,000. A new ground record attendance of 15,363 was established on the second day of the game with Derbyshire.

The total income for the first year of post-war cricket was £14,349 5s 4d, with members' subscriptions amounting to £4,762 7s 6d, and a satisfied treasurer was able to announce a surplus of £424 2s 0d.

Better players were becoming available but, despite an improved professional staff, which included three class new-ball bowlers in Grove, Pritchard and Hampshire-born Vic Cannings – engaged after service in the Palestine Police – Warwickshire had a poor season in 1947 in which they finished 15th in the County Championship table, after being in sixth position by mid-July.

They had then won six matches but, disastrously, failed to win another game, and ended what looked like being a season of progress with five defeats.

The annual report was critical in its review of a season it called one of extremes, with gate money and subscriptions reaching a record £19,477 16s 8d but 'playing results can only truthfully be called very disappointing'. Chairman Colin Langley went on to point out that the advent of Grove, Pritchard and Aubrey Hill, together with the discovery of Cannings, suggested that a team might develop that could place the Club high in the Championship.

The bowlers did their bit, with the new pace trio securing 249 wickets from 2,452.1 overs, the 809 bowled by Pritchard being more than any other cricketer ever bowled for Warwickshire in his first season. In theory this should have enabled Hollies to be used more selectively with greater success, but his final figures of 1,042.4–232–2,598–107 wickets at 24.28 were a disappointing follow-up to his magnificent return from the previous season when his 180 wickets came at an average cost of 15.13 and, just as significantly, from only an additional 252 overs bowled. Only in the matches against Yorkshire (home and away), Essex, Northamptonshire and Kent did he take five wickets or more in an innings, compared with nine times in 1946. The Old Hill spinner took his 1,000th first-class wicket in the match against Worcestershire, when he dismissed Kenyon on 49.

The standard of county cricket undoubtedly improved, with sides forced into makeshift selections on fewer occasions, and a fine second half of the summer produced better batting wickets, although the side produced some erratic batting performances which Cranmer publicly attributed to over-confidence. Ord's improved form brought 1,484 runs in all games, and Taylor, Hill and Cranmer also passed the 1,000 mark. So did Dollery, but his comparatively poor 1,206 aggregate at an average of 26.21 was a major reason behind the general batting fallibility. He took over the wicket-keeping duties from Goodway mid-way through the season in circumstances which were not to the latter's satisfaction, but the Report insists that the decline in Dollery's form was more due to 'his insistence on playing too risky shots which continually cost him his wicket' rather than any extra responsibilities behind the stumps. The shots were not specified. A natural games player, Dollery claimed 49 victims, despite not having worn the gloves for some 16 years, and in a topsy-turvy season for him, was selected for England in the first Test against South Africa. He was promptly dropped after scoring 9 and 17, but Hollies played in three of the five games, and took 5 for 123 from 55.2 overs at Trent Bridge.

More improbably, at Trent Bridge in what was his first home Test match, Hollies saved the match by sharing a last-wicket stand of 51 with the Kent amateur fast bowler, Jack Martin. It was Martin's only Test, and when he came in to join Hollies (being one of a select band to bat behind one of the game's natural number 11s) England were only 178 ahead with 200 minutes remaining in the game.

Warwickshire were dismissed for fewer than 200 on 17 occasions, despite good home pitches, and all too often the good work of the bowlers was dissipated.

Grove did the hat trick against Somerset at Taunton – seven for 48 – and his 93 wickets, the same total as Pritchard, showed what a fine career was disrupted by the war. Essentially a rhythm bowler with a lovely easy action, he appeared to have a run-up which was too long for the medium pace it generated but, wisely, when experiments failed with a shorter approach, he reverted to the method which served him best.

Like all opening bowlers, the Brummie and the Kiwi loved batting, and benfited by an inspired piece of tactical wizardry from Cranmer and Dollery at Brentwood. The first innings scores were tied, but with the pitch taking a progressive amount of spin, Grove and Pritchard opened the second innings to make what hay they could off the new ball before the Essex spinning cousins, Ray and Peter Smith, got to work. Cranmer's hunch paid off with an opening stand of 107, and with both bowlers passing fifty, Warwickshire went on to win the game by 34 runs, with the second-innings wickets shared by Pritchard, Grove, Hollies and Cannings.

Hill's determination earned him 1,197 runs, but official praise was qualified with the comment 'that it must be almost unique for a first-class batsman to be run out four times in six innings. He ran himself out through slow starting far too frequently'.

Cranmer, who earlier scored 111 at Dudley against Worcestershire, hit his fourth and last hundred for the County against the South African tourists in 90 minutes in a whirlwind display of hitting which delighted the large crowd, who paid £2,245 5s 10d to see the visitors win by an innings and 114 runs. A second-innings collapse was brought about by seamers Tucket and Dawson, with Cranmer and Jack Hossell, a left-hander who played for Aston Unity and Stratford, scoring 58 between them out of the side's 76.

Later in August, the start of the second day of the match against Northamptonshire was marked by a silent tribute to the former opening batsman, Arthur Croom, who had died aged 50 two days earlier. After being severely wounded in the First World War, Croom went on to score 17,662 runs for Warwickshire at an average of 31.70, and passed 1,000 in every season from 1927 to 1939, except for 1936. His son, Leslie, was to be engaged for the 1949 season, but failed to make the step from Birmingham League cricket with West Bromwich Dartmouth.

Names which were to play a significant part in the fortunes of Warwickshire in the next decade began to appear. Coventry-born Fred Gardner, still a Bevin boy, followed up his spectacular 2nd XI performances the previous year – 432 runs from three completed innings – with six innings for the 1st XI which brought him 129 runs, including his first half-century on his debut against Gloucestershire at Edgbaston. Among the 'also batted' was A. V. 'Bert' Wolton who, at the age of 28, was another cricketer whose entry into the first-class game was delayed by the war. His two innings yielded two runs, and gave little indication of the ability with which he was to charm and delight Edgbaston supporters for the next 13 years.

Amateur Thompson played eight delightful innings which put him clear at the head of the averages with 378 runs at an average of 47.25, and Oxford blue Ron Maudsley made useful all-round contributions for the second successive year. The number of club players pressed into emergency service declined, with one of the 1946 stalwarts, Jack Marshall from Leamington, playing in only two games, and Lin Clugston – whose three appearances the previous year came 18 years after his previous three first-team games – none at all.

So, the first two crucial post-war seasons were completed on a basis which, from necessity, was a hand-to-mouth one, and one which could only have been tolerable under a captain like Cranmer. He announced his resignation at the end of the season because of business reasons, and the annual report paid a fittingly generous tribute to one of the most ebullient personalities ever to play for the County:

> The Club owes Peter Cranmer a great debt for taking over at a difficult time in the pre-war era, and again for resuscitating Warwickshire cricket after the war, but most of all for the exhilarating *joie de vivre* which he brought to Edgbaston, and instilled into the team playing under him. His was the cricket of which the real game is made, and long will he be remembered, and vivid memories of his exciting career recalled at Edgbaston.

The tribute illustrates Cranmer's complete disregard for personal glory by referring to the match against Sussex in May 1938, when he declared with his own score on 98 and all but snatched an improbable win.

His career figures at that point of 5,151 runs from 235 completed innings at an average of 21.91, with his four hundreds divided equally between Edgbaston and Dudley, are no just reflection of his overall contribution to the cause of Warwickshire cricket.

Cranmer's own views on his time as captain are interesting. He emphasised how helpful Wyatt had been to him before the war, despite the circumstances which brought about the change at a time when he felt that many of the professional staff were too old. In 1946 and 1947, he rightly felt he was unfortunate to be able to call on only three players – Dollery, Hollies and Ord – with pre-war experience, but as always, he insists that, given his time again, he would not change anything. Cranmer's great strength was that he always let it be known that he enjoyed playing, whatever cards the fates dealt him.

When stock was taken of the year, the increased membership caused the committee to consider additional accommodation and also a restriction of the right to introduce guests. Notable among ground improvements was the new area on the north side of the ground on which new hard-practice pitches and a turf nursery had been laid. This pleased 'Tiger' Smith who, in commenting on the team's disappointing form, attributed it to the players' 'casual attitude to the game' which he said was largely due to poor practice conditions, including lack of nets, as well as the lack of serious competition for places from a professional staff which, numbering only eleven, was well under strength.

The Annual General Meeting in February 1948 revealed that six other professionals would be added to the previous year's staff, all of whom had been retained. The official introduction of the new boys said:

> Bromley, Gardner and Woodroffe are quite well known at Edgbaston; Spooner and Kendall are both wicket-keeper-batsmen from Durham and Coventry respectively, while Townsend is an all-rounder from Durham. The engagement of players has been further complicated recently, for in addition to the liabilities under the National Service Act, the Control of Engagement Order now seriously affects the position.

In addition Alec Hastilow had secured the services of the New Zealand Test batsman, Martin Donnelly, whose five hundreds the previous season earned his nomination as one on the 'Five Cricketers of the Year' in *Wisden*. Also the Indian Test all-rounder Abdul Hafeez Kardar would play some 2nd XI cricket, and the foundations of the 1951 Championship side were thus shrewdly laid.

Of even greater significance was the decision taken the previous month to appoint Dollery and Maudsley as joint captains. Although Les Berry had led Leicestershire in 1946, Dollery's appointment as the first nominated professional captain was an historic step by a committee which, increasingly in the coming years, was to make other long-sighted decisions which would benefit cricket in general, as well as the Warwickshire Club.

Hollies, who was awarded a benefit that year, warned that such a long-range division of the captaincy duties could prove embarrassing should the side be at the top of the table in mid-June when Maudsley's University Trinity term would be over. Dollery saw it differently:

> 'If the short period of my 12 matches was unsuccessful, I could return to my role as a player pure and simple, and no harm would have been done. I was to be a stop-gap with the possibility, if all went well, of succeeding Ron Maudsley when he had to give up.'

He hesitated only because: 'It seemed that I had reached the straight leading to the finish of my career, and I was not keen on suffering any interruption or disturbance. But someone had to head the side for the first 12 matches, and I was very conscious of the honour Warwickshire did me.'

Dollery swept away any doubts, either on his part or in the minds of other people, with an emphatic return to his best form. He scored 1,692 runs at 47.00, even though he managed only two hundreds, 167 against Derbyshire and 102 against Lancashire.

His first two games in charge at Trent Bridge and Old Trafford produced an eight-wicket defeat against Nottinghamshire despite a hundred in each innings from Ord, and the wrong end of a draw against Lancashire, but the new captain's splendid 167 at Derby set up the first of three successive wins which were to help take the side to third place in the table in June.

The first home match of the season brought the first-ever victory over Yorkshire at Edgbaston in first-class cricket, the 34-year-old new captain leading from the front with a fighting 95 on a tricky pitch. Taylor's dogged approach brought him 11 priceless runs in the match, and newcomer Townsend complemented Hollies, Grove and Pritchard with three for 18 with his lively fast-medium bowling in Yorkshire's second innings to wrap up a convincing win by 54 runs.

The side went from strength to strength, with Pritchard enjoying what was to be his best season by far. He took 166 wickets from 1,186.3 overs at an average of 17.93, and was well ahead in strike ratio and fitness of any other new-ball bowler in the country. His final tally also took him past the previous record number of wickets by a Warwickshire fast bowler – 152 by Howell in 1923. Like all good pace bowlers, whose speed is just below the very top bracket, Pritchard was capable of producing bursts of genuine hostility which made him, on several occasions, unplayable. He clean bowled six Essex batsmen at Edgbaston in first-innings figures of seven for 71 in a victory, in which he finished with 11 for 141. In June he took 11 for 80 against Leicestershire, including the first of his four hat-tricks for the County, and followed up with six for 59 in the match against Worcestershire. Then he registered his greatest triumph, against Northamptonshire, with 13 for 153 including eight for 43 in the first innings.

So well were things going that Maudsley offered to stand down, but his offer was rightly refused. Decisions like that should not be altered in mid-stream, although the review of a season in which the Club finally finished seventh said: 'The fluctuation in form was attributed by many competent onlookers to the division of the office of captain, and the consequent mid-season switch over. To some degree it undoubtedly was.'

Maudsley's team only won one match in July, a thumping victory by 183 runs against the subsequent Champions Glamorgan, who finished the season only 40 points ahead of Warwickshire. The key match was the return when the home side scored 104 for seven to sneak home by three wickets, with Hollies nearly denying them with seven for 55.

Disappointing though the final position was in the table, important advances were made by several players. Ord had his best season with five hundreds, and maiden hundreds came not unsurprisingly from Gardner (126 against Kent) and, more unexpectedly, from Grove, whose 104 at Leicester enabled his side to reach 443.

Spooner made the wicket-keeping position his own with a wonderfully consistent first season which brought him 60 victims and 823 runs scored in the attractive left-handed style that was to serve his adopted county so well in the coming years. Townsend and Wolton showed glimpses of their undoubted potential, with the Durham all-rounder taking 21 slip catches to show why he was soon regarded as one of the best close fielders in county cricket, but amateurs Donnelly and Thompson disappointed. The New Zealander scored 772 runs in 25 innings, but his attacking style proved fallible on pitches which were more variable than he had previously batted on at Oxford. Thompson's 78 from eight innings underlined the dangers of the practice prevalent at that time of bringing in amateurs in mid-July, irrespective of current form among the professionals whose positions they filled. Grove's support bowling brought him 60 wickets, but Cannings suffered a marked decline, with only 16 wickets from 317.1 overs, at an average cost of 46.25 each.

The Test scene was made historic by Hollies bowling out Bradman second ball for a duck in the Oval Test match. Hollies had not wanted to play in the game, because the Ashes series was lost and it meant missing two key Championship matches. Happily, the Warwickshire committee insisted that he accept the invitation, and so the spinner was able to spring the trap he had baited in the match against the tourists at Edgbaston early in August. He returned the remarkable figures in the Australian first innings of 43.5–8–107–8 and, because he was not convinced that Bradman had identified his googly, kept it hidden from him in the second innings when, although the visitors needed only 41 to win, their captain came in to have another look at Hollies.

So to the Oval and the dramatic second-ball dismissal, about which two facts can be added to those already known. Bradman *was* bowled by a googly from Hollies, but *not* from round the wicket, as a clumsy piece of film editing shows in the BBC archives. Clearly the cameraman who captured the unforgettable sight of Bradman being bowled, never bothered to film the bowler, and when this was done later Hollies had switched to round the wicket. And it is said that the camera never lies. The second fact is that Bradman was not *clean* bowled, but got an inside edge to leave himself just four runs short of securing for himself a Test career average of 100.

Anxious to maintain the spectacular progress initiated by Dollery's captaincy, it was not surprising that the committee decided against repeating their experiment of appointing joint captains in 1949. Their nomination of Dollery to the post in his own right proved the accuracy of his remarks at the beginning of the year, when he saw the initial shared responsibility as a possible stepping-stone to a long-term appointment. The ship was now his, and following several rough voyages, was now poised to enter exciting and more rewarding waters.

Hollies' benefit realised £4,896 12s 11d, easily a Club record. Of the 21 previous beneficiaries, starting with Shilton in 1895, only Charlesworth with £1,050 in 1920 had exceeded four figures. Benefits at that time were run completely differently to today's, with the emphasis completely on cricket matches and members' donations and collections, with no trading or large promotions. So £3,543 came from the receipts of Hollies' benefit match against Kent, and donations from members.

Following his success at the Oval, Hollies was invited to tour South Africa with England under George Mann, but a troublesome knee injury forced him to decline.

The annual report by the committee to the members was rightly optimistic, pointing out that four of the six sides which finished higher in the table had been beaten by Warwickshire at least once. The absence of a slow left-arm spinner was noted, but it was felt that Kardar, who would be available in 1949 after the end of the Oxford University season, 'would make a great difference to the team's potency'.

Regarding the 2nd XI, the Club deferred their application to join the Minor Counties for another twelve months, but under their new captain, Lloyd Robinson from Moseley Ashfield, who succeeded Alec Hastilow, they enjoyed an unbeaten season against other county second teams, including three victories. With a bigger staff, the Club and Ground XI played 39 matches, and suffered only one defeat.

With the added interest of the Australian tour, the Warwickshire membership was closed for the first time in the Club's 66 years of existence. The subscriptions were a record £11,041 16s 0d with gate receipts boosted to £12,273 5s 10d, thanks to a paying attendance for the game against Australia of 37,893. The final surplus was predictably modest at £274 0s 10d, with professional wages now up to £6,908 0s 8d, and a further £9,671 6s 6d going on restructure, repairs and seating. Telephone costs had soared to £65 11s 2d!

The sudden death occurred of the chairman, Colin Langley, who died in the middle of the 1948 season aged 59. He played intermittently from 1908 to 1914, in which time his lively pace bowling brought him 54 wickets at the useful average of 25.75. His best performance was against Worcestershire when at 23 in 1912 he took eight for 29 off 16 overs. After the First World War, in which he was injured, he joined the committee, and assumed the offices of chairman and honorary secretary in 1942. His library of books, numbering over 400, were happily bequieathed to the Club to form the nucleus of the present library. Alec Hastilow was appointed to succeed him in both offices in August, and so commenced another distinguished chapter in the chairmanship of Warwickshire.

Several changes in the playing staff for 1949 were announced. The Club did not retain the services of Fantham, Hill, Mitchell, Watkins and Woodroffe, and Bromley was away on National Service. Donnelly would also be unavailable because of anticipated touring duties with New Zealand. Croom and Roberts would join the Club, while the promising 16-year-old pace bowler from Leamington, Roley Thompson, would be available as an amateur, because of misgivings his parents had about one so young becoming a professional.

Dollery was granted a richly deserved benefit in 1949, a year which held rich promise for him and his Club. The tributes to him in the annual report were deservedly generous. The Club president and benefactor, Dr Harold Thwaite, wrote: 'He has completely re-modelled his style to meet changed bowling fashions, and has remained a master of batting competence and elegance.'

The chairman of the England selection committee, Group Captain A. J. Holmes, went even further:

> Tom Dollery has been the backbone of Warwickshire batting, both before and since the last War. As Captain of the XI in the first half of the last season, he displayed splendid qualities, and when you see a whole side gather round the skipper, from the youngest to the oldest, when a wicket falls, there must be 'something' about that skipper. I won't attempt to name that 'something' but we all know inside just what it is. Tom has it to the full, and we admire him the more for having it.

CHAPTER FOURTEEN

DOLLERY'S PATH TO THE SUMMIT

SO OFTEN, OPTIMISM IN SPORT is misplaced. There are so many variable factors, particularly in cricket where the normal human frailities which produce inexplicable vagaries of form can be compounded by equally human umpiring errors, as well as interventions of the weather gods.

But the accession of Dollery to the full-time captaincy defied all the elements so successfully that the Club had its best all-round season, both on and off the field, for many years.

The final placing of fourth in the Championship table was the club's best achievement since 1934. They finished just 24 points behind the joint Champions, Yorkshire and Middlesex, and a frustrating four points adrift of neighbours Worcestershire, whose third place was their highest since 1907, and only the eighth time they had finished in the top half of the table in 40 attempts. An interesting comparison shows that while Warwickshire had managed 17 top-half finishes in 45 attempts, 11 of those coming before the first World War, Yorkshire's lowest finish in 50 years was eighth out of nine in 1891, and eighth again in 1910 when 16 counties contested the Championship.

Dollery fashioned 12 wins, with eight draws and five defeats in the programme of 26 matches, the match against Glamorgan at Swansea being abandoned because of rain. He scored 2,084 from 44 completed innings, including six hundreds – the first time he had achieved 2,000 runs or six centuries. More important, like Cranmer before him, his batting was always selfless, with his runs invariably scored in the manner best suited to the needs of his side. *Wisden* said: 'He never lacked courage, and his tact and genial disposition made harmony complete. Though still young in a cricket sense, he was the "father" of the side.'

The Club's annual report was similarly generous: 'He was the country's outstanding captain, and at all times led the side with quiet dignity, marked technical skill and splendid personality. The side was everywhere described as one of the happiest in England and certainly one of the most attractive to watch.'

Of his six hundreds, including his first double at Gloucester, three were crowned by wins – against Derbyshire, Gloucestershire and Leicestershire. His side's narrow failure at Maidstone on a wearing pitch to turn his 95 and 118 to maximum advantage was especially disappointing. His hitting at Bournemouth, when 50 of his 121 came in 11 minutes as part of one glorious crowded hour in which he, Ord and Pritchard added 161 was, according to Hollies, the fiercest he had ever seen. Just three weeks later, the 200 which set up the win at Gloucester came in just 205 minutes, and his second innings 73 in 65 minutes came out of 157 for nine.

Dollery was at his most masterly in the low-scoring match at Edgbaston against Derbyshire, when his 100 out of the 172 enabled his side to squeeze home by one wicket in a tense game, in which 39 wickets fell for 757 runs.

His golden year included a new record benefit of £6,362 17s 0d, and his selection to the committee marked the beginning of a period of seven years in which, arguably, he exerted a greater influence on Club affairs than any of his 13 predecessors.

Hollies was once again, at his very best with 144 wickets from 1,399.1 overs at 19.84 each, despite playing in all four Test matches against New Zealand. He took five wickets or more in an innings nine times in the Championship, with six of these performances clinching victories against Worcestershire, Derbyshire, Gloucestershire, Northamptonshire, Hampshire and Surrey.

Pritchard's 1,043 overs – 143 fewer than the previous season – brought him 113 wickets at 24.72 apiece including the second hat-trick of his career, at Maidstone against Kent. The understandable relative decline in his strike rate compared with 1948 – his seven for 63 in the home defeat by Surrey, together with seven for 96 in the drawn game at Old Trafford, were the only times he managed five wickets or more in the Championship – was offset by the dependable Grove's 95 wickets at 23.61 each, and encouraging progress shown by Townsend and Kardar.

The 28-year-old Townsend complemented his attractive 1,056 runs with 44 wickets at 23.90 from 435 lively overs, with his most telling performance one of five for 37 in a Gloucestershire total of 347 at Edgbaston, in Warwickshire's first win of the season. He set a new club record with 33 catches, which prompted the prophetic official club comment that : 'He should be an England all-rounder of the future if he allows this form to be the basis of his subsequent improvement.' The remainder of his 13-season career was to be marked by flashes of brilliance with bat and ball which were frustratingly in contrast to his superb consistency as a slip fielder, where he took 409 catches.

Kardar fulfilled the high hopes held of him with nearly 'half a double' in half a season. He scored 471 runs from 18 completed innings and his attacking slow left-arm spin bowling brought him 48 wickets at 23.91 each. He had his own ideas about field placings, a particularly eccentric tactic being to do away with a mid-on. He was a magnificent fielder, particularly to his own bowling, and he believed that by

Tom Pritchard bowling Laurie Fishlock of Surrey. Note the short follow-through, indicative of the whirlwind arm action from the New Zealander generated by his pace and hostility.

leaving such a large on-side gap, he could engineer the occasional run-out. A somewhat breathless Hollies quickly disabused him of the brainwave, after he was forced to leave his usually safe dug-out at mid-off to chase a succession of on-drives.

Spooner claimed 60 victims to add to 587 attractive runs and, like his great friend Townsend, reflected credit on the sound judges, both at Edgbaston and the north-east, who had faith both men would adapt quickly to regular county cricket, despite their late entry because of the war.

Among the batsmen Gardner made the most pleasing progress, ending a fine season with 1,657 runs at 34.52, including two hundreds. Ord's model consistency brought 1,308 runs, and Thompson scored

609 from ten completed innings, helped by 97 and an unbeaten 102 against the Combined Services.

Jamaican-born Derief Taylor, who was soon to devote his great love of cricket to coaching, proved his point as nightwatchman in the home match against Leicestershire in which he kept the fire stoked so well he scored a rare hundred. At lunchtime he disappeared from sight, and when a somewhat worried Dollery walked out after the interval with Taylor, who had reappeared just as the bell went, the captain offered a word of caution about taking risky singles when Taylor got into the 90s. A muttered reply revealed the reason behind the lunch-time disappearing act, with aromatic evidence that Taylor had taken a little medicinal dose of a liquid which had its origins in his native Jamaica.

His fielding was always done at his own pace, with the highlight at the St Helens ground at Swansea. A packed crowd had spilled over the ropes, when a towering catch was hit wide of Taylor on the boundary edge. He ran among the encroaching crowd, finally tripped over and disappeared among a group of Welshmen. To the amusement of everyone, a dark arm slowly emerged from the bottom of the scrum, triumphantly to claim the catch.

Total revenue for the season was £29,381 19s 1d – an increase of nearly £4,000 – with 152,000 spectators paying to see home matches, plus 35,000 more for the match against New Zealand. These figures were exclusive of the record membership, and the Club was quick to point out that as Warwickshire was fifth in the attendance list of the 17 counties, Edgbaston supporters could justifiably look forward to the day when Test cricket would return to the ground.

The Report explained the loss of £1,113 thus: 'Maintenance of a big playing staff, plus the exceptional development of the ground which is taking place, has more than absorbed the whole of the Club's revenue, and also eaten deeply into the reconstruction fund. The time is now imminent when this fund will need additional support, if it is to finance adequately the plans your committee has in mind.'

Dr Thwaite said that the 25,000 tons of bomb-site rubble dumped on the ground earlier in the year was the first instalment towards providing additional seating for between 15,000 and 20,000 people, without which the Club could not expect to be allocated a Test match. The *Birmingham Post* congratulated the Club on concentrating its efforts on extending the facilities for the general supporters, rather than for 'even so important a section as the members'. Captain Cowan then understandably felt it necessary to forestall any criticism from the members by assuring them that their turn was next.

The reference to the larger playing staff was interesting, a new pay structure having been implemented for that year. Players who had appeared in representative cricket received between £500 and £600; capped players got between £400 and £500, with uncapped players an unspecified lower amount. An even more interesting decision, particularly when compared with modern trends, was the decision not to undertake to find employment or accommodation for players as a preliminary to an engagement.

As in the previous one, the year was sadly marked with the death of one of the great pillars of Warwickshire cricket history. On 1 September 1949 Mr Rowland Vint Ryder died at his Birmingham home aged 76. Despite an association with the Club which began in 1895 after his first application had been rejected the year before, when he died there was nothing on the ground which carried his name in memoriam. Happily that omission was remedied 40 years later when the West Wing Stand was renamed the 'Ryder Stand'.

Dr Thwaite paid tribute to Ryder in the *Birmingham Post*, in which he outlined the many qualitites of the Yorkshireman who ran the Club in his inimitable way for nearly half a century. Of his loyalty, he said:

> Several times he had tempting offers to take attractive and lucrative appointments outside the game – on one notable occasion through the good offices of Dr W. G. Grace – but he remained steadfast and loyal to the game and his County. Tall, dignified and almost austere in appearance, he nevertheless was possessed of great charm and manner and a delightfully dry sense of humour, which only those very close to him were privileged to observe and appreciate.
>
> He served the Club through the difficult adolescent period when Warwickshire was lifted to first-class status; he organised single-handed the first Test match allocated to Edgbaston in 1902; he had raised a Championship Eleven by 1911; and finally he has left Warwickshire cricketers and legislators of today a heritage of which they are justly proud and upon which they are building up the Club in the way he would have wished.

At the time of his death, Warwickshire were thus poised to enter the second half of the 20th century with higher hopes than at any time since the first Championship title win in 1911.

A much changed staff reported for duty in April 1950. Gone were Taylor, Croom, Flint, Kendall and Brindle, in addition to which Cannings was granted his release to join his native Hampshire. He fell away so markedly after a fine first season in 1947, when he took 63 wickets, that the following two seasons yielded only 25 wickets at an average of 41 from 481 overs.

There were six new youngsters, including Bromley whose National Service ended in May, Roley Thompson and the New Zealander,

Ray Hitchcock, who was so determined to break into county cricket that he volunteered to work his passage on the voyage to England. Together with Bromley, summer engagements were also offered to two other demobilised RAF National Servicemen, slow left-arm spinner Ray Weeks from Camborne in Cornwall, and Jack Bannister, a pace bowler from Wolverhampton who had been under the watchful eye of 'Tiger' Smith during his previous three seasons in the Birmingham League with Mitchells and Butlers.

Other names who were to feature prominently for the Club in later years included David Heath and Ray Carter, with Kings Heath keeper Esmond Lewis ready to enhance the reputation he had established with a record nine victims in his first-class debut the previous year.

The wet summer saw Warwickshire enjoy a brilliant start to the season, with the fixture list now extended to 28 Championship matches. Their first three matches were away, and thanks to match returns of nine for 158 and eleven for 91 by Hollies, convincing wins were registered against Hampshire and Middlesex.

Another two victories against Essex and Sussex produced 15 more wickets for Hollies, and successive wins away against Leicestershire and Worcestershire took the Club to the top of the table by the third week in June.

The eventual joint Champions, Lancashire and Surrey, were held at bay, thanks to wins in the middle of July against Middlesex and Somerset, but the only other victory from the last 12 matches was, improbably, against the all-conquering West Indies side in one of the most thrilling games ever seen at Edgbaston.

There were home defeats by Worcestershire, Somerset, Derbyshire – for whom the old firm of Jackson and Gladwin finished with combined match figures of 18 for 187 – and Nottinghamshire, with five of the other seven games drawn, and two abandoned. It is a measure of the optimism engendered by the previous season that the same final position of fourth was considered disappointing; so much so that the annual report said:

> If your committee had reported in the years between the wars on a season in which the County side had finished fourth in the Championship, and the subscription and gate receipts both constituted new Club records despite a generally wet summer, it would have been regarded as highly successful. In 1950 this was the case, but on all sides it was treated as a disappointing result, and not even the fact that the three years 1948, 1949, and 1950 constituted the most successful and progressive period in the Club's history from every standpoint, mitigated the fact.

Then followed the definitive statement of ambition:

> The yard-stick of success seems to fluctuate with prevailing conditions and circumstances, and the distance which Warwickshire cricket has travelled in the post-war era demands a different standard of measurement.

The victory over the West Indies was the only match lost by the tourists to county opposition, and a paying attendance of 45,442 watched an enthralling seesaw game in which the home side was left a modest-looking 95 to win on a pitch which was tricky, but by no means difficult.

Warwickshire got into this good position thanks to some magnificent bowling by Grove on the first day, when he returned career-best figures of 26.4–9–38–8 to earn from Frank Worrell the praise that it was the best piece of seam bowling the West Indies had seen on tour. After Wolton, with 89, and an unbeaten 66 from Spooner gave Warwickshire a lead of 128, Hollies got to work with six for 57 to help bowl out the tourists for 222, and the stage was set for a grandstand finish.

The second day had been watched by an estimated 25,000 people (a paying attendance of 19,174) and around 15,000 watched the final drama unfold. Stollmeyer instructed his fast bowlers, Prior Jones and Lance Pierre, to bowl leg theory to a field of seven fielders on the leg-side and only two on the off-side. With most of the bowling directed well outside leg stump to an inner and outer ring of fielders, run scoring was so risky that only a batsman who could pull and hook well, like New Zealander Don Taylor, could make any impression. He stood firm while his colleagues perished, but even his unbeaten 36 owed much to a 'sitter' of a dropped catch on the long leg boundary by Roy Marshall.

Pritchard went in with a handful of runs needed, under strict dressing-room instructions not to move his bat or feet against the leg-side bowling. But the fast bowler reverted to nature and backed away with a wavering bat which edged the winning runs between his body

Top left: Frank Worrell batting with Jeff Stollmeyer in Warwickshire's historic win over the West Indies. Tom Dollery and Fred Gardner in the slips are the only Englishmen in the picture, with New Zealander Don Taylor at forward short leg, and in the gully is Hafeez Kardar, who first played for India before captaining Pakistan.

Bottom left: A rare picture of the famous 'three Ws' in action together, with Clyde Walcott behind the stumps and Everton Weekes and Frank Worrell in the slips at Edgbaston in 1950. Charlie Grove, who took 8 for 38 to set up the win, is the batsman. Weekes did not play in the game but came on as a substitute.

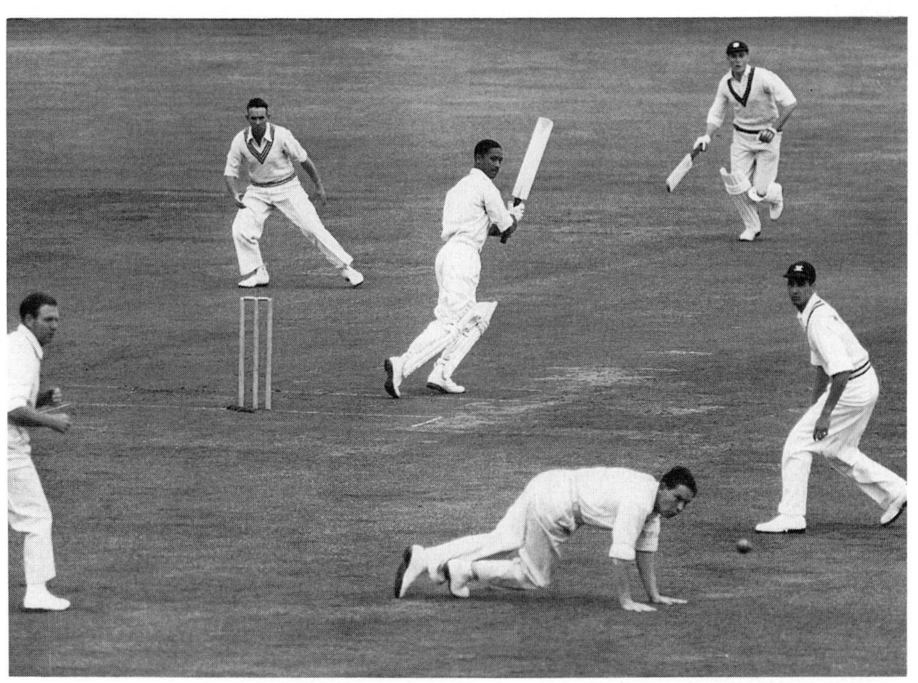

and the leg stump and, more important, past the despairing dive of the wicket-keeper.

The win was only the fourth by Warwickshire against touring sides in 35 matches, the other three successes being against South Africa in 1901, All-India in 1911 and the West Indies in 1928.

Giving Pritchard batting orders had proved unsuccessful on several previous occasions, notably at Swansea when he was sent in to play for a draw and waste time in an unobtrusive way. He promptly hit the Glamorgan spinners into the sea twice and defended his action by saying 'it just seemed the best way of wasting time'.

Most of the County players had good seasons, with Hollies (126 wickets), Pritchard (104) and Grove (97) sharing the work together with Kardar, whose first full season – and his last with the Club – brought 60 wickets as well as 849 runs.

Gardner continued to progress with 1,911 runs at 45.50, with four hundreds including his first double (215 not out at Taunton) and, for the first time in his career, two hundreds in the same match, against Essex at Ilford. He also carried his bat for 73 against Glamorgan at Swansea, the second time he had achieved this rare feat.

Dollery had another magnificent season, which earned him the last of his four England appearances at Old Trafford, and but for a disappointing August he must surely have gone to Australia under Freddie Brown, together with Hollies. The spinner played in two tests and both senior cricketers were honoured by selection for the Players against the Gentlemen at Lord's. Dollery marked his captaincy with a lovely 123 to add to the four other three-figure scores which were among the best of the 49 he went on to score by the end of his career. Going in at Derby with the scoreboard showing one run for three wickets, he hit 163, and a month later at Edgbaston his 100 in 100 minutes all but brought a win against Kent after his side had been set a target of 282 in 170 minutes. Other treats for Edgbaston fans were the 185 out of 341 he scored in Ord's benefit match against Middlesex, and 150 out of 261 against Somerset, which still could not stave off a ten-wicket thrashing.

Spooner passed 1,000 for the first time, and although he did not score a hundred his final aggregate of 1,328 runs came at an average of 30.88. Wolton and Townsend disappointed, as did the diminutive Ord, whose service to the Club was rewarded with a benefit return of £4,833 18s 4d.

In the 2nd XI, Heath and Hitchcock were the best of the batsmen, with Thompson and Bannister both taking over 40 wickets, which earned the latter selection for the Minor Counties XI in their three-day game against the West Indies at Norwich.

Revenue rose by nearly £6,000, but with reconstruction and new ground development projects going full steam ahead, the loss for the year was £4,267 16s 4d.

The Club lost three former captains with the deaths of T. S. Fishwick, A. C. S. Glover and G. W. Stephens, who between them led Warwickshire for five seasons between 1902 and 1919. Other deaths included F. R. Santall at the early age of 47, senior committee member Sir Leonard Parsons and Mr A. C. Baker, who had served on the committee for the previous two years.

So ended a 'disappointing' year for Warwickshire, with fourth place in the Championship not considered good enough.

CHAPTER FIFTEEN

CHAMPIONS FORTY YEARS ON

WARWICKSHIRE STARTED THE SEASON which was to be their most triumphant for 40 years, with criticism mounting about the policy of importing 'foreign' players. Kardar had gone, but the presence on the staff of two New Zealanders and a West Indian, with Tasmanian Keith Dollery commencing a two-year qualifying period, not unsurprisingly resulted in Warwickshire being given a 'League of Nations' tag in some quarters.

Dr Thwaite had made the Club's position clear at the 1950 annual general meeting, claiming that the introduction of cricketers from outside the county boundaries was stimulating interest locally and 'breeding a spirit of emulation in Warwickshire youth in town and village'.

English cricket's attitude towards overseas cricketers playing in county cricket was to change dramatically in the next three decades. One specially registered player per county was acceptable in 1968, but this increased to an unacceptable total of over 70 among the 17 clubs five years later. Because of the insular policies of some counties, allied to British law, it was a further 20 years before the 1968 ration was in force again.

Following two successive fourth-placed finishes, optimism at Edgbaston was high, and this time Dollery and his players made no mistake. The balance of the side was the best of any Warwickshire team in living memory. The final piece of the jigsaw so carefully compiled by the Club in the six post-war years fell into place with the advent of Ray Weeks, whose debut the previous year was marked with five wickets for 42 against Cambridge University. The slow-speaking 21-year-old Cornishman provided Hollies with the ideal spin support that had been missed so badly in previous years. He completed a magnificent first full season with 94 wickets at 21.75 each from 1,002.2 overs.

It was the most promising debut by a young bowler in the Club's history, and nobody could have forecast that, so dramatic was to be the inexplicable decline in his form, the next seven seasons would produce the woeful figures of 1,833–701–3,959–134. However, nothing must detract from the part he played in bringing the County Championship title back to Edgbaston after a break of 40 years. Coincidentally, the opposition against whom the title was clinched was the same – Northamptonshire.

With Hollies spearheading affairs yet again to obtain 145 wickets at 17.69 each and Grove, for once, outbowling Pritchard to secure the 100 wickets he had so narrowly missed in each of the two previous seasons, Dollery had an attack of four men who complemented each other superbly. Townsend's 22 wickets, which cost only 23.59 each, were the most expensive of the front-line attack. It proved once more the old adage that 'bowlers win matches', with six of the 16 wins coming inside two days. The final margin of 30 points over second-placed Yorkshire, and 80 over Lancashire in third, was the most conclusive since the points scoring system was changed yet again, to award 12 points for a win.

The batting, so inconsistent in previous years, invariably did just enough. Nobody approached 2,000 but of the six batsmen who averaged over 30, Spooner was the star with 1,767 at an average of 43.09. It was a remarkable performance from the wicket-keeper, who also claimed 73 victims, to sustain the tremendous twin concentration needed to open the innings and keep wicket throughout the season. Many times he was back in the field shortly after playing a long innings or, conversely, back at the crease only minutes after completing a tiring spell behind the stumps.

Spooner's maiden hundred, against Worcestershire on 26 May, was the first to be recorded on the new memorial scoreboard, donated the previous August by Dr Thwaite in memory of his late wife.

Dollery's 1,491 runs at 41.41 always, as usual, had a big influence on the outcome of many games, and with Gardner getting 1,388 and a revived Ord 1,311, Wolton's welcome advance with 1,011 at 30.60 ensured that the bowlers would mostly have a worthwhile total to work with. Invaluable support runs came from a slightly disappointing Taylor, who had spent two years qualifying, and Hitchcock who made a big impact when he replaced his compatriot. Also of occasional significance were the 1,192 tail-end runs from bowlers Pritchard, Grove and Weeks.

Pritchard was inconsistent, with only 38 wickets at 31.55 coming from the first 13 games, before he caught fire so sucessfully that in the next four, against Gloucestershire, Somerset, Worcestershire and Glamorgan, he was largely responsible for three victories with 36 wickets at 10.88 each, including match figures against Glamorgan at Edgbaston of 14 for 93. Injury then kept him out of all of the August matches except two, but the promising 18-year-old Thompson deputised admirably, particularly in the crucial away match against Northamptonshire, when he took three for 11.

The fielding was superb, with Townsend breaking his own Club record with 41 catches, and everyone playing a supportive part behind their deadly attack. Only 13 players were used, thanks to the national

A typical example of Dick Spooner's positive wicket-keeping, as he catches Ken Smales of Nottinghamshire off the bowling of the Warwickshire beneficiary, Charlie Grove. Alan Townsend watches Tom Dollery in close support.

selectors who chose to ignore the cricketers of the best team in the land.

Dollery deserved the accolade paid him in the Club Report:

> The team was deservedly popular wherever it played, for their cricket possessed a lively and vital quality that appealed to all. While bowling was the actual keystone of success, it was backed by admirable fielding and batting that was equal to the demands of most occasions, and free and attractive whenever reasonably possible.
>
> It was success in the best traditions of the game for a team playing perfectly together as a co-ordinated entity, under the man who has proved himself the greatest professional captain the game has known, and one of the greatest natural cricket leaders of all time – H. E. Dollery. He led this side, which he himself described as 'an extraordinary team of ordinary cricketers playing purposeful cricket' and when necessary he inspired them with the brilliance of his own personal achievement – magnificent slip catches, great fighting hundreds against the near rivals Lancashire and Yorkshire, and superlative cricket judgement. Such was the man – and such his cricket genius.

The season began pleasantly with a match on 30 April between a Warwickshire XI and an Old England XI which was organised by Councillor Edgar Hiley of Solihull, then appeals organiser for the

Birmingham and Warwickshire branches of the National Playing Fields Association. Hiley's name was soon to feature prominently in the history of the Club.

Many great names from the past turned out, including Wyatt and Canon Jack Parsons, Donald Knight, Alf Gover, Laurie Fishlock and 'Gubby' Allen, with Knight delighting everyone with 112 out of a total of 206 – and that within a fortnight of his 57th birthday.

The game was a perfect curtain-raiser for the season, which began in ideal fashion with an eight-wicket home win over Sussex.

After two draws against Glamorgan and Derbyshire – the latter a thrilling game with Hollies coming in at 157 for nine, the team needing 174 to win, and playing out the last over – the side travelled to Huddersfield to begin a unique double over Yorkshire. On a rain-affected pitch, all 40 wickets fell for 440 runs, with the winning margin no less than 86 runs. Needing 136 to win, the home side were bundled out for their lowest score of the season – 49, with Hollies and Grove doing the damage. Hollies rated his analysis of 20.5–12–12–5 as the best performance of his career, and with Grove only marginally less destructive and frugal with figures of 18–8–25–4, it was small wonder that their bowling wrung a tormented *cri de coeur* from a Yorkshire member who was unused to such rough treatment: 'For God's sake Tom, take one of 'em off'.

Back to Edgbaston and a last-gasp win against Worcestershire, with an inspired piece of 'diddling' bowling from Hollies, taking the last six wickets for 24, the final wicket coming with five minutes of extra time remaining.

Then came the sort of improbable win which Champions need to pull off. Needing 343 to win at Lord's, a major innings was needed from a side which had already collapsed once for 185, with only Spooner's 96 preventing a debacle. The wicket-keeper completed a marvellous match, in which he was on the field for all but an hour, with 158 to steer his side home by three wickets.

That was the win that convinced Dollery's side that it was going to be their year, and the match had an amusing postscript for Weeks. With time running out after tea on the third day, Dollery sent the later batsmen to wait their turn by the pavilion gate. Due to bat at number 10, a relieved Weeks ran back through the Long Room as soon as the winning hit was made, and was quite puzzled to receive a standing ovation from the cognoscenti among the members, who clearly did not know one Warwickshire player from another.

A break from the Championship took a much-changed side to Fenner's, where they admired innings of 156 and 42 from Peter May in a high-scoring draw.

A draw at home against Essex was followed by another win 'out of

Warwickshire v Worcestershire. Dollery and Ord dance with glee, Spooner chortles and Townsend embraces Gardner, who has just thrown the ball in the air with delight after taking the catch to dismiss Yarnold off Hollies. Warwickshire had won with two minutes to spare.

the blue' so to speak, with Nottinghamshire apparently cruising to victory, having scored 100 in under an hour and chasing 243 to win in 190 minutes. It was Grove's benefit match, and provided a double fairytale twist – for him with receipts of £1,353 1s 3d helping towards a final rewarding figure of £4,469 2s 6d – and for the team when a brilliant piece of fielding from the midwicket boundary by Hitchcock ran out Stocks, after which Hollies again wove his spell to take five for 60 and earn a win by 83 runs.

Warwickshire's only defeat before the Championship was won came next at Old Trafford, but Warwickshire then shook off their northern rivals with a staggering run of ten wins in their next 12 games, in which Gloucestershire and Somerset were beaten twice, with doubles completed against Nottinghamshire, Middlesex and Yorkshire, and other wins against Leicestershire, Glamorgan and Kent.

It was a terrific run, with the first win at Trent Bridge marked by an overdue maiden hundred from Townsend and a career-best seven for 70 by Weeks. Pritchard started his remarkable return to form in the next match at Coventry against Gloucestershire with five for 42 to set up a comfortable win by eight wickets, before Grove's match figures of eleven for 74, ably backed up by seven for 63 from Hollies, bundled Leicestershire to a six-wicket defeat in another low-scoring game at Edgbaston which produced just 609 runs.

A fluctuating home game at Coventry against Gloucestershire, in which Wolton scored a career-best 157, saw Hitchcock pull the Warwickshire chestnuts out of the fire when, with 179 needed for victory, the home side slumped to 26 for four and 80 for five. The left-hander came in to play the first of several crucial innings and smashed a match-winning fifty in just 38 minutes, receiving good late support from Pritchard (20 not out) and steering his side home by three wickets.

Each side of a draw at New Road with Worcestershire Dollery's bowlers brought off home wins by an innings against Somerset and Glamorgan, and the title was beckoning. Pritchard was at his most lethal with five for 26, plunging Somerset to 13 for seven – they 'recovered' to 50 all out to lose by an innings and 115. Pritchard followed this with eight for 55, including his third hat-trick, against Glamorgan to nail down another crushing win by an innings and 68.

The following match at Maidstone followed a similar pattern, with the home side managing to avoid an innings defeat – just, with Warwickshire winning by the next best margin, ten wickets, although determined second-innings resistance from Arthur Fagg and Brian Edrich meant that the winning runs came with only minutes to spare.

Middlesex were the next to be slaughtered – again by ten wickets, although they were without Compton, Edrich and Robertson who were playing for the Players. Occasional pieces of good fortune like that always seem to go to sides who are already playing well, and the players' belief in themselves and their captain grew.

Surprisingly, the crowds would not come, but following comment in the *Birmingham Post* and also from Leslie Deakins, the Birmingham public excelled itself in the vital home game against Lancashire. An estimated 28,000 watched the first day – a ground record that will never be broken, with the maximum attendance nowadays around 10,000 less – and although the crowds on Monday and Tuesday were understandably smaller, they saw a thrilling rearguard action which succeeded in denying victory to the visitors, thanks to an unbeaten 108 from Dollery, following a Washbrook double hundred.

The next match, at Wells, brought another two-day win by an innings and 122, with Weeks supporting Hollies on a slow turning pitch with a marathon second-innings spell which gave him match figures of six for 62 off 59 overs. The game ended in unusual fashion, the extra half-hour being claimed with five Somerset second-innings wickets remaining. Hollies took two wickets with successive deliveries, but with play seemingly certain to go into the last day, the extra cost of paying gatemen and other staff was miraculously avoided when the Somerset number 11 conveniently hit his own wicket. He was apparently mindful of the shoe-string budget on which his club ran their affairs.

Another huge crowd turned up at the next home match against Yorkshire, the fixture planners and England selectors again helping out Warwickshire, with Hutton, Lowson, Watson and Brennan on Test duty. On a pitch which became worn during the Warwickshire first innings, when Dollery scored a superb 111, Hollies was always too much for the weakened Yorkshire batting, and a match analysis of nine for 110 brought the first-ever double over the visitors, and the first to be achieved against them since Gloucestershire beat them twice in 1947.

Including members, an estimated 55,000 watched the game which put their side in a position at the head of the table which was all but unassailable – happily so, with the next three games being drawn. A high-scoring draw at Leicestershire, in which Thompson underlined his potential with an impressive six for 63, was followed by two rain-interrupted games at Derby and Wellingborough, but a return to the home soil of Coventry was to prove decisive.

With Gardner delighting his home-town supporters with 139, Warwickshire reached their highest score of the season – 456 for five declared – with Ord (74), Hitchcock (60), Spooner (57), Townsend (46 not out) and Dollery (42) all making solid contributions. The second day was the last one, with Northamptonshire tumbled out twice for 117 and 170. Hollies six for 98 in the match, Grove, five for 22 in the second innings, and Thompson, three for 11 in the first, were the most successful bowlers.

Mathematically, the title was not yet won, unless Yorkshire failed to beat Warwickshire's neighbours Worcestershire at Scarborough. With everyone at Edgbaston on tenterhooks on the third day, Yorkshire were apparently cruising home on 232 for five, needing 250, and 30 minutes to get them. But Dick Howorth mopped up the tail and at 3.50pm Warwickshire were officially Champions for the first time since 1911.

The flag was flown at Edgbaston, and the obligatory champagne corks were popping by 4pm. Hundreds of supporters gathered at the ground, and reporters and photographers came for the quotes and photographs.

Dr Thwaite said: 'I am gratified and overwhelmed with feelings of satisfaction and delight. Tom Dollery has established a new epoch in cricket, the brilliant success of a professional captain.' Dollery contented himself with a tribute to teamwork, with Leslie Deakins confessing that 'this is the day I have been waiting for for 25 years'.

Strangely enough, the last player to find out the news was Hollies, who vainly tried to make contact by telephone with the offices of the Club and the local newspapers. He even went to a newspaper office near his home, but the staff refused to disobey their instruction which forbade them to pass on any news to the public. Only when a frustrated Hollies returned home did a call from Edgbaston bring him the news he wanted to hear.

Wisden later joined in the praise of the Warwickshire team and their captain:

> Warwickshire's triumph emphasised the importance of skilled leadership, for in Tom Dollery they possessed a man able to get the best out of his side on and off the field. Dollery, a professional, led an all-professional eleven, and while 20th-century conditions rob the game of the real amateur, Dollery showed that a paid player can become a captain in the real sense of the word. By his astute work, Dollery has raised the status of the professional just as Hobbs did in the days when every county had one dressing-room for the paid, and another for the unpaid.
>
> Much credit for Warwickshire's achievement must also be given to the committee and secretary, L. T. Deakins, for shrewd team building.

Celebratory functions came thick and fast, the main one being the official Championship dinner given by Lord Iliffe and the directors of the Birmingham Post and Mail Ltd at the Grand Hotel in Birmingham on 25 October. Various players were absent, including Spooner, who was touring India with England, Ord and Hitchcock, on coaching duty in South Africa, and Thompson, in the RAF. W. G. Quaife enjoyed the second Championship win, but died ten days before the dinner.

The guest list was a distinguished one, including the Lord Mayor, Alderman R. C. Yates, the Lord Lieutenant of the county, Lord Willoughby de Broke, the England captain, F. R. Brown, and Neville Cardus, who listened to the reading of a telegram from Sir Pelham Warner saying: 'Tom Dollery has created a band of brothers and everyone will acclaim him.'

Finally Dollery spoke and, like his leadership, his speech was a model of incisive appraisal of the team he had moulded so brilliantly:

> I am proud not only of the fact that we won the Championship, but of the way we won it. We did not resort to any tactics other than those which were in the true spirit of the game. You will see many

The County Championship winning team to Edgbaston.
Standing: Don Taylor, Jack Bannister, Ray Weeks, Tom Pritchard, Roley Thompson, Alan Townsend, Ray Hitchcock.
Seated: Fred Gardner, Charles Grove, Eric Hollies, Tom Dollery (capt.), Jimmy Ord, Dick Spooner, Bert Wolton.
Only thirteen players were used before the title was won, with Bannister playing at the end of the season, when Pritchard was injured.

better cricket teams, but I doubt if you will see a keener one. And I know there has never been a more loyal one, not only to the Club, but to its captain.

A nice gesture followed when Dollery presented Dr Thwaite with a silver cigarette box, suitably inscribed, from the players and administrative staff.

Other receptions included those given by the Lord Mayor of Coventry, Councillor Harry Weston, and the Mayor of Warwick, then the Earl.

Members and the general public contributed nearly £1,000 to a testimonial fund, which the Club made up to £1,350 and distributed among the players in proportion to appearances made.

Dollery never lost sight of the importance of Hollies' contribution: 'You knew he was never going to let you down. All the team seemed to pull out a bit extra when we were in trouble. But Eric – well against Yorkshire he even opened the bowling on a bad wicket. He told me "I can spin a new ball as well you know."'

The committee wisely decided to press ahead with their plans to develop the ground and hasten the day when they would stage a Test match once again.

A loss of £5,396 6s 8d was announced, despite gate receipts topping £20,000 for the first time, and the closed membership subscriptions yielding £15,453 11s 0d. Over £16,000 had been poured into repairs, renewals and extensions, and Alec Hastilow, then a vice-president of Birmingham Chamber of Commerce, announced a new appeal to industrial and commercial organisations for funds to permit further ground developments. This was to bring in over £10,000, and was another example of how well the Club has always been served by its officers.

The committee also suggested that, in the absence of any trophy for the County Championship, they should initiate a pennant, and this idea was accepted at Lord's.

Warwickshire's daily average attendance of 5,389 paying spectators was the highest in the country. So ended the most successful year in the history of the Club, although the final three games proved to be anti-climatic, with two draws and a defeat.

Bannister took the first of a tally of wickets which, in the next 19 years, was to become the third highest in the history of the Club. His first wickets were those of Jim Parks and Brian Close in the match at Edgbaston against the Combined Services, his first Championship wickets coming on his 21st birthday at Clacton against Essex. The game provided Warwickshire's second defeat of the season, and Bannister likes to tell an amusing story concerning a piece of advice given him by Grove: 'We were all out towards the end of the first day for 204, and before we went out for the last half-hour, Charlie warned me about their attacking opener, Dickie Dodds. He told me that he threw the bat at everything, but told me not to worry and get upset if I was hit about. In fact, I nipped in with three maidens to his partner, "Sonny" Avery, while Dodds hit Charlie all over the ground.' Announcing the professional staff for 1952, the Club said that Thompson and Carter had been called up for their National Service, with slow left-arm spinner Ian King, now demobilised, rejoining the staff. Possibly the most significant sentence in the annual report's section of the future staff simply said: 'T. W. Cartwright (a 16-year-old all-rounder from Coventry) has been engaged.'

CHAPTER SIXTEEN

THE END OF THE DOLLERY ERA

JUST AS HAPPENED AFTER the 1911 Championship title win, the following season was a disappointing one for Warwickshire. They dropped to 12th place, winning eight matches in a lopsided season with seven of those wins coming in July and August. The season was the first of Dollery's final four playing years at Edgbaston, with final placings in 1953, 1954 and 1955 of ninth, sixth and ninth. It marked the beginning of the rapid reduction in the effectiveness of the team, who were soon to lose three of the four main bowlers who did so much to win the Championship.

After flying so high the previous year, a crash-landing was almost inevitable. A tied game against Sussex at Hove provided the only tangible success in the first ten matches, five of which were lost due to some woefully inconsistent batting. The side topped 300 only once, in a high-scoring drawn home match against Northamptonshire, and exceeded 250 on only two other occasions. Only Gardner, and to a lesser degree Hitchcock, were immune from a loss of form which resulted in Dollery scoring 562 runs in his first 22 innings, Spooner 489 in 21 and Ord 655 in 21. Wolton and Taylor aggregated 621 runs in the entire season from 39 innings, and with the bowlers failing to reproduce their 1951 sparkle, it did not take long for the press and members to read more into the slump than simply a widespread loss of form and confidence.

Even Dollery's captaincy came under the hammer, and the next Annual Meeting was marked by a counter-attack from the president who said he 'bitterly resented the unfair criticism, veiled innuendoes, and general attitude adopted by some Club members and a section of the public in attempting to attribute the team's failure to dissension among themselves.'

Dollery admitted that half-way through the season the sharp decline in his own batting form prompted thoughts of resignation, but happily he dismissed them to such good effect that his last 29 innings produced 1,511, including a career best 212 at Edgbaston against Leicestershire, and three other hundreds: in the return game with the same county, and against Derbyshire and Yorkshire.

With hindsight, the poor season could have been anticipated. Among the bowlers, Hollies and Grove were 40 years old and Pritchard 35. For them to have maintained peaks of fitness and form for a second successive year was expecting too much, and although

Thompson and Bannister deputised with eleven wickets at 13.81 and 32 at 20.71 respectively, they were still learning their trade.

And of course, with Ord 40, Dollery 38, Wolton 33, Spooner 32, Townsend 31 and Gardner 30, the success of the previous year was a level of performance which could only be short-lived.

The committee had achieved a minor miracle in building a title-winning side, effectively in five years, but longer-term planning was now necessary.

The 1952 season began pleasantly with Mr W. Findlay, President of the MCC, opening the new Thwaite Gates two days after the tied match at Hove.

On a pitch which afforded generous assistance to seam and spin alike, each team scored 254 runs in the match, with Warwickshire's first innings 138 the highest of the four innings. That earned a lead of 15 which, after a disastrous start to their second innings of 13 for five, they extended to 131 thanks to a seventh-wicket stand of 60 between Townsend and Grove. At 82 for three, Sussex seemed certain to win, but Grove and Hollies tilted the game the other way so decisively that the last-wicket pair came together with 12 still needed.

During a tense lunch interval, Hollies slipped unnoticed into the home dressing room and, after listening to the many different tactics proposed by all and sundry, laughingly revealed his presence and said: 'Talk as much as you like – you won't win.'

The leg-spinner was promptly ejected, but within minutes proved his point by trapping the last man, Webb, lbw with the scores level to give Warwickshire eight points compared with four for Sussex, because of that small first-innings lead.

Another remarkable game but for vastly different reasons, was that at the Oval towards the end of May. The season was to see the beginning of Surrey's invincible run of seven consecutive Championships, with the Oval pitch starting to offer unusual assisitance to bowlers of all types. Nothing untoward therefore, in the home side managing a match total of only 292 runs, it still winning by 69. The Bedser twins and Tony Lock took 14 wickets for 115 between them, with Hollies, Weeks and Pritchard responding with 16 for 175, and Dollery scoring the only fifty in the match. With 20 wickets falling on the first day, and the pitch forecast to break up even more next day, both teams were astonished, before the start of play on the second day, to find that the worst holes in the surface had been repaired, and now were a different colour from the rest of the strip. Rather than pursue what would have been a major scandal, Dollery agreed to play on and, by so doing, again displayed the dignity and innate feeling for the overall interests of cricket which marked his whole career.

The gloom of a poor season which saw gate receipts drop from £20,318 to £12,438 was only relieved by the individual performances of Dollery (2,073) Gardner (1,826 runs at 37.26) and Spooner (1,325 at 29.44) in the batting department, and the efforts of Hollies and Grove, who both took 118 wickets – the best seasonal haul for the seamer. Their only real support came from Townsend, who had a superb all-round season. In addition to his 74 wickets at 17.70, he scored 940 runs and easily topped the catching list with 38.

Despite his figures at the Oval, Weeks put the first question mark against his long-term future with only 48 wickets at 29.43 from 691.4 overs, although at the time it was felt that he had suffered the slow bowler's normal reaction to a successful first season.

Encouraging signs for the future included maiden hundreds for Bromley, against Essex, and Yorkshireman Norman Horner, against Oxford University at The Parks.

Dollery's 1000 runs came on 25 July, and the 2,000 mark was passed on 30 August. Both Grove and Thompson took nine wickets in a Championship innings, the senior man for 39 runs at home against Sussex, and Thompson for 85 against Nottinghamshire, also at Edgbaston. Gardner batted throughout an innings for the third time, scoring a magnificent 184 not out from Liverpool against Lancashire at 286, and Spooner also carried his bat for 98 out of 210 at Worcester. Hollies claimed his 1,000th first-class wicket since the war – the first bowler to do so, and a remarkable performance in seven seasons. Coincidentally, his 1,000th wicket was that of his nearest rival in the race, fellow leg-spinner Doug Wright of Kent.

A total of 120 points, compared with 256 the previous year, told its own tale, and with the fickleness of the Birmingham public self-evident, the committee kept a tight rein on the ground development. Nevertheless, it was still able to announce to building of the new Stanley Barnes stand, as well as the long-term intention to erect a house on the ground for the assistant secretary because 'with the growing importance of the Edgbaston ground, it is becoming increasingly necessary to have an administrative official of the Club in permanent residence'.

An application to stage a Test match against Pakistan in 1954 was turned down, but the committee said 'It will renew the request until granted, as it is a duty owed to the great sporting public of the County.' There would not be much longer to wait. Ground admission for 1953 would be increased from 1s 6d (7½p) to 2s 0d (10p).

The benefit granted to the cheerful Pritchard realised a net £3,816 0s 6d, with the award of a second one to Hollies in 1954, meaning that the joint testimonial originally awarded to 'Tiger' Smith and scorer George Austin would be deferred.

Leslie Deakins' vision of the £250,000 needed to transform Edgbaston seemed a pipe-dream – until the advent in 1953 of a scheme which was to produce over £2,000,000 for cricket in general in the next 20 years. Over half that amount would be spent on building projects at Edgbaston, which more than fulfilled that young man's dream, conceived on those lonely war-time dog watches in Scapa Flow.

The unlikely vehicle was to be an amended form of football pools which, after careful monitoring of similar schemes run by Worcestershire and Hereford United Football Club (who in turn had copied the original idea of St Ambrose Roman Catholic Church in Kidderminster), was to be the basis of some strong recommendations from Deakins. Understandably, all sorts of reservations held back the final decision to proceed, including one from the advisory committee 'that it was an undignified method of raising funds, that the legal aspect was uncertain, and that the officials of a supporters' club would undoubtedly in time wish to influence County Club policy'.

The Warwickshire secretary would not be deterred, and having persuaded his committee to appoint a sub-committee, consisting of Cyril Goodway, the subsequent treasurer, James McDowall, and Ran Smith, to investigate the possibilities, the gravy train was under construction. A nine-point treatise from the sub-committee did not go so far as making a firm recommendation, and the committee became even more hesitant about dipping its toe directly into the waters of commercial fund-raising.

Guy Heaton and John Lones proposed and seconded the following resolution: 'That while this committee would be very thankful to receive donations legally obtained from any source, it does not see its way clear to sponsor a supporters' club at the present time.' A majority of 17 votes to three in favour might have deterred most secretaries, but not 'L.T.D.' as he was now affectionately known by players and office staff alike.

An astute lobbying exercise brought in a letter to the committee, signed by five prominent members, seeking official blessing for an association, with Ray Hitchcock, whose playing popularity was considered an advantage in selling the idea to members and the general public, as the paid organising official. The 'Five Wise Men', to whom the Club will eternally be in debt, were M. F. K. Fraser, the Club's publicity officer, Councillor Edgar Hiley, Aubrey Lewis, a prominent local business man, Councillor E. H. Richardson and Derek Salberg, of the Alexandra Theatre.

Their initiative pushed the committee into appointing another sub-committee including, most significantly of all, the chairman, Alec Hastilow, and the rest is now an integral part of Warwickshire history.

The 'Famous Five' were able to convince the Club that the role of the association would always be one of non-interference in Club affairs, and despite many changes in staff and committee since their launch date in August 1953, that admirable policy has been rigidly adhered to ever since.

The first three weeks produced £240, to be devoted to the development of the ground. By the end of the winter the turnover was £46,000 and a new Bituturf wicket had been laid for early season practice. A total of £8,170 had already become available for developments, and was in addition to the cost of erecting temporary offices on the ground, offering £5,000 towards a new Indoor Cricket School and entertaining the Pakistan and Canadian touring teams to dinner.

Early teething troubles included one brush with the law which Fraser, inimitably, described as 'an archaic and inequitable law which operates in such a way that one man may steal a horse, while another cannot look over the stable door'.

Progress was so rapid in the next few years that, with successive office accommodations proving inadequate, the new William Ansell stand was built with a triple purpose: to provide a ballroom and dining complex to generate additional income, to improve and extend the accommodation for members, and to house the staff and equipment of the association. Although in the late 1970s and the 1980s income declined, the staggering success in the previous two decades ensured the future of Warwickshire cricket, and provided Deakins with exactly the financial fillip he and his committee needed to ensure that once Edgbaston had regained its Test match status it would retain it.

Many clubs, in and outside cricket, vainly tried to copy the biggest successful post-war fund-raising scheme in sport, but there was never a magical formula to adopt. It was a case of the right person, Hitchcock, having the right ideas at the right time in the right industrial climate to launch a scheme which, like most successful concepts, was simple and yet appealing to the public.

His first assistant was Miss Winifred Crook, daughter of a Birmingham solicitor and former Birmingham League cricketer, and she was quickly joined by assistant secretary-treasurer of the Club, David Blakemore. The two married, and when Hitchcock moved on Blakemore became secretary of the association and his wife the organiser, and their diligence, conscientiousness and foresight played an increasing part in the success of the association as the gravy train rattled on.

The 1953 season was one of transition, with younger players like Horner, Bromley, Bannister, Keith Dollery and Cartwright forcing their way into the First XI, and the three senior bowlers, Hollies,

Grove and Pritchard, consequently playing a less prominent part in the attack, although Hollies was handicapped by injury.

Only six matches were won out of 28, with seven defeats and 15 draws completing a frustrating season in which first-innings advantage on 11 occasions could not be converted into victories. A final position of ninth in the table, 60 points adrift of Champions Surrey, was a fair reflection of the team's effort, with several batsmen having a successful season.

Dollery's 1,889 runs at 44.97 took him past 20,000 runs for the Club – only Quaife and Wyatt had done this before – and Gardner's 1,557 aggregate took him past 9,000 in his seventh season. Horner established himself with 1,479 runs at 34.39 and with Spooner, Wolton and Townsend also topping 1,000 – the all-rounder for the first time – the side was rarely short of runs. Hitchcock's appearances were limited by injury, the young Cartwright played 16 innings for 260 and the promising amateur David Heath played 14 innings for 265 runs.

In the final match of the season at Trent Bridge, Cartwright had batted patiently for over four hours until, just before the tea interval, he lost concentration and swept ambitiously at several deliveries. As he walked off, a pleasing gesture from Joe Hardstaff saw the former England batsman pull the youngster on one side and tick him off for taking such risks just before the interval. Cartwright's 83 promised a bright future although, at that stage, nobody could have guessed that he would mature into arguably the best medium-pacer in post-war cricket.

Bannister and Dollery took 70 and 74 wickets respectively, with the side's innings victory over Gloucestershire at Bristol yielding them 18 of the 20 wickets.

An amusing story concerns the close friends, Hollies and Grove. The veteran opening bowler had been advised that, with the younger bowlers pressing hard for experience, the committee would rest him for a game, which he could choose. Hollies advised him to miss the Bristol match, because the low, slow pitch had proved a graveyard for fast bowlers all season. With Bannister taking six for 31 in the second innings, and Dollery four for 22, including the hat-trick, to add to his six for 38 in the first, Grove was not too impressed by the advice given him, particularly as Hollies took good-natured advantage of his friend who, for the first time since the war, was made twelfth man.

Worse was to follow for Grove, for with Bannister and Dollery again among the wickets in the next match at Hinckley, he did not regain his place for five matches.

An even more remarkable match took place at the Oval than in 1952, when the nature and colour of the pitch changed so mysteriously overnight. This time, despite a delayed start on the Saturday because of rain, Surrey launched their charge for a second successive Championship title with a win over Dollery's side by an innings and 49, clinically completed in less than one day.

The dramatic events on 17 May thus provided the first instance of a match being all over in a day since 1857. Starting at noon, Warwickshire were all out for 45, with Alec Bedser's ability to bowl medium-paced leg-breaks, genuinely cut off the third finger, making him unplayable. He took eight for 18. Keith Dollery and Hollies restricted Surrey to 146, and a nasty lifter from Grove caused Lock, top scorer in the match with 27, to retire hurt. The visitors' second innings started just after 5pm, with Townsend, due to bat at number 7, optimistically running himself a hot bath. He need not have bothered. Because before the bath was full, he was in and out for the second time that day. Bedser completed devastating match figures of 12 for 35 with four for 17, and Jim Laker took five for 30.

Laker's five included the hat-trick, with left-handed Hitchcock self-mockingly claiming that, when the Surrey fielders spotted him coming into bat after Laker had taken two wickets with successive deliveries, they immediately shook hands with their off-spinner, because in their minds the hat-trick was a certainty.

Proof of the unplayable lift that the pitch provided all day was that not one Warwickshire batsman was bowled in either innings. Second time round, there were five consecutive ducks in the middle of the innings while that hot tap was filling Townsend's bath.

Hollies provided a bit of light relief when he batted at the end of the match. Having toured Australia with Bedser, he knew him well enough to ask for one off the mark to avoid the dreaded 'pair', in return for which he would give his wicket away. Not much of a deal for a Test match bowler of Bedser's class, but he obligingly gave Hollies a friendly leg-side long hop which was clumped away, only for Lock to bring off a spectacular catch at backward short leg.

Further embarrassment followed, because the side was due to be entertained in the House of Commons by a local MP on Monday evening, and permission had to be obtained from an unbelieving set of Edgbaston officials for the players to stay in London over the week-end.

A year that was to end in controversy, with a special members' meeting called to debate the dismissal of Grove, was notable for what the Annual Report described as 'the playing highlight of the whole season – the game with the Australians'.

In this match Dollery was at his tactical best. Gardner and Horner – who had earlier scored his maiden Championship hundred against his native Yorkshire – put together an opening stand of 143, with Gardner going on to score 110 to become the first Warwickshire batsman ever to score a hundred against the Australians. Dollery declared at 270 for 8 – one of the few occasions this was done against an attack including Lindwall and Miller – and with the pitch taking some gentle spin, Hollies with five for 45, and Wolton, with three for 20, bowled the tourists out for 181.

There did not seem sufficient time for Dollery to press home the advantage of the lead of 89, but the Warwickshire captain made just about the most inspired declaration of his career. During his side's brief second innings on the third day, he spotted that the pitch was starting to deteriorate and promptly, to the surprise of everyone, including his own players, closed at 76 for three. What a cheeky challenge to the pride of Australia. They were asked to score 166 in 170 minutes, but Hassett's comment to Dollery before Australia batted was revealing: 'You bastard.'

Hollies initially thought that the match had been given away, but Dollery knew his pitch and, even more important, he knew his leg-spinner. Early wickets fell to Hollies and Wolton, but Hassett had opened the innings, and he was not going to risk a morale-shattering defeat so soon before the final Test in an Ashes series which was still all square. Spotting the terrible tangle Graeme Hole and company were getting into against spin, he decided to 'take' Hollies for the rest of an astonishing innings which was to produce 53 runs from 59 overs, 31 of which were maidens.

The crowd of 22,000 – at least three times that figure paid record receipts of £8,323 1s 10d in the match – never came to grips with the tactical battle waged between the two captains and Hollies, and barracked throughout at what they saw as a negative approach from the tourists. Hollies frequently switched ends, but whenever he took the ball at one end after having apparently finished bowling at the other, there smiling at him was Hassett. Never averse to the odd bit of chat, Hollies jokingly warned the little Aussie that the noisy crowd would not stand much more before they came over the ropes.

Hassett replied: 'The first one who comes near me gets my bat around his ears.' Hollies' reply was a classic: 'It's not the first one you'll have to worry about.'

The dramatic game ended in a draw with Hassett on 21, and so strict were his instructions to his players that even Miller batted 27 minutes for 10. The match figures of Hollies show what a masterly rearguard action Hassett conducted: 55.3–31–59–7.

The financial report announced a profit of £3,061 14s 3d, achieved despite the number of paying spectators for Championship cricket dropping to under 50,000 – less than a quarter of the number who came through the gates in 1951.

Lindsay Hassett is applauded off the field by Warwickshire captain Tom Dollery. The scoreboard in the background tells the story: Hassett 21 not out, scored in 170 minutes. The young player who was nought not out is the young Richie Benaud on his first tour of England.

The surplus was brought about by record membership subscriptions – £20,321 4s 0d – and the overdue decision by the Chancellor of the Exchequer, Mr R. A. Butler, to remove the crippling Entertainments Duty. In seven post-war years, during which the Club had suffered overall losses totalling £9,439, Warwickshire had paid £8,356 to the government.

The Club announced that additional ground developments would include the improvement of the two practice areas, cover for the popular side, a new members' dining room and new offices for the new supporters' association. An interesting innovation was the starting of direct broadcasting of play at Edgbaston to the Yardley Green and West Heath sanatoria, and among several players who volunteered their services was Bannister, whose experience gained in those early days was to stand him in good stead with the BBC over 30 years later.

The report concluded with a reference to the acrimonious special general meeting at the Grand Hotel in Birmingham, called by 20 members under Rule 29 who sought to 'pass a vote of no confidence in the committee', because of the decisions to sack Grove, Lobb and groundsman Boak, and the fact that 'the methods employed by the committee in advising the men concerned, and the time lag in the case of the players, was quite unreasonable'.

Bannister was the unwitting catalyst of what was soon known as 'the Grove affair'. With the typical impetuosity of a 23-year-old who thought that 70 wickets in a season deserved a county cap, he wrote to the committee to say that he had received an offer from the Central Lancashire League club, Werneth, to play for them in 1954, and felt obliged to take up the offer unless he could be more sure of regular first-team cricket.

The immediate result was a letter dated 14 September 1953, informing Grove that he would not be retained because of the wish to give younger players an opportunity. Had he received the same letter at the end of July, as was normal practice, it is probably that would have been the end of the matter, but the timing led to his dismissal being irrelevantly linked with the departure of Lobb and Boak for different reasons. The letter became public knowledge via the *Birmingham Post* three days later, and an uncomplaining Grove was promptly offered a two-year contract with Worcestershire the following week. But a section of the membership, headed by the Club's honorary statistician Ted Hampton, was unhappy about the decision, and letters appeared in the local newspapers saying that 'the members have it in their own hands and it is up to them to act in the proper way at the proper time'.

Alec Hastilow defended the decision by pointing out that the committee had been faced with the responsibility of deciding which of seven pace bowlers should be re-engaged: Grove, Pritchard, Dollery, Bannister, Lobb, and Thompson and Carter, who were about to finish their National Service. He reminded the members, also with no great relevance, that because Grove's career was seriously interfered with by the war, he was granted a benefit after only five years in the first eleven. Nobody was complaining about the treatment afforded Grove in his playing career – only the method of his dismissal. The bowler's fitness for six-days-a-week cricket was also questioned, but Hampton – a close friend of Grove – was adamant that an injustice had been done.

Although Grove distanced himself from the rebellion, the necessary requisitioning notice was lodged, and Hampton resigned as statistician until the special meeting was held. The committee naturally deplored such a move, but instructed the secretary to include on a subsequent agenda the whole question of the committee's approach to players' engagements, with particular reference to much earlier notice being given.

It was also decided to include the question of more rapid release of information to the press after decisions at meetings, so as to avoid 'scoops when leakages occur'. Whatever action was taken on the latter point, the same dissatisfaction among the members 34 years later about how the Club dealt with its 'man-management' of staff was to bring about two more costly and disruptive special general meetings.

The cost of the meeting was £100, and the committee went into a packed hotel – 1,600 members were present – prepared to resign *en bloc* if the resolution was carried. Dr Thwaite presided, but said that as a member of the committee it would be better if he vacated the chair and that Alderman Yates, the former Lord Mayor, should deputise for him. This was agreed and Councillor Denis Howell, later to become a distinguished MP, moved the motion on the grounds that it was not the decision to sack Grove which had brought the storm of criticism, but the method used to dispense with the services 'of one of the greatest bowlers to come out of Warwickshire'. Howell went on to say that the public reference to Grove's benefit had introduced an unnecessary and offensive element into a matter which should have been dealt with by a meeting between a Club official and the player.

Howell was right, and it remains an inexplicably sad part of professional cricket that so many potential awkward situations are not de-fused by sympathetic foresight from men who so often as committee men fail to bring the same principles to bear which stand them in such good stead in their own professions.

Lobb and Boak were next to be drawn into the argument, with Howell revealing that Somerset were told on 22 August that Lobb would not be released. Happily, for the player, the delay in reversing the decision made no difference to the subsequent offer from the west country club, which he accepted.

Boak received a letter pointing out that if he did not apply for a vacancy in the Coventry area 'you may well be exposing your family and yourself to serious risk'. The implied threat – that his home and job were inseparably linked, was criticised by Howell, who made the telling point 'that all three cases are bad enough individually; taken together they present to us an extremely doubtful attitude of mind in which to deal with players and other professional staff in this mercenary manner'.

Alec Hastilow's reply made several valid points, particularly the one concerning the medical advice that, after sustaining an Achilles tendon injury at Derby at the beginning of August, Grove was unlikely to go through another complete season. Even so, the points he made about fitness, other new-ball bowlers, and the generous recompense Grove had always received, did not meet Howell's main argument that it was not the decision to sack Grove that the members objected to, but rather the manner and timing of it.

Those points were never satisfactorily answered, but with the argument lost, Hastilow played his trump card. He outlined the administrative chaos which would follow the resignation of the whole committee if the requisition was carried, because it was a critical one only, with no constructive alternative to bridge the gap.

This ensured the safety of the committee, although not before Edgar Hiley said that as well as hoping that, in future the committee would consider making an earlier announcement concerning the re-engagement of players, he wished that the committee were not quite so aloof from the membership, and also that it were not so high-handed.

Wise words, and ones which were to be repeated by other critics in 1987.

The most succinct press comment came from Dick Knight in the *Birmingham Evening Despatch*: 'The Committee can sack whosoever they like, but not howsoever they like.'

At least the meeting prodded the Club into reviewing various of its procedures concerning the re-engagement of players, as well as appointing the secretary as the Club's public relations officer.

The committee, having escaped the axe, perversely decided not to take any action on Hiley's suggestion that it was too aloof from the membership, or on a member's suggestion that a questionnaire should be circulated annually to all members on which they could register complaints or suggestions. Another malaise which has always affected cricket is that too many clubs fail to recognise that their club belongs to the members.

Let Grove bring down the curtain on the 1953 season. Several years later he said: 'I was deeply hurt at the way I left, but this has long been forgotten, and I would rather it remain so. My association with Warwickshire was always a happy one, and if it were possible to start all over again, I would not hesitate to join the Edgbaston club.'

His career figures for Warwickshire speak for themselves: 6,553.4 overs; 15,484 runs; 697 wickets; average 22.21.

Dollery, as usual, provided the perfect tribute: 'Charlie had the great quality of getting the good players out.' Bannister never forgot the great debt he owed Grove, who passed on more sound, hard-headed advice than any other player: Charlie's greatest asset was that he never really believed any batsman could play well. 'Hutton? Not bad but nothing special', was a typical answer to a question about how best to bowl to the great man.

Such an ugly meeting did not augur well for the 1954 season, but

Dollery's team shrugged off the administrative problems with one of the best starts in the Club's history – eight wins out of the first 12 matches played, although this was eventually washed away in the wettest summer ever recorded. Previously the seasons of 1903, 1907, 1912, 1924 and 1936 were the wettest in the 20th century, but in 1954 Warwickshire lost 163 hours and 39 minutes to rain, with two-thirds of that at home. Only nine of the 34 games constituting the full fixture list were unaffected, and the equivalent of 18 full days were lost at home – roughly a third of the entire programme.

The side's final improved position of sixth was entirely due to its explosive start, in which the first four matches were won, including a splendid win over reigning Champions Surrey at the Oval, with the now established new-ball attack of Bannister and Dollery sharing 13 wickets. The run came to a halt at Headingley, where in a rain-ruined drawn match on a lifting pitch, Gardner played one of the best and most courageous innings of his career. Struck all over the body by the hostile Trueman, Gardner was persuaded to seek treatment from the Yorkshire physiotherapist after withstanding the onslaught while scoring 70 in an innings which was spread over two days.

Gardner enhanced his reputation for unconscious humour with a remark which reduced both dressing rooms to helpless laughter. When the masseur gingerly touched one particularly livid weal, Fred stopped him with : 'Don't bother with that one. That's one of yesterday's.'

Trueman and Appleyard were too much for the Warwickshire batsmen a week later at Edgbaston, bowling them out for 142 and 83 to win by ten wickets, but after successive away wins over Somerset and Leicestershire, with a still deadly Hollies taking 17 wickets for 196 in the two games to push his side to the top of the table, the remainder of the season was dismal.

Only Gloucestershire and Glamorgan were beaten in the last 16 games with the fixtures against Kent, Lancashire and Middlesex abandoned because of rain.

The main features of the season were, perforce, of an individual nature, with Wolton finally fulfilling his potential with 1,770 runs at an average of 41.16, which put him at the top of the batting averages. Gardner, who by now had established himself as one of the most dependable openers ever to play for the County, was second with 1,509 runs at 35.09, and Dollery's 1,265, including hundreds against Essex, Leicestershire and Middlesex, took him past Wyatt to become the second heaviest run scorer for Warwickshire behind Quaife.

Hitchcock staged something of a revival with 714 runs, but Horner disappointed with 1,166 at the modest average of 22.86. Spooner and Townsend topped 1,000 again, with the all-rounder taking 39 catches – nearly twice as many as anyone else. His contribution with the ball was a minimal one (eight wickets for 460), and with Pritchard playing only a handful of matches, Hollies had to spearhead a relatively inexperienced attack in which Bannister, with 85 wickets, Dollery with 72, and slow left-arm spinner Ian King with 71, did best.

A pleasing recognition of the brilliant wicket-keeping of the amateur Lewis was the first of two selections – the other was three years later – for the Gentlemen against the Players at Lord's. Warwickshire were indeed fortunate to have his services on the few occasions when Spooner was injured, and he was undoubtedly among the best amateur wicket-keepers in post-war cricket.

One note for the modern player who doubts many of the facts told him about yesteryear: Bannister bowled 844 overs and Keith Dollery 688, yet the side still averaged 21.20 overs per hour. The modern professional will say in defence that, of course, the game nowadays is much more scientific, with more thought given to strategy. He would never offer such a specious theory had he been privileged to watch H. E. Dollery captain a side. He saved time by ensuring that his players knew where they would be fielding at the start of a session before they left the dressing room, and such was his authority that, even in front of big and noisy crowds, he seldom had to attract the attention of any fielder to move him. They were disciplined enough always to watch him for a sign after every delivery, and bowlers were also encouraged to walk back to their marks briskly.

His decision at the end of the season to retire was a big blow to players and committee alike. The two reasons he gave were increasing business responsibilities and a decline in his playing ability now that he was 40. With Hollies also expressing doubts about carrying on, because of a wish to secure his future, the Club chairman needed all his persuasive powers to ensure both players would play in 1955. Dollery finally accepted a contract for five years – the first year as a player and the other four as head coach.

Hollies was promised every effort to find him a job and, significantly in view of the treatment meted out to his friend Grove, given an assurance that the public would be given six weeks' notice when his retirement was announced.

Bromley announced his retirement – a sad case of a brilliant young talent which failed to flower. Cartwright's absence on National Service was balanced by the return of his Coventry colleague, Jim Stewart. Khalid Ibadulla continued the qualification period which enabled him to play Championship cricket in 1957.

Dr Stanley Barnes gave the Club £5,000, the largest single donation ever received, specifically for work to begin on the reconstruction of the pavilion.

Work was also to start on the west wing, and with the completion of the assistant secretary's house, and the announcement of plans to build a new indoor cricket school, the year ended on a much more optimistic and positive note than had seemed possible during the monsoons of July and August.

The following year brought to an end the Dollery era, but as though to compensate the Edgbaston supporters, the Board of Control at Lord's finally rewarded the non-stop efforts of Leslie Deakins and his committee with the award of a Test match against the West Indies in 1957, following an acceptance at headquarters of a rota plan submitted from Warwickshire which would give the usual grounds, Lord's excepted, four Tests in five years and seven in ten years.

The Club presidency sadly changed hands twice in the year. Dr Thwaite decided not to seek re-election because of ill-health, and Dr Barnes accepted the nomination, though he was to hold office for only a few months before, at the age of 80, he died. He was a distinguished figure in the pre-war field of medicine, who after becoming a leading European neurologist relinquished his practice in 1931 to become Dean of the Faculty of Medicine at Birmingham University, where he played a leading part in the development of the Queen Elizabeth Hospital.

Dr Barnes' short term of office was marked by the start of preparations for the 1957 Test match. The ground and building sub-committee was instructed to make its priority the extending of accommodation on the popular side, and a special Test match sub-committee was appointed to deal with matters which, although considered routine nowadays, were then part of uncharted waters. Reservation of seats, extra catering and toilet facilities, car parking, dressing-room accommodation, hotel and dining arrangements in the city, press and TV facilities, the pitch, and many other items comprised the agenda of that sub-committee.

The new groundsman, Ted Williams, had to resign within a few months because of ill-health, and his successor was to hold the post for over 25 years. Largely on the recommendation of D. J. Insole of England, Essex and Cambridge, Bernard Flack was appointed and he took up his duties at the end of the summer.

The Championship was won for the fourth successive time by Surrey, with the unique record of winning 23 of their 28 games, with the other five games lost. That the side was not involved in a single drawn game says much for their ability and positive approach under the lively leadership of Stuart Surridge. In winning their four titles, Surrey lost only 13 games, with Warwickshire, perhaps improbably, beating them four times.

Although Dollery's side, in their captain's final year, won only ten games to finish joint ninth, one of those wins was against the Champions at Coventry, where Hitchcock scored a brilliant unbeaten 123 in even time on a turning pitch. The small boundaries enabled the left-hander to deal out some unusually heavy punishment to Laker and Lock, although he was helped by the decision by the Surrey captain, Surridge, to bowl only his spinners. Hitchcock did not receive one ball from a seamer in his innings, and this strange strategy was highlighted when Bannister took seven wickets in the match to help his side to a convincing win by 131 runs.

Hitchcock topped the batting averages with a career-highest aggregate of 1,695 at an average of 34.59 and, restored to full fitness, played several thrilling innings, including a hundred in 78 minutes at Derby in the days when the Lawrence Trophy was decided on time rather than the much fairer system subsequently adopted of balls received. He scored 128 out of a stand of 191 with Townsend against Essex at Edgbaston, with the other hundred – his maiden in first-class cricket – coming at Hinckley in the nine wickets win against Leicestershire. The 25-year-old New Zealander also chipped in with 45 useful wickets, and the improvement in his leg-break bowling helped to compensate for the decline of King and Weeks, who managed only 25 wickets between them for 1,018 runs.

The constant post-war failures of promising young Warwickshire spinners to fulfil their potential after a promising start was to be a recurring problem for successive captains and coaches, and one for which there is still no sign of a solution. Among those who came and went too quickly after a good start were Weeks, King, Hill, Bridge and Tidy.

Wolton had another excellent season with 1,809 runs, and Dollery (1,595), Spooner (1,347) and Horner, whose 1,192 was slightly disappointing from 45 completed innings, all passed 1,000. Townsend fell away with 898 runs at 19.52 and only 17 wickets, but his 35 catches underlined what an indispensable role he filled in the side.

Hollies just went on and on, taking 115 wickets at 17.69 at the age of 43 from 1,053.1 overs and was belatedly named as one of the *Wisden* 'Five Cricketers of the Year'. With Bannister and Thompson – who kept Keith Dollery out of the side – taking 91 and 92 wickets respectively, the attack only needed a good off-spinner to turn it into a unit capable of challenging for the title.

Individual landmarks reached were the 2,000th wicket of Hollies, Spooners' 10,000th run, the award of a county cap to Thompson, and Bannister becoming the first Warwickshire bowler to take a hat-trick against Yorkshire in a return of nine for 35 in the first innings at Bramall Lane. Curiously enough, the only wicket he did not take was that of Brian Close – his first first-class victim four years earlier.

The year belonged to Dollery who, despite another fine season with the bat and as captain, refused to change his decision to retire, even after being honoured with the offer of the captaincy of the England A side to tour Pakistan that winter. His final representative appearance was for the Players at Lord's, where he fittingly signed off with 82. His 151 in the home win at the end of June against Nottinghamshire was his 50th hundred, and made him the second player in the country to reach 1,000 runs, with Insole pipping him by a few hours.

Dollery's final match, after 21 years, was a comedy of errors at Neath against Glamorgan. His players decided that a fitting farewell present would be the £300 prize money for the fastest first-innings total of 300 in the County Championship. To the astonishment of the Glamorgan side, against whom Gardner had always been at his most dogged, the opener waltzed down the pitch to the first ball of the match to set the tone for a frenetic pre-lunch session which did not go quite according to plan. Then a maiden hundred from Wilf Wooller, which took over seven hours, was enough to set up a crashing defeat by an innings and 80 to complete a sad ending to the season of three successive defeats. Wooller was partnered for part of his marathon innings by a 17-year-old from Neath Grammar School called Tony Lewis, later to captain club and country.

The most difficult of all slip catches – the one to the left of first slip off a slow bowler. Alan Townsend's consummate catching skills dismiss Worcestershire's Roy Booth.

The party given by the players to mark the farewell of their captain was full of fun and affection, because they knew better than anyone the enormous contribution made by Dollery to cricket in general, as well as to the Warwickshire cause. Bannister, for one, has never altered his view that Dollery was not only the best captain he played under, but also the best leader he has seen in county cricket, and is on record thus:

> Quite simply, he never missed a trick. Although he would always keep us involved in decisions, I can remember plenty of occasions when his thinking was so far ahead of the rest of us, that he took us by surprise.
>
> His ability to read a pitch was unsurpassed, and although he apparently did not make a great study of the opposition, my path into county cricket was eased enormously by his advice on the strengths and weakensses of opposing batsmen. I count myself lucky to have played the early part of my career under such a man,. and without him, I doubt whether I would have enjoyed the same success.

The committee recorded that:

> Few counties have been blessed with a player of the personality or ability of H. E. Dollery, and he has undoubtedly left his mark for all time, not only at Edgbaston, but in the game generally, where he has given a new status and dignity to the professional player, both as a cricketer and a leader.
>
> During his 21-year association with the county game, he has earned the respect and admiration of all cricketers and cricket lovers up and down the country. His cricket, more than most players, was sharply divided by the war, which cost him so much in opportunity, for he was due to make his initial tour abroad with an MCC team to India in 1939.

Figures only scratch the surface of one of the game's great personalities, but they are worth noting (only 36 innings and 949 runs were scored in representative cricket): 715 innings; 65 not out; 24,406 runs; highest score 212; 50 hundreds; average 37.54.

The following season, 1956, continued to change the familiar face of the post-war Edgbaston, both on and off the field. Lord Bennett had become the third president of the year when he was elected on 20 September 1955. Missing from the playing staff when it reported back in April, in addition to Dollery, were Ord, Pritchard and King. Ord joined Dollery on the coaching staff, while Pritchard and King took up business appointments. Both players were subsequently to play briefly for other counties, with the 39-year-old fast bowler turning out for Kent, and King joining Essex.

Pritchard took 695 wickets at 23.22 each in his eight-year career, with a strike rate of a wicket every 53 deliveries. He made an important contribution towards the rapid rise of the Club after the war, when they built a Championship-winning side from scratch in six seasons. No more cheerful man has ever played for the Club, and it is a tribute to his popularity and unfailing unselfishness that he left the game without a bad word ever said about him.

Ord had always been a model professional. A small, neat man, his 20 years as a player brought him 11,788 runs including 16 hundreds, and he was another batsman whose career was seriously affected by the war.

Newcomers on the staff included Barry Fletcher and a Barbadian fast bowler called Shirley Griffiths, who had to qualify, and their pre-season practice was held under the watchful eye of the new captain, Hollies.

When the MCC failed to approve the special registration of M. J. K. Smith, the Club had no alternative but to ask Hollies to step into the breach for 1956. It was only the third time in the Club's history that a captaincy appointment turned out to be for one year only – H. J. Goodwin in 1910 and G. W. Stephens in 1919 were the others – and it was a reluctant Hollies who bravely took over the reins at a time which would have taxed even the enthusiasm of someone like Cranmer.

Nothing went right. In the absence of Dollery, much was expected of Hitchcock but a dramatic decline resulted in the left-hander's form and he scored only 834 runs from 46 innings. Only Gardner, who performed heroically for most of the season with a fractured finger to score 1,311 runs before he finally fractured an elbow, and Wolton, with 1,425, averaged over 30. The constant shortage of runs saddled Hollies with an impossible task. Only five wins meant a slump to 14th position in the table, which was yet again headed by Surrey, for the fifth successive year, although another rain-ruined summer meant they had to win only 15 matches out of 28.

Warwickshire topped 300 twice only, and of greater significance failed to reach 200 in Championship cricket on 25 occasions, including twice each in the away matches lost to Worcestershire, Lancashire and Middlesex, as well as against Yorkshire and Northamptonshire at home. That meant a catastrophic start to the season of six defeats in the first nine matches. Even Oxford University bowled them out twice at Edgbaston for 155 and 159, with the subsequent MCC secretary, Jack Bailey, taking six for 78 in the match.

Horner improved to score 1,411 at 27.76, but with younger players like Cartwright, Stewart and Leach understandably returning moderate figures, too much responsibility was thrown on an attack

At the 1972 Championship winning celebration these three players combine the three times that Warwickshire have won the County Championship. On the left, 'Tiger' Smith, who played in the first Championship team of 1911 and also was County Coach in the 1951 Championship season and watched the 1972 victories. In the centre is Dennis Amiss, who played in the 1972 win. On the right is Tom Pritchard, the New Zealand fast bowler who helped to bowl Warwickshire to victory in the 1951 Championship team and retired at the end of the 1955 season.

which was not up to it. Bannister and Thompson had indifferent seasons with 73 and 60 wickets respectively, and although Townsend bowled well for his 32 wickets, his 25 catches showed the marked drop in the penetrative powers of the attack.

Hollies' bag of 82 wickets was his lowest since the war, and underlined the difficulties facing a specialist bowler leading the side. Keith Dollery, whose last season this was to be, performed his second hat-trick, this time against Kent with, piquantly, Pritchard one of the victims.

Thompson also did the hat-trick, at Horsham against Sussex in a rare Warwickshire victory which was notable for two incidents in the second innings. In a much-shuffled batting order following the early season traumas, Horner was asked to bat lower down, but so badly affected was the opener by having to wait, that captain Hollies decided to quieten the nerves with a large brandy It made little difference when, with only 89 needed to win, the super-charged Horner went in with his side in trouble, and apparently ran out Wolton, who looked to be the last hope. Wolton was called for an impossible single, and was well out of his ground, when the Sussex wicket-keeper triumphantly claimed the run-out, which was promptly given by umpire Fred Price.

Only then was it noticed that the home keeper had missed the stumps with his gloves, and a relieved Wolton was recalled to score an unbeaten 53 – his second fifty of the game – to steer his side home by four wickets. As Hollies said in the nail-biting last few overs: 'I reckon I shall need the brandy soon.'

Other individual highlights included Spooner, taking his 500th victim, and Horner joining the short list of Warwickshire players to score a hundred before lunch. Like Diver in 1899 and Fishwick in 1904, Horner did it against Leicestershire.

The newly appointed addition to the Edgbaston administrative staff, with a five-year contract, M. J. K. Smith, played four non-Championship innings during his qualifying year and scored 146, including 55 against the Australians, for whom Benaud took eleven for 75 in the win over the home side by an innings and 127.

The annual report, commenting on the poor season in which £6,680 5s 11d was taken in the Australian match compared with £4,606 11s 6d from all the other home games, apportioned the blame thus:

> The game was in general disfavour with the public because of the slow tempo of the game which was often characterised by tedious strokeless batting, brought about, as batsmen claim, by negative bowling down the leg-side to a packed on-side field.

At least the year was notable for the progress made in developing the ground, with the long-awaited Test match only a year away. The new pavilion suite was opened by the Lord Mayor of Birmingham, Alderman Lummis Gibson, and the new dressing-room accommodation was popular with the players, as was a new Club room with the members.

Just as important was the new indoor cricket school, which was handed over by the now thriving supporters' association, and the building was justly described as the best in the country. In that winter work was commenced on a new kitchen, a new ladies room in the east wing, the erection of new gates adjacent to the Thwaite Gates, and a new press box to seat 160 journalists.

Not surprisingly, Hollies announced that he intended to retire at the end of the following season, and his final season was happily to be an outstanding personal success.

CHAPTER SEVENTEEN

THE START OF THE SMITH YEARS, 1957–59

THE 1957 SEASON WAS EAGERLY anticipated on two fronts by a membership which was impatient for success. They naturally expected much from the new captain, Mike Smith, who had been appointed at the suggestion of Hollies, and of course Test cricket was due back at Edgbaston for the first time in 28 years.

Pride of place must go the historic match against the West Indies, which brought to fruition all the dreams and hard work of Warwickshire officials in the eleven previous seasons since the war.

The weather was fine throughout, and 64,977 people on the popular side joined 26,500 members to pay £31,571 to watch an enthralling game in which England came close to winning after being on the very brink of defeat.

Ramadhin was too much for a strong-looking England batting line-up, which was bundled out for 186. With the little West Indian returning figures of 31–17–49–7, a slightly apprehensive groundsman Flack watched the West Indies reply. He need not have worried. With Collie Smith scoring 161 and Walcott 90 the tourists made 474 for a seemingly match-winning lead of 288. The West Indies opening batsman, Pairaudeau, had the frustrating experience of being dismissed for one, and then spending the next 8½ hours at the wicket, running for the injured Walcott, and then Worrell.

The famous partnership of May and Cowdrey, which added 411 for the fourth wicket, effectively killed off Ramadhin for the series, and an excited crowd saw the West Indies reeling at 72 for seven, after a declaration at 583 for four had left them 140 minutes' batting time.

The administrative organisation earned Warwickshire much praise, with the *Birmingham Post* saying that 'the Warwickshire Club and the secretary and his staff in particular have acquitted themselves triumphantly, as well as the groundsman and his staff'. The claims for Edgbaston to become a permanent Test match ground were considerably strengthened. The press box was also an outstanding success, with the *Coventry Evening Telegraph* having the foresight and generosity to underwrite the construction costs. In the years to follow, the facilities and position of the box were to attract envious praise from visiting correspondents from all round the world.

As soon as the Test match was over, work began on a four-year plan of reconstruction involving the replacement of the 55-year-old double-decker stand in readiness for the Test match against Australia in 1961.

M. J. K. Smith was particularly strong on the leg side, thanks to the correct open positioning of the front foot and leg.

On the county front, Smith got off to an awful start with the bat, registering three successive ducks, two of them for the MCC against Yorkshire. The third one was at Dudley, where Jack Flavell persuaded him to offer no stroke, and won the lbw decision, but then he settled into the prolific form which was to make him the heaviest scorer in county cricket during the next ten years.

He reached his 1,000 runs for Warwickshire by 10 July, although his first hundred did not come until 20 days later against Middlesex, and the 2,000 mark was passed on 24 August. His final aggregate of 2,074 at 38.40 placed him top of the batting averages, just ahead of Gardner, whose return to full fitness brought him 1,658, averaging 36.04.

Horner's aggregate of 1,545 was his best to date, and although Townsend was the only other batsman to pass 1,000 runs, both Stewart and the newly qualified Ibadulla played well, with Stewart scoring his maiden hundred against Leicestershire.

The bowling department was dominated by – who else? – Hollies. He marked his final season with 128 wickets at 19.03 from 1,200.3 overs – an astonishing workload for someone aged 45, and he played a major part in a wonderful first half of the season which brought nine wins in the first 14 matches. These included six successive wins against Gloucestershire twice, Derbyshire, Glamorgan, Kent and Sussex.

Hollies had match figures of ten for 99 against Derbyshire, nine for 128 in the return match at Edgbaston against Gloucestershire, seven for 113 against Glamorgan, five for 84 against Kent, and seven for 95 in the second innings against Sussex. He found unexpected spin support from Carter, who had switched to off-spin from his former fast-medium style, his final tally of 70 wickets promising a much longer and more successful career than was the case when, four years later, he left Edgbaston with 241 wickets at 27.79 to his name.

The two wins against Gloucestershire failed to restore Bannister's popularity with his colleagues following a remark made at Bristol before the start of the first match. He said to the Warwickshire team: 'I've just told Tom Graveney that I've never seen him score a hundred yet. That will put the pressure on him.' To this day Bannister maintains that there was just no need for Graveney to score 122 on 3 June, followed by 106 and an unbeaten 101 in the return game two weeks later.

In the new-ball department Bannister, with 73 wickets at 22.16, was the most successful until a back injury in the middle of August threatened his career for nearly a year. The newly qualified Ibadulla had a successful first season with a mixture of seam and off-spin which brought him 54 wickets at 17.88. Among Townsend's 35 catches was the one to catch Bill Alley off Hollies at Edgbaston, which established a new record of 307 for the Club.

At the half-way mark, Warwickshire were a deserved second in the table, but with injuries to Spooner, Ibadulla and Stewart, as well as soft wickets because of rain which caused two matches to be abandoned and severely curtailed two others, not another match was won, and the side slid to a final 11th place. This time, they were 178 points behind Surrey, who marked their sixth successive Championship with a staggering margin of 94 points over second-placed Northamptonshire.

The season saw the introduction of batting bonus points, as well as a limitation to five fielders permitted on the leg-side – a sad blow to off-spinners.

Spooner's injury caused him to miss his benefit match against Middlesex, and the wicket-keeper's final return of £3,784 10s 0d was disappointingly affected by the inclement weather in the last two months of the season. At least the wicket-keeper's injury gave Lewis sufficient opportunities to earn selection for the second time, for the Gentlemen against the Players.

One of the most significant post-war bowling performances was achieved in the 2nd XI by a player who, for six seasons, had been regarded as a specialist batsman. The 22-year-old Cartwright, whose progress since his debut in 1953 had been slow, turned in some remarkable figures in the second innings of Warwickshire's Challenge match in the Minor Counties against Yorkshire at Scarborough: 26–17–19–7. He had worked at his bowling in the nets, and the new career of Warwickshire's most successful seam bowler was ready to be launched.

The newly acquired status of a Test ground increased the telephone expenses from £216 to £434, which was still a far cry from the astronomical charges in 1988 of £21,890.

Just as the end of the 1955 season belonged to Dollery, so was the last month of Smith's first year dominated by the pending retirement of Hollies. That the last three matches were lost – two to Surrey within ten days – by ten wickets and by an innings and 70 – did not affect the warmth of the reception he got everywhere from players and spectators alike.

As he went out to bat at Edgbaston for the last time, the players formed a guard of honour for one of the greatest slow bowlers of all. He signed off in typical fashion with seven runs, compelling Surrey to bat again to score 13 to win. He then asked to bowl, and his last two overs on the ground he had graced for 25 years were maidens.

In his penultimate match against Lancashire at Old Trafford, he took five for 53 – the 182nd time he had achieved five in an innings, and the last of his 2,323 wickets came in the final game at the Oval when he dismissed Lock to return an analysis of 15–2–35–2.

The record books show that only 16 bowlers have taken more wickets in history, and of course he dominates all the Warwickshire bowling records. His 180 wickets in 1946 remains the highest ever total for the Club, and almost certainly will do so for ever. he bowled more overs in 1949 – 1,399.1 – than anyone else has done in a season.

To put that physical feat into perspective, the aggregate number of overs bowled for the Club in 1988 was 3,090.1, spread among ten bowlers who bowled more than 100 overs each. Hollies virtually would have been on at one end throughout that season.

He took 100 wickets or more in a season 14 times, only missing the target twice after the war – in 1953 and 1956. He was a captains'

Eric Hollies leaves the Edgbaston ground for the last time in 1957, with the opposition, Surrey, the same as his first game on the ground in 1932. L to r: Alan Townsend, Ronnie Pratt, Esmond Lewis, Ray Hitchcock, Norman Horner, umpires Charlie Elliott and Syd Buller, Clive Leach, Swaranjit Singh, Shirley Griffiths, Ossie Wheatley, Mike Smith.

treasure in the dressing room, as well as with the ball in his hand. His sense of fun was joyous, and many a dull and boring day has been lightened by those unerringly aimed shafts of Black Country wit. He once explained his reluctance to share a car with Dollery: 'I'm not saying he drives fast. It's just that he makes the telegraph poles look like a sheet of corrugated fencing.'

The annual report said:

> We shall always recall his enthusiastic approach to the game, which never dimmed with the passing years, his good fellowship, his gentle repartee and the constant desire to help his colleagues to enjoy it all to the full as much as he was doing. No cricketer ever had a greater love for the game than Eric.

The 1950s were a decade full of change, off and on the field, with the Club presidency particularly affected.

After only eight changes in that office between 1882 and March 1955, the death of Lord Bennett on 29 September 1957 brought a fourth president in $2\frac{1}{2}$ years. The Seventh Earl of Warwick was elected on 15 November 1957, just 20 days after the death of Dr Thwaite at his home in Surrey, aged 74.

Leslie Deakins included in his tribute to the man who held the premier Office for longer than anyone else except Ludford C. Docker, the following appreciation:

> His death marks the passing of a man who, more than any other, was responsible for the resuscitation of Warwickshire cricket from the doldrums of the 1930s to the Championship of 1951, and the restoration of the Edgbaston ground as a Test match centre in 1957. He will long be remembered at Edgbaston by the scoreboards and gates erected in his honour and bearing his name, but to the initiated, more as the man who pointed the way and led the Club forward, reviving by his personality the flagging fortunes of the early 1930s and creating a bright future, redolent with opportunity, for those privileged to follow in his footsteps.

This was a particularly generous tribute from a man who, as history would later recognise, had a greater influence than anyone on the post-war progress made by Warwickshire.

Other deaths included Sydney Santall, whose 1,206 wickets and 6,490 runs held the team together around the turn of the century during the Club's first years in the Championship, and the Club's senior vice-president, Sir Fitzroy Hamilton Anstruther Gough-Calthorpe, who had sold the freehold of the second section of the ground to the Club in 1945.

The gloom thus cast over Edgbaston was not to lift throughout the 1958 season that was, by some distance, the most dismal and unsuccessful since the war. The weather was poor and the team no better, occupying 16th position in the Championship, equalling the previous worst finishing position in 1921.

Only three of the 28 matches were won, the first against Sussex, and two out of the last three against Somerset and Middlesex. The annual report was justifiably critical, but the comments on the state of county cricket were even more scathing:

> The tempo of the game slowed down to a degree where in the early stages of many games it was difficult to define actual movement. The laws of the game were more than ever disregarded, and throwing and dragging by bowlers became all too commonplace, and most depressing of all, no apparent action was taken to rectify the position.
>
> There was a very great diminution of public interest, and County match aggregates fell from just over a million in 1957, to practically half that figure. If cricket is to continue as a spectacle to interest a public and provide them with entertainment, the great majority of

players will have to show far more zest and attacking ability. Your committee is at one with the authority that declares there is nothing wrong with the game, but only with the players' approach to it.

With the team highlights able to be counted on one hand, those of an individual nature were just as scarce, Mike Smith was asked by the England Selectors to open the innings, but the move failed, both at Test level, where he made 57 in four innings before he was dropped after the first three Tests against New Zealand, and with Warwickshire, where his stability at number 4 was missed.

That was no fault of Horner, who dropped down the order, and his aggregate of 1,476 was second only to that of his captain. Smith eventually passed 2,000 runs in all cricket, with 1,631 at 46.60 putting him well clear at the top of the County averages.

Gardner suffered what seemed to be an inevitable decline in a player's benefit year, scoring 1,332 with an average of under 30, and his benefit realised only £3,750, thanks in part to a public appeal by Dollery after the weather had ruined the match against Lancashire. Wolton, with 1,186 runs at 34.88, was the only other batsman to pass 1,000, although Cartwright advanced to 902, including his highest innings to date, 128 out of 263 at Edgbaston against Kent.

In his last full season Spooner's form declined, and with deputy Lewis also announcing his retirement, the cricketers were fast disappearing who had served Warwickshire so well in the post-war years.

Leadbeater, signed from Yorkshire as the leg-break successor to Hollies, took 42 wickets in the wet season, and underlined his all-round abilities with 116 as nightwatchman against Glamorgan at Coventry, but the other all-rounder, Ibadulla, fell away with bat and ball.

The leading wicket-taker was Carter, whose dual-purpose bowling of seam and off-spin brought him 81 wickets at 20.01 each, but with Bannister missing for over half the season with his back injury, only the new left-arm spinner Geoff Hill, with 59 wickets, enjoyed any success. He joined the staff after completing his National Service with the RAF and bowled well in the second half of the season.

Bannister returned against Oxford University towards the end of June, but although he took seven for 43, his remodelled action brought about such a drop in pace that for that year he could be regarded only as a support seam bowler. Carter and Cartwright were capped, the latter agreeing reluctantly to stay at Edgbaston after his request to seek another Club who would give him greater opportunity to open the innings was refused.

The second post-war Test match to be staged on the ground gave England a convincing win against New Zealand by 205 runs, with

39,549 spectators defying the weather to produce receipts of £18,941, and provide an overall attendance, with members, of 61,000.

The financial year as a whole was disastrous. A mere 35,805 people paid to watch Warwickshire, and the Club decided to postpone further ground development plans, as well as to make every effort to reduce the large overdraft incurred through financing part of the west wing development. The secretary recorded his complete disagreement with the decisions, and the mood of the unhappy year was further darkened by the deaths of Frank Foster, the Rev E. F. Waddy, who played briefly after the First World War and the Club's honorary treasurer, Captain C. F. R. Cowan.

One happy note on which the year ended was the inaugural meeting of the Warwickshire Old Cricketers' Association, soon to grow into the largest and strongest of its kind throughout the world. There were 30 former players present to elect J. Ernest Hill, then 91, as the first president, Cyril Goodway as chairman, and J. M. A. Matshall as treasurer. The first committee included four former England players: Sydney Barnes, then 86, 'Tiger' Smith, 72, Tom Dollery, and Eric Hollies.

The association membership, confined to anyone who had played first-class cricket for the Club, soon rose to over 100, and the defined aims included an annual dinner which quickly developed into the highlight of each year.

At the annual meeting, chairman Hastilow forestalled any criticism from the members concerning the poor playing record with a commitment to build up a Championship side, and although that promise was not to be fulfilled until 1972, a spectacular improvement took the side from sixteenth to fourth.

The 1959 season was played on covered pitches and Smith responded by taking his side to fourth place in the Championship, 20 points behind the Champions Yorkshire, and two points adrift of Gloucestershire and Surrey.

The 26-year-old captain had a magnificent season in which he became only the fourth batsman since the war, and the second for ten years, to pass 3,000 runs in first-class cricket. Compton, Edrich and Hutton were the others, and his aggregate of 3,245 from 67 innings has been exceeded by only nine other players – Hammond twice.

He scored 2,417 for Warwickshire, to set up a new record, and hit six hundreds, including a superb unbeaten 182 out of 318 for six on a turning pitch at Stroud to bring off an improbable victory against the strong Gloucestershire spin attack.

He set another Club record with 43 catches, most of them taken in the forward short leg position 'discovered' following the new restricted leg-side legislation.

The win at Stroud was the third of 13 wins by a rejuvenated side, which was constantly spurred on by the vastly improved performances, compared with the previous year, of Horner (1,806 runs at 35.41), Stewart (1,799 at 40.88 including an historic 155 at Blackpool), Wolton (1,449 in a benefit year which brought him £3,542 16s 4d), Townsend (1,154) and, most welcome of all, Cartwright, with 1,264 runs at 26.89 and 75 wickets at 25.96.

Add the effective seasons in the new-ball department of Thompson and Cambridge Blue Wheatley, who took 97 and 95 wickets respectively, together with 85 wickets from off-spinner Bridge, now back on the staff after National Service, and it is easy to see why the Club had such a fine season.

So keen was the competition for places that Bannister, slowly returning to his previous pace and form, found that even by taking all ten wickets in an innings against the Combined Services on his 'home Mitchells and Butlers pitch, he could not force his way into the Championship side'.

In the same match Stewart scored the first hundred of his subsequent 151 in 85 minutes, and as his magnificent season unfolded, the runs came at an even quicker pace. He scored a hundred before lunch against Lancashire in a match which he crashed into the record books by hitting a total of 17 sixes in one of the most astonishing displays of hitting ever seen in county cricket.

The second was the lowest of his five hundreds (125), the other four all being over 150. In his two innings at Blackpool, at one point he scored 39 from eleven consecutive scoring strokes, including two sixes and six fours in the first innings, and 45 runs from twelve strokes in the second innings, which included five sixes and two fours.

The run glut was helped by the first ever compulsory covering of pitches, and the Birmingham public responded by more than doubling the gate receipts of 1958, even though the aggregate sum of £7,945 8s 4d was a long way from the £20,318 taken in 1951.

Only five matches were drawn, with Smith's the positive approach fashioning several unexpected wins, notably against Somerset at Edgbaston, when a first-innings declaration as soon as the follow-on was avoided led to Warwickshire scoring 264 for four to win the game.

Another first-innings deficit of 117 in the home match against Middlesex was reversed, with Horner scoring 173 out of 314 for four to bring off an unlikely win. Throughout the season, the self-belief of the players was there for all to see.

Spooner and Fox shared 83 victims between them, but although the skill of the former showed no decline after twelve seasons, he decided to announce his retirement. As the committee put on record: 'As a batsman-wicket-keeper, he has had few equals in the history of the

In 1959, on 29–31 July, at Blackpool, W. J. (Jim) Stewart hit 17 sixes in the match against Lancashire: ten in his first innings of 155 and seven in his second innings of 125.

game, and it was nothing short of tragedy that the war robbed him of six vital playing years'.

His career figures are outstanding. He scored 12,037 runs at an average of 26.86, including eleven hundreds, and claimed 686 victims, including a Club record of 155 stumpings. No more honest or enthusiastic cricketer has ever played for the County, and he was unlucky that one of England's greatest wicket-keepers, Godfrey Evans, limited his England appearances to seven.

At Test match level, Smith scored his first hundred for England at Manchester against India, and he followed this with 98 in the next Test at the Oval.

To round off the Club's best playing season since 1951, Dollery led the 2nd XI to win the Minor Counties, and it was a much happier annual report that year, although the financial position was not helped by a stiff increase in the ground rates to £7,548.

A long-standing complaint of the players concerning the lack of a sightscreen at the City end of the ground was finally redressed with the decision to install one for the 1960 season. In particular, the views of players from both teams in the home fixture with Northamptonshire were noted, after Frank Tyson had proved especially difficult to pick up, with the ball delivered against a background of a packed crowd.

Other winter decisions included that of Dollery to resign after one season as an England selector.

Smith enjoyed a successful tour with England of the West Indies, scoring 308 runs in the five-match series including 108 and 96 in the two tests at Trinidad.

Mike Smith and Jack Bannister win two of the six national awards of the 1959 season. Abbas Ali Baig won the Visitor's Award for scoring a hundred in his first test at Manchester; Peter Walker's 64 catches won the fielding award, while Jim Parks scored the fastest hundred of the season in 61 minutes and also claimed 91 wicket-keeping victims. They each received a trophy and a hundred guineas, as did Smith for being the first batsman to score over 3,000 runs since Len Hutton in 1949, and Bannister for his 10 for 41 against the Combined Services. (Credit t.b.c.)

CHAPTER EIGHTEEN

A LORD'S FINAL

THE NEXT FIVE SEASONS were to bring wildly contrasting fortunes, with Warwickshire's final Championship position fluctuating from 15th to second, and the side reaching the second final of the Gillette Cup – the first domestic knock-out competition to be introduced in county cricket.

Mike Smith would win 17 more England caps to add to his ten appearances already and, as with Wyatt 30 years earlier, the Club would have to adjust to his regular absence.

Wolton, Townsend and Gardner, of the old order, were nearing the end of their careers, and new players like Amiss, Jameson, Barber and Brown would replace them.

A reversion in the points scoring method to a percentage basis, allowed a cumbersome championship season in 1960, in which eight clubs, including Warwickshire, Worcestershire, and the eventual Champions, Yorkshire, played 32 matches, with the remaining nine counties playing 28.

Despite another season of heavy scoring from Smith, who scored 2,551 runs in all cricket, Horner (1,902), Stewart (1,725), Hitchcock (1,554) and Ibadulla (1,289), only four matches were won, compared with 12 defeats, and a frustratingly high figure of 16 draws.

Significantly, in view of the experimental scoring system, the first eight positions in the table were decided in the order of the number of matches won, which is usually the case.

Warwickshire were penalised by the weather, and the refusal of opposing captains to play them in the same open manner as the previous year, when two high-scoring matches were won after declarations, and two others by achieving big totals batting last.

Smith's biggest handicap was the failure of Hill and Bridge, with the young spinners suffering from what was becoming a traditional Warwickshire malaise of failing to build on a promising first season. Between them they could manage only 52 wickets for 2,081 runs from 745.1 overs, and until Carter finished the season well with 29 wickets at 21.37 each, the lack of spin support placed too much responsibility on the new ball bowlers.

Bannister, now restored to full fitness, deposed Thompson, and both he and the indefatigible Wheatley took over 100 wickets. Had Cartwright repeated his 1959 form, results might have been better, but his 543 runs at 20.88, together with only 25 wickets at 46.72, left a hole in the all-rounder department which Townsend and Ibadulla could not fill.

The wicket-keeping duties were shared between Fox and A. C. Smith, who took over the gloves at the end of the Oxford University term and impressed with sound work behind the stumps, as well as some competent batting.

Stewart hit only one hundred – 129 at Northampton – but scored so heavily that he attracted the attention of the England selectors, who named him twelfth man for the final Test at the Oval against South Africa to give him his first sample of the big match atmosphere.

It was on the same ground in the first week of July, that in a three-day match against Surrey unaffected by rain only six wickets fell, with neither side batting a second time. Horner opened with Ibadulla – promoted earlier in the season because of an injury to Gardner – and they proceeded to share a stand of 377, which was higher than for any wicket, for or against Warwickshire, in the history of the Club. It established a new world record for an unbroken opening stand. Horner scored 203, a career best, and Ibadulla 170. On a good batting strip Lock showed the advantage he enjoyed in the years before he was forced to remodel his action after being no-balled for throwing, when he reverted to his former method for a couple of deliveries in mid-afternoon. Horner recalls: 'He hadn't turned anything, until he suddenly ripped in a couple with his old action, and they pitched middle and off and turned sharply. He smiled at me and then went back to normal bowling.'

Townsend was due to bat at number 3, but after lunch, different batsmen took over in 'the waiting chair', until acting captain Wheatley declared at 5.30pm, 'in order not to spoil the game by getting too many runs'.

He need not have bothered, with Surrey grinding their way to a first-innings lead after tea on the third day. A statistic which Bannister claimed ought to be a record, even if it was not, was that he took the first wicket of the match at 12.50pm on the second morning, when he dismissed opening bat M. J. Stewart.

The young Amiss made his debut at the age of 17, and did well enough with 135 runs from six completed innings and two wickets, to earn the comment in the annual report that 'his form suggested he will prove a more than useful allrounder in the future'. Only partly right, because although the Birmingham-born teen-ager in the next 27 years was to score an additional 43,288 runs, he could manage only 13 more wickets.

The Edgbaston Test match was a dull affair, with England beating South Africa by 100 runs after five days in which 890 runs were scored at 2.2 per over. The attendance was a lowly 43,147, and with receipts only £16,664, the rumblings concerning the viability of Edgbaston as a Test match centre grew louder.

Smith played in four of the five Tests, against South Africa scoring 99 at Lord's, and together with A. C. Smith, played for the Gentlemen at Lord's in a fixture that would be played only twice more.

With the supporters' association having financed a dozen reconstruction developments, and another five in the pipe-line, concern was expressed at so much capital outlay on facilities which could be used only infrequently and, significantly, the report said that 'the answer may lie in dual purpose construction, so that buildings may prove revenue-earning in some form in the winter months'.

Despite an increase in members' subscriptions to £3 3s od, which produced an extra £5,637, the committee felt bound to warn its supporters that the Club must be run on its normal revenue, with the bountiful supporters' association making no contribution to its income. It also said that the ultimate joint intention was to establish an endowment trust, the income from which would go the Club, largely to cover increased maintenance costs and rating assessments created by the structural development of the ground and premises. A fine distinction perhaps, but one which has rarely been appreciated by the unknowing who have been too ready to level a charge of 'money-bags' at Warwickshire.

Wolton and Townsend, whose benefit realised £4,143 2s 4d, had played their last games for the Club, and with Gardner to retire twelve months later, the old order had almost gone. Also leaving Edgbaston before the start of the 1961 season was Wheatley, who would take up a business appointment in Wales which would allow him to play for Glamorgan. Hill, whose contract was ended by mutual consent after two disappointing seasons, also accepted a good business offer. Wheatley took 237 wickets in 63 games to underline that Glamorgan's gain was Warwickshire's loss.

The following season, 1961, which at one time promised much for Warwickshire, tailed off in August with two defeats and four draws in the last six matches, leaving them in 12th position in the table. This was an improvement on the previous year, thanks to nine wins, including doubles against Leicestershire and Somerset.

Smith again was head and shoulders above most batsmen in the country, with 2,587 in all cricket at an average of 41.72. His aggregate for Warwickshire of 2,099 was followed by 1,774 from Horner. Particularly pleasing were Hitchcock's 1,678, and Cartwright's total of only eight runs fewer. Cartwright's 77 wickets marked his breakthrough as a front-line bowler. Stewart was not so consistent as in the two previous years, with 1,312 at 30.51, but his batting at Street in the victory over Somerset, in which he scored 104 and an unbeaten 55, contained 11 sixes and 14 fours underlining that he was arguably the best selective stroke-player in county cricket.

With Ibadulla scoring 872 and A. C. Smith marking his first full season with the Club with 881 runs and 67 victims, the side was seldom struggling for runs.

The most encouraging bowling performances came from Bridge and Thompson, with the latter filling the gap left by Wheatley with 77 wickets to support Bannister, who bowled more overs than any other seam bowler in the history of the Club (1,197.3) to complete his best-ever season with 131 wickets. The off-spin of Bridge took him to 100 wickets before any other slow bowler in the country on 1 August, and he bowled so well on all types of wickets against the best batsmen in the game, that not even people who had seen other post-war young spinners like Weeks, King and Hill lose their form could possibly have guessed that seven years later he would leave the Club with only 281 wickets in his career of 12 years.

He took five wickets or more in an innings seven times in 1961, and his full figures of 1,131.1–392–2,753–121 make impressive reading. The spin outlook was also brightened by the first appearances of Ron Miller, a tall left-arm spinner from Durham, and with Walsall Grammar schoolboy David Brown also showing much promise, the season was more encouraging than the results showed.

Smith's ability at short leg profited by the success of Bridge, and when he took four catches in succession off the slow bowler, at Northampton he established another Club record with 53 catches in the season.

Mike Smith bringing off a superb short leg catch in the Sydney test in January 1966, to dismiss David Sincock off David Allern. Bob Barber and Jim Parks admire the catch.

The Australians played their first Test match on the ground since 1909, and the match was happily a financial success. The third day, Saturday, had been sold out for two months, and despite rain on three of the five days 83,000 spectators, including members, turned up to watch a high-scoring draw, in which in his only Test appearance in the series, Smith scored 0 and 1 not out, although there was a doubt about whether or not he had hit the delivery from Mackay in the first innings from which he was given out.

Receipts were £38,482, a ground record, and the profit second only to that from the Lord's Test. Nevertheless, the MCC decided to elevate Headingley to the same status as Lord's and the Oval, which meant that in future, Edgbaston would receive six, instead of seven, Tests every ten years.

Not for the first time – or the last – Cartwright's idea of his worth differed from that of the Club, but after lengthy correspondence, he accepted the original offer, after the committee had debated whether or not to make him an exception to the general pay structure of the staff.

With the receipts for home Championship games totalling only £5,740 3s 2d, the financial position made the establishment of an endowment fund even more important, particularly as the Test match had produced criticism about the inadequacy of covered seating.

The annual report marked the retirement of Gardner, Townsend and Wolton with an appraisal of three men 'who were entirely different in technique and temperament'.

Their loyalty was commended, and the joint tribute ended with: 'Cricketers all, you will ever be welcome at Edgbaston, and while you remain nowadays in the Pavilion to watch, may your successors prove worthy in manner and performance at the crease.'

So the last links with the 1951 Championship team were broken. Gardner was just about the most under-rated batsman of his time. In a different era, possibly blessed with fewer 'fashionable' looking openers, he would have played Test cricket. His career figures are: 593 innings; 66 not outs; 17,826 runs; average 33.82. He hit 29 hundreds. Few of those runs came easily, and of course he opened the innings throughout the 1950s when English cricket was particularly well blessed with fast bowlers of high quality and hostility.

Perhaps unfairly, Townsend was criticised from time to time for failing to realise his full potential, but 11,965 runs, 323 wickets, and 409 catches are not figures which need any apologies. A graceful batsman, and a lively fast-medium bowler who was hindered on occassions with back trouble, he was, in the opinion of Alec Bedser, 'one of the best slip fieldsmen I have seen'.

Wolton's entry into county cricket was delayed by the war,

Warwickshire's Alan Townsend took some magnificent catches during his career (1948 to 1960). This was a typical athletic catch at full stretch to dismiss Doug Slade off Tom Cartwright in 1958 at Dudley.

otherwise his career figures of 12,896 runs from 477 innings, including 12 hundreds, would have been much better. A batsman who could play with great freedom, he seemed to play with a little too much caution at times, but whichever approach he adopted was characterised with unfailing grace and style.

The 1962 season was the final year of the three-year experiment in which Warwickshire and Worcestershire were two of the eight sides in the Championship to play 32 games, with the remaining nine clubs playing 28. The format provided Edgbaston supporters with a feast of individual performances which lifted the Club to third place in the table – their 12 wins were two fewer than Yorkshire and Worcestershire who finished above them.

Cartwright did the first double for the Club since Foster in 1911 and 1914, and although only seven previous Warwickshire batsmen had reached 2,000 in a season, Stewart (2,318), Ibadulla (2,098) and Smith (2,090) headed a batting line-up in which Hitchcock, Horner, and A. C. Smith, in addition to Cartwright, also passed 1,000. Add the continued promise of the steadily developing Amiss, and the impact made by the 21-year-old, robust Jameson, with 383 runs from 14 innings, and it can be seen how well the players accepted the chances afforded them by the extra innings available from the experimental Championship format.

Smith and Stewart were the only ones to average over 40, with the latter hitting seven hundreds. He reached 1,000 runs on 12 June, the

Above left: One of Warwickshire's leading all-rounders, Tom Cartwright, who scored 10,781 runs and took 1,058 wickets for Warwickshire in the 1950s and 1960s; he also played for England. Note the classical sideways wind-up of the body in preparation for the away swinger.
Above right: The seam has been released in the perfect plane away-swinger, pointing towards the slips.

first batsman in the country to do so, and the earliest date ever for any Warwickshire player. He hit a career-best unbeaten 182 at Hinckley in a win by eight wickets against Leicestershire, and he also scored 79 not out in the second innings. Warwickshire lost only four wickets in the match.

In a thrilling game at Nuneaton, Warwickshire were 208 for nine at the end of the match – just three runs short of beating Middlesex, following a remarkable first innings recovery brought about by Cartwright and A. C. Smith. They came together at 67 for six and put on 244, with the all-rounder scoring his first double hundred – 210 – and the wicket-keeper 94.

The bowlers also excelled themselves, with Bannister taking 100 wickets for the third successive season, and Cartwright and the 21-year-old Wright, who reached the mark for the first time, established another record for Warwickshire, who had never had three bowlers achieve this feat in one season before.

The enthusiastic and hostile Brown was hampered by injury, but his 53 wickets marked the start of what was to be a distinguished career. The spin department was not so well served, with Bridge able to play only six matches because of an operation. Hitchcock strove manfully to bridge the gap with 35 wickets, and the promising Miller took 54, as well as 34 catches which marked him as a slip fielder of the highest class.

The wins came unevenly, with seven coming from 12 matches between 1 June and 10 July, and only one victory from the last nine matches, from 1 August onwards.

The win in early June was against Yorkshire at Bramall Lane, Sheffield, and was only Warwickshire's eighth win from 115 matches against the white rose county. In that time, Yorkshire won 57 games, 46 were drawn and four abandoned.

The advance by Cartwright and Wright was impressive, with the latter taking five wickets or more in an innings on nine occasions, including twice in the same games at Edgbaston against Gloucestershire and Surrey. Their success decided Thompson, at the age of 30, to retire, and he finished a frustrating career spanning 14 seasons, including two on National Service, with 472 wickets at the low cost of 23 each. Always faced with keen competition, Thompson was unlucky when Keith Dollery and Wheatley were preferred to him in their short stays at Edgbaston in the 1950s, just at the time when an extended run in the first team would have benefited Club and player alike. Instead, the natural ability which marked him as a young bowler of immense promise at 16 was finally subjugated by a defensive approach.

The Edgbaston Test match against Pakistan produced an England win by an innings and 24, but the attendance of 35,000 yielded receipts of only £11,000 – comfortably the lowest figure since the return of Test cricket.

The overall attendances in county cricket were 933,871 – well under half of the golden year figure in 1947 of 2,200,910. Warwickshire were fourth in the attendance figure, but the most worrying factor was a decline in the number of members, which resulted in a loss for the year of £5,327 11s 1d.

Lord's announced sweeping changes for the 1963 season, including 'the introduction of a knock-out competition to be called the Gillette Cup', and the most radical announcement of all, the abolishment of amateur status.

Alec Hastilow retired as Club chairman and was succeeded by Edmund King. Hastilow held office for 14 years, and his considerable influence at Lord's marked the beginning of links between Edgbaston and the headquarters of cricket which were to become even stronger in the 1970s and 1980s. Hastilow combined his great love for cricket with a distinguished business career, which was fittingly marked with the presidency of the chamber of commerce, and his period in office gave the Club a chairman whose foresight and conscientiousness has never been surpassed.

The Smith era was now firmly established, and despite injuries to himself, Stewart and Bannister, the side won ten matches to finish fourth in the 1963 Championship table, which had now reverted to a uniform format of each club playing 28 games.

Indifferent weather brought a further decline in crowds, with a pathetic attendance figure of 48,785 paying spectators (£4,067 16s 9d), but even that was sufficient to put Warwickshire fourth in the attendance list of 17 clubs. Smith's marvellous run of topping 2,000 for six successive seasons was only halted because of a broken wrist sustained when fielding at short leg in the second match of the season at Edgbaston, against Yorkshire. Even so, having missed six matches, he returned in such splendid form that his 1,566 runs at 47.45 enabled him to top the national averages.

Incidentally, the match against Yorkshire proved unlucky in every way, with an exactment of swift revenge by the visitors for that win at Sheffield the previous year. They bowled out Warwickshire for 35 (Cartwright and A. C. Smith were joint top scorers with 11) and 55, and won by an innings and 171 runs. Warwickshire's match aggregate of 90 was the lowest in their history.

Only three of the first 13 games were won, with three fixtures abandoned, and the handicap of injuries to key players proved difficult to overcome. Cartwright's batting declined in proportion to the progress he made with the ball, and this was to be the pattern throughout the 1960s. His 100 wickets came at only 17.86 each, and although West Indian seamer Rudi Webster gave him magnificent support with 80 wickets in the last 17 matches at a similar cost, the absence of Bannister and Brown, together with a loss of form by Wright (8 wickets at 39.55) meant that the lack of a good support seamer prevented several winning opportunities being taken. Roger Edmonds, a 21-year-old physical training student, bowled well with a mixture of seamers and off-cutters to take 35 wickets at 21.25.

The occasional failure to press home a winning advantage was no fault of the spin department which was excitingly headed by new signing Bob Barber, the former Lancashire captain, whose leg-break bowling earned him 65 wickets at 22.44 each, in addition to which he also scored 1,291 runs at 32.37, although not in the flamboyant style he was to adopt so successfully for club and country the following year.

He was a magnificent natural athlete, and his bowling was an old-fashioned throwback to an era when an attacking philosophy was more common-place. He was a genuine spinner, as opposed to a 'roller'. His seven seasons for Warwickshire were to be interrupted by business demands but, it is more a comment on his occasional curious reluctance to bowl than a lack of opportunity that he was to take only another 132 wickets from 1,183.5 overs in the next six years.

He formed a successful opening partnership with Horner, whose aggregate of 1,531 runs was the highest for the County, but with only Hitchcock the only other to reach 1,000, the effect of the absence of Stewart for the first half of the season cannot be over-emphasised. An operation the previous winter for the removal of a bunion led to the amputation of Stewart's left big toe, and although he courageously overcame severe pain to win back his first team place, he was never the same batsman again. Crucially, the loss of his point of balance seriously affected his batting style, which was mainly based on a front-foot technique that had previously enabled him to hit the ball hard and often in the 'v' between mid-on and mid-off. Now he found that, by being dependent upon the position of his second toe, he was forced to play more around his front leg than alongside it, and the former glorious free stroke play with a perpendicular bat was impossible to recapture. It says much for his determination and ability that he rebuilt a successful career, albeit at a lower key, which was to continue at Edgbaston until 1969.

Miller fielded brilliantly and took 44 catches, while an individual highlight was the hat trick by Barber against Glamorgan at Edgbaston.

Successive finishes in the table of third and fourth encouraged the Committee to forecast even better things in 1964, when the hoped for return to full fitness of Bannister and Brown, together with progress from Amiss and Jameson, would mount a genuine title challenge.

The Edgbaston Test match against the West Indies extended England's successful record on the ground. Seven for 24 by Trueman, including the last six wickets in 24 balls for four runs, bowled out the tourists for 91, victory coming by 217 runs. The gates were closed on the Saturday, with an estimated 25,000 spectators swelling the final attendance figure to 86,500, and receipts of £36,349 showed that, given attractive opposition, the Birmingham public would still turn up to watch.

The new Gillette Cup competition proved an outstanding success, with 25,000 at Lord's watching Sussex beat Worcestershire by 14 runs. The annual report made the prophetic point that, with Warwickshire receiving £773 after being eliminated in the first round, and the winners receiving £2,000, 'the competition could possibly prove a financial salvation for many clubs'.

Hitchcock's richly deserved benefit brought him £6,410 19s 7d, second by only £54 to the sum raised for Horner, and the committee decided that the 1964 beneficiary would be Bannister. The supporters' association went from strength to strength and in the year covered the full cost of the press box stand and the second phase of the west wing extension.

The Club suffered heavily with several deaths, including J. Ernest Hill, scorer George Austin, and Miss Mabel Ansell, the last survivor of the William Ansell family.

Hill died aged 96. He scored the first first-class hundred for the County in 1894 – 139 not out against Nottinghamshire at Trent Bridge. Austin, aged 73, had been a scorer at Edgbaston for 52 years, having been associated with the Club for seven years before that as a junior office boy. He became ill in the third match of the season at Edgbaston against Essex, and died a week later. A quiet, small man, he possessed a wonderfully dry sense of humour, and was unfailingly kind to younger players. It is doubtful whether anyone associated with Edgbaston inspired so much affection as 'Chico', about whom no unkind word was ever said. Fittingly, he remains the only 'outsider' to be invited by the old players' association to attend their annual functions.

The optimistic forecasts for the 1964 season were justified, with Smith's side runners-up both in the County Championship and the Gillette Cup and, for good measure, they beat the Australians for the first time in the Club's history. They won half of their 28 Championship games, including an astonishing win at Worthing. Despite Sussex seamer Ian Thomson taking ten for 49 in the first innings and 15 for 75 in the match, the home side was bowled out in their second innings for 23 to lose a match by 182 runs, in which neither side scored 200 in either innings.

The pitch disintegrated and, following the umpires' report, county cricket was taken away from the ground. Bannister (6–2–16–6) had Lenham lbw with a shooter the next ball after the batsman had been struck in the chest by a full length delivery which pitched in the same area. A rueful Lenham whispered to Bannister, as he walked off: 'I don't reckon I was out because the ball would probably have gone under the stumps.' When the score was 23 for eight after 12 overs, Cartwright talked himself on instead of Brown (6–4–7–2) and took a few seconds to prove his point with an analysis of 0.2–0–0–2.

Cartwright dominated the bowling throughout the exciting season, taking 128 wickets including match figures of 50–20–84–10 in Bannister's benefit match against Worcestershire, and secured five or more wickets in an innings on seven other occasions. His wickets cost

13.78 each, and his successful advance to the top bracket earned him the first two of his five England caps. He was chosen to tour South Africa under his county captain, and they were joined by Brown, whose 81 wickets at 19.35 earned him the trip, and Barber.

Webster could not repeat his previous season's prodigious success, but his 44 wickets, together with 55 from Bannister at under 20 each, ensured that the usually strong seam unit was up to standard. Barber chipped in with a valuable 47 wickets from only 389 overs, and his newly adopted attacking style brought him 1,455 runs at 32.33.

Smith was the heaviest scorer with 1,629, and although good support came from Ibadulla (1,547), Horner (1,079) and, most pleasing of all, Jameson, whose 1,068 at 32.35 included 165 against Oxford University, the team often displayed a fatal inconsistency which was the difference between them and Champions, Worcestershire.

Stewart continued his come-back with 916 runs from 28 completed innings, and passed 10,000 runs in his career.

Spinners Miller and Bridge were disappointing, with the latter now but a shadow of the off-spinner who was so successful three years earlier.

The Gillette Final at Lord's was embarrassingly one-sided, with Sussex taking full revenge for the earlier debacle at Worthing. In conditions which were unusually hazy – Warwickshire supporters travelling down the M1 that morning were delayed by heavy mist – Thomson wrecked the early batting with four wickets for 17 in his first eight overs, and the match was virtually won and lost in that vital hour.

The match which took Smith and his team to Lord's was marked by controversy at Old Trafford, in which the Lancashire players refused to attend the Man of the Match ceremony, and the Warwickshire team decided to have their victory drink on the journey back to Birmingham. A huge crowd of over 20,000 took exception to Smith's tactics when, after Warwickshire had scored 294 for seven, the Lancashire openers had rattled up 70 from nine overs before tea. On the resumption, Smith deployed eight of his nine fielders on the boundary edge, with an indignant David Green answering Bannister's point that there were plenty of ones and twos available thus: 'one day cricket is about hitting boundaries, not running up and down the pitch'. Limited-overs cricket was indeed still in its infancy.

The Lancashire wicket-keeper, Clayton, decided to protest by scoring 17 runs in as many overs, not, it was later said, without the knowledge of his captain, Ken Grieves. The crowd turned ugly, and the match finished in an unpleasant atmosphere with Lancashire on 209 for seven.

Earlier, Bannister had been fielding on the boundary in front of half-a-dozen Manchester United players, and he asked them how they managed to concentrate when the crowd made such a lot of noise. The reply was: 'It's easier for us, because if they barrack us, we only get it in the neck for 45 minutes at a time. You've got another two hours to go yet.'

The changing times brought a change of attitude by the Australian tourists in a match at Edgbaston, which they lost by nine runs after three declarations. On the first day, Barber hit the first hundred of his final brilliant 138 before lunch, and batted only 135 minutes in all. With over three hours lost to rain on the second day, only a contrived result was possible, and after being left to score 195 at 76 an hour, the Australians batted adventurously to be bowled out for 185 in the final over of the match, with the injured Grout not bothering to bat. Shades of Hassett's side 11 years earlier!

Bannister's benefit produced a record £8,846 8s 7d, thanks to his good fortune in choosing as his benefit game the fixture against Worcestershire. With both sides then running neck and neck at the top of the table, receipts were £2,956 1s 0d, with over £500 being taken on the third day.

The supporters' association produced a surplus of £167,891, thanks to a membership of their football pool which was three times that of the combined total of all other supporters' associations. Their altruistic approach to cricket was characterised by an interest-free loan of £20,000 to enable the Essex club to buy the Chelmsford ground, and thus establish a long overdue headquarters.

The Club advertised a £500 'reward' for any submitted plan for a new pitch-covering system which was successfully constructed and used. Although the idea of a big cover was subsequently shelved for 17 years, the criteria laid down in the annual report was almost Wellsian in its glimpse into the future:

1. The ideal aim is to cover an area of some 60 yards by 40 yards
2. The unit employed should be easy and quick to put on to the ground and remove from it, and this suggests it should be mechanically operated
3. It should be strong and durable in use in construction, and yet be capable of folding or contracting to small dimensions when out of use
4. It should be light in weight so that it would not mark the turf as it passed over when the ground was wet or soft
5. It should not lie flat on the turf as this might have damaging effects on grass growth
6. The scheme should include a ready means of disposing quickly of water

Brumbrella was clearly in somebody's mind's eye, however futuristic the idea seemed then.

Although Horner was to play three innings in 1965, Hitchcock and he effectively retired at the end of the season. Their distinguished careers almost ran parallel, with the New Zealander joining the Club in 1949, and the Yorkshireman signing two years later. In neither case did a final career average of under 30 do justice to the big part they played in Warwickshire cricket, once they established themselves in the First XI.

Both men were naturally free-scoring batsmen, who were always prepared to sacrifice their wicket for the benefit of the side, in addition to which they were both fine fielders. Horner, in particular, soon won a reputation as one of the finest fielders in the covers in post-war cricket. Hitchcock possessed a good arm, and his occasional leg-breaks broke many a stubborn partnership. Even more important than runs and wickets, was their unfailing cheerful approach to a professional game that can be cruel in its demands. They treated the twin impostors of Kipling alike, and both men were of the stuff that trustworthy cricketers are made.

Horner scored 18,217 runs from 647 innings at an average of 29.66, and he scored 25 hundreds.

Hitchcock scored 12,269 runs from 511 innings at an average of 27.82, and he scored 13 hundreds. He also took 182 wickets at 28.56.

The Warwickshire dressing room might have been a quieter place without them, but it could not have been a happier one.

CHAPTER NINETEEN

FROM ONE SMITH TO ANOTHER

THE REMAINDER OF THE 1960s brought a change of Club Captain which was eventually to lead to the Club's third Championship title. Mike Smith decided to retire at the end of the 1967 season, after an 11–year period as captain which was as happy as any in the Club's history. His final three seasons followed three successful years, but the 1965 season produced a slump to 11th place in the Championship and only five games were won. The weather was dismal, particularly during June and July, when no fewer than nine out of 12 matches were abandoned as draws because of rain on the final day. Smith and Barber missed 12 matches because of Test match calls, and with Brown and Cartwright also playing for England, plus the decisions of Hitchcock and Horner to retire, it was small wonder that the side was usually short of runs.

Stewart hit the only Championship hundred of the season – 102 against Surrey at the Oval in the second match of the season – and topped the averages with 1,187 runs at 38.29. Smith and Jameson were the only other batsmen who averaged over 30, with the captain failing to score a hundred for the first time, and he did not complete his 1,000 runs until the last match. Amiss, now in his sixth season with the Club, but still only 22, responded to the enforced promotion in the batting order with 1,433 runs, and the only other encouraging performance came from Jameson who scored 1,428, including hundreds against New Zealand and Oxford University.

A. C. Smith accepted his responsibilities as captain in the absence of M. J. K. with 924 runs, and took off his pads to open the bowling so successfully at Clacton against Essex, that he took a hat-trick of great merit, with Barker, Smith and Fletcher being the first three wickets to fall in a match which Essex managed to save with their last pair at the wicket in a tense finish.

Cartwright was now at the height of his bowling powers, and his 100 wickets for the Club from only 684.4 overs at the astonishingly low cost of 13.85 earned him two England caps against New Zealand and South Africa. In the latter game, he alone withstood a magnificent hundred from Graeme Pollock at Trent Bridge, where he returned his best Test match figures of six for 94, albeit at the cost of a broken thumb in stopping a return drive from the powerful left-hander. He had match figures of 30.4–19–48–10 in a game against Essex at Coventry which was spoiled by rain with Warwickshire well on top, and 36–9–100–12 in the home win against Middlesex. He took five or more wickets in an innings on six other occasions, and spearheaded a strong seam attack in which Bannister took 77 wickets at 18.83 and Brown 61 at 25.91. Nobody else took 50 wickets, with Edmonds and the still disappointing Miller the best of the other bowlers.

Another unusual hat-trick came from Jameson to wind up the Gloucestershire innings at Edgbaston, in a spell of 26 deliveries in which he took four wickets for three runs.

The Club progressed to the semi-final in the Gillette Cup competition, only to throw away the game to Yorkshire at Edgbaston when, after limiting the visitors to 177, they committed suicide with five batsmen run out, and lost by 20 runs a match they should have won.

The Edgbaston pitch came under fire for its lack of pace from many eminent cricketers, including Brian Statham and New Zealand captain, John Reid. Flack had already relaid one pitch, and although it could be tried only in practice, he was instructed to relay one third of the main square, which was excavated to a depth of two feet.

Bannister took his 1,000th first class wicket against New Zealand and his 1,000th for Warwickshire a month later at Leicester. When he dismissed Graham Dowling, he was congratulated by his team mates to the puzzlement of non-striker Trevor Jarvis, who asked the umpire: 'that's a lot of fuss over one wicket. Is it his first?'

The Edgbaston Test match against New Zealand was a disaster, relieved only by the England victory by nine wickets. The enjoyment of the 21,000 people who attended the match was hardly helped by an innings by Barrington of 137 in $7\frac{1}{4}$ hours, for which he was promptly dropped as a disciplinary measure. How times have changed. Nowadays, such an innings would guarantee selection for the series.

Warwickshire's income dropped by £10,784, and with the magnificent William Ansell Stand now completed and opened, it was little wonder that the deficit for the year was £13,781.

In addition to the appointment of the Club president, Lt-General Sir Oliver Leese, as president of the MCC, the Club's links with Lord's were further strengthened by the appointments to various committees of Edmund King, Cyril Goodway and Alec Hastilow.

A disappointing season ended on a high note, with Brown and Barber selected to tour Australia with England under the captaincy of Smith. This was their second successive major tour, and brought to 16 the number of Warwickshire players who, since Quaife went to Australia in 1901–1902, had been selected for 24 different MCC tours. These included eight tours of Australia, five of West Indies, four of South Africa, three of India, two of East Africa, and two of New Zealand. Smith could not regain the Ashes, but his side drew the series in which Barber's 185 at Sydney ranks among the most memorable innings ever played in the history of the Ashes.

In 1966 Warwickshire won the Gillette Cup under captain Mike Smith. The team is shown here with the trophy, having just defeated Worcestershire at Lord's. Abberley, Edmonds, Ibadulla, Cartwright, Amiss, Jameson, Alan Smith, Webster, Brown, Mike Smith, Bannister and Barber.

Back home, a much better season ended with Warwickshire winning the Gillette Cup for the first time, and winning eight games in the County Championship to move up to sixth place in the table. Smith was cruelly deposed as England captain after the first defeat by the West Indies at Old Trafford, and so was able to play much more county cricket than the previous year. His 1,663 runs included three hundreds, and as his average of 43.76 shows, he restored much needed stability to the upper order. Amiss progressed so well (1,632 runs at 37.09) that, despite not having scored a Championship hundred in 162 innings, he was chosen for the final Test match at the Oval following an unbeaten 160 against the West Indies a week earlier at Edgbaston. His seasonal boundary count of 164 fours and 13 sixes showed that his orthodox technique, developed under the still watchful eye of 'Tiger' Smith, was now reinforced with controlled power, and although a career record at the end of the season of 4,277 runs at 28.32 was not a startling one, the prevailing county system allowed him to develop at a pace which was to stand him in such good stead for another 21 years.

Stewart headed the averages, but could play only 14 innings because of a pre-season operation on the knuckle joint of the right index finger.

His experience was missed, particularly as Barber decided that, because of a wish to devote more time to his family business, he would limit his appearances to 11 matches, including the fixture with Cambridge University at Fenners.

Understandably anxious though Warwickshire were to take advantage of Barber's talents whenever they were available, the situation was clearly unsatisfactory on several counts. Even if the Club could justify a player picking his matches before the start of a season, Barber's form was likely to suffer because of playing on an intermittent basis, and of course problems would arise in the dressing room with someone having to step down on a pre-determined basis. Significantly, although he had scored four hundreds in his first 125 innings for the Club, he was to score only one more in 89 remaining innings. A breakdown of his overall performances for Warwickshire in his nine-year period at Edgbaston reveals a marked decline with the bat and a much reduced output with the ball after he went part-time:

Full-time, 1962–65: *Batting*: 125 innings; 3,613 runs; average 31.14; four 100s

Bowling: 1,152.3 overs; 3,240 runs; 136 wickets; average 23.82

Part-time, 1966–69: *Batting*: 89 innings; 2,365 runs; average 26.57; one 100

Bowling: 516.3 overs; 1,614 runs; 61 wickets; average 26.45

The Club could justifiably claim that the presence of such a talented all-rounder frequently unsettled opposing sides, and of course he played his part in the two Gillette Cup successes in 1966 and 1968.

Abberley scored 1,281, including an unbeaten 117 at Edgbaston against Essex, but his most valuable innings came at Hull where, in a low-scoring match in which neither side reached 200 in either innings on a difficult, slow pitch, Warwickshire needed 106 to win. Deep in trouble at 17 for three, Abberley played the best fighting innings of his career to score an unbeaten 54 in 150 minutes, and take his side to victory by three wickets.

For the second successive season, Cartwright took exactly 100 wickets with the last 13 coming in the final match at Edgbaston against Northamptonshire. Less responsive pitches meant that he needed 842.5 overs compared with 684.4 the previous year. The main support came from Brown and Webster who took 73 and 70 wickets respectively, with the 36-year-old Bannister managing 43.

Former Oxford Blue J. M. Allan had been engaged to bolster a woefully weak spin department, but 37 wickets at 28.75 did not redress an imbalanced attack. Miller took 40 wickets, of which only 25 were in the Championship. He decided to leave the first-class game at the early age of 25.

An experiment with a limitation of 65 overs to the first innings of Championship matches was unpopular with the players, particularly the middle-order batsmen, whose opportunities were severely restricted.

Another experimental rule forbidding the polishing of the ball simply forced swing bowlers to pitch a shorter length, and long debates concerning Sunday cricket ended in a Club referendum producing an overwhelming majority of 2,420 in favour, 668 against, and 460 in favour with reservations.

The Warwickshire committee decided against Sunday cricket until better methods had been worked out for taking gate monies and remaining inside the complex law on the subject.

The financial report was again gloomy, with a deficit of £19,786 5s 10d which, following the substantial losses of the two previous years, led to a long overdue increase in membership subscriptions from £3 3s 0d to £5 0s 0d. The committee also recorded its full support for the Clark Committee Report which called for a reduction in the amount of cricket played, and would thus greatly reduce a players' wage bill which now stood at £26,697 16s 7d out of a total expenditure of £85,990 15s 6d. This compared with a figure of £13,964 15s 5d out of £55,173 3s 5d in 1960, and £9,352 0s 0d out of £35,380 3s 10d in 1952. Namely players' wages now accounted for 31 per cent of income compared with 25 per cent in previous years.

A further sombre note on which to end the year was the statistic that the overall Championship attendance figure in the country had sunk to 513,578, and every county match at Edgbaston produced receipts of under £500 – the figure taken on the third day of the match against Worcestershire two years earlier.

The winds of the year were indeed chilly – so much so that Smith's final year as captain was one in which the game's authorities finally acknowledged that first-class cricket could no longer survive in the form which had seen it safely, if at times precariously, through the first two-thirds of the 20th century. More one day cricket was necessary, but an even bigger departure from tradition brought the corporate decision by the counties to persuade MCC to devolve the authority of administering first-class cricket in England to the newly formed Test and County Cricket Board. Within five more years, the three-day Championship was reduced, to accommodate two more one-day competitions and the first-class game was never to be the same again.

Although Smith's appetite for the game had been dulled sufficiently for him to announce his retirement at the age of 34, he still scored 1,656 attractive runs in 1967 and finished this part of his career – he was to return for three seasons in 1970 – in second place in the Club averages (41.40), behind Amiss, whose advance with 1,693 runs at 62.70 put him second in the national averages behind Barrington.

The wettest May on record meant that four of the first seven Championship matches were abandoned, two with only one side batting, and the other three games were drawn.

The side was handicapped by a spin department that was almost non-existent, and only a staggering season by Cartwright enabled the side to win five matches and thus finish tenth in the Championship table, 68 points adrift of Yorkshire, whose success was tarnished by a deplorable display of time-wasting in the middle of August at Edgbaston. Its basis was in the oft-flawed and much-changed points system, which now afforded eight points for a win, four for first-innings lead and two for a draw, a dreadful imbalance giving little incentive to press for victory.

The match went badly for Brian Close who, on hearing an abusive remark addressed to him as he left the field at lunch on the first day, tackled the wrong man in a manner which provided grist for the mill of a Sunday newspaper ten days later. The incident was irrelevant to those towards the end of the match, but the authorities predictably took the view that any man who could react in such prickly fashion to one of a sparse Edgbaston crowd, might not be the ideal captain of England in the West Indies, where the volatile crowds are always a problem.

Yorkshire were bowled out for 145 after tea, leaving Warwickshire 102 minutes to score 142 for victory. The current mandatory requirement to bowl 20 overs commencing one hour before the scheduled close was not then in existence. The incidents of the final minutes of the match forced the authorities to recognise the need to prevent any repetition of tactics which, however Close defended them, were not only outside the spirit of the Laws, but the letter as well.

Amiss and Jameson went for the runs, but even though 100 came in 82 minutes, the odds were still against Warwickshire, although with 20 minutes remaining, they could justifiably expect five, and possibly six, more overs. Instead, only two overs were bowled in the last 22 minutes, which included a brief stoppage for rain. So brief that before all the players had left the field, Umpire Elliott had turned them round because the rain had stopped. Close and Trueman, however, had reached the pavilion, and play did not restart for 11 minutes, with only a further 11 minutes remaining. Despite enjoinders by Elliott to Close, only two overs were bowled in that time, with one from Trueman containing two no-balls, three bouncers and a wicket, taking six minutes. Trueman later claimed that Yorkshire were unfairly treated, because one of the deliberate no-balls he bowled to prevent another over, was not called!

Warwickshire finished on 133 for five and an incensed crowd made so much noise that one of Close's defences was that he had to walk nearer to players to make orders heard. He also claimed that the wet ball had to be wiped, which accounted for his side bowling only 24 overs.

The recriminations were many, but an objective comment, penned by the respected cricket correspondent of *The Yorkshire Post*, J. M. Kilburn, was scathing about the Yorkshire players:

> Yorkshire players made no effort to hide their delaying tactics. They walked slowly to bowling marks, to positions in the field and between overs. They were provocatively tardy in retrieving the ball from the boundary and returning it to play. Spectators grew increasingly discontented and abusive and the whole atmosphere of the game degenerated to disillusion with the basic principles of sport.

Cartwright took seven for 62 in the match, a relative failure in a season in which he took five wickets in an innings or more on 13 occasions, including four matches in which he took ten or more wickets. His 15 wickets for 89 against Glamorgan at Swansea equalled the performance of Hargreave at the Oval in 1903, and his 147 wickets at 15.52 from 1,194 overs took his tally for the Club to 783 in the eight seasons of the 1960s. His skills were helped by several unsatisfactory pitches at Edgbaston, notably in the match against Derbyshire, where Warwickshire's match aggregate of 186 was good enough to win a game by 59 runs. Ibadulla and David Cook were top scorers with 22 and 20. Bannister took ten for 83 and Cartwright eight for 18 with Jackson's eleven for 69 and seven for 37 by Rhodes of no avail.

Another home victory over Hampshire by ten wickets was helped by Cartwright's first-innings analysis of 9.4–7–6–5, and with the Lord's pitch inspector, Bert Lock, called in after the Test match against India, as well as after both Warwickshire's wins over Gloucestershire and Nottinghamshire at Coventry, it was not a happy season for the chairman of the ground sub-committee, Cyril Goodway. He admitted 'a slight error of judgement' in using part of the re-laid area too early, but defended the Test strip by saying that the criticism 'was without reasonable foundation', and with the match producing 860 runs, the spectators were given 'infinite pleasure and saw an excellent contest'. India were bowled out for 277 to lose by 132. Jameson, Abberley and Ibadulla all reached 1,000 runs for the season although all three averaged less than 30.

Bannister took advantage of the sub-standard home pitches to take 75 wickets at 20.86, and Brown took 74 at 20.31, but the season belonged to Cartwright who, in the last three games, took eleven for 93 in the drawn game with Somerset, ten for 163 in the defeat at Dover by Kent, and six for 95 in the first innings of the defeat by Yorkshire at Middlesbrough.

Stewart scored only 492 from 17 completed innings in his benefit year, but he reaped a deserved harvest for the enormous enjoyment he gave spectators around the beginning of the 1960s, with final recepts of £8,346 4s 2d.

Alan Smith was appointed as M.J.K.'s successor, and an exciting addition to the staff in 1968 was announced – the West Indies' off-spinner, Lance Gibbs.

At the break in M. J. K. Smith's career, he had scored 19,748 of his 31,580 first-class runs for Warwickshire, and in that time had captained England in 25 of his 47 Test matches. He scored a hundred against each of the other 16 counties, only four of which he had not scored at least 1,000 runs against. As a captain, he had the knack of getting the best out of players without making a fuss, and easily sustained the tricky balance between being 'one of the boys' and maintaining the unswerving respect of his players. The appearance he gave of vagueness was sometimes, but not always, misleading, and he was one of the few post-war captains, both in County cricket and at international level, who finished as he began – without an enemy in the world.

Following the formation of the Test and County Cricket Board, the players formed the Cricketers' Association during the winter, with Bannister becoming the first paid secretary in 1970, following two years as chairman.

The following season, 1968, was one of transition, in which the new Club captain welcomed two overseas Test players, Kanhai and Gibbs, who were to play such an important part in Warwickshire cricket in the following ten years. Kanhai ended the season at the head of the averages, with six hundreds among his 1,819 runs at 46.64. Thus, Mike Smith's stability and flair was replaced, although Gibbs showed, with only 72 wickets at 25.11, that he needed time to adjust to the everyday demands of county cricket.

Starting the season somewhat anxiously, Kanhai's top score in the Championship was 48 before the match at Trent Bridge which transformed his season. Another failure in Warwickshire's first innings of 93 was then followed by a piece of history.

He came in to bat before lunch on the second day and was dropped before he had scored off West Indian left-arm seamer, Carlton Forbes by, of all people, Kanhai's Test captain Garfield Sobers, with the scoreboard showing six runs for three wickets. Ibadulla was his partner, and they were still there at lunch on the final day. They added 402 thrilling runs, with Ibadulla scoring an unbeaten 147. When Kanhai was finally out for 253, he returned to the dressing room to take the wind out of the sails of his appreciative colleagues with a complaining remark which underlined to them just how limitless were his horizons: 'that's the third time I've got out in the 250s'. What a bogey score!

His rare skill, although well supported by over 1,000 runs from Stewart, Amiss and Jameson, could not prevent the side slipping one place in the table to 11th with seven wins in a season which saw the 23rd different points scoring system in under 40 years.

This time, there were more bowling points to be won than for batting, and the immediate result was that most clubs decided to take advantage of the loose regulation which allowed a club to decide whether or not to cover its pitches. For once, the Champions, Yorkshire, whose 31st title it was, did not win most matches. Their 11 victories was one fewer than second placed Kent, but their 19 extra bowling points – 114 compared with 95 – tipped the balance, with a final victory margin of 14 points.

They beat Warwickshire at Middlesbrough by an innings and 42 runs, after a masterly unbeaten 180 by Boycott was more than the visitors aggregated in either of their innings of 129 and 137. Off-spinner Ray Illingworth's match figures of ten for 71 underlined the lack of penetration in the Warwickshire spin department, which the arrival of Gibbs had not yet redressed. Used to bowling on firmer and drier Test pitches, the Guyanan displayed a reluctance to bowl from round the wicket which was to limit his success for another three years, and the side had to soldier on for yet another year with a seam-orientated attack.

At Hove, Barber hit 125 of his final total of 432 runs from 21 innings, and with his bowling, and the batting of Cartwright now contributing little, the absence of an all-rounder meant that Alan Smith had a difficult task in trying to help select a balanced team.

He had a good first year in charge, culminating in a splendid Gillette Final win over old rivals Sussex who, at one stage near the end, looked to have the game won. His unbeaten 39 out of a seventh wicket stand of 60 with Amiss deservedly won him the Man of the Match Award after he had gone in with the score at 155 for six.

The injuries to Bannister and Cartwright, which prevented their appearance in the final at Lord's, meant reduced success for the two seamers who had shouldered so much work in the 1960s, but Blenkiron took his chances with 51 wickets at 25 each.

Cartwright suffered from knee and shoulder injuries, but although

Gillette Cup Final at Lord's on 7 September 1968. Alan Smith with the Gillette Trophy, after the presentation. In the background is Bob Barber.

he could bowl only 607.4 overs from which he took 71 wickets at 16.12, he still became the first Warwickshire player to score 10,000 runs and take 1,000 wickets in first-class cricket, although 50 of those wickets were not taken for the Club.

His benefit realised a record £9,592 17s 4d, and it is a tribute to both bowlers to say that he dominated the Warwickshire bowling in the 1960s in the same way as Hollies had done in the late 1940s and 1950s.

On the Test scene, Amiss, Barber and Brown were called up for various Tests, with Barber's selection for the last of his 28 England appearances illustrating perfectly the fault in the policy which had allowed him to play intermittently for Warwickshire since 1966. His list of matches, agreed before the start of the season, did not include the fixtures in June at the Oval or against Gloucestershire at Coventry ten days later. A spate of injuries and Test calls meant that Alan Smith was given such a weak side at the Oval he asked Barber if he would help out.

The all-rounder felt he could not vary his schedule, but all ended well when a side short of Amiss, Cartwright and Brown still managed to win by eight wickets, thanks to Bannister taking eight for 82 in the match and Smith taking the pads off to take three for 52 in the second innings.

Barber, who had played in 'Kanhai's Match' at Trent Bridge, was not scheduled to reappear for three weeks, but a call from the England selectors asking him if he could play before they chose the side for the Lord's Test changed his mind. Now a problem arose, with someone having to step down to make way, and the victim was the unfortunate Abberley, who had scored 38 against Yorkshire and 44 against the Australians the previous match. To complete the chain of bizarre events, the chairman of the England selectors, Alec Bedser, travelled to Coventry to watch Barber fail twice in a match where they were bowled out for 150 and 75 to lose by 112. But he still chose the left-hander for one more Test, before deciding that even the prodigious talents of 33-year-old Barber could not be persevered with on a part-time basis.

The Edgbaston test was Cowdrey's 100th, which he marked with 104 in a drawn game in which the first day was washed out. The total attendance, including members, on the other four days was a healthy 56,069, and the recepts of £35,393 were £10,000 more than the returns of Old Trafford.

The financial pattern of the previous years continued, with a loss of £9,161, but the committee felt that with a proposed reduction in three-day cricket in 1969 to 24 Championship matches to accommodate the new Sunday League, and the benefits from the investments of monies from the supporters' association, the trend could be halted with prudent house-keeping.

The last season of the decade provided the side with mixed success. They rose to fourth place in the newly reduced County Championship, with their seven wins from 24 matches bringing them to 55 points, behind surprise winners Glamorgan. They shared several close finishes, including one against Somerset, who had one wicket to fall and were still 74 runs behind; one against Lancashire when, with three wickets in hand, Warwickshire were two runs short of victory; and one at Edgbaston against Nottinghamshire when the scores were level with the last Warwickshire pair at the wicket.

In the John Player League, six wins from 16 matches secured ninth place, with Lancashire pipping Hampshire by one point for the first title. Essex beat Warwickshire by seven wickets in their only Gillette Cup match.

The name of Cartwright was to dominate the year. With Alan Smith now an England selector, he took over the captaincy after early opportunities afforded Amiss did not prove successful, and handled the team with predictable shrewdness. Brian Timms from Hampshire was taken on and deputised admirably for Smith behind the wicket with 26 victims in seven matches, with McDowall batting and keeping well in the other games.

Back to tolerable fitness, Cartwright bowled 880.5 overs and took 108 wickets at 16.18, and nursed the improving Blenkiron (79 at 21.85) and impressive newcomer from Lincolnshire, Norman McVicker (74 at 20.05) through the arduous season in which the faster bowlers were forced to operate within the constraints of an artifically shortened run-up in Sunday games.

It has never been fully appreciated that the determination of the authorities and television to compress the 40-over format into a rigid period placed an increasing physical strain on bowlers whose natural actions have evolved from a different length approach to the wicket. For instance, the Sussex and England fast bowler, John Snow, was at such a loss that he did not take a single wicket in the first season of the John Player League.

Brown completed a strong seam atack with 51 wickets at 22.58, but with Gibbs absent for half the season on tour with the West Indies, the spin department again made no significant contribution.

Kanhai once more topped the batting averages with 1,044 runs at 41.76, after missing the first month with knee trouble, and Amiss was second with 1,503 runs at 31.97. Both batsmen scored one Championship hundred, with Kanhai's 173 out of 323 on a lively pitch at Peterborough against Northamptonshire, another of the many remarkable displays he was to produce for Warwickshire.

A wet May saw four out of the first five Championship matches abandoned, with the other match at Bradford producing a thrilling win by five runs in a low-scoring match in which Boycott was the only batsman to reach fifty. Even he could not prevent Cartwright bowling Warwickshire to victory, taking seven for 34 to bowl out Yorkshire for 115 and return splendid match figures of 39.4–21–55–12. He took five wickets or more in an innings on six other occasions, as if to underline that he was still an indispensable member of the team. Events were to prove otherwise for, at the end of the year, he was to be one of three stalwarts who had played their last game for Warwickshire.

Bannister and Stewart were also to depart the Edgbaston scene they had been a part of for nearly 20 years – the last two decades of county cricket to be played in the time honoured format before one-day cricket was introduced in such quantities. Cartwright was, after much controversy, to continue his career with Somerset and Glamorgan, and while Stewart played a few games for Northamptonshire, Bannister, who played only two Sunday League matches in his final year, made a break so final that he never played in another serious game of cricket.

Ibadulla's long career, starting, after a three-year qualification period, in 1954 was rewarded with a benefit figure of £7,797 12s 11d.

Cartwright's final match for the Club, although it was not known to be that at the time, was against New Zealand, and he signed off with match figures of eight for 96. On 15 October it was reported that he had decided to give up playing first-class cricket because, at 34, he was now injury prone and wanted to spend more time with his family. This was amended three weeks later, when he was quoted as saying that he would be happy to continue playing county cricket for Warwickshire if they could offer him the job he was looking for. He wanted a job which would lead to a coaching appointment at a public school, and although chairman Edmund King suggested that he might apply for the position of Club coach in succession to Dollery, the player said that he 'would not be so presumptuous'.

A curious remark if correctly reported, but it seemed that the differences between him and the Club were not only difficult to pinpoint, they were even more difficult to reconcile. He was given permission to negotiate with other counties, although this would not preclude Warwickshire trying to block his special registration some months later. Finally, the offer of the post of senior coach at Millfield swayed him towards Somerset, and the matter was finally resolved in a registration sub-committee meeting in April 1970 which made history.

Prior to Cartwright, any cricketer whose services were still wanted by his club had to miss at least one year, and sometimes two, in county cricket, before he could play for another county. Tom Graveney, Peter Richardson, Mike Smith and Barry Knight are just four examples who paid such a high price for changing their employers. Such a draconian and antedeluvian restriction was clearly unenforceable in law, and it is not coincidental that, since the formation of the Cricketers' Association, there has not been an instance of a cricketer who changed clubs missing an entire season. The nearest was Imran Khan who, when he moved from Worcestershire to Sussex in 1977, was not allowed to play until 1 August.

But the climate was changing, with the Test and County Cricket Board and the Cricketers' Association having come into being in the same year – 1967, agreeing a more sensible approach. The Association's chairman, Jack Bannister, was able to persuade the authorities that an instant move was equable if a player had good reason to move, and he allayed their fears that such a move would lead to a soccer-type transfer system.

Bannister by then had left Edgbaston, after a final season in which he travelled with the team as official Club vice-captain. He completed 20 years with Warwickshire, and the committee officially thanked him 'for his very great efforts for the Club over the years. His record on the field is a most impressive one, and his standing off is extremely high.'

His 1,181 wickets remains the third highest total ever taken for the Club, with over half coming after a back injury he sustained in 1957 caused him to develop a more 'open' action which, although it reduced his penetration, allowed him to go on to bowl more overs (11,296) than any opening bowler in Warwickshire history. He openly confesses that he only realised just what an art seam bowling could be when he was 30:

> Tom Cartwright provided me with a fascinating insight into just what could be achieved with a good hand action. I saw him take 1,000 wickets in the 1960s with an old ball, just because he perfected every refinement available to a seam bowler. In the end he could bowl both inswinger and outswinger with the same body action, simply because he had worked out how to retain control of the hand action, irrespective of where his feet were. Hollies was the greatest slow bowler I ever saw. Cartwright was the best seamer.

Cartwright finished with 1,058 wickets for the Club at 18.75, including 100 wickets in a season seven times, and he scored 10,781 runs at 22.09 including five hundreds.

An all-too-familiar financial loss was announced at the end of the 1969 season – this time of £8,740 – and the membership was told that, although the new Sunday League half-day matches produced £3,267 from six home matches, the revenue from 17 three-day games, including matches against both touring sides, the West Indies and New Zealand, had shrunk to a derisive £1,842. Now that the total expenditure had reached £106,705, it was vital to maximise alternative sources of income, particularly as membership subscriptions had dropped by £3,785 to £33,891.

The Warwickshire supporters' association reported a slight drop in income and profit, although these early warning signs of a problem which was to become acute in the late 1980s were regarded as only a temporary set-back.

At the annual meeting, the members were given the enticing prospect of the return to the first-class arena of M. J. K. Smith, with the former captain happy, at the age of 37, to play purely as a batsman under the captaincy of Alan Smith.

CHAPTER TWENTY

CHAMPIONS A THIRD TIME

THE 1970S BEGAN WITH SWEEPING CHANGES in the Edgbaston cricket personnel. Cartwright, Stewart and Bannister had left the playing staff, Barber did not play in a single game, and with Dollery and Hitchcock retiring as senior coach and 2nd XI captain respectively, the old order of the 1950s and 1960s had gone.

The decision of Dollery was unsurprising, as he had disagreed the previous year with the decision taken on financial grounds, to reduce the staff and withdraw from the Minor Counties. What was unfortunate from every point of view was that the decision to appoint Alan Oakman as senior coach was one of the major causes in Dollery and Hollies cutting all links with the Club for most of the 1970s. Hollies believed that he had been let down, following assurances given him regarding a paid position on the coaching staff. Whether or not either former player did have a genuine grievance, it is sad that they were allowed to drift away from the Club and ground which had been so much a part of their lives for nearly 40 years. Surely two of the greatest names in Warwickshire's history should have been dealt with in a more sympathetic and thoughtful matter. Both men were to return to the fold before the end of the decade, but the gap in their attendance at Edgbaston reflected badly on the Club.

The committee and the supporters' association felt obliged to redefine their working arrangements, following differing views on priorities, and a special liaison committee was established to prevent the crossing of any wires in the future.

The cancellation of the South African tour of England contributed towards the heaviest loss in the Club's history – £28,253. The annual report called 1970 'the most unfortunate year in the game's long history'. In a comparison with the bodyline controversy of the early 1930s, the point was made that then cricket's troubles came from within the game, whereas this time the enforced cancellation of the tour meant that cricket faced an entirely different problem. The substitute matches against a Rest of the World team provided some magnificent cricket, but the public, understandably, were not keen to support an 'abstract' series.

The Club drew little consolation from the fact that although a loss of £19,000 had been forecast, at least part of the additional £9,000 would be met by compensation from the Labour government, at whose firm request the tour was cancelled. The eventual compensation figure was £25,054 – well short of the £200,000 the TCCB asked for. The Test and County Cricket Board's net surplus from the substitute tour was £64,000 – approximately a third of the expected figure from the scheduled tour by South Africa, and the budgets of the counties were badly affected.

The team had a predictably lop-sided season, with Kanhai heading one of the strongest top orders in the Championship, but the bowling department, without Cartwright, and also Brown because of injury for the first five matches, was among the weakest in the country. The final position of eighth in the Championship table – 38 points behind Kent – would have been improved by at least three places had the side's total of 71 bowling points been better. Only Middlesex, with 69, secured fewer, and they finished 16th.

Kanhai was at his brilliant best, and despite missing ten matches because of playing for the Rest of the World, he scored, 1,529 for the Club from 23 completed innings, including six hundreds. His unbeaten 187 at Coventry against Derbyshire ranks among the best and most remarkable ever played in county cricket. He batted for 185 minutes, hitting seven sixes and 26 fours, but it was his total domination in the second half of Warwickshire's first innings which was extraordinary. From a score of 169 for six, the West Indian smashed 124 out of 126 in 96 minutes.

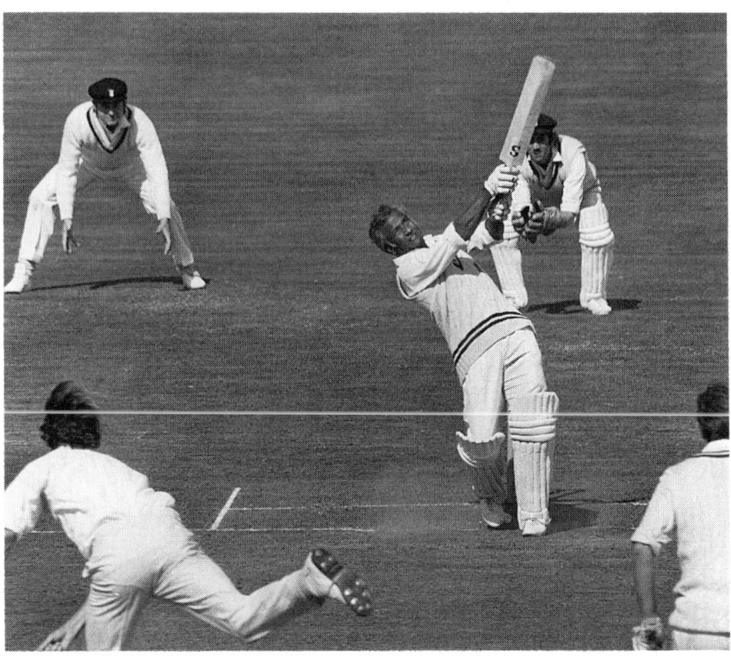

Rohan Kanhai hitting Derbyshire's Alan Ward for six in his remarkable unbeaten 187, including 124 out of the last 126 runs scored. Bob Taylor is the wicket-keeper.

Earlier in the season, no less a judge than Leslie Ames of Kent and England said that he had never seen a better innings than Kanhai's 107 on a pitch at Gravesend perfectly suited to the destructive talents of Derek Underwood. The left-arm bowler took 14 for 213, but Kanhai's mastery over him earned his side one of their seven wins – this one by 93 runs.

M. J. K. Smith made a triumphant return with 1,644 at 40.09, and with Amiss and Jameson also consistently heavy scorers with 1,476 at 44.72, and 1,821 at 40.09, runs were rarely in short supply.

A perfect example of why Kanhai deserves the over-used epithet 'great', is that in his 26 innings, having reached fifty on ten occasions, he converted six of these into hundreds. Smith increased only two of 12 fifties to three figures, Jameson four out of 13, Amiss one out of nine, and Abberley, whose 1,212 runs were scored at the disappointing average of 26.34, one out of seven.

Brown headed the bowling averages with 70 wickets, but their average cost of 24.18 contrasted sharply with the previous efforts of Cartwright. Blenkiron managed 76 wickets at 26.81, but the 806.5 overs he bowled revealed the same lack of penetration that marked the disappointing returns of Gibbs. The off-spinner bowled 698.3 overs, but took only 50 wickets at 32.00 each.

The one redeeming feature was the bowling of young leg-spinner Warwick Tidy, whose line and length was unusually accurate for a bowler of his type. His final figures of 535.2–120–1,494–48–31.13 suggested that, at long last, the Club had found a top-class spinner, but his flame was to flicker out within three years, when he left county cricket still with only 82 wickets to his credit.

Considering the lack of a spearhead bowler, the side did well to finish in the top half of the Championship, and even better to finish fourth in the John Player League after winning half their 16 matches, although they lost to Nottinghamshire in their first Gillette Cup match.

For once, a series of close finishes went Warwickshire's way, with two wins over Northamptonshire by two runs, and by four wickets with eleven balls to spare, a last-ball wicket to beat Lancashire by 31 after a daring declaration which left only 26 overs in which to take ten wickets, and the closest finish of all, when a bye off the last ball enabled Warwickshire to take half the win points with the scores level at the Oval.

Cranmer captained the 2nd XI at the age of 56, and led a side including the name of J. Whitehouse from Nuneaton, whose 617 runs from 17 innings was to provide a prelude to a fine debut season in county cricket in 1971.

In that season, Warwickshire put the problems of 1970 behind them so successfully that they finished with 255 points, the same number as the declared Champions, Surrey, who took the title because of their 11 wins, compared with nine by Alan Smith's side.

This was the first time that the title was not shared under those circumstances, but although Warwickshire felt frustrated because the positive approach instilled by their captain was denied a share of the major spoils at the last gasp, the Championship is nearly always taken by the side which is good enough to win more matches than anyone else.

The improvement came about because of Gibbs. Single-handed, he hauled the side to the top with 131 wickets at 18.99 each from 1.024.1 overs. That represented a staggering difference of striking rate compared with 1970 – best illustrated by the startling statistic that he took 81 more wickets from 325.4 more overs. He took five or more wickets in an innings on nine occassions, one more than the rest of the attack managed between them, and he spun the side to two convincing victories against Glamorgan and Essex with match figures of 41.4–14–75–10 and 42–15–84–10, respectively. He also took ten for 135 at Middlesbrough, where a second innings 110 from Boycott steered Yorkshire to a narrow win by three wickets.

Alan Smith was unstinting in his praise of Gibbs: 'His was the outstanding individual championship performance of all 17 counties in terms of value to the side and the winning of points.' Certainly the players thought so, with the West Indian winning the Reg Hayter Award for 'The Cricketers' Cricketer', an award which is voted for by all the county cricketers.

Smith added: 'Before the season began, he promised me a hundred wickets and paid with interest. Undoubtedly more relaxed than in previous seasons, he has come to terms with county cricket and has overcome several technical problems that have restricted him in previous years.' Given such an outstandingly successful spearhead, the remainder of the bowlers all chipped in so well that the 93 bowling points gained were three more than Somerset, eight more than Essex, and at least ten more than most other sides.

McVicker filled a big gap left by the injured Brown and an out-of-form Blenkiron – 56 wickets between them – with the former Lincolnshire bowler taking 74 wickets at 26.34. Tidy fell away, but Gibbs ensured that it did not matter by invariably capitalising on many good situations created by the repeated success of Smith (1,951 runs at 50.02), Kanhai (1,529 at 47.78), and Jameson, whose 1,765 at 41.04 included a career best 231 against India and brought him his first selection for England.

The revelation was Whitehouse, who made 173 on his first-class debut at the Parks against Oxford University, and finished a splendid

Lance Gibbs, now much happier to bowl from round the wicket. The umpire is Eddie Phillipson.

first season with 1,295 runs at 38.08, including a maiden Championship hundred at Trent Bridge. Aged 23, Whitehouse showed 'an uncomplicated and positive approach to batting, including a rare facility in being able to hit the ball off front and back foot'. So said the annual report, which contained happier news than for some while, with Mike Smith back to his very best.

But still the crowds would not come, although a telling statistic revealed that marginally more money – £3,518 compared with £3,297 – was taken from eight home Sunday games than from 36 days of Championship cricket. Not that either figure was other than derisory, with 15,116 people paying to watch Championship cricket, 13,743 on Sundays, and a miserable 13, 332 for the Test match against Pakistan.

The side finished bottom of the Sunday League with five wins, and were beaten by Kent at Canterbury on a difficult pitch in the semi-final of the Gillette Cup.

Barber made himself available on seven Sundays, but an aggregate of 100 runs at 14.28 showed that even players blessed with considerable talent cannot flit in and out of first-class cricket.

The declared loss rose to £29,097, with one of the biggest expenditure increases being the players' salaries – now £41,154. The Club reiterated its longstanding view that too much three-day cricket was still played, and the figures are difficult to refute, with the cost of running Championship cricket £13,000 (exclusive of salaries) for a return of £3,000, compared with one-day cricket which needed an outlay of £3,800 to bring a return of £3,500.

What might have been said was that the future of the England Test team, the success of which materially affects the counties' share-out from Lord's, is dependent upon a strong, thriving three-day competition, and the steady decline of England in Test cricket can be traced to three factors: the growth of one-day cricket; the regular flow of overseas players into county cricket; and the subsequent improvement of countries whose players were able to develop their skills in county cricket. However, the Test and County Cricket Board, which body the Clubs comprise, listened to their treasurers and decided to accommodate a new Benson and Hedges 55-over competition, including both zonal and knock-out matches, by reducing the Championship programme for 1972 to 20 matches per county.

The death occurred early in the year of Len Bates, aged 75, after several years of ill health during which both legs were amputated. He was born in the Head Groundsman's house at Edgbaston. When he left the staff in 1935, he became Head Coach and Groundsman for 25 years at Christ's Hospital School in Horsham. As the Committee tribute to him said:

> He was the classical exponent of the art of real batting in the era between the two wars. No man, from birth to death, was closer to the game or understood its message better. No man in consequence will be more closely linked to cricket for all time.

Having climbed to the Championship summit, only to be pushed back a pace, the Club captain was determined that the 1972 season would leave no room for argument, and the players responded to his positive leadership in magnificent fashion.

Smith became, arguably, the most successful captain in Warwickshire history – certainly if judged on results alone. The Championship was won for the third time – this time without defeat – and in addition to his side losing in their fourth appearance in a Gillette final, they also reached the semi-final of the new Benson and Hedges competition.

The Championship win must take pride of place, with the margin of 36 points leaving no room for argument. The side won nine games – two more than Kent, Gloucestershire and Northamptonshire – with the new truncated programme of 20 matches still giving the spoils to the sides who won most matches. The annual report paid a deserved tribute to Smith: 'He led the side with his customary zeal and marked ability. Captaining a county side these days is an intense and demanding occupation, and he showed rare courage in some of the decisions he had to take.'

E. W. Swanton in the *Daily Telegraph* wrote: 'Day in and day out, there has scarcely been a better side to watch.' This view was supported by two facts. First, the four players who led the side – Mike Smith was recalled to the England colours against Australia at the age of 39, which led to Brown and Kanhai deputising for the deputy – won only four tosses out of 20. Secondly, the side's combined total of 137 batting and bowling bonus points was at least 16 points ahead of any of the contending sides.

Only one of the first six games were won – at Old Trafford where Lancashire were beaten by an innings and 41 after Brown, McVicker and Rouse capitalised on a marvellous 199 from Kanhai.

Conclusive wins in a week against Middlesex and Hampshire

The 1972 Warwickshire County Championship winning team at Edgbaston. Standing (l to r): Deryck Murray, John Whitehouse, Norman McVicker, Bill Blenkiron, Bob Willis, Steve Rouse, Warwick Tidy, Alvin Kallicharran. Seated: Dennis Amiss, Rohan Kanhai, Mike Smith, Alan Smith (capt.), David Brown, Lance Gibbs, John Jameson.

The unsung hero, Norman McVicker. In the 1972 Championship winning side Norman McVicker was the top wicket taker: he took 66 wickets in Championship matches only at an average of 23.80 to top the bowling averages. The nearest wicket-taker was Lance Gibbs with 52 wickets. Note the dangerous away swinger which made McVicker such a dangerous bowler.

announced the Warwickshire challenge for the title, and a fortnight later came the decisive thrust with three successive wins against Glamorgan, Lancashire and Kent.

The victory march was temporarily halted by a wet first week in August and both games against Gloucestershire and Somerset were abandoned, before two more successive wins against Nottinghamshire and Surrey – both by nine wickets – opened up a conclusive lead. For good measure the season ended on a high note at Trent Bridge, where Warwickshire took advantage of a third day declaration which would not have been made had the Championship still been at stake, to win by four wickets.

Oddly enough, the highest wicket taker was McVicker with 66 at 23.80, while Gibbs was next with 52 at 27.46. So what about the old maxim that it is 'bowlers who win matches'? The captain says: 'What happened was that on seven occassions, fielding first, the bowlers got the side into a good position early in the game, and our strong batting displayed much more consistency, and was thus able to consolidate the early breakthrough.' This, in turn, meant that priceless extra time was bought for the bowlers to bowl out the opposition for a second time. In the wicket-keeping department, the West Indies' player, Deryck Murray was signed, and in addition to his 42 victims, he scored 412 valuable runs at 27.46.

The batting had been further strengthened by the signing of Alvin Kallicharran, although the long term adverse effects on English cricket of a Club being allowed to play four overseas cricketers in the same side were to be far-reaching. The diminutive left-hander scored 1,153 at 42.70 – an average which was good enough only to place him fourth in the averages, behind the prolific Kanhai (1,607 at 64.28), Amiss (1,219 at 55.40), and Mike Smith, whose 1,107 came at 50.31 per innings. Smith did himself justice in his three Tests, particularly at Lord's in Massie's match (16 wickets for 142 on debut), where he scored 34 and top score of 30 in England's second innings of 116. Whitehouse and Jameson had moderate seasons, which meant the chance for Amiss to establish himself as an opener, and he took it so emphatically that he played for England in the one-day internationals, and won a place on the winter tours of India and Pakistan.

He scored an unbeaten 151 in his new position against Middlesex, and four more Championship hundreds came against Lancashire (a career best 192), Worcestershire (156), Kent (121 not out), and 120 against Nottinghamshire. The innings against Middlesex marked the relaunching of a career which had produced until then, only nine Championship hundreds from 366 innings, although he had also scored five other first-class hundreds. Compare that ratio with the 88 hundreds he was to score from 833 innings before the end of his career.

Kanhai's insatiable appetite for large scores was evidenced, yet again, by his success in converting eight of his 11 fifties into hundreds, with Amiss showing how fast he was maturing, with five of his six fifties leading to hundreds.

Brown made something of a comeback with 37 wickets, but although they came at the high cost of 26.29, he was able to be used as a strike bowler in partnership with Bob Willis, whose controversial special registration from Surrey enabled him to play from 1 July onwards, and his 28 wickets played their part in the title win.

Having beaten Yorkshire, Leicestershire, Glamorgan and Worcestershire – the last three at Edgbaston – Warwickshire had high hopes of beating Lancashire in the Gillette Cup final at Lord's, but a magnificent 126 from Clive Lloyd shattered their bowling and their dreams.

Bob Willis. The end product of weight training and running – the last straining arc as the ball is propelled at 90 miles per hour plus. Compared with McVicker, Willis's more open action releases the ball with the seam angled towards leg slip, which means an inswinger, or the ball moving off the seam.

In the new Benson and Hedges Cup, zonal qualifying wins against Northamptonshire, Worcestershire and Cambridge University, followed by a quarter-final win over Glamorgan gave them a rare chance of another Lord's final. It was not to be, with Illingworth's Leicestershire bowling them out for 96 in 39.5 overs.

Only three matches were lost out of the 30 played in the Championship and the two knock-out competitions, but the John Player League provided a more unsuccessful story, although the side's seven wins lifted them six places to 11th. Alan Smith admitted: 'Too much could not be read into this, because four of the wins were so narrow that only a slight measure of ill fortune would have left the side once more at the foot of the table.'

The committee agreed: 'The lack of any measure of success continued. This is doubly unfortunate since this competition is so popular with the public, and it is essential that the team should make every effort to establish a better approach and pattern to its play.'

The emphasis on the importance attached by the committee to limited overs cricket was repeated in the financial report: 'Only 12,923 spectators paid to watch the 30 days home cricket in Warwickshire in the County Championship, compared with 204,000 in 1951.'

The point was hammered home with one statistic which seemed to make the argument an irrefutable one: 'To prove that interest in the game (played in a manner the public wants and appreciates) still exists, 9,075 paid in a single afternoon to watch the semi-final tie in the Gillette Cup against Worcestershire.' In 1989, nearly double that crowd watched another 60-over semi-final with, for the first time, every ticket presold, to emphasise the financial dilemma which has faced English cricket in the intervening 20 years; the success of the domestic one-day game can only properly be assessed in inverse proportion to the declining appeal of the national team.

Any objective comparison must acknowledge the considerable difference in appeal to the public of a knock-out semi-final, and a day's play in a county championship match – even involving the ultimate Champions.

For the record, the respective receipts were £4,249 and £4,129 from three-day cricket and Sunday games. Players' salaries totalled £49,573 from a total expenditure of £148,110 – an increase of £8,419 out of the extra £15,013 it took to run the Club.

The combined share from the Test and County Cricket Board from Test matches, and the Gillette and Benson and Hedges Cups, together with other sponsorships, amounted to £45,841 – an increase from 1971 of £20,348. Income from the now flourishing endowment fund of £373,298, was £19,156, and with members' subscriptions yielding £35,579, thanks to the introduction of a shareholder membership, it can be seen how well Warwickshire had come to terms with the much-changed demands of budget-balancing in the modern game.

The members were warned that, although the level of subscriptions would remain unaltered, VAT, which was shortly to be introduced, would have to be added in 1974. The committee also warned that, with the West Indies due to tour in 1973, the Club would probably lose Kanhai, Gibbs, Kallicharran and Murray, and although this would create opportunities for young players, the success of 1972 could not reasonably be expected to be repeated. Much would be expected of Willis, who would be available for the whole season.

The Club's statistician for most of the post-war period, Ted Hampton, was presented with an inscribed silver cigar box from the Club and the supporters, following his recovery from a serious operation the previous year. It is doubtful if any other county club was able to call on a more able and devoted statistician in a period when that particular 'art' was, relatively speaking, still in its infancy.

Ibadulla announced his retirement after playing at that time, more post-war matches for the Club than any other player. Forced to qualify for three years because he played for the Pakistan Eaglets on their tour of England in 1951, the all-rounder scored 14,766 at 26.36, including 17 hundreds, and he took 418 wickets at 30.01 with a mixture of off-cut and seam. In addition, he was a brilliant fielder, usually close to the wicket, and took 311 catches.

Bannister, who played in most of Ibadulla's games, paid the Pakistani this tribute: 'He was the archetypal "bits and pieces" cricketer, who was never out of the game. Even on the rare occasions he failed with bat and ball in the same game, his superlative catching – particularly at forward short leg – could turn a game. Who can ever forget his great catch in 1966 in the Gillette Cup Final against Worcestershire, to get rid of Tom Graveney off Tom Cartwright. That was just one example of a man who, more than any other overseas cricketer in my experience, made himself "at home" in county cricket.'

An equally important retirement at committee level brought Cyril Goodway into the chair in succession to Edmund King, who decided to make way after ten distinguished years in office. King was the perfect example of a traditionalist, who nevertheless became one of the game's first enlightened administrators in a decade when the face of cricket changed completely. He retained his links with Lord's where, as chairman of the finance and general purposes sub-committee, he was to play a leading role in helping the Cricketers' Association to bring in a minimum wage scale in 1979. His also was the guiding hand behind the historic decision of the Test and County Cricket Board, in the absence of a sponsor for the Championship, to make prize money available in 1973, with £3,000 going to the Champions, £2,000 to the runners-up, £1,000 to the third team and £500 to the fourth.

Another nettle to be grasped was the implementation for the first time of over-rate fines, with £500 per team, to be paid by the players, for a rate below 18.5 overs per hour. This was subsequently increased to £1,000, with the important addendum, insisted upon by the Cricketers' Association, that the Clubs must pay half, as they were responsible for the appointment of the captains, who had an important role to play in trying to speed up the flagging over-rates.

Not surprisingly, the results in 1973 did not match those of the previous golden year. Kanhai played in the first five Championship games only, Gibbs in the first four, with Kallicharran and Murray playing in the first seven, and the left-hander returning with Gibbs for the final game against Lancashire. The depleted side finished a respectable seventh in the Championship, 79 points behind Hampshire, but were 15th in the John Player League and failed to survive a knock-out round in the Gillette and Benson and Hedges Cups against, on both occasions, Worcestershire.

Shorn of the brilliant batting of Kanhai, and with Brown the leading wicket-taker with 68 wickets at 25.00 each, the side lacked a cricketer with the flair to mount a serious challenge for any of the four competitions. Only five matches were won in the Championship, with the same number of defeats, and only Worcestershire were beaten of the sides above them in the table. Even the final position of seventh was achieved only with the help of two wins over Lancashire in the last three games, and individual highlights were few.

Alan Smith certainly led from the front, and did more than anyone to fill the vexed all-rounder position with 435 runs at 25.58 and 40 wickets at 21.37 to add to the important 22 he took the previous year. He had now given up wicket-keeping, and in the absence of Murray, the duties were shared between Barry Flick and Jamie McDowall, with Flick disappointing – he was released at the end of the year.

Amiss, Jameson and the ever-dependable Mike Smith carried the batting, with Jameson's magnificent revival bringing him 1,948 runs at 48.70. He scored five of the side's ten hundreds and, as usual, always scored his runs at such an entertaining rate that he earned selection, together with Amiss, on England's winter tour of the West Indies.

Amiss played in all three Tests against Kanhai's West Indies side, and delighted everyone at Edgbaston by scoring 56 and 42 in the drawn Test, which was marked with the unfortunate incident between Kanhai and umpire Arthur Fagg. The annual report curously criticises the media for magnifying the dissent shown by the West Indies' captain following a disallowed appeal for a catch. Whether or not Fagg should have refused to continue unless he received an apology is a

The all-rounder Alan Smith takes to bowling, with his 'windmill' action after turning over the gloves to Deryck Murray. Here he is in action during the 1972 Championship year when he took 22 wickets for 24.54 each, to come second in the bowling averages.

moot point. What cannot be argued, is that without the over-reaction from Kanhai, there would have been no incident for the media to 'magnify', and the crowd 'exaggerate'.

The financial return of £40,224 was more than from any previous Test match at Edgbaston, but the attendance figures were well below the best so far recorded.

Willis made the hoped-for impact with 51 wickets at 19.35, although his history of proneness to injury was beginning at an unusually early age. McVicker's 52 wickets at 24.53 underlined his value as a support seamer, and it was a blow when he decided to join Leicestershire. Five seasons had brought him 300 wickets, as well as 1,701 valuable lower order runs from 96 completed innings.

The major loss was, of course, Gibbs, who decided to take advantage of a cricket coaching appointment in Guyana. Although he only really fulfilled his great off-spinning talents in his golden year of 1971, his total of 338 wickets played a major part in holding the attack together in its transitional period around the start of the 1970s. His departure would at least give extended opportunities to Peter Lewington, whose performance in taking 48 wickets at 27.89 each from 527.5 overs was among the more encouraging features of the season.

The staff for 1974 would not include Whitehouse, whose accountancy examinations would preclude his availability, but an interesting addition was Geoff Humpage, a 20-year-old all-rounder. The financial report showed a deficit of £12,863, with the loss 'only' that amount because of a decrease in players' salaries brought about by the absence of the West Indies' quartet on tour, and a life-saving increase in investment income of £11,237 to £30,393.

The annual message was repeated to the players regarding their performances on the Sabbath: 'The John Player League gates can be improved upon so much more, if only playing results also improved.'

One man who enjoyed the financial aspect of the year was David Brown, who profited both from his own popularity and the break in benefits for four years with a Club record return of £21,109.30.

The shift in emphasis in fund raising, necessarily so since the inception of the John Player League in 1969 ended a previously prolific source of income from Sunday games against local clubs. This meant that whereas Brown only received £183.77 from the three-day match against Worcestershire, he received £16,605.24 from 'out matches, dances and special efforts', as well as £4,216.89 from 'a Caribbean ball'. Times had indeed changed.

The Club awarded a benefit in 1974 to John Jameson, with the season much anticipated because of the full-time availability of the three West Indies Test players.

However, despite the return of Kanhai, Kallicharran and Murray, Warwickshire had their least successful season under the captaincy of Alan Smith – falling to ninth place in the Championship, struggling to eleventh place in the John Player League, failing to reach the last eight of the Benson and Hedges, and again losing their first Gillette Cup match.

In the latter competition, Warwickshire's performances in 12 years were of an extreme nature. A total of four finals and two semi-finals were in sharp contrast to their six first-round eliminations.

Of the poor season, Smith said: 'The batting's apparent positive quality (second in the overall run-rate table) was not frequently enough concentrated upon the achievement of results. All too often the best batting was achieved at non-critical times. There was also a question mark over the bowling, and it is a miserable fact that only in the first Championship match did either Warwickshire have full complement of bowlers, or the team's bowling was not disrupted by injury to at least one of the bowlers during a game.'

The averages bear this out, with the strike attack of Brown and Willis taking 56 and 53 wickets respectively – both at a cost of under 20.5 each – but they bowled only 870 overs between them.

Fortunately Hemmings, still only 25 despite this being his ninth season on the staff, finally delivered the sort of all-round performance his talents had promised, with 84 wickets at 22.08, as well as 645 runs at 23.88. He bowled 738 overs, and despite another useful season from the captain – 26 wickets at 28 and 368 runs from 19 completed innings – the side would have been in a mess without Hemmings.

Rouse played in only nine matches, and his 27 wickets at 18.11 emphasised how much his vastly improved left-arm seam bowling was missed.

The flattering batting was again headed by Kanhai although, again because of his battered knee, he missed seven Championship matches. His 22 innings brought him 936 scintillating runs at 52.00, with three hundreds including the second historic double hundred, when he partnered Jameson to what is still a world record second-wicket partnership of 465, against Gloucestershire at Edgbaston.

Both batsmen were unbeaten – Jameson with 240 and Kanhai with 213, and all that after poor Abberley had gone for a duck. The fortunate few among the crowd who paid the grand total of £173 in the three days (the Sunday receipts against the same opposition were £451), watched a breathtaking display by two of the game's most destructive batsmen. It is rare for a side to be blessed with two such stroke-makers, and even more unusual for them to share such a huge partnership. They batted for only 310 minutes and faced 598 deliveries – a highly creditable over rate from the savaged Gloucestershire bowlers. For once, the fireworks resulted in a win, with Hemmings (six for 87) in the first innings, and Blenkiron (four for 18) and Willis (four for 31) in the second, completing a win by an innings and 61 runs.

Amiss all but added a third double century in the home match against Middlesex, with his 195 setting up a win by ten wickets.

Behind the stumps, Murray had a good season with 51 victims and 707 runs at 22.09, and Humpage marked his debut against Oxford University with three victims and thirteen runs.

Kallicharran's 1,309 runs at 35.37 were slightly disappointing, and all in in all, everyone at Edgbaston was glad to see the end of the season.

For Blenkiron, it was also the end of a career, which, like that of so many promising young bowlers since the war, petered out after a

John Jameson and Rohan Kanhai, in front of the scoreboard that shows the world record second wicket partnership of 465 (unfinished) completed in 100 overs, Warwickshire v *Gloucestershire at Edgbaston in 1974. Jameson scored 240 not out and Kanhai 213 not out.*

bright start. His final total of 298 wickets was an inadequate return for his ability in a stay at Edgbaston of 11 seasons.

The captain called for a greater athleticism in the field, particularly in Sunday cricket, where a 'stronger defensive inclination and intent' must be adopted. He announced his own retirement, and David Brown was appointed to succeed a man who contributed enormously to Warwickshire cricket in his 17 years association with the Club.

Judged by the highest standards applicable to any cricketer who played six times for England, Smith might have had his limitations as a wicket-keeper, but he amply compensated for any shortcomings with an attitude which more talented players would do well to emulate. Always full of courage, his head never went down, and like Trevor Bailey, it could be truly said of him that he extracted every ounce out of his cricketing ability. In addition he was an inspiring captain who was never afraid to take, and stand by decisions. Any air of eccentricity, accentuated by his well known knock-kneed pads, was probably cultivated, because as he was to demonstrate through the rest of the 1970s and the 1980s, his able and astute mind served him well in the secretaryship of Warwickshire, and the managership of two England tours, before he was appointed as the Test and County Cricket Board's newly created chief executive on 1 October 1986.

Smith was a man of much style, whose period of captaincy was marked by a never-flagging determination to do things his way. He was always approachable but, having listened to ideas and suggestions, he was unafraid to back his own judgement.

CHAPTER TWENTY-ONE

A LATE 1970s DECLINE

THE YEAR OF 1975 WAS ONE OF CHANGE at Edgbaston. It started with Alan Smith's appointment as assistant secretary in succession to Sydney Harkness, who retired after 29 years yeoman service and David Brown becoming the 18th appointed captain of the Club. The year ended on a sadder note with Leslie Deakins suffering a stroke, the death of Alec Hastilow, a new Club president, and the final retirement of M. J. K. Smith.

On the field, England staged the first Prudential World Cup, and the Australians retained the Ashes in a series of four matches, thanks to their win in 3½ days at Edgbaston.

The County side had a moderate season, with the only highlight their highest final place to date in the John Player League of joint fifth. Brown's side won nine matches, four fewer than the title winners, Hampshire. A successful campaign in the Benson and Hedges Cup ended with a tantalising defeat by three runs in the home semi-final against Middlesex, with the same club increasing Warwickshire's first-round exits in the Gillette Cup to seven two weeks later – also at Edgbaston.

A sign of the times, with the ever-growing emphasis on the one-day competitions, was the absence in the captain's report to the members of any direct reference to the County Championship. Warwickshire finished 14th, the lowest position for 15 years, and the Club's fourth-lowest finish since the war. The team won only four matches, with three of the victories coming in the first five matches, and the final one three matches later on 24 June. Significantly, all four matches were won by high-scoring batting totals in the fourth innings – and only in the one-wicket win over Somerset did Warwickshire bowl out the opposition twice. In the other victories, Surrey, Nottinghamshire and Sussex all declared twice, thus pinpointing the bowling weakness of an attack in which no regular bowler took his wickets at a cost of under 26 each.

Rouse and Willis played only four and three matches respectively, and manfully though Brown (73 wickets), Perryman (49), Hemmings (79) and Lewington (66) battled, the balance of the side was woefully lop-sided.

Kanhai topped the national batting averages, with his 1,073 runs coming at the remarkable average of 82.53, and he hit three hundreds. He also passed 10,000 for Warwickshire in only his 218th innings, with an average of 55.62, including 32 hundreds. Amiss was the heaviest run-maker, with 1,545 at 49.83, and the hundreds continued to stream from his bat, with four more, including a lovely unbeaten 143 out of the 355 for two that the side scored to beat Sussex at Hastings. Kallicharran topped 1,000 runs, but Smith did not. His final season brought him 703 runs from 23 completed innings, and fittingly his last first-class hundred was against Oxford University at The Parks. In the last match of the season, he delighted the Edgbaston spectators with 89 against Northamptonshire, who won by three wickets.

Smith ended a magnificent first-class career with 39,832 runs from 1,091 innings at an average of 41.84. Only 14 batsmen have scored more runs, and he must go down in history as the most successful run-scorer in post-war county cricket. He scored 69 hundreds, and undoubtedly only his consistently selfless approach denied him entry into the exclusive set of batsmen who have scored 100 100s. For example, in the six seasons of his 'second' career, he reached the 90s seven times, and the 80s a further 11. Alan Smith said of M. J. K.:

> Purely as a batsman and also a close-to-the-wicket fielder, he has earned the respect, admiration and gratitude of players and spectators around the world. But, more important, wherever he has been, whomsoever he has met, he has instantly made friends. No player in the last 25 years has been more universally popular. Hard-bitten professionals have been prepared to walk over a cliff if he so decreed as captain.

He was indeed a player's player.

Among the other first team regulars, Whitehouse returned 970 runs at 33.44, but Jameson had a moderate season with 931 at 25.86. Humpage and Oliver showed promise, but all too often the team was out-gunned, particularly in both games against Lancashire which resulted in defeats by an innings twice – the first time this had happened to Warwickshire since Derbyshire achieved the same feat in 1936.

Alec Hastilow died aged 80, and Brigadier Sir Richard A. G. Calthorpe succeeded Lt General Sir Oliver Leese as president after the latter retired, following a period in office of 16 years.

The annual deficit was little changed at £9,108, despite a similar increase in revenue from members' subscriptions, and the side's improved Sunday form. The overall income increased by £45,670, but inflation increased expenditure by a similar amount.

The benefit granted to Amiss realised £34,947, and it was announced that long-serving Derief Taylor had been awarded a testimonial in 1976.

New captain David Brown brought the same enthusiasm and honest endeavour to the post as characterised his bowling and his personal example led to a much better season in 1976. He led his side to fifth place in the Championship, sixth in the John Player League, and to both knock-out semi-finals. The captain took his 1,000th wicket in first-class cricket and although he was again denied the services of Willis through injury, he juggled his limited resources with impressive expertise. Willis played in only five games, with his 22 wickets at 21.50 showing how much he was missed. Brown shouldered most of the extra responsibility nobly with 66 wickets at 25.80, and in the spin department Hemmings bowled 960.1 overs to take 81 wickets at 30.72.

Rouse took 44 wickets, with the promising West Indian pace bowler, Bill Bourne coming through with 57 wickets, as well as a maiden hundred against Sussex. The attack was always steady rather than deadly, but the batsmen, headed by Amiss with 1,547 runs at 61.88, performed consistently well. For the first time, Kanhai was below his best (864 runs at 36.00), but a tremendous final season from Jameson eased the way for Humpage and David Smith to pass 1,000 runs for the first time. Humpage was particularly impressive, totalling 1,329 runs at 44.30, and he hit his first two hundreds for the Club. Behind the stumps he claimed 63 victims to complete a splendid first full season, which won him both his county cap and the Warwickshire tankard for the all-rounder award.

Jameson's aggregate of 1,727 at 43.18 was the highest by any player in his last season for the Club, and his seven hundreds in the Championship included 103 before lunch in the last match of the season at Edgbaston against Glamorgan. As usual his runs were scored at a rapid rate, with the hundreds against Worcestershire and Northamptonshire coming in 83 and 92 minutes respectively, three more in under $2\frac{1}{2}$ hours, and only his 112 in the win against Kent at Tunbridge Wells took him longer than three hours.

Amiss was in similarly prolific form, with five hundreds deservedly earning his recall to the England side for the final Test at the Oval, where he alone defied Michael Holding (match figures of 14 for 149) with an innings of 203 which said as much for his temperament as his technique. Whitehouse progressed to 1,363 runs at 35.87, including an unbeaten 169 in the home win over Yorkshire.

The side reversed the previous year's double defeat by Lancashire, beating the northern side twice in a fortnight, by 36 runs at Edgbaston and four wickets at Blackpool, and the total of 70 bowling points gained was surprisingly beaten by only two sides, and was three more than the total of the Champions Middlesex. In fact Warwickshire's combined bonus points total of 135 was the highest in the table, but their total of six wins, compared with Middlesex's 11, indicated the vital difference of penetration between the two sides.

Warwickshire won the only two games of the season, at Tunbridge

Wells and Bournemouth, in which one of their bowlers took ten or more wickets in the match. Hemmings took ten for 101 against Kent and 13 for 237 against Hampshire.

In the John Player League, the side won three of its first four games, but successive defeats by Lancashire, Leicestershire and Surrey left them with too much leeway to make up. In the Benson and Hedges semi-final, a high-scoring match saw Worcestershire's 281 prove 12 runs too many, while the Gillette semi-final against Lancashire at Edgbaston produced a similar scoreline to the 1972 final with, this time, a Barry Wood 100 taking Lancashire to 234 for four, and a win by six wickets.

The side's progress in those two lucrative competitions meant a share-out from Lord's of £27,462, compared with £15,200 the previous year, and the Club proudly announced its first surplus – £9,108 – for 12 years. This was more than satisfactory, with the expenditure for the year passing the £250,000 mark for the first time. Two more happy financial announcements concerned the £6,056 raised for Derief Taylor, and the success of the executive suite, with its membership closed now that 100 firms were paying £200 each for the year.

Jameson's decision to retire at the age of 35 in order to take up a school appointment in Taunton was a blow to committee and members alike. As he proved in his final season, when he should have been picked for England, his batting skills were undimmed, and those people who watched pre-war county cricket likened him to Gloucestershire's Charlie Barnett. Together with Roy Marshall, Dickie Dodds and Colin Milburn, Jameson must be bracketed as one of the most destructive of post-war batsmen, and the bit seemed to be taken hold of even more firmly when he opened the innings. Like all entertaining batsmen, his career figures tell only part of the story, but they are still impressive enough in their own right: 581 innings; 43 not out; 18,149 runs; average 33.73. He hit 31 hundreds including two doubles. His total of only four appearances for England says more for the short-sightedness of the selectors than any shortcomings on his part.

After leaving Edgbaston to return to Taunton School, Jameson later became a first-class umpire, following which he spent one year as head coach at Sussex in 1988 before he was appointed to the assistant secretaryship of the MCC in 1989.

An even sadder departure from the regular Edgbaston scene was that of Leslie Deakins who, although he made a good recovery from the stroke he suffered, decided in March 1976 to resign as general secretary after 32 years. He had joined the Club in 1928, and served his apprenticeship under the watchful eye of R. V. Ryder before his naval service in the war enabled him to plan a new Edgbaston, and the present ground stands as a permanent reminder of what one man, blessed with the necessary imagination, drive and conscientiousness, can bring about. As the committee tribute said: 'Throughout his long career, his fellow secretaries held him in high esteem. he was the man they went to for advice and this was as great a tribute as the game could give him.'

Former player Bannister said:

> I signed for Warwickshire in 1950 only because Leslie was able to dispel family misgivings about the insecurity of professional sport. In my 20 years at Edgbaston he was the perfect administator. Even if you disagreed with any of his many strong views, you had to respect the burning love the man had for cricket in general and Warwickshire cricket in particular.
>
> I only saw him at a loss for words once. Alan Smith and I accompanied him to take part in 'A Warwickshire night' at the Wombwell Cricket Society in Barnsley. An early question came from the back, asking 'Mr Deakins, do you still hold the same view about Committees as the last time you were here?'
>
> Replied Leslie: 'I can't remember what I said.'
>
> 'You said that the average committee is like a bunch of bananas. They start off green, turn yellow, and end up with not a straight one in the bunch.'
>
> Although he has not travelled much, his name is respected all over the cricketing world.

Brown's final season as Club captain in 1977 was a poor playing one for his team, which finished tenth and eleventh respectively in the Schweppes County Championship and the John Player League, in addition to which their failure to survive the first knock-out rounds of the Benson and Hedges and Gillette Cup competitions meant that from 14 July onwards, the Warwickshire season was a 'dead' one, of academic interest only.

Overshadowing everything else was the Packer affair, which burst upon the unsuspecting cricket world in the third week in May. The annual report made pointed reference to the fact that the committee's first knowledge of the signings of Dennis Amiss and Alvin Kallicharran was after the contracts were signed: 'In neither case was the Club advised that anything was being considered by the two players.'

The following comment was even more pointed:

> Some $2\frac{1}{2}$ months later Bob Willis also received an offer to play in this series of cricket matches, but in his case he came to the Club saying that he had received an offer, and had not made up his mind as to

what was the right thing to do, therefore giving the Club opportunity to assess the situation, and perhaps make a counter suggestion.

The Warwickshire Club was to remain at the eye of the Packer storm for two years, despite the subsequent withdrawal of Kallicharran from his involvement, after he had sought the assistance of the Cricketers' Association.

An indication of the unpleasant pressures created during the season was an incident in the away match against Derbyshire at Chesterfield between Kallicharran and a photographer which nearly resulted in the West Indian withdrawing from the match.

Small wonder that, although Brown typically kept his side on an even keel throughout the traumatic season, the playing results were so poor. Only four games were won, although the side actually won more bonus points – 133 – than any other county, which showed the difficulties encountered in trying to convert advantageous situations into wins.

The biggest bowling advance was made by Perryman, whose 73 wickets at 26.41 included one performance of ten wickets in the win against Middlesex (11 for 150), and on four other occasions he took five or more wickets in an innings, including six for 30 in both home victories over Leicestershire and Lancashire.

He deserved the award of his county cap, and other good figures were returned by Brown (57 wickets at 21.21), Rouse (49 at 27.04), and Willis, whose 11 matches brought him 31 wickets at 20.94, including match figures of 11 for 72 in the drawn game at Bristol. Hemmings took the first ever hat-trick for Warwickshire against Worcestershire, but his 46 wickets came at the high cost of 36.74 each.

Amiss and Whitehouse topped the batting averages, scoring six hundreds each, and although Kallicharran converted only one of his 11 fifties into a hundred, his 1,343 runs at 41.97 put him fractionally behind Whitehouse, whose 1,543 aggregate was scored at an average of 42.86.

Amiss scored 1,470 runs from 26 completed innings to average 56.54, and with Humpage passing 1,000 again (67 victims as well) and Kanhai and Abberley scoring consistently, if not heavily, it was not surprising that the side topped 400 twice in the Championship, and exceeded 300 on eleven other occasions.

Amiss's unbeaten 144 against Glamorgan at Nuneaton completed a unique record for Warwickshire – giving him a hundred against the other 16 counties, both Universities, MCC and Scotland. M. J. K. Smith was then the only player to have scored hundreds against every other county but, although he also reached three figures against both Universities, he did not accomplish the feat against MCC or Scotland.

The Essex fixture at Edgbaston produced a bizarre first session which brought the visitors 204 for one wicket in 135 minutes from 62 overs bowled. Warwickshire were below the minimum over rate for the first half of the season, hence the frenetic attempt to redress the balance, with bowlers operating off reduced run-ups, and fielders sprinting between overs. The loophole in the legislation which allowed such a farcical approach was subsequently blocked by a ruling that over-rates would be calculated only to a maximum of 22 overs per hour.

In limited-overs cricket, the attack could rarely sustain a satisfactory containment policy, and their season generally lacked any impetus.

The second Prudential Trophy Match between England and Australia was staged at Edgbaston, resulting in England winning a low-scoring match by 101 runs, with 35 from Amiss and Old the highest scores on a difficult pitch.

For the second successive year, the committee announced a small surplus (£7,753), after 12 years of successive losses, with one significant footnote concerning the £10,000 deducted from the test and County Cricket Board's share-out to each Club, to allow for the possible liability of the Club's share of legal costs incurred in the Packer case. Events were to show that this figure was too low by around £2,000 per Club.

Another disappointing financial announcement concerned the benefit receipts of Rohan Kanhai, which amounted to only £11,500. Even though there were several contributory factors to the low return, including Kanhai's absence from the country for five months of his benefit year, it was a poor reward for a player whose magnificent record for Warwickshire at the end of the 1977 season was 11,615 runs from 225 completed innings in 173 games, for an average of 51.62, including 35 hundreds.

Considering the generous returns of other less notable players, both before and after 1977, Kanhai is entitled to regard himself as unlucky.

The season began under the Packer cloud, and skies darkened throughout the winter, with the result that the second year of the World Series affair was undoubtedly the unhappiest in the Club's history. The dressing room atmosphere was impossibly unpleasant, with Amiss the target of much bad feeling because of his continued involvement with World Series Cricket, which many of his colleagues, particularly Willis, felt posed a direct threat to the structure of Test and county cricket.

The new captain, John Whitehouse, could scarcely have taken office under more difficult circumstances, and it was small wonder that the side dropped one place to 11th in the Championship, and slumped even further to 16th in the John Player League. Only eight of 38 matches in the two competitions were won, and although Warwickshire reached yet another Benson and Hedges semi-final, they again went out first time to Somerset at Taunton in the Gillette Cup.

The determination which had served Amiss so well at various other crisis points in a career (which was now into its 19th season) helped him through a period which ranks among the most depressing any player has ever endured. He ignored the arguments and, even worse, the silences to which he was sometimes subjected, and decided to let his bat do the talking. He reached 2,000 runs for Warwickshire for the first time in his career, becoming the first player to pass that mark since 1962. Another first for him was a hundred in each innings of the home match with Worcestershire, the first time this had been done by a Warwickshire player since Stewart at Blackpool in 1959, and the first time at Edgbaston since Charlesworth did it against Surrey in 1913.

The committee had announced at the start of the season that, notwithstanding Amiss's service to the Club and the fact that his skill was unimpaired, he would not be offered a contract for 1979 unless his contractual commitments with World Series cricket re-established his availability for England throughout the year. Therefore, the more runs he scored, the more he was proving the Club's point that it was not his ability that was in question, but rather the fact that Warwickshire wanted all their players to be available for Test cricket, home and abroad.

A group of members, some of whose motives were not as selfless as others, became incensed as the Amiss run stream flowed on its way to 2,030 runs from 41 innings at a splendid average of 53.42. He scored seven hundreds as well as 11 other scores over fifty. He was persuaded to lend his name to a requisition for a special members' meeting, which was arranged after the end of the season at the Locarno Ballroom in Birmingham. The season simmered to an ugly finale, with the members, as it transpired, much keener to attack the committee than was Amiss. As events proved, some of the requisitioners were looking for a convenient stick with which to beat the Committee, and Amiss provided the ideal vehicle.

The Cricketers' Association had been making strenuous efforts to break the deadlock between Packer and the International Cricket Conference, and they became involved at Edgbaston just before the end of the season through their secretary, Jack Bannister. He spoke with Amiss in the final match of the season at Edgbaston against Derbyshire, and managed to persuade him to ask the requisitioners to defer the special meeting until later in the winter, to allow negotiations which were privately taking place to progress unhindered by a meeting which could only be emotive and unpleasant.

Amiss agreed, but his supporters did not. They wanted to go ahead with their attack on the committee but, after Bannister was called by Amiss to talk to them, they reluctantly agreed to defer to the wishes of the man they insisted they were trying to help.

The Association, through its president, John Arlott, extracted from Packer's representatives a promise that, if Amiss were offered another contract, they would begin meaningful negotiations to restore peace to world cricket. Conversely, the Warwickshire Club insisted that they would offer a contract only if negotiations had already started. Impasse.

The chairman, Cyril Goodway, was particularly reluctant to trust the Australians, and his intransigent stance was understandable, in view of the fact that the previous agreements among the county clubs to stand together, had all been broken, leaving Warwickshire as the only Club which was prepared to adhere to its original stance on the matter. Other Clubs in 1977, notably Kent, had also refused to offer contracts to Packer players until they were available for Test cricket all the year round, but by the end of the season, they had all changed their minds.

Finally, Goodway relented after hearing a tape recording of a telephone conversation between Arlott and Linton Taylor in Australia, and in late March, after the other players were already back in training, the absent Amiss was offered a contract. To the Club's

Jack Bannister, John Arlott and David Brown, Secretary, President and Chairman of the Cricketers' Association at a press conference after one of their important meetings during the Packer affair.

astonishment, he asked for time to think things over, but good sense prevailed all round, and Amiss came back, thankfully, to a more congenial atmosphere – created it must be said by the insistence of players like Willis, who had been his most implacable opponent in 1978, that a new start must be made.

Bearing in mind the handicap with which the team had burdened itself in 1978, no proper appraisal of their record is valid. Suffice it to say that, other than Amiss, only Kallicharran, whose season was disrupted because of injury and illness, and David Smith passed the 1,000 mark, with Abberley (625), Lloyd (526), Humpage (663) and Whitehouse (740) all falling well short of an average of 30.

Despite the increased programme of 22 matches, only Perryman took 50 wickets, and other than Willis' 40 wickets in 12 matches at an average of 18.38, the next most economical bowler was the persevering Brown, with 40 wickets at 29.00 each.

An increasingly out of sorts Hemmings played in only 14 matches, and his 275 runs and 28 wickets at 40.79 each meant his impending departure to Trent Bridge was inevitable. It is doubtful that the success which he achieved in the next decade would have been his at Edgbaston, where he felt the crowd was over-critical. He was 29 when he departed with a career return from 177 matches played of 441 wickets at 31.87 and 4,294 runs at 21.80.

The Club broke even in a year when expenditure had now reached £321,956, with players' salaries £76,180 – an increase from 1978 of £21,494 – and the books were balanced due to an increase of £14,049 to £65,146 from members' subscriptions and an extra £12,253 from the Executive Suite hiring charges.

Among the deaths of former Warwickshire stalwarts were those of the former president, Lt General Sir Oliver Leese, aged 83, and George Paine, who was 70.

Chairman Cyril Goodway ended his message to members before the 1979 season with: 'The split among the members and therefore the Club, was a grave and serious matter. 1978 was a year it might be best to forget, though that is unlikely to be so.' How right he was with the 1979 season proving to be a disaster.

It might have been a happier dressing room, but the playing record was one of the worst in the history of the Club. The side's dismal record was 15th and 16th respectively in the Championship and John Player League, a quarter-final exit in the Benson and Hedges Cup, and the all-too-familiar one-match appearance in the Gillette Cup.

The side managed only three wins in the Championship, and two in Sunday cricket, even though the season had started brightly with all four zonal games won in the Benson and Hedges Cup. A total of nine wins from 44 matches played tells its own story, and the awful weather completed a depressing season for Whitehouse in his second year as captain.

He was handicapped by his three leading pace bowlers, Willis, Brown and Rouse, bowling only 424.1 overs between them out of a team total of 2957.1, and Perryman and Clifford were forced to shoulder an impossible burden. Surely never before have the bowling averages been headed with an average of 31.10 per wicket, which was effectively the case, although Rouse was nominally at the head with six wickets for 80 in his only match.

Small wonder that the team struggled, and their normally strong batting was also well below standard. Amiss held things together to a limited degree with 1,672 at 49.18, and Kallicharran scored 1,098 at 52.29 in the 17 matches to which he was limited, because of World Cup duties with the West Indies. The two Test batsmen scored ten of the eleven hundreds hit for Warwickshire, with Lloyd's maiden 104 against Nottinghamshire at Edgbaston the other one.

Maynard and Humpage shared the wicket-keeping duties, and both scored good runs, Lloyd progressed steadily, but the captain and David Smith had disappointing seasons. South African all-rounder Anton Ferreira showed promising form, but the rare personal highlights of the catastrophic season belonged to Amiss and Kallicharran, with the former hitting a career best unbeaten 232 at Bristol.

On the international scene, Edgbaston staged two World Cup games – those in which West Indies beat India by nine wickets and Australia beat Canada by seven wickets – before the first Test of a four-match series against India. An unbeaten double hundred by David Gower, together with 155 from Boycott, enabled England to score a massive 633 for five wickets declared, before they bowled India out twice for under 300 to win by an innings and 83 runs.

At administrative level, the presidency changed hands, with the Rt Hon The Earl of Aylesford, Her Majesty's Lord Lieutenant for the County of West Midlands, succeeding Sir Richard Calthorpe, who retired after holding office for four years. David Brown was appointed cricket manager to assume 'in conjunction with the captain, overall executive responsibility for the playing of the game by Warwickshire teams, and through the direction of the coaching staff, will organise the development of players at all ages and levels with the aim of ultimately producing cricketers for the County XI'.

A sweeping brief, and one which Brown would undertake in partnership with a new captain. Whitehouse, understandably was keen to step down after two disastrous seasons, and Brown's close friend Bob Willis accepted the invitation to captain the Club.

The 1980s were certainly going to be different.

A loss for the gloomy year of £6,095 was described, not unfairly, as not unsatisfactory, with the double negative seeming fitting. The worst losses sustained by Warwickshire, were the personal ones of 'Tiger' Smith, Norman Kilner and Fred Gardner. The last died at the early age of 56, just after a hip operation encouraged thoughts of a return to local league cricket in his beloved Coventry.

The Club also lost two stalwarts in James McDowall and Edgar Hiley. McDowall had been a committee member since 1948 and held the Honorary Treasurership for 17 years, in addition to being vice-chairman from 1972 until his death. Hiley was 76, and made a considerable contribution towards the success of the supporters' association, for whom he was chairman for 20 years.

'Tiger' Smith's death at 93 had a happy postscript. He was buried on the final day of the Kent match at Edgbaston, and at the funeral Cyril Goodway succeeded in persuading Eric Hollies to revisit Edgbaston for the first time since the beginning of the 1970s.

'Emotional blackmail' was how Goodway described his offer to Hollies in the churchyard, but it worked. Hollies watched the side wind up their dreadful season with a win by an innings and 174 runs, and happily was a frequent visitor to the ground until his death two years later.

CHAPTER TWENTY-TWO

THE WILLIS ERA, 1980–1984

AS 1970 HERALDED A PERIOD OF change at Edgbaston, so did 1980 begin a decade which must rank among the most turbulent in the history of the Club. In appointing Brown as cricket manager, the committee said that they 'ultimately concluded that such an appointment was desirable to help cope with the increasing pressures of the modern game'.

Put another way, Warwickshire were conceding that the modern game, with its four domestic competitions, drew a much sharper distinction between success and failure than ever before. Before the inception of the John Player League and the Benson and Hedges Cup in 1969 and 1972, the County Championship was the premier competition, with the Gillette Cup providing the ideal occasional spice.

In the 1960s, only a handful of sides would still be in contention for one or other trophy by the middle of July, and so the tempo of a professional cricketer's way of life was slower and steadier. A young player could ease his way into the first-class game, and a sympathetic captain could nurse him through his first few seasons. The first-class programme allowed a batsman anything up to 60 innings, and a bowler would only bowl a handful of overs in limited-overs cricket.

Compare that scenario with the one facing the new management team at Edgbaston of Brown and Willis. The County Championship programme was one of 22 matches, after shrinking to 20 in the mid-1970s, and each side was committed to at least 21 one-day games in the three competitions. The ratio was 66 days of three-day cricket to a minimum of 21 days of limited-overs competition, in which youngsters were thrown in at the deep end – frequently batting and bowling in situations which would tax the resilience of the most experienced players.

When Brown started playing in 1961, his comparative ratio of cricket played was one of between 84 and 96 days in Championship cricket, and no more than four one-day games. Now, he knew that the sort of steady, lengthy apprenticeship served by him and colleagues like Amiss, Jameson and Abberley, now had to be replaced by a force-fed method which, although it might bring the better players through more quickly, would certainly kill off the marginal cricketers – some of whom would, in earlier days, have been 'late developers'.

Brown's own career had ended with 1,001 wickets at 23.85, with only Hollies, Santall, Bannister, Mayer and Cartwright taking more wickets for the Club, and his first decision was to appoint Abberley as 2nd XI captain and assistant coach to Oakman.

Abberley received £39,752 from his benefit, to reward him for a loyal career in which his final figures of 9,825 runs at 24.20, including only three hundreds, were a disappointing return from a player who was thought good enough to go on a Young England tour of Pakistan at the age of 21. He was unlucky to be injured on that tour, and also to be denied the established place he was seeking in the First XI at the same time, because of the strength-in-depth of the batting talent available, and of course he suffered from the decision to allow Barber to play on a part-time basis.

Brown and Willis agreed that the Club's playing strengths were better suited to one of the limited-overs competitions, with the bowlers particularly limited in sufficient penetrative ability to mount a serious challenge for the Schweppes County Championship. In this, although they beat Hampshire and Worcestershire in their first three games, they were not to win any of their next 18 games, before they beat Somerset by ten wickets in the final game at Taunton in September.

They were out of the Benson and Hedges Cup by 22 May, which realistically concentrated the minds of everyone on the John Player League, in which of course the Club had such an appalling record in the previous 12 years. Brown and Willis succeeded in instilling consistency into the bowling and fielding departments, and with Lloyd and Amiss scoring heavily at the top of the order a new record of eight successive wins was established. Even more encouraging, only the wins against Surrey and Essex, by 16 and five runs respectively, were remotely close games and the side enjoyed a self-belief that more than justified the committee's decision to leave all cricket matters in the hands of the profesionals.

The first Sunday home game against Sussex produced record receipts of £2,705, and that figure was to be surpassed three times, with the final match of the season against Somerset yielding £6,208 from a crowd who came to see the John Player trophy which by then had been clinched the previous week-end at Leicester.

In the Sussex game, the *Birmingham Post*'s new cricket correspondent, Jack Bannister, referred to a 'Warwickshire display of fielding and bowling which was both well organised and athletic'. The next win by eight wickets over Lancashire at Liverpool, brought this comment from the Club's former bowler: 'Four wins out of four are convincing last year's critics that no longer are Warwickshire the doormat of one-day cricket.' The side extended its winning run to eight games, with the eighth win against Middlesex at Edgbaston on a slow pitch marked by the only hundred scored for Warwickshire in the competition that year. Humpage hit a magnificent unbeaten 108 in a display of improvised stroke play against Emburey which, for once,

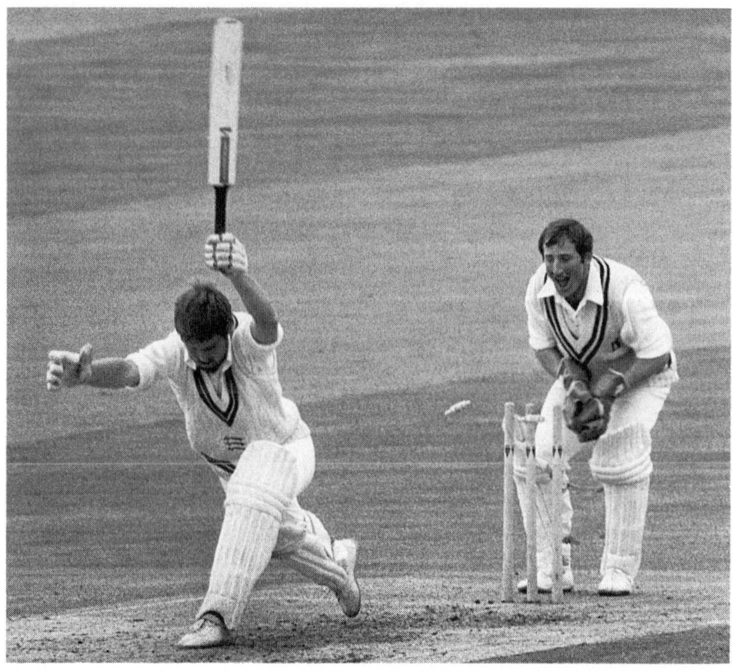

Out? 'No', said the umpire as Mike Gatting is beaten and apparently stumped by Geoff Humpage off Dilip Doshi. Thanks to Humpage's magnificent 108, Warwickshire unexpectedly won the match.

rattled the England off-spinner, and his captain Brearley. Few better one-day innings have ever been played for the Club.

After the opening burst of eight wins came a traumatic run of five games, in which games were lost to Worcestershire, Nottinghamshire and Derbyshire, Gloucestershire were defeated by one run at Edgbaston, and the next home match against Kent was tied, despite Lloyd being 89 and on strike for four balls of the final over. He could manage only a single off the fifth ball, and John Snow, who had been signed to bolster the attack when it flagged in mid-season, ran his partner out off the last ball as they tried to steal a bye.

The next home match against Glamorgan was crucial, but although the visitors scored an impressive 235, Whitehouse with 77, and Lloyd, who scored 51, helped secure a win by four wickets. The penultimate match was at Leicester and hundreds of supporters made the short motorway trip to watch the side win its first trophy for eight years. A typical solid display of out-cricket limited the home side to 180, and Humpage (47), Lloyd (46) and Kallicharan (36) took the side over the finishing line with a stylish flourish.

Geoff Humpage hitting out for Warwickshire against the West Indies at Edgbaston in 1980. Deryck Murray is the wicketkeeper.

The most economical bowler throughout the season was Dilip Doshi, an inspired signing to replace Kallicharran, who was on tour with the West Indies, and like the rest of the attack, he was brilliantly supported in the field throughout the triumphant campaign, with Claughton, Oliver and Lloyd outstanding.

In the Championship, Doshi's 961.2 overs were nearly a third of the total bowled by the team, and his 101 wickets at 26.73 came out of 279 taken by the other bowlers. Willis and Ferreira were the best of the others, with Gladstone Small making a promising start with 24 wickets.

The batting averages were more respectable, with Whitehouse marking his final season with 725 runs at 65.91, including a career best innings of 197 at Edgbaston against Glamorgan. Amiss was his usual solid self with 1,686 at an average of 42.15, and Smith (1,582), Lloyd (1,423), and Humpage (1,339) all averaged over 30.

Doshi and Lloyd were capped, to crown the opener's most successful season, and although the Championship record was poor, at least Edgbaston supporters were able to watch one of the most astonishing innings ever played on the ground.

It came early in May from Ian Botham, whose 126 out of 306 for eight in Somerset's second innings contained six sixes and 16 fours – exactly 100 in boundaries. During 21 overs after lunch he scored 119 out of 136 in 80 minutes, including 30 in two overs off Ferreira, 19 off a Small over and 16 off single overs from both Willis and Hopkins.

The players benefited in every way from the intensive physical training programme they were given in April, and a new agreement with the Club gave them a share in the vast increase in Sunday receipts. The 1979 figure of £8,430 rocketed to £29,500, with the players receiving a percentage once £9,000 had been taken.

Bob Willis holds the John Player League trophy with the winning squad and Cricket Manager David Brown around him.
L to r: Geoff Humpage, Steve Perryman, John Claughton, Alvin Kallicharran, Gladstone Small, Chris Maynard, Dennis Amiss, David Smith, Steve Rouse, Bob Willis, Dean Hoffman, David Brown, Anton Ferreira, Dilip Doshi, Phil Oliver, John Snow, Andy Lloyd, John Whitehouse.

Warwickshire declared a profit of £23,872, thanks to the increase in gate monies (swelled to £40,000 compared with £13,012 in 1979, with the help of £7,084 taken in the match against the West Indies), and a share of £83,867 from the Test and County Cricket Board. The beginning of the decade ushered in an expenditure figure in excess of £500,000, and the Club expressed its gratitude again for the investment income, which the current high interest rates had pushed up to a massive £87,540.

The annual report's obituary section included tributes to, among others, committee member Derek Foster (73), honorary statistician Ted Hampton (83) and New Zealander, Don Taylor, who died at the early age of 57. He shared with Bert Sutcliffe the then unique feat of two double century opening partnerships (220 and 286) in the same match for Auckland against Canterbury in 1948.

Whitehouse and Claughton decided to retire, the latter because of a worrying knee injury. He was a brillant fielder, and made a vital contribution to the side's success in the John Player League. Whitehouse decided that he could no longer keep pace with the demands of accountancy as well as play cricket, and so a fine career came to a premature end. He played in 179 games for Warwickshire, and scored 8,689 runs at an average of 32.30, including 15 hundreds.

Willis was awarded a benefit in 1981 after ten years at Edgbaston, during which period his appearances were limited to 98 matches because of injuries and test match calls, but the John Player title was a fitting reward for the strenuous efforts made by him and Brown to maximise the ability of a staff which was short of class players.

This deficiency was exposed in the following season (1981), even though the side was again successful enough in the John Player League to win nine of its last ten matches and finish third to Kent and Somerset. Had they beaten the latter side in the final game they would have been second, but their third successive poor season in the Schweppes County Championship revealed the true strength of the playing staff.

Warwickshire won two matches only, with both victories, against Kent at Nuneaton and Northamptonshire at Northampton, coming in high-scoring matches in which the batsmen scored 326 for six and 365 for nine, following demanding declarations. Kallicharran's 135 helped win the first game, with Oliver's magnificent unbeaten 171 dominating the other victory.

The bowling averages made sorry reading, with only Willie Hogg, signed from Lancashire, taking 50 wickets. The average cost of 35.88 was good enough to put him second behind Willis who, in a benefit year which brought him £44,951, could play in only seven matches after returning from the tour of the West Indies needing knee surgery. His 13 wickets cost 28.54.

Warwickshire were forced to juggle their overseas trio of Kallicharran, Ferreira and Doshi to comply with the new regulations. The two bowlers took a combined 77 wickets at the high average cost of 45.35 – indeed the paucity of penetration among the entire attack is shown by the grisly statistic that from an aggregate 2913.5 overs bowled, the bowlers conceded 10,915 runs (practically 3.75 runs per over), and took 234 wickets at 46.55 each.

In the previous three seasons, comparisons reveal that the average cost of each wicket was 35.07, 40.54, and 35.05, so it was clear that the emphasis placed on one-day success was not helping bowlers to learn the art of wicket-taking in three-day cricket. Small wonder, therefore, that combining the Championship results of 1979, 1980, and 1981, a pitiful picture emerges of eight wins out of 66 matches, with 27 defeats, and 31 draws. The batting department was among the strongest in the country, with Kallicharran (923) and Oliver (554) averaging over 50, Humpage (1,657) and Amiss (1,722) over 40, and Lloyd's 1,445 coming at 34.40. No fewer than 20 hundreds were scored, with six each from Amiss and Humpage, whose best season this was. Further encouragement came from Asif Din, who marked his first season with 878 attractive runs.

Humpage showed that he had matured into one of the best selective stroke-makers in English cricket, but although he was selected for the three one-day Prudential matches, the selectors wasted a golden opportunity by batting him at number eight, where he did not get a chance to play properly.

His 146 at Gloucester was a career best, with Oliver (twice) and Lloyd also hitting their highest scores. The one failing concerned run-out dismissals. Lloyd and Doshi were run out twice in the same match. Most run-out dismissals have a bizarre aspect, but none more than Lloyd being run out by Amiss's runner, David Smith, while one of Doshi's two suicides occurred when he forgot he had a runner and set off for the other end. An end of season count gave Lloyd nine run-out dismissals in all games, thus equalling his own record of the previous year. Manager Brown could not afford to be too critical, with only five of Lloyd's dismissals coming in first-class cricket, in which Brown succumbed seven times in 1970.

To complete a season which was dominated by the batsmen, the 1,361 runs scored in the Glamorgan defeat at home by 35 runs was the highest-ever aggregate for a Warwickshire match, beating the previous record of 1,351 at Worcester in 1908. Brown's report only directly criticised the team performance once: 'I feel I should say that in my opinion, the side only once lost direction and fell apart – against Nottinghamshire.' In an extraordinary turn around, after strange captaincy by Willis which saw Doshi (four for 94) and Ferreira (three for 121) come on and bowl unchanged while the visitors raced to 303 for nine declared, Warwickshire were bowled out for 49 and the subsequent Champions won inside two days. Not for the first time, criticism was heard of Willis' captaincy, because of the fast bowler's inability to readjust to county cricket after a Test match.

In the two knock-out competitions, Kent knocked the Club out of the Benson and Hedges Cup in a match transferred to the Oval because of rain, and Sussex spun them out of the Gillette Cup at Edgbaston in the first match.

The Prudential match staged at Edgbaston against Australia was notable not only for Australia's victory by two runs, but also for the complete vindication of the Club's foresight in installing the country's first giant cover 'Brumbrella'. The generosity of the supporters' association, who underwrote the cost of £50,000, enabled a capacity crowd to watch the game completed after a heavy fall of rain for over an hour, which under normal circumstances meant that the game would have been carried over to the second day.

The fourth Test match ended on the fourth day – Sunday – with Botham electrifying the crowd with a decisive spell of five wickets for one run to bring victory by 29 runs to England. Notwithstanding that after three days, with Australia only needing 151 to win, a small Sunday crowd seemed inevitable, the spectators turned up in such numbers that the final receipts were more than three times the previous ground record.

This helped towards Warwickshire's share of the Test and County Cricket Board's profits rocketing to £140,878, but with the county gate monies down by £8,007, and total expenditure up to £581,276, the Club announced a small loss of £1,672.

The enormous extra costs of administering a Test match ground resulted in 'postages and telephone' costs amounting to £19,241 – rather different from the £48 0s 6d figure in the accounts of 1946.

Rouse and Doshi left the staff at the end of the year, Rouse because of long-standing knee trouble and Doshi because of the registration rules which forced the Club to choose between either him alone, or Kallicharran and Ferreira together.

Rouse played 124 games during his 11 years at Edgbaston, and took 266 wickets at 30.33, while Doshi's two seasons yielded 146 wickets at 31.84.

The obituary column was sadly the longest for many years with the deaths of former players Hollies, Mayer and Maudsley, as well as leading committee figures, Edmund King and Roy James.

Hollies died just before the start of the season, but as the committee tribute said : 'Eric Hollies, master-spinner, will always bowl at Edgbaston for the initiated, and our summers will be made the brighter by his eternal presence, for he was the very spirit of the game'.

Maudsley was 63 and no more gentlemanly cricketer – in every possible sense of the word – ever played for the County.

Edmund King was tragically killed in a car crash, and at the time of his death was still playing a leading part in controlling the finances of the test and County Cricket Board. A cheerful and unfailingly courteous man, he at times deliberately cultivated a sense of vagueness which was belied by his keen brain. He introduced one of the few light-hearted moments during the High Court action to settle the Packer affair. Under strong cross-examination about a complicated reciprocal arrangement for tours between countries, he cheerfully confessed an ignorance of the minutiae, but added 'whatever it is, it seems to work'. Even his legal adversary had to smile and that is how King will always be remembered in cricket – with a smile.

Roy James rendered the Club long and loyal service on the committee for 30 years, and it was his financial expertise which maximised the growth of the returns on the interest from the endowment fund.

The 1982 season was another poor one – the side finished bottom of the Schweppes County Championship and the John Player League – and suffered the worst financial loss in its history – £80,230.

The financial report pointed out that, under the new catering contract with Chef and Brewer – a subsidiary of Grand Metropolitan Hotels Ltd – the shown drop in income of £22,876 compared with 1981 was not a true figure because of a different account method, but it was the drop in overall income from cricket and sponsorship which was mostly responsible for the huge loss.

In particular, there was a drop of £34,828 in income from perimeter advertising on the ground, because of the collapse of the company, Sports Space Advertising, who were contracted by several counties to sell space on the perimeter fencing for them.

Cricket income decreased by £53,022, with the Test and County Cricket Board share-out down by £36,127, although the Club's own drop in gate receipts of £9,945 to £20,148 from 46 days cricket was more than balanced by the extra £22,119 received from the newly named NatWest Trophy, thanks to the team getting to the Final at Lord's. Significant factors in the expenditure included increases of £9,883 for players' salaries, and £14,420 for 'general secretary and office staff', which now included a new commercial manager.

Hundreds by Kallicharran and David Smith helped Warwickshire to the NatWest Final, with the West Indian's unbeaten 141 at Taunton rightly applauded as one of the best innings of his career. Thanks to 85 from Botham, Somerset totalled a commanding 259, and with Joel Garner in typically hostile form, it looked a winning total. But first Amiss (59), who hit Vic Marks out of the attack and thus forced a change of bowling strategy, and then Kallicharran took over. When Garner was brought back, the left-hander was in full flow and pulled and hooked his former Test colleague in a manner to which Garner was clearly unaccustomed.

Smith's 113 in the home semi-final against Yorkshire, was well supported by 66 from Lloyd on a pitch which was far from straightforward, and the side travelled to Lord's with high hopes that their strong batting would enable them to beat Surrey. It was not to be, with Warwickshire literally 'on the back foot' against Sylvester Clarke and David Thomas, from the moment Smith trod on his own wicket. Any claim of 'bad luck' must be weighed against the modern custom of wearing footwear which is lighter and less comprehensively spiked than used to be the case. Even a total of 158 was achieved thanks only to some determined lower order batting from Din with 45 and Small, who scored a stylish 33.

As invariably happens in a September final at Lord's, batting conditions were considerably easier later in the day, and Surrey cruised home by nine wickets to drive the final nail into the coffin of a season which the Warwickshire players must have wanted to bury as quickly as possible.

The club had finished bottom of the Championship the previous year, but at least then the side won two games. This time the second successive wooden spoon came after a record of no wins, eight defeats and 14 drawn matches, and again it was the bowlers who were simply not up to the demands of three-day cricket.

Willis captained the side in 13 games, compared with seven the year before, but 26 wickets at 34.31 showed that the mental transition from Test to country cricket was just as difficult for him.

Small carried the attack, but the average cost of 30.56 for his 63 wickets underlined the lack of a good new ball partner, in the absence for most of the season through injury of Hogg and Ferreira. Small was called into the England party for the Edgbaston Test match against India, but was left out and allowed to rejoin the game he had left the day before at Southport, where changed regulations allowed Brown to deputise and bowl for him.

The match was made even more remarkable by Warwickshire losing by ten wickets, after a fourth-wicket partnership of 470 between Humpage and Kallicharran rushed their side to 523 for four declared. Humpage hit a career best 254 in just under five hours, including 13 sixes and 24 fours. Only New Zealander John Reid and Pakistan's Majid Khan have hit more sixes in an innings – 15 each.

Kallicharran was unbeaten with 230, one of three double hundreds he hit in a magnificent season in which he scored 2,120 runs at an average of 66.25. His eight hundreds equalled the club record, shared by Wyatt in 1937 and Kanhai in 1972.

After Lancashire kept the game open by declaring at 414 for six, Warwickshire were quickly bowled out for 111, and Graeme Fowler's second hundred of the match – an unbeaten 128 following his first innings 126 – took his side to 226 without loss and an amazing win by ten wickets.

Humpage emphasised his claims to be regarded as one of the best wicket-keeper-batsmen in the history of county cricket with another prolific season in which he scored 1,407 runs at an average of 38.03, including four hundreds.

Amiss scored 1,404 at 37.95, and Lloyd maintained form with 1,432 at 35.80. Din's second season was worth 855, but David Smith's decline in form gave him a moderate return of 591 runs from 28 completed innings.

Not only did the side fail to win a match, on only one occasion did they come even close. That was when, needing 273 to win, Surrey ended the game on 234 for nine.

Brown was justifiably scathing in his report to the members:

> I don't intend to single out individuals for criticism, but I am sure that with the possible exception of Alvin Kallicharran, no-one on the Warwickshire staff in 1982 can possibly look back upon the season with professional pride and say that they did as well as they possibly could, and even worse, look back and say 'I gave the season everything I had.

Harsh words, and possibly too harsh regarding Humpage, Amiss and Lloyd, but understandable from a man who knew only one way to play his cricket, and that was firstly to give everything he had, and then somehow dredge up something else. He realised that the young bowlers needed time to develop under the rigours of the modern game, and so he decided to buy them time by signing the experienced Chris Old from Yorkshire and Norman Gifford, whose departure from Worcestershire was sadly tinged with acrimony after 22 years' magnificent service to the Club.

The year was notable for Willis becoming captain of England, and Amiss again ruling himself out of Test cricket – this time for three years – by joining a disapproved tour of South Africa before the start of the season. Humpage also joined the tour, probably in disappointment at having failed to secure a place in England's party which toured India.

Ironically for Keith Fletcher, who was captain for the tour, he distanced himself from the South African venture, only to be replaced in April by Willis who was within a few hours of getting on the plane with Graham Gooch, John Emburey and the rest of the party. He withdrew at the last moment, and so history was changed.

The Test and County Cricket Board announced that the programme for the County Championship in 1983 would revert to one of 24 matches, with a view to experimenting with four-day matches in the near future.

The death took place of Charlie Grove on 15 February 1983 aged 70, bringing to four the number of the Championship side of 1951 to have died. He had been the first team scorer since 1971, and was president-elect of the old players' association when he suffered a stroke three weeks before his death.

The report also carried obituaries for Norman Partridge, and T. E. Hurst, who served on the committee between 1951 and 1975.

The criticism mounted of the Brown-Willis partnership but Warwickshire's fourth year under them went some way towards answering it after the worst three-year record in the County Championship in the history of the Club.

From 66 matches played in that time, the side won five, lost 23 and drew 38, but the injection of bowling expertise and experience by Gifford and Old achieved the desired object. The bowlers exercised sufficient control to avoid the previous depressing pattern which invariably meant that the efforts of the batsmen were, more often than not, directed at saving, rather than trying to win, games.

Gifford, who led the side in Willis' absence, brought qualities of leadership to Edgbaston which had not been seen since the retirement of Brown and, astonishingly, the side established a Club record with seven successive wins between 4 June and 12 July – one fewer than had been gained in the previous 93 matches stretching back to the beginning of the 1979 season.

Curiously enough, in the golden run of 38 days, the matches against both Oxford and Cambridge University were drawn but there can be little doubt that but for the injuries to Small – he played in only six matches because of a thigh strain – and Ferreira, who missed the last eight matches with a broken finger, the final placing of fifth with 276 points (48 behind Champions Essex), would have been much better.

As it was, with ten matches won and only three lost from the 24 games played, the committee welcomed the improvement thus: 'To jump from 17th to fifth was a great achievement in itself. The manner of achieving this dramatic improvement was most entertaining and surely a source of great pleasure to all Warwickshire members and supporters.'

The one-day competitions all provided disappointments, with progress in both knock-out tournaments halted at the quarter-final stage, and the side finished bottom of the John Player League for the second successive season.

Brown blamed the poor showing on a 'non-committal approach to Sunday cricket, once we were in a challenging position in the County Championship'.

A welcome feature of the ten victories in the Championship was that six sides were bowled out twice, and the final aggregate bowling record of 326 wickets at an average cost of 33.96 was a considerable improvement.

The successive home wins against Yorkshire and Middlesex were triumphs for team spirit as well as ability. Following a declaration from Illingworth at 184 for nine, Warwickshire were left 299 to win on an untrustworthy pitch, and at 180 for eight, the target looked an impossible one. Humpage, the last hope, played one of the best bad-wicket innings seen on the ground for many years, and aided by noble defensive support from Gifford and Willis, his unbeaten 141 in four hours and 24 minutes brought a thrilling last-wicket victory.

In the following match, also on an unsatisfactory pitch, Gifford outbowled Emburey and Edmonds, and with Willis taking six for 22 in the match, Middlesex totalled 152 in aggregate and lost by 167 runs.

Before those two wins, the victory over Lancashire provided members with their first win at Edgbaston for three years and nine months.

As often happens, once the winning streak began, the confidence which had drained away during the previous three seasons came flooding back, and among the batsmen, Kallicharran took his number of double hundreds to five with a career-best unbeaten 243 in the home win against Glamorgan, and Lloyd also hit a career-best unbeaten 208 against Gloucestershire in the drawn game at Edgbaston.

Amiss, now 40, enjoyed another fine season with 1,721 runs at 44.13, including three hundreds, and in completing 1,000 runs for the sixteenth time – only Quaife was ahead of him on 20 – he overtook M. J. K. Smith's aggregate for Warwickshire of 27,672 runs. Coincidentally, Smith played 741 innings for the Club, and Amiss overtook him in his 741st innings.

With Humpage and Smith also passing the 1,000 mark, the wicket-keeper for the sixth time and the opening batsman for the fourth, and 19-year-old Paul Smith scoring a promising 458 at 32.72, the batting regained its dependability, while not sacrificing its usual, attractive approach.

But it was the bowling 'cement' provided by the 166 wickets of Gifford and Old, at an average of 25.34 from 1,700.1 overs which deserves most of the credit for the side's revival. The 43-year-old left-arm spinner silenced the critics who thought his signing was a retrograde step with magnificent figures of 1,043.4–347–2,393–104 wickets at 23.01, and Old's 656.3 overs helped the new ball department to create and maintain stability.

Ferreira's good all-round season – 465 runs at 25.83 and 40 wickets at 31.92 – earned him his cap.

The third Prudential World Cup brought three preliminary matches to Edgbaston, with England losing a thrilling game to New Zealand by two wickets.

The Club's finances took a further battering, with a record loss of £93,618, despite increases in gate monies and the share of TCCB profits, which raised cricket income by £64,756 to £373,486.

The biggest increase in expenditure was one of £43,522 to £214,116 paid in salaries to cricketers – an inevitable consequence of signing Gifford and Old.

The committee forecast a brighter picture for 1984, when a Test match against the West Indies would be staged, and plans were announced for the completion of new executive boxes in the Priory Stand.

The one troubled note of the year was the resignation as chairman of Cyril Goodway after 11 distinguished years in office, in protest about the decision of the Test and County Cricket Board's discipline sub-committee to suspend and fine Old for the unauthorised publication of articles which appeared under his name in a national tabloid newspaper. Goodway's decision was particularly sad, because of the strong relationship he had helped establish between the authorities at Lord's and Edgbaston. The player did his best to stop the offending material appearing, and when he failed, the Club committee immediately fined him a record £1,000.

The Board refused to accept the Warwickshire action as satisfactory, despite Alan Smith being able to show how he and the Club had done all they possibly could to remain at one with the regulations. Old was fined £2,000 and suspended for three days, and it was this decision, which punished the Club by denying them the player's services, that led to Goodway's resignation on what he viewed as a matter of principle. As it happened, Old was injured for his suspension period, but Goodway refused to ignore what he viewed as a slight on Warwickshire and himself.

Goodway had joined the ground and house sub-committee in 1946 and, in the words of the committee tribute to him: 'was virtually the leading light in the enormous development of the ground. Cyril, together with Percy Whitehouse and Leslie Deakins, and helped by the huge success of the supporters' association, was able to lead the

Club to a creation of a stadium which is the envy of cricketers from all over the world'.

He was succeed by Tony Steven, a courteous, kindly man, who deserved better than to be in office during a period of unrest at Edgbaston which was to produce two special members' meetings in the following four years.

In 1984, a slump from the beginning of August resulted in Warwickshire winning only two of their last nine Britannic Assurance County Championship matches, and none of the last five, but the Club enjoyed a season of all-round success, with defeats in the Benson and Hedges Final at Lord's and the NatWest semi-final underlining how close the players came to a major achievement.

A final placing in the Championship of ninth, and seventh in the John Player Special League, renamed as such the previous year, was a meritorious performance, considering the injuries which kept out Willis, Lloyd and Hogg for most of the season, and Old for part of it.

Lloyd's eye injury, suffered in his test match debut on his home ground against the West Indies, was horrific. He had played in only six matches before the accident, but superb seasons from Amiss, Kallicharran and Humpage compensated for his absence, with all three batsmen achieving personal bests in one way or another.

Amiss' 2,137 runs in the Championship has been beaten only once for Warwickshire – by Mike Smith's 2,169 in 1959 – and with Kallicharran also topping 2,000 Championship runs, this was the first recorded instance of two Warwickshire batsmen achieving this in the same season. The West Indian's aggregate of 2,301 was his highest for the Club, and his nine hundreds also set up a new record.

The 1,891 runs by Humpage at an average of 48.49 was the seventh time he had passed 1,000 runs in a season, and was his highest aggregate. Only two other full-time wicket-keepers in history had ever scored more runs – Les Ames and Jim Parks.

As Humpage also scored 777 in one-day cricket, it can be seen that his performance deserves to rank with that of any other wicket-keeper batsman in the history of cricket and quite deservedly, he was named as one of *Wisden*'s 'Five Cricketers of the Year'. He hit five hundreds, including 205 against Derbyshire at Chesterfield, and also claimed 66 victims behind the stumps to complete his best season for Warwickshire.

Robin Dyer snapped up the chance afforded him by the injury to Lloyd, and scored a stylish 1,187 in the season at 34.91 including his maiden hundred – an unbeaten 106 at Cardiff.

Small, Old and Ferreira carried the new ball attack, with one or others making telling contributions in the wins over Middlesex at

Andy Lloyd scored his first double century, 208 not out in 414 minutes, including 35 fours and one six, for Warwickshire v Gloucestershire, County Championship at Edgbaston on 27 May 1983. In this picture Lloyd hits a boundary off Phil Bainbridge with wicket keeper Jack Russell looking on.

Lord's, Gloucestershire and Kent at Edgbaston, Lancashire at Old Trafford, and Yorkshire at Headingley. Not surprisingly, Old excelled himself against his former colleagues, taking 11 for 99 in the biggest victory margin of the side's six wins – 191 runs.

Gifford had an easier season, thanks to the success of the seamers, but still took 65 wickets at 29.52, and Ferreira enjoyed his best all-round season with 79 wickets at 27.94 and 777 runs at 29.88.

The bowlers were largely responsible for the improved performances in the John Player League, where four closely fought victories in the last five matches lifted the side to seventh. Humpage and Amiss hit unbeaten hundreds in the wins against Gloucestershire and Nottinghamshire, with Warwickshire's victory margin at Trent Bridge the minimum one of one run.

The Benson and Hedges campaign was one of undisturbed success, with six straight wins until Lancashire outplayed the Club in the final at Lord's – helped, it must be said, by having the fortune to bowl first on a pitch which contained an unsatisfactory amount of moisture before lunch. Even so, a total of 139 reflected yet another Warwickshire batting display at Lord's which lacked application, with Kallicharran's 70 deserving of more determined support. As he stood helplessly at one end, his side lost their last eight wickets for 37.

In the NatWest Trophy, after crushing home wins against Oxfordshire, Shropshire and Surrey by 127, 103 and 110 runs, with Kallicharran again leading the way with 206 and 101 in the first and third rounds, the left-hander's 86 in the home semi-final against Kent was once more denied responsible support. Conditions again favoured seam and swing earlier, compared with later, when Mark Benson's unbeaten 113 steered Kent home by six wickets.

Kallicharan's splendid season – 3,439 runs in all competitions from 67 completed innings – was rewarded with a benefit return of £34,097, and it was announced that Amiss would receive a testimonial the following year.

A remarkable financial recovery produced a surplus of £66,198, thanks mainly to a huge increase in revenue from match sponsorship and room hire, as well as from perimeter fence advertising, due to the Test match against the West Indies. Altogether £271,485 was taken compared with £79,753 in 1983 when Edgbaston did not stage a Test match.

Other significant increases in income, included one of £21,926 from the success in the two knock-out competitions, and an additional £41,861 from the catering contract.

The forecast for 1985 was similarly healthy, and the committee authorised the purchase of a completely new telephone system, as well as the installation of new seating in the Raglan Stand and pavilion west wing. The report included this definitive view: 'The Club's finances are in a thoroughly sound state, and as far as can be reasonably anticipated, should remain so for the foreseeable future. 1984 and 1985 will turn out to have been important years during which the Club's finances have stabilised.'

Gifford, having led the side in 19 of the 24 Championship games, was appointed captain for 1985 in succession to Willis, who never regained full fitness after the illness which forced him to come home from Pakistan during the Faisalabad Test match.

The annual report paid a lengthy tribute to the fast bowler, placing great emphasis on the courage and determination that enabled him to return to cricket from a series of injuries and illnesses which would have deterred many cricketers. Reference was also rightly made to the fact 'that he has always been a great defender of the ethics of the game. Never once did he engage in those wretched verbal slanging matches that ocasionally regrettably occur between cricketers'.

What must be questioned was the wisdom of the original decision to appoint Willis as captain, knowing that if fit, he would be absent on international duty for many matches. His normal difficulty in motivating himself for three-day cricket after his Test match experiences was exacerbated by his appointment in 1982 to the England captaincy. During his five years as Club captain, he played in 53 out of a possible 114 Championship games with the following result: 1,153.3 overs; 272 maidens; 3,387 runs; 104 wickets; average 32.56.

He played 136 first-class matches for Warwickshire in 13 seasons, and took 353 wickets at 24.84 each. His final figures of 3,137.3–747–8,769–353–24.84 compare with his magnificent Test record of 2,892.5–8,190–325–25.20. He took five or more wickets in an innings on 16 occasions for England, and 14 for Warwickshire.

Willis will go down in history as a man who, despite not seeking – or probably wanting – the captaincy of county and country, was given both. The normal difficulties confronting a specialist bowler under such circumstances were compounded by a nature which was too introspective ever to come to terms with the many demands of first-class cricket.

Paradoxically, it was much to Willis' credit that, knowing his shortcomings in communication and man-management, he uncomplainingly accepted both posts. The truth is that he was a captain's man, and not a man's captain.

Life membership was conferred on him, although just three years later, he was to be plunged into one of the most acrimonious sequences of events ever known at Edgbaston.

CHAPTER TWENTY-THREE

FROM STRIFE TO PEACE, 1985–1989

ALTHOUGH THE UPSET WHICH was to end with Willis virtually severing his connections with Warwickshire was not to occur until 1987, the first warning shots were fired by the members after the 1985 season, which was in such marked contrast to the previous year.

The side won only two Britannic Assurance Championship matches, and dropped from ninth to 16th in the table, after losing eight matches and drawing the other 14. In the John Player Special League, a bright start of five wins from the first seven matches was spoiled by a combination of bad weather and poor cricket which resulted in two matches being abandoned, five defeats and the only two wins coming in the last two fixtures. With the side failing to qualify for the last eight of the Benson and Hedges Cup, and losing to Nottinghamshire in the second round of the NatWest Trophy, a section of the membership requisitioned a special general meeting 'to pass a Vote of no confidence in the cricket sub-committee and coaching'.

A somewhat confused meeting took place on 16 December when, despite one of the members' spokesmen, Dr 'Red' Walker, intimating that the purpose of the meeting was more to let the Committee know of the increasing unrest among the membership than to force any resignations, the resolution was passed by 352 to 330. The requisitioners had ample opportunity to prevent a vote, and by not so doing, revealed that their strategy had not been properly thought through.

The cricket sub-committee under the chairmanship of Jamie McDowall resigned *en bloc* the following day, with a re-constituted body formed several weeks later with David Heath as chairman. The only change in personnel was R. J. Evans instead of McDowall.

Brown was deeply upset by the result of the meeting, and only after several days did he decide to carry on, little knowing that a chain of events had started which, nearly two years later, would result in the termination of his employment at Edgbaston, Heath as a paid employee being relieved of his role as Chairman of Cricket, Willis severing his connections with the Committee and Evans becoming the new Chairman.

One of the strongest criticisms of the management and coaching staff concerned the lack of progress, particularly with the ball, made by young players like Paul Smith, Lethbridge, Wall and Hoffman. Even allowing for youngsters needing time to mature, the average runs conceded per over by each of them was too high at over 3.5, and with only Lethbridge's 77 wickets costing less than 40 – marginally so at 38.91 – the comments were difficult to rebut.

It was further suggested that the time bought by the signing of Gifford and Old had not been usefully deployed, because none of the younger bowlers had taken advantage of the breathing space afforded them to improve their techniques. Did the fault lie with the players or with the coaching methods? The one positive result to come from the meeting was an offer from Chairman Tony Steven to the members in answer to the complaint that, in the absence of a special meeting, they had no opportunity to air any grievances between the end of one season and the Annual General Meeting just before the beginning of the next one. Steven offered to meet the members, together with other officers of the Club, during the winter months.

It was subsequently decided to hold the Annual Meeting in January, thus giving the committee the chance to take into account the views of members before finalising policies for the following year. The change of dates was implemented on 27 January 1988.

Small (69 wickets), Ferreira (77) and Gifford (46) carried the attack, but the inability of Old to play more than seven matches was the biggest blow to the new captain, Gifford.

The batting, under the constant pressure of trying to compensate for the bowling frailties, finally crumbled as well, although Dyer impressed again with 1,242 cultured runs at 28.88. His inability to raise the tempo of his game was a handicap, particularly in one-day cricket, and he provided a good example of the difficulties facing young cricketers trying to make their way in the modern cricket world.

Amiss scored most runs, and his 1,555 at 39.87, including five hundreds, took his total in first-class cricket to 96, as well as his overall aggregate past the 40,000 mark – the first Warwickshire batsman to achieve this. Another record for Amiss was his final Testimonial figure of £85,000, well over double the amount he recieved from a full benefit in 1975 (£34,947).

Lloyd returned with 1,230 at 38.44, and marked his first innings at Edgbaston since he had been carried off in the Test match against the West Indies, with 160 against Glamorgan.

Humpage and Ferreira had satisfactory seasons, with the South African all-rounder taking 77 wickets at 28.14 and scoring 805 runs at 28.75, including his second hundred for Warwickshire. This was an unbeaten 101 at Taunton in the match in which Viv Richards secured maximum batting bonus points single-handed with 322 – the highest score ever recorded in a Warwickshire match.

In addition to Humpage's 1,361 runs at 37.80, he set up a new wicket-keeping record for Warwickshire with 80 victims to beat the previous total of 79 set up by Jack Smart in 1932.

The Club hosted the fourth Test match against Australia as well as the second of the Texaco one-day internationals. Despite several

Derek Randall was caught by Geoff Humpage, bowled by Dean Hoffman in each innings (twice in the match). Here, in the second innings, Randall is out to a very good diving catch by Humpage. Warwickshire v *Nottinghamshire at Edgbaston 1985.*

interruptions from rain, record receipts were taken from the Test which England won in exciting fashion on the final day by an innings and 118 runs.

A year of contrast for the Edgbaston Committee ended on a note of financial triumph. The surplus for the year was a record £88,015, thanks to further considerable increases from the peripheral benefits of staging a Test match. Steep increases in membership fees yielded an extra £40,882, with the overall figure of £154,413 having more than doubled the 1979 figure of £62,189, and the profit from the catering contract had risen from £52,713 to £87,907. Small wonder that with the total annual expenditure now £1,040,450, the decline in gate receipts to £19,107 was of no great significance.

The most significant happening in 1986 was the departure of Alan Smith to Lord's to take up his duties as the newly appointed chief executive of the Test and County Cricket Board, in succession to the former secretary, Donald Carr. Only after his departure, was it appreciated just how well he had established a system of administration at Edgbaston which would function smoothly, even during his lengthy absences which, on the occasions he was abroad with England in a managerial capacity, could amount to five months in a calendar year.

In other years, his duties as an England selector – in 1986 he completed his second term of four years – together with his executive committee responsibilities at Lord's meant an absence of around 60 working days. The organisation he built at Edgbaston in his 10½ years as secretary was a tribute to a man who, in addition to possessing a combination of a love and feel for cricket which made him an outstanding administrator, also possessed the rare quality of the ability and willingness to delegate.

Smith was the fifth secretary at Edgbaston in 104 years, and the shortest serving by six months, but he deserves to rank with any of his predecessors for the way he ensured that the Warwickshire Club was not left behind during the sponsorship explosions of the 1970s which lifted cricket into the world of big business. When he took office on 1 April 1976, the total annual expenditure was £256,013, with income an additional £5,072. When he left Edgbaston, expenditure and income had reached £1,000,000, with the biggest increases in revenue coming from advertising (£221,183 from £16,893), membership subscriptions (£162,269 from £46,240) and the catering contract (£87,907 from £22,103). On the expenditure side, the cricketers' salaries were now £253,658 compared with £54,217, while those of the office staff had risen to £101,356 from £26,372.

The figures which revealed most about the need for County Clubs to maximise the return from alternative sources of income than cricket was the one in the 1986 accounts which broke down the main income. From cricket income, Warwickshire received £519,650, with £373,09 coming from 'other activities'. That is why Smith's period in office at Edgbaston was one of the most important in the history of the Club. His appointment at Lord's was announced by the Board's chairman, Raman Subba Row, at Worcester in April, and the Warwickshire committee set about finding a successor to Smith during the early part of the summer.

The playing staff for 1986 had been strengthened by a trip by Brown to South Africa to sign all-rounder Brian McMillan, who had impressed the coaching staff the previous year when his twelve matches in the 2nd XI produced 367 runs at 40.78 and 25 wickets at 23.32, with pace bowling that appeared to border on the category of 'genuinely fast'. It was as a strike bowler he was engaged, but rather than solving a longstanding problem, he created another one by heading the batting averages with 999 runs at 58.76, while he took only 17 wickets from 220 overs at a cost of 47.52 each.

It was small surprise therefore that, with Gladstone Small and Norman Gifford the only regular bowlers of real quality, the side could improve its 15th place in the 1985 Championship table by only two places. Only bottom-placed Glamorgan, with 47, obtained fewer than Warwickshire's 51 bowling points. Four matches were won, with five lost and 15 drawn.

In the John Player Special League, the reversion to bad habits by the support bowlers meant a drop from sixth to co-ninth, with only bottom-placed Gloucestershire, with three wins, securing fewer than the five by Warwickshire. The side won three of its first five games, and four out of the first eight but, as in the Championship where two of the four wins came in the first nine games with no defeats, the second half of the season was notable only for individual performances.

Pride of place must go to Amiss and Gifford for completing 100 hundreds and 2,000 wickets in first-class cricket, and seldom, if ever, can two cricketers with the same club have passed such historic personal landmarks within five weeks.

Starting the season with 96 hundreds, Amiss scored an unbeaten 108 in the first match of the season at home in the drawn game with Essex, and after six more games in May, he notched numbers 98 and 99 at Bristol and Swansea by 20 June. After the win over Glamorgan by 284 runs, Amiss reached 54 in the next game at Edgbaston against Leicestershire before he sportingly walked off for a catch at the wicket down the leg-side which the umpire had not given out. He was 'rewarded' for his sportsmanship in the following match at Headingley when he was given out on 83 to a short leg catch, about which there was a strong element of doubt.

Like many of the 20 batsmen before him who had faltered in sight of the winning tape, Amiss had to endure another six matches and four weeks in which he passed fifty only once in ten innings before he scored an unbeaten 101 in the home drawn game against Lancashire. Nothing should detract from a magnificent achievement, but Amiss would certainly have preferred to have scored the last hundred under more competitive circumstances. In a 'dead match', Clive Lloyd agreed to play on through the final hour in order to help Amiss into three figures, but nevertheless the Warwickshire batsman deserved the plaudits he received from far and wide. His 76 hundreds for the Club constituted a record, and of course he became the fist Warwickshire player to join the elite club of players with 100 100s, whose membership he increased to 21.

As for Gifford, his 2,000th wicket came in an extraordinary match at Folkestone, in which Warwickshire lost by an innings and 30 runs after they were bowled out in their second innings on an impossible batting strip, with Underwood returning the astonishing figures of 35–29–11–7. On occasions on the final day the prodigious turn and lift available for one of cricket's all-time great bad-wicket bowlers sent the ball past the wicket-keeper to first slip, and batsmen were fighting

The historic scoreboard which says it all.

just to survive against deliveries which would leap throat high off a slow bowler's length.

Gifford became the 33rd bowler in history to reach this mark, and his unabated enthusiasm and undimmed skill, even under the strain of captaining such a moderate side, underlined the wisdom of the committee in backing Brown's judgement when the former Worcestershire captain was signed three years earlier.

He was handicapped throughout the season by being forced to omit Kallicharran and Ferreira every time he chose McMillan, and in desperation, the Club committee began a campaign to get the West Indian declared 'English' at Lord's, because he owned a British passport and had been resident in Birmingham for over ten years.

Even though strong arguments were put forward several times before the start of the following season, Kallicharran's career was hindered in a way that eventually proved costly to him and Warwickshire.

McMillan suffered a minor back strain in the early part of the season, but batted so well that he retained his place for 12 matches, which meant, of course, that Ferreira could not play. Especially after his splendid two previous seasons, in which he had not missed a game and scored 1,582 runs to supplement his 156 wickets, it was unsurprising that his all-round value was sorely missed. Whatever the growing restrictions in the legislation regarding overseas cricketers, it seemed that the Club committee felt under irresistible pressure from the membership to sign an overseas strike bowler, with the result that the treatment afforded to Kallicharran and Ferreira was unfortunate.

The South African decided to retire at the end of the season. His record with the Club was: 138 games in eight seasons, 4,088 runs at 28.99 and 335 wickets taken at 32.51. It is doubtful if any cricketer has been held in greater esteem by Committee, players and members alike. Unfailingly cheerful, he was a model professional sportsman who never ignored an opportunity to enhance the name of Warwickshire cricket, either by talking to the public or playing with children in their games of boundary cricket. He deserved some reward from the game to which he contributed so much, and although his stay at Edgbaston was too short to warrant a benefit, he was awarded one by Northern Transvaal in 1988 which brought him about £45,000.

One player to be released at the end of the year (there were eight in all) – was the 27-year-old Dyer. The committee took the view that as he could not command a regular place, it would be wrong to keep him, at that age, as a replacement. Like K. D. Smith, who was released the previous year, Dyer was a correct batsman who became a victim of the demands of one-day cricket. After all, both batsmen had career averages of 27, the same figure as Bates, Fishwick, Hitchcock, Ibadulla, Ord, Spooner and John Thompson, all of whom gave long and distinguished service to the Club.

Warwickshire failed again to qualify for the Benson and Hedges Cup knock-out stages, and in the NatWest Trophy they followed a good performance against Essex in the second round with a poor effort at Worcester where, admittedly on a difficult pitch, they could score only 136 for eight from their 60 overs.

Tim Munton, a 21-year-old seamer from Melton Mowbray, made a good impression with 32 wickets at 28.28, but with Parsons taking only 31 wickets at 38.03 in 21 games, the bowling cupboard looked depressingly bare.

No fewer than eight batsmen averaged over 32, with the division between McMillan and Kallicharran of the number 3 spot yielding a combined 2,004 runs from 39 completed innings, including eight hundreds.

Just behind them was 24-year-old Andy Moles, who took his chance so well after an unfortunate facial injury to Lloyd – received while fielding at slip to Gifford at Portsmouth – that he scored 738 runs from 15 completed innings, including two hundreds and five fifties. Together with Paul Smith, who responded to his promotion to open the innings with 1,508 runs at 37.70, he shared in four opening partnerships of over 100, with their 161 and 155 at Weston-super-Mare providing the first instance of two stands over 150 for Warwickshire, the fifth instance in the history of the County Championship, and only the twelfth in the history of cricket.

Humpage's three hundreds took his total to 28 – the eleventh highest for Warwickshire – and he scored another entertaining 1,462 runs at 38.47.

The search for a new secretary produced an original short list of three, including the Club's immensely popular commercial manager, Jim Cumbes, the Worcestershire secretary, Michael Vockins, and former Warwickshire captain, John Whitehouse. The new chairman of cricket, David Heath, was invited to submit a later application after he had been made redundant, and was finally chosen after the committee interviewed him for the first time, and the other three candidates for the second time, on the same day.

Cumbes was particularly disappointed to learn from the chairman next morning that the post had been filled from within the Club, and came close to joining one of his former football clubs, Aston Villa, who were keen to engage the services of a man who not only had proved his worth in the commercial side of cricket since 1982, but was one of the most popular men in the midlands sporting world. Cumbes was soon offered a new three-year contract, although he was to seek release from the agreement within twelve months.

The Club hosted the third Cornhill Test match against India in early July 1986, with the final drawn outcome brought about by an untimely interruption for rain during the tea interval on the final day. So for the second successive year, an Edgbaston Test match lasted into the fifth day, after every previous match going back to 1973 had produced a quicker result.

The Club announced a surplus of £40,402 – the third successive year a profit had been announced – which helped turn an accumulated fund deficiency of £161,707 on 31 October 1983 into a plus figure of £37,908 three years later. A. C. Smith was enrolled as a honorary life member – the 28th in history, and only the third former player to have played all of his cricket in the post-war period (the others being M. J. K. Smith and Willis).

CHAPTER TWENTY-THREE

The first rumble from the storm clouds which were to burst over the Club in twelve months time came immediately after Smith's departure. A sentence in the annual report pinpointed the start of a series of events which culminated in the most divisive special general meeting of Warwickshire members ever held; 'David Heath, the new general secretary, who had served on the general Committee since 1979, automatically relinquished his position on assuming office on 1 October.'

But Heath did *not* relinquish the chairmanship of the cricket committee, despite the unease felt by some of the committee members about the principle of a paid administrator holding an office which, previously, had always been held by an honorary committee member. This criticism, together with many subsequent events, would have been avoided had it been more widely known that, on taking up his secretarial duties on 1 October 1986, Heath immediately offered his resignation from the chair of cricket. Club Chairman, Tony Steven and the committee decided to defer the matter for several reasons, the most important of which was, in their opinion, the absence of an obvious successor, once M. J. K. Smith decided not to stand for office because his son, Neil, was about to join the playing staff.

A recommendation from the chair wsas accepted that Heath should continue to be chairman of cricket until the Annual General Meeting the following April. Subsequent events indicated that the decision not to make public Heath's resignation offer was an error of judgement which was compounded with the membership labouring under a misconstruction of the facts.

Coincidentally, the first decision by the General Committee was the refusal of permission to Brown and Gifford to approach Ian Botham, who had announced that he was leaving Somerset. Some of the former cricketers on the committee, like the captain and manager, were in favour of talking to the England all-rounder, and the decision was a bitter blow to Brown and Gifford, as well as to Cumbes, who was already aware of the tremendous commercial advantages Botham would bring by the number of provisional bookings and sponsorship offers he had received, some of which were conditional upon Botham appearing at Edgbaston in 1987.

The seeds had been sown which would soon result in a change of personnel in all three offices of Club captain, manager and commercial manager, although the change in the captaincy was certainly not connected with the growing troubles.

The biggest administrative upheaval ever experienced at Edgbaston undoubtedly contributed to an abysmal playing record in 1987 which must rank with the worst overall performance of any previous Warwickshire side. Sadly for Amiss, in his last season, and Gifford, in the last of his three years as captain, the side finished in 15th place in the

Britannic Assurance County Championship with two wins and bottom of the John Player Special League with three wins. They failed to qualify for the knock-out stage of the Benson and Hedges Cup after winning one of three qualifying games, with the match against Lancashire at Old Trafford abandoned, and after beating Staffordshire and Buckinghamshire in the first two rounds of the NatWest Trophy, they were easily beaten at Bristol by Gloucestershire.

In the four competitions, they won six out of 44 matches against first-class opposition.

Undoubtedly, the absence of Gladstone Small for 12 of the first 14 matches, due to a back strain he sustained while playing for England in Sharja in April, was crucial. But the effects of the growing unrest off the field were bound to seep into the dressing room, and any criticism of the team's poor showing must take that into account.

The membership recognised this by requisitioning the second special general meeting within 23 months, only this time they levelled their displeasure at the general committee by tabling a resolution expressing 'a vote of no confidence in the chairman and the general committee'.

The annual report to the membership was signed, as usual, by the chairman and secretary, Tony Steven and David Heath, but an addendum signed by the secretary only announced that the chairman had resigned on 9 October, and his successor was R. F. Evans. The final paragraph said:

> Thus the message in the opening paragraph of the 1986 Annual report which referred to 'unity of purpose throughout the Club', has been shortlived and additional pressure is again being imposed on those striving day by day to build a happy and successful County Club.

An arguable view, bearing in mind that as well as two men holding office as Club chairman, the Warwickshire Club also had three separate chairmen of the cricket sub-committee in three months, and after Jim Cumbes and membership secretary Keith Cook left Edgbaston, cricket manager David Brown had his employment terminated after 27 years at Edgbaston. Cook was to return within 12 months as assistant marketing manager, just before a further loss from the administrative staff saw the departure of assistant treasurer, Roger Arthars, after 14 years service.

Neither of the annual reports of 1987 or 1988 went into any detail of the sequence of events which led to the special general meeting held on 11 November 1987, and the 1988 report carried only three paragraphs, including the voting result, about the stormiest meeting in Warwickshire history.

The growing disquiet about the apparent disinclination of David Heath to vacate the chairmanship of the cricket sub-committee was at the heart of the troubles. A member at the annual meeting questioned the compatibility of a paid administrator holding that office, and was told by Chairman Steven that, together with the chairmen of various other sub-committees, the position of Heath would be reviewed 'in the next two or three weeks'. How much better if the committee had then revealed that Heath had already offered to resign.

A general committee meeting on 27 April made no decision, partly because they were waiting for the completion of a report by Peter Bromage and Tony Cross into the possible altered structure of the cricket committee, as well as a considered view about its current and future role. For this and other reasons, no cricket committee meeting was held until 13 July, although the Bromage report became available on 5 June, when it was presented to the Finance and General Purpose Committee.

The meeting on 13 July was contentious, with the dual role of Heath at the heart of the three-hour debate. It is difficult to understand how, with the committee so evenly divided, the issue was allowed to go to a vote, but it did, with a narrow majority – ten–eight, it is believed – producing an unnecessary division of the meeting.

Willis accepted the offer to succeed Heath, but in typically forthright manner added to his acceptance the remark that, in his view, the whole matter had not been handled well.

Presumably, Heath was instructed to make a press release about the change in office affecting one of the most important sub-committees in the Club, but nothing was said until the news predictably leaked during the following weekend when the team was playing at Bournemouth. Yet again, instead of influencing events by making a considered statement immediately after the meeting, the Club found itself in the backs-to-the-wall position of responding to rumours, and a golden opportunity was missed to minimise the implications of the committee row.

Brown, Gifford and Amiss vainly tried to concentrate the minds of the team on cricket, but within a week, another link appeared in the chain of events leading to the inevitable special general meeting. The *Birmingham Post and Mail* cricket correspondent, Jack Bannister, was making his way to the BBC commentary box in the Edgbaston pavilion, on the first day of the Test match against Pakistan, when three members independently told him that the popular Jim Cumbes had informed the committee that he wished to leave Warwickshire at the end of the season to take up similar commercial managerial duties at Old Trafford. A considerably larger salary figure was reported in a newspaper, but as that was still below the one offered by Aston Villa the previous year, the reasons for Cumbes moving were clearly not solely financial.

The story was confirmed by the secretary, but at his request, Bannister agreed not to publish the story until after the weekend because of the difficulty of putting together a Club statement during the first three days of the Test match. It was not made clear that Cumbes had not been 'head-hunted', but had instead immediately applied to Lancashire after the post was first advertised. When Bannister and Heath met after play on Saturday to discuss the matter, it also transpired that Cook was shortly to vacate the membership secretaryship after ten of his 18 years service at Edgbaston had been in that office.

Bannister also discovered to his surprise that the members had not been informed of the resignation of the Club's honorary treasurer, Philip Gough, which took effect from 27 April 1987. There is no doubt that this resignation was in no way connected with the troubles of the year, but came after Gough had given the committee ample notice of his wish to stand down because of business pressures, after eight years of valuable service in office. Even so an announcement of Gough's resignation should have been made to the members, when it happened.

Heath made it clear to Bannister that the decisions of Cumbes and Cook were unconnected, and the timing coincidental. On the face of it, the decision by Cumbes to move from one Test match ground to another of approximately the same standing could hardly have been made because the commercial possibilities at Old Trafford were any better than those at Edgbaston. Also, the disruption involved in moving house and family after 20 years in the area made his decision a difficult one to understand – particularly in view of his success at Edgbaston, where his drive in extending the sponsorship facilities in the private boxes and chalets for Test matches had pushed up the income in 1987 to £127,056, compared with £22,383 in 1983, the year before he promoted the first chalet village at an Edgbaston Test match.

Cumbes had been particularly disappointed by the decision the previous winter not to talk to Botham, so it must be assumed that his request for early release from his three-year agreement was partly because of this, together with what he described as a wider range of responsibilities with the Lancashire club, under its new chairman, Bob Bennett, with whom Cumbes had a longstanding friendship.

Ironically, the final departure of Cumbes was to be followed within three months by those of Willis and Brown.

If a list were drawn up of the men at Edgbaston who were least likely to do anything to precipitate a members' rebellion, the names of Dennis Amiss and Jim Cumbes would be at the top. Yet they were the unwitting causes of the biggest eruption within committee to date. This surfaced during the last week of Championship cricket at Edgbaston at the beginning of September. Amiss had been interviewed by Chairman Tony Steven about the possibility of him succeeding Cumbes. His magnificent career was at an end, and several people, including Heath, believed that the high level of esteem in which he was held in the Birmingham area would be of considerable advantage. Following a lengthy talk with the new chairman of cricket, Bob Willis, during Warwickshire's away match against Middlesex at Uxbridge in late August, Amiss expressed an initial interest, which waned once it was made clear that his accountability would be on a wider basis than he wished.

An executive committee meeting followed shortly, attended by Willis. When Steven offered a different explanation for Amiss declining the job from the one Willis believed to be the truth, he challenged the chair forcefully, and left the meeting after a total lack of support for his views.

In order to publish his version of events, Willis resigned as chairman of cricket the next day, although he did not resign from the general committee until 8 October. He chose the *Birmingham Post* as the vehicle for his message to the members, and the call for a special general meeting was inevitable.

Minutes of the general committee meeting held on 14 September, and chaired by M. J. K. Smith in the absence of Steven (who was on holiday), reveal that Willis was given the opportunity to propose a vote of no confidence in Heath, but declined to do so, saying that he had not been given sufficient time to substantiate such a proposal.

Steven resigned as Club chairman on 7 October, hoping that this decision might cause the cancellation of the costly special meeting, and Ken Kelly, who had been a member of the committee since 7 April 1975, resigned in order to help the requisitioners, among whom Dr Walker and W. A. Hammond were subsequently elected to the committee in January 1988.

The special meeting was held at the Metropole Hotel at the NEC on 11 November with, seemingly, more members present than the 957 votes cast. In the previous week, both sides had plenty to say in the local newspapers, with new chairman Evans calling on Willis to sever all links with Warwickshire if the vote went in favour of the committee. That it did so by 507–450 owed much to a powerful winding-up speech by Evans. So ended a traumatic 12 months in which Heath was incorrectly accused of clinging to the office of chairman of cricket. This, together with several other issues, including the rejection of a unanimous wish by Brown, Gifford and Cumbes, the three men appointed to run the cricket and commercial affairs of the

Club, to approach Botham, must pose a question mark about the judgement of the committee.

With hindsight, Willis would probably concede that, although he acted from what he believed to be the best interests of the Club, he would have won the day at the Metropole had he initially made his protest in a more restrained manner. Had this happened, it is probable that certain members of committee would have kept an open mind, rather than feel forced to close ranks because of the speed with which the unseemly affair became dominated by personalities.

It was doubly unfortunate for Amiss that the closing weeks of his wonderful career should have been played out in such an unpleasant atmosphere, with him unwittingly drawn into the controversy. He was given affectionate farewells around the country, with the public address announcer at Bournemouth unwittingly paying him a double tribute.

On the final day of a rain-ruined match, he walked off just before tea after enduring a peppering from Malcolm Marshall on a lifting pitch. The crowd applauded loudly when the announcer told them that was the last time Amiss would bat on a Hampshire ground, not knowing that a Gifford declaration, followed by a daring forfeiture of his side's second innings by Mark Nicholas, the Hampshire captain, would bring Amiss back to the crease fo face a second barrage from Marshall.

In the next game at Southport, a surprised Moles was also to get a standing ovation when the public address announcer mistakenly identified the 26-year-old opener as his 44-year-old colleague.

Amiss's final game was at Scarborough where, although he escaped a 'king-pair' by good luck, his final two innings were worth four runs from four deliveries in four minutes. The speed of his second innings dismissal so bemused the next man in – Humpage – that the wicket keeper misread the clock by an hour, and puzzled cricketers from both sides saw the normally attacking batsman playing for the close of play an hour early.

In the last of his 28 seasons with Warwickshire, Amiss scored 1,300 runs – the 20th time he had passed the 1,000 mark – and scored two hundreds. Sometimes the career figures of a cricketer do not do him justice, but those of Amiss unquestionably do.

First, his Test match record. In 50 games for England he scored 3,612 runs from 78 completed innings for an average of 46.30. His highest score was the never-to-be-forgoten unbeaten 262 at Kingston, Jamaica, in 1973 to save the game. Of his ten other Test hundreds, only three were under 150.

For Warwickshire he played 547 matches and his 946 innings (102 not outs) produced a record 35,146 runs at 41.64 and he hit 78 hundreds.

A typical powerful cover drive from Dennis Amiss, Warwickshire's most prolific batsman.

His overall first class record was even more massively impressive: 1,139 innings; 126 not outs; 43,423 runs; average 42.86. This put him in 11th place in the all-time list of run-scorers behind Hobbs, Woolley, Hendren, Mead, Grace, Hammond, Sutcliffe, Boycott, Graveney and Hayward. Of equal significance are the names immediately below him: Cowdrey, Sandham, Hutton, M. J. K. Smith, Rhodes, John Edrich, Wyatt, Compton and the Tyldesley brothers.

Amiss also scored 11,082 runs in limited-overs cricket.

It was a long road from an elementary school Docker Shield Final at Edgbaston 30 years previously to a deserved place in the all-time batting Hall of Fame. Nothing came easy for Amiss, and his success was a tribute as much to courage and determination as technique.

Moles finished the season strongly with hundreds in each of the last three matches – with 137 and 151 on successive days at Edgbaston against Worcestershire and Kent preceding 101 at Scarborough.

Lloyd passed 1,000 for the sixth time, and Humpage for the tenth in a benefit year that rewarded his outstanding performances and service for 14 seasons.

Din was promoted to number 3 in the absence for the entire season of Kallicharran, who could not be registered once it was decided to play either Merrick or Donald as the permitted overseas player. Din scored a fluent 1,056 at 33.00 and scored hundreds against Gloucestershire and Sussex. Paul Smith suffered, from either, or both, a loss of form and a switch to the middle of the order, which seemed hard on him after his excellent season in 1986.

The combined 96 wickets from the two overseas fast bowlers showed what a difference the absence of Small made, but in truth the side had little chance of realising its potential once the internal problems started.

The Club staged the most exciting Cornhill Test match of the series, and also the closest of the Texaco one-day internationals. England won the latter by one wicket with three deliveries to spare, in front of a capacity crowd wich produced some of the worst scenes of violence seen on the ground, after several hundred of the tourists' supporters succeeded in gaining entry without tickets.

Additional revenues from these two games, together with an increase of £49,885 from fencing advertising and the team sponsorship of over £20,000 from Mitchells and Butlers Ltd, contributed to a huge record surplus of £191,880 – the one bright feature of the most depressing year at Edgbaston within living memory.

The old cricketers' Association lost three of its most respected and best loved members – Tom Dollery aged 72, Jack Buckingham aged 84, and Derief Taylor, who smilingly concealed his age throughout his 35 years with the Club, spent mostly on the coaching staff, where his ability to improve young cricketers without stifling their natural talents marked him as a born teacher.

The saddest postscript to the year was the sacking of David Brown who, within a few weeks received the good news and bad news that he had been made a life member, together with Amiss, but the committee had decided after the special general meeting that sufficient of the responsibility for the happenings of 1987 lay with him, for a change to be made.

To his eternal credit, Brown accepted the decision without complaint, but he must have wondered at the justice of an outcome which left him as the only real casualty. His record as cricket manager during eight seasons was rather like his bowling – honest, conscientious and scrupulously fair, although perhaps lacking the little spark of flair that would have lifted him even higher.

Tributes were paid to him and the retiring chairman, Tony Steven, in the 1988 annual report.

The lessons of a year that drained committee, players and members alike, were many. If, despite recorded minutes that show that Heath was prepared to resign from the chair of cricket, some members of the committee were unaware of this – and this seems to be the case – there was a breakdown in communication between the membership and the Committee, so the problems needlessly escalated, inevitably to provoke the calling of a divisive special meeting of the Club membership, at which the committee had to fight off the ultimate challenging motion.

Since then, the lesson that the Club belongs to the members, not to the committee or the players, seems to have been learned, and a much more open administration, with Heath leading the way, has made great progess in righting a ship that was beginning to founder. The wishes and needs of the members should always be actively sought, and not just taken into account when they have to be. To this end, the Annual General Meeting is now held in January instead of April, at which time the membership had little chance of influencing policy decisions for the year, which are usually taken much earlier. Also, a programme of social evenings for members is now proposed each year, and a successful innovation is an 'Open Day' when members meet the committee and the players.

The response to these, and other enlightened moves, was such in 1989 that for the first time since 1972, there was a net gain of members of 1,000, and a comparison of the Club's overall income in 1989 and in 1985 reveals and increase from £892,749 to £1,819,034.

In this period, eight new boxes were built, the Rea Bank stand was re-seated, a new Stanley Barnes stand built together with a new Thwaite scoreboard, and the wonderfully positioned press box was refurbished.

On the other side of the ground, the Executive suite was refurbished and the Members' bar extended to include a restaurant. On the cricketing side, the Indoor School was given improved lighting and heating, and the ground staff were given the most sophisticated equipment available to improve and maintain a playing area suitable for Test cricket.

Evidence of the Warwickshire Club's ability to stage a successful Test match is provided by the gross receipts of the game against Australia, which were the highest of the four provincial grounds.

The leap year of 1988 started briskly at Edgbaston, with the annual meeting brought forward from April to 27 January, when the membership was officially told of the changes which ensued from the special meeting, held, aptly enough, on Armistice Day, 75 days earlier.

Chairman 'Bob' Evans, who succeeded Tony Steven on 9 October 1987, gave details of the new appointments of Club captain and cricket manager, which meant that Andy Lloyd and Bob Cottam would take over the running of Warwickshire cricket from Norman Gifford and David Brown.

M. J. K. Smith had succeeded Willis as chairman of cricket, and with Dr Walker and W. A. Hammond elected to the committee, all parties expressed the view that the time was long overdue for the bickering to stop, and all energies should be concentrated on the *raison d'être* of the Club, the playing of attractive and successful cricket.

Lloyd turned out to be a good choice, and his 'new broom' enthusiastic approach brought early success, with his side winning four of the first seven Championship matches, and qualifying for the quarter-final stage of the Benson and Hedges Cup. With Cottam stepping back from the sort of full-time dressing-room involvement with the County side that can easily lead to a dilution of the captain's responsibility, the members were soon aware that Edgbaston was a much happier place than in recent years. Cottam saw as one of the most important parts of his job the need to instil unswerving adherence by players to his rules of discipline, fitness and, just as important, attitude. The new chairman improved public relations, and with Alan Oakman soon settling into his new job of assistant secretary (cricket), the season ticked over smoothly.

Although only two more three-day games were won after the middle of June – at Edgbaston against Hampshire and Northamptonshire – Warwickshire finished in respectable sixth position with 218 points, even though several close finishes went against them.

At Northampton in the middle of May, they contrived to lose a game by six runs, scoring only 112 in their second innings after making the home side follow on 235 behind. They took nine of the ten wickets they needed to beat Somerset at Bath a month later, and after

Leicestershire won by one wicket at Edgbaston in August, they lost by four runs to Glamorgan after Small and Gifford had added 82 for the last wicket. Had Warwickshire won, the stand would have been the biggest tenth-wicket stand to win a match in the history of cricket.

To round off a season that was only a few runs and wickets away from being an outstanding one, Small's third fifty of a season in which he scored 521 runs at 24.80, took his side to 290 for nine – just eleven runs short of victory against Somerset.

Small returned to top form with 76 wickets for Warwickshire, although he disappointed in the Lord's Test. His contribution in partnership with either Merrick (65 wickets at 22.10) or Donald (26 at 20.53) was the essential difference between Warwickshire's performances in 1987 and 1988.

The batting was underpinned by Lloyd who, in his view, played as well as at any time in his career. He scored 1,448 runs at an average of 36.20 and two of his four hundreds led to victories. He scored an unbeaten 160 in the innings win over Hampshire at Edgbaston and, significantly, scored the only other hundred at Edgbaston against Northamptonshire, out of the eight scored for Warwickshire in the season. The reason for this was the one unsatisfactory aspect of the season – the awful pitches which were produced, despite the edict from Lord's to all Clubs to produce trustworthy surfaces.

Almost perversely, having decided to experiment with six four-day matches in the Championship, several Clubs deliberately prepared 'results' pitches which led to the Test and County Cricket Board's unprecedented decision to punish any proven transgressions in 1989 with a deduction of 25 points.

At times, Merrick was unplayable and revealingly he took 42 of his 65 wickets in eight out of his 16 matches at Edgbaston. Even so, his most remarkable spell came at Derby in a high-scoring drawn game where, in Derbyshire's first innings, he took six wickets in ten deliveries, including the hat-trick, and did not concede a run.

Munton made pleasing progress, to take 46 wickets at 22.76, and Paul Smith's 23 wickets at 23.47 represented his best return so far in a career which was still tantalisingly short of fulfilment.

Much was expected from Dermot Reeve, who was a contested signing from Sussex. His bowling was severely handicapped by a shoulder injury which was known about when he signed, and which eventually needed surgery, but even so, a total of 24 wickets at 31.25 from 292 overs was disappointing.

Gifford bowed out quietly with 31 wickets, to take his total for Warwickshire to 341 at an average of 27.44 from 139 games. His contribution cannot be measured by figures alone, and had he not joined the Club for his six seasons, the troubled times at Edgbaston would have been immeasureably worse. He was elected to the committee in January 1989 but resigned within a few days when he was appointed head coach to the Sussex Club.

Other than Lloyd, only Din passed 1,000, and he further established his right to the number 3 position by heading the averages with 1,425 runs at 38.51, including a career-best unbeaten 158 against Cambridge University.

Moles was one of several players whose season was curtailed by injury, but his 968 runs at 33.37 was enough to put him third in the averages. Kallicharran was plagued with a back injury which forced an operation the following winter, and he also sustained a broken finger, as did Moles, Reeve, Paul Smith twice and Banks.

After missing the whole of the 1987 season because he was not reclassified 'English' until December of that year, Kallicharran played only eight Championship matches, and a return of 301 runs from 14 innings sadly posed a question about his future at the age of 39.

With the retirement of Amiss, much had been expected from Kallicharran and Humpage, but cricket being the perverse game it is, the wicket-keeper had a disastrous season in which he scored 411 runs from 25 completed innings. He was dropped for 17-year-old Piran Holloway, but ironically in his worst-ever season he passed 'Tiger' Smith's aggregate of 15,911 runs to become the highest scorer of any wicket-keeper for Warwickshire, and his 57 victims took him past 'Dick' Lilley and Alan Smith into third place in the Warwickshire list behind 'Tiger' Smith and Dick Spooner.

At the end of 1988, in addition to his 16,174 first-class runs he had scored 5,844 in limited-overs cricket, and at the age of 34, it seemed unlikely that his career was coming to a close.

In Sunday cricket, the side's six wins lifted them to joint tenth, and there was a welcome improvement in the bowling, with the side's average of runs conceded per over down to 4.25 compared with 4.94 the previous season.

Warwickshire were beaten by nine wickets at Chelmsford in the Benson and Hedges Cup, and a seven-wicket victory by Kent in the second round of the NatWest Trophy at Canterbury was just as easily gained, following poor batting under good seam bowling conditions when Warwickshire failed to use their 60 overs in scoring 144.

The first Texaco Trophy one-day international against the West Indies was staged at Edgbaston, as was the first Refuge Assurance Cup Final at the end of the season, with near-capacity crowds turning up for both games. In the first, Small delighted the crowd with splendid bowling against the West Indies which brought him four for 31 in 11 overs and the Man of the Match Award, as well as victory for England by six wickets.

The lack of a Test match reduced the financial surplus to £7,623, but the new treasurer, Neil Houghton, forecast a better year for 1989, when a Test match against Australia would be staged, and he anticipated 'the improved performances this season will continue and provide the basis for a sound financial year in 1989'.

At the start of the year, Amiss' retirement was marked with a visit to Buckingham Palace to receive the MBE. Winnie Crook also announced her retirement from the supporters' association. She, together with her husband, David Blakemore, played a leading part in raising the necessary monies to fund the development of the ground, and had either of them been less dedicated to the cause of Warwickshire cricket the nation-wide decline in the success of fund-raising activities in the previous ten years would have had a much greater, and earlier, effect at Edgbaston.

If only from a feeling of relief, following the release from the internecine activities of the previous two years, everyone at Edgbaston impatiently awaited the 1989 season with a rare optimism.

The side, indeed, had a much better season – one of their best of the decade – even though their final County Championship results were remarkably similar to those of the previous year. This time they had five wins compared with six, and 44 and 75 batting and bowling bonus points compared with 48 and 74. The final position in the table was eighth – a drop of two places – but the captain could justifiably claim that, after a poor spell which lasted throughout the first three months, a remarkable run of form from the end of July onwards indicated that at long last a side of formidable all-round strength had been welded together.

After failing to qualify for the knock-out stages of the Benson and Hedges Cup, and not managing to win one of the first 13 Championship matches, despite earning more bowling points at that stage than 12 other sides, at the end of July the side was in 16th place, just five points ahead of bottom-placed Kent.

The turning point was a successful run-chase against Gloucestershire at Edgbaston, in which Dermot Reeve scored an unbeaten 86. After the side went on next day to beat the strong and much-fancied Northamptonshire side on their own ground in the quarter-final of the NatWest Trophy, a momentum was established that made a mockery of the earlier tentative efforts by, mainly, the same players.

Successive away wins at Canterbury and Bournemouth followed, and another win at Swansea gave Lloyd and his players just the fillip they needed for their home semi-final NatWest game against Worcestershire.

With the visitors badly hit by injuries – their attack was without Dilley, Botham, Newport and Pridgeon, Warwickshire delighted the first-ever all-ticket capacity crowd for a domestic game at Edgbaston by bowling and fielding superbly, after an unbeaten 94 by Asif Din steered his side to 220 for nine – good enough in the end to win easily by 100 runs.

The main reason for the emergence of Warwickshire from the shadows was that the batsmen remedied the early season weakness of a lack of runs from numbers 3 to 6. Their cause then was hardly helped by the curious decision to bat Humpage at number 7 in the early games, and that certainly cost what slim chances there were of wins against Lancashire and Leicestershire in the Benson zonal games.

In both cases, one of the best natural hitters on the staff came to the crease with so few overs remaining, that he had little chance to make an impact, and the same can be said of the thrilling home Championship match against Worcestershire, in which the sides finished with equal scores in a drawn game, but Warwickshire took half the win points because they had four wickets in hand.

Had Moles, who scored a solid 85, had any sort of support, the home side would have won anyway, but even so it made no sense for

South African fast bowler, Allan Donald, who made such rapid progress in 1989.

Warwickshire captain, Andy Lloyd, holds the NatWest trophy aloft after the presentation on the balcony. Andy Moles and Tim Munton are on the right of the picture, with Gladstone Small behind Andy Lloyd's right arm.

Humpage to be undefeated with seven and not face a ball in the final over.

He finished the season with 1,041 runs at an average of 38.55, and with Alvin Kallicharran scoring his first two Championship hundreds for three years, and Lloyd and Moles both passing 1,100 runs, the bowlers were given the sort of support which had not been previously forthcoming.

Allan Donald had a wonderful season, with his 86 first-class wickets at 16.25 each sandwiching the South African fast bowler in second place in the national averages between Terry Alderman and Malcolm Marshall. Donald made such progress that the other overseas pace bowler, West Indian Tony Merrick, had few opportunities and he was released at the end of the year.

In addition to getting good players out, Donald developed the true fast bowler's ability to rip through the tail, as he showed at Canterbury and Taunton in particular, when he mowed down a succession of lower-order batsmen, and three times was on a hat-trick.

Gladstone Small survived a niggling side injury which cost him an England cap at Trent Bridge before he bowled well enough in the final Test match at the Oval to earn selection for England's tour of the West Indies the following winter, and his 51 wickets at 23.56 support the view of those who claim that he and Donald formed the best new-ball attack in county cricket.

Munton made sufficient progress with 59 wickets to earn his cap, and with Paul Smith's 33 wickets giving him his best season with the ball, and Reeve chipping in as often as his injured shoulder would allow, Lloyd had a penetrative and varied seam attack at his disposal.

Off-spinner Adrian Pierson did well with 32 wickets before a shoulder injury gave Neil Smith his chance. Whether his future lies with bat or ball is unclear, but he looks the sort of cricketer who will make every scrap of his ability count, as shown by his marvellous display of concentration at Headingley in the match before the NatWest final when, going in as nightwatchman, he batted all the next day for an unbeaten 161.

And so to the big day at Lord's where, against all the odds, including those of the bookmakers, Warwickshire won their first knock-out trophy for 21 years. Although the result was a triumph for much solid teamwork throughout most of the game, it took an individual flash of inspiration from Neil Smith to clinch a last-over win which seemed to have slipped away, despite earlier excellent innings from Reeve, Paul Smith and Humpage. He hit the second ball from Hughes for a towering six over long-off to crown a splendid finale to the season, and give particular pleasure to the ailing Leslie Deakins who sadly died seven weeks later, aged 80.

Much will depend in the near future on the ability of the first six batsmen to score sufficient runs to enable the side to challenge as hard for trophies as the ability of their bowlers suggests is possible, and the inter-changeable value of Reeve, Din and Paul Smith holds the key.

For the first time in his eight seasons, Paul Smith averaged over 30 with the bat and under 30 with the ball, and as he was 26 at the beginning of the 1990 season, he still had time to fulfil the glowing forecasts made about him as a teenager.

There is enough young talent on the Warwickshire staff to suggest that the side is about to begin a period in the Club's history which during the next few years should be much more successful than previously, and thus provide the long-suffering membership and public more of the entertainment and results that have been denied them until the last few weeks of the 1989 season.

EPILOGUE

IF A POET IS ALLOWED AN occasional licence, an author should enjoy the same privilege, and I have decided to claim mine to finish the history of a Club with which I have been associated in one form or another since 1947.

My licence is stamped 'Selector', and having voiced the odd criticism of selectors at all levels from school to international in that time, I now volunteer myself as a similar target.

This history of the Warwickshire County Cricket Club has provided a parade of players, some of whom will for ever be on any list of the game's most noted players, and I have devised a competition which will embrace four teams from the past, covering the period from when first-class status was first conferred on the Club to the present day.

My teams are selected from the years 1894 to 1914, 1919 to 1939, 1946 to 1968, and 1969 to 1989. The criteria for selection is that the chosen players are picked on their best form, when they performed at their peak, and the pitches on which the games will be played will conform with those prepared according to the Test and County Cricket Board on high, in the Groundsman's Valhalla, where sunshine and rain are always available in the right proportions.

The Strips will therefore start solid, with a touch of greenness for the first session. They will then be good to bat upon, albeit with pace and even bounce before, sometime after lunch on the second day, the surfaces will start to take spin as the top gradually dusts. Even in the last session of the three-day games, the pitches will not be impossible to bat upon, but the wear and tear will be sufficient to discourage the captains winning the toss from fielding first.

The weather will be fine, but not too hot throughout the three days, and the grounds will be packed with cricket enthusiasts, anxious to see the best pitted against the best. All these conditions are mine to decide under the terms of my licence, although the modern selectors would probably think that their task was complicated, rather than simplified, by having to choose players best fitted for conditions in which pure skill would be the deciding factor.

Each captain is co-opted to the selection committee of one, and their influence can be seen in the choice of certain players, whose figures might be less impressive than those of some omitted players but balance and team spirit are major considerations, so let the arguments begin.

A happy moment at the Edgbaston Test of 1989 was the handing over of a long lost treasure to Bob Wyatt, the 1929 MCC Touring blazer, found in the loft of a house that was occupied by his brother in Cheltenham. Test captains David Gower and Allan Border hand over the blazer to the 88-year-old Test veteran.

1894–1914	**1919–1939**	**1946–1968**	**1969–1989**
S. Kinneir	A. Croom	F. Gardner	D. Amiss
T. Fishwick	N. Kilner	R. Barber	T. Lloyd
C. S. Baker	J. Parsons	W. Stewart	R. Kanhai
W. Quaife	R. Wyatt	M. J. K. Smith	A. Kallicharran
J. Devey	L. Bates	H. Dollery	J. Jameson
C. Charlesworth	F. Calthorpe	A. Kardar	G. Humpage
P. Jeeves	E. J. Smith	A. Townsend	K. Ibadulla
F. Foster	N. Partridge	R. Spooner	G. Small
A. Lilley	G. Paine	T. Cartwright	D. Brown
S. Hargreave	J. Mayer	C. Grove	A. Donald
F. Field	H. Howell	T. Pritchard	N. Gifford
S. Whitehead	D. G. Foster	W. E. Hollies	L. Gibbs

The four captains are Foster, Wyatt, Dollery and Brown, and what a Festival Week 'Rusty' Scorer could make of their four sides, with 12 players from each era to parade skills which delighted cricket followers all over England and, in some cases, abroad as well. The odd 'wild card' has been chosen at the particular captain's request – like Stephen Whitehead, Percy Jeeves, Derek Foster and Hafeez Kardar, with all four possessing a wicket-taking flair that, for varying reasons, their relatively short careers did not allow to flourish.

If the competition were played on a round-robin basis, which side would win? Who knows, but as my licence allows one final team to be chosen to play the rest, the authorial neck is willingly placed on the block with:

> Dennis Amiss, Sep Kinneir, Rohan Kanhai, Mike Smith, 'Tom' Dollery (capt), Bob Wyatt, Percy Jeeves, Frank Foster, Dick Spooner, Frank Field, Harry Howell, Eric Hollies and Sam Hargreave.

The party numbers 13 because try as I may I cannot reduce it satisfactorily without omitting Wyatt, Jeeves or Field, and my studies and research convinces me that all three are worthy of inclusion in any Warwickshire 'team of all time'.

The choice of captain was easy, with Dollery head and shoulders above any other captain I have seen in first-class cricket. His finger was always on the pulse of a game, and his unselfish batting was an inspiration to his players. Also, his selection would release players like Foster and Wyatt from the problems which occasionally appeared to inhibit them.

The writing of this book has been a fascinating and rewarding exercise, particularly this epilogue. Since William Ansell had a dream in the last quarter of the last century, the Bear and Ragged Staff has experienced times of triumph and trouble – notably in the 1980s when the Club was beset with internal strife that, thankfully, fell short of open civil war.

The wounds have healed, and with the playing success of the 1989 season to build on, Warwickshire cricket is poised, with a promising young side, to go forward to the next century in the hands of an enterprising committee and captain who should ensure a period of welcome success.

STATISTICAL SECTION

BIOGRAPHICAL DETAILS OF WARWICKSHIRE PLAYERS

NAME AND EXTENT OF CAREER	BIRTHPLACE	DATE OF BIRTH	DATE OF DEATH
Robert Neal Abberley *1964–1979*	Birmingham	22. 4.1944	
Roy Beverley Abell *1967*	Birmingham	21. 1.1931	
Charles Henry Adderley *1946*	King's Heath, Birmingham	16. 9.1912	28. 2.1985
James Moffat Allan *1966–1968*	Leeds	2. 4.1932	
Dennis Leslie Amiss *1960–1987*	Harborne, Birmingham	7. 4.1943	
Mohamed Asif Din *1981–*	Kampala, Uganda	21. 9.1960	
Harry Austin *1919*	Moseley, Birmingham	17. 4.1892	28. 8.1968
Herbert William Bainbridge *1894–1902*	Gowhatti, Assam, India	29.10.1862	3. 4.1940
Charles Shaw Baker *1905–1920*	Moss Side, Manchester	5. 1.1883	16.12.1976
David Andrew Banks *1988–1989*	Pensnett, Staffs	11. 1.1961	
John David Bannister *1950–1968*	Wolverhampton	23. 8.1930	
Eric George Barber *1936*	Bishopsgate Green, Coventry	22. 7.1915	
Robert William Barber *1963–1969*	Withington, Manchester	26. 9.1935	
William Henry Barber *1927–1933*	Nuneaton	23. 7.1906	13. 1.1980
Alfred Edward Barbery *1906–1907*	Marylebone, London	13.10 1884	23. 5.1973
Maurice Percy Barker *1946*	Leamington Spa	4. 2.1917	
Sydney Francis Barnes *1894–1896*	Smethwick	19. 4.1873	26.12.1967
Terry Peter Barnes *1956*	Coventry	13.11.1933	
Joseph Barton *1895–1896*	Smethwick	10. 1.1860	31. 1.1945
Leonard Thomas Ashton Bates *1913–1935*	Edgbaston, Birmingham	20. 3.1895	11. 3.1971
Samual Harold Bates *1910–1912*	Edgbaston, Birmingham	16. 6.1890	28. 8.1916
Martin George Bayley *1969*	Leamington Spa	10. 7.1952	
Robert Geoffrey Baynton *1921–1923*	Moseley, Birmingham	5. 3.1900	26. 8.1924
Harold Lewis Benjamin *1919*	St. Thomas Parish, Birmingham	13. 4.1892	7. 8.1942
Joseph Emmanuel Benjamin *1988–*	St. Kitts, West Indies	2. 2.1961	
Gwynfor Leonard Benson *1959–1961*	Birmingham	7. 1.1941	
William Blenkiron *1964–1974*	Newfield Estate, Bishop Auckland	21. 7.1942	
William Anderson Bourne *1973–1977*	Clapham St. Michael, Barbados	15.11.1952	

NAME AND EXTENT OF CAREER	BIRTHPLACE	DATE OF BIRTH	DATE OF DEATH
Carl Louis Breeden *1910*	Moseley, Birmingham	10. 2.1891	2.11.1951
Vincent Crescedo Brewster *1965*	Bridgetown, Barbados	2. 1.1940	
Walter Basil Bridge *1955–1968*	Birmingham	20. 5.1938	
Reginald Gordon Brindle *1949*	Warrington	3.10.1925	
Ralph Francis Broberg *1920*	Balsall Heath, Birmingham	21. 7.1899	3. 9.1938
Philip Harry Bromley *1947–1956*	Stratford-upon-Avon	30. 7.1930	
Albert Brown *1932*	Birmingham	29. 7.1911	
David John Brown *1961–1982*	Walsall	30. 1.1942	
Edward Brown *1932–1934*	Newcastle-on-Tyne	27.11.1911	14. 4.1978
John Dowell Brown *1913–1914*	Coventry	25. 8.1890	18. 3.1968
John Buckingham *1933–1939*	Grimethorpe, Yorks	21. 1.1903	25. 1.1987
Reginald Henry Markham Buron *1919*	Leamington Spa	23. 3.1900	19.10.1980
Harold Aston Busher *1908*	Sparkhill, Birmingham	2. 8.1876	10.1954
George Robert Byrne *1912*	Northfield, Birmingham	28. 5.1892	23. 6.1973
James Frederick Byrne *1897–1912*	Penns, nr. Birmingham	19. 6.1871	10. 5.1954
Victor Henry Douglas Cannings *1947–1949*	Bighton, Hants	3. 4.1919	
Raymond George Carter *1951–1961*	Small Heath, Birmingham	14. 4.1933	
Thomas William Cartwright *1952–1969*	Alderman's Green, Coventry	22. 7.1935	
Crowther Charlesworth *1898–1921*	Swinton, Lancs	12. 2.1875	15. 6.1953
William Clarkson *1922–1923*	Lancashire	not known	not known
John Alan Claughton *1979–1980*	Leeds	16. 9.1956	
Christopher Craven Clifford *1978–1980*	Hovingham, Yorks	5. 7.1942	
David Lindsey Clugston *1928–1946*	Belfast	5. 2.1908	
Thomas Collin *1933–1936*	South Moor, Stanley, Co. Durham	7.. 4.1911	
David Roland Cook *1962–1968*	Birmingham	2. 9.1936	
Michael Stephen Cook *1961–1962*	Birmingham	19. 2.1939	
Robert Cooke *1925–1926*	Selly Oak, Birmingham	25. 5.1900	14. 1.1957
John Pruen Cordner 1952	Diamond Creek, Victoria	20. 3.1929	
Robert Henry Cotton *1947*	Birmingham	5.11.1909	17. 1.1979
Charles Frederic Roy Cowan *1909–1921*	Glangrwyney, Brecon	17. 9.1883	22. 3.1958
Peter Cranmer *1934–1954*	Acocks Green, Birmingham	10. 9.1914	
Alexander Basil Crawford *1911*	Coleshill	24. 5.1891	10. 5.1916

NAME AND EXTENT OF CAREER	BIRTHPLACE	DATE OF BIRTH	DATE OF DEATH
Joseph Cresswell *1895–1899*	Denby, Derbys	22.12.1865	19. 7.1932
Henry Thompson Crichton *1908*	Edgbaston, Birmingham	18. 5.1884	1. 7.1968
Eric Bertram Crockford *1911–1922*	Birmingham	13.10.1888	17. 1.1958
Alfred John William Croom *1922–1939*	Reading	23. 5.1896	16. 8.1947
Leslie Charles Bryan Croom *1949*	Wybunbury, Cheshire	20. 4.1920	
Anthony John Cross *1969*	Fulmer, Bucks	5. 8.1945	
Eric Percival Cross *1921–1923*	Handworth Wood, Birmingham	25. 6.1896	27. 2.1985
James Cumbes *1982*	East Didsbury, Manchester	4. 5.1944	
Arthur Charles Curle *1920*	New Milverton, Leamington Spa	27. 7.1895	2. 2.1966
Gerald Curle *1913*	New Milverton, Leamington Spa	7. 6.1893	4. 3.1977
Conrad Stephen Davies *1930–1936*	Birmingham	27. 6.1907	
Richard John Davies *1976*	Selly Oak, Birmingham	11. 2.1954	
Charles Stewart Dempster *1946*	Wellington, N. Zealand	15.11.1903	14. 2.1974
John Henry George Devey *1894–1907*	Newtown, Birmingham	26.12.1866	11.10.1940
Frederick Dickens *1898–1903*	Stratford-upon-Avon	23. 4.1873	20. 2.1935
Edwin James Diver *1894–1901*	Cambridge	20. 3.1861	27.12.1924
Frederick Dobson *1928*	Olton, Solihull	12.10.1898	15.10.1980
Kenneth William Cecil Dobson *1925*	Shardlow, Derbys	28. 8.1900	3 3.1960
Ludford Charles Docker *1894–1895*	Smethwick	26.11.1860	1. 8.1940
Horace Edgar Dollery *1934–1955*	Reading	14.10.1914	22. 1.1987
Keith Robert Dollery *1951–1956*	Cooroy, Queensland	9.12.1924	
Allan Anthony Donald *1987–*	Bloemfontein, S. Africa	20.10.1966	
Martin Paterson Donnelly *1948–1950*	Ngaruawahia, N. Zealand	17.10.1917	
Dilip Rasiklal Doshi *1980–1981*	Rajkot, India	22.12.1947	
Paul Renton Dunkels *1971*	Marylebone, London	26.11.1947	
Thomas Wilfred Durnell *1921–1930*	Cannon Hill, Birmingham	17. 6.1901	10. 4.1986
Robin Ian Henry Benbow Dyer *1981–1986*	Hertford	22.12.1958	
Roger Bertram Edmonds *1962–1967*	Birmingham	2. 3.1941	
Geoffrey Elson *1947*	Coventry	19. 3.1913	
Russell Stanley Everitt *1909*	King's Heath, Birmingham	8. 9.1881	11. 5.1973
Arthur Hugh Fabling *1921*	Grandborough	6. 8.1888	11.10.1972
William Edward Fantham *1935–1948*	Birmingham	14. 5.1918	
George Clement Farren *1912*	Rugby	1873	2.11.1956

NAME AND EXTENT OF CAREER	BIRTHPLACE	DATE OF BIRTH	DATE OF DEATH
Anthonie Michal Ferreira *1979–1986*	Pretoria, South Africa	13. 4.1955	
Charles Anderson Fiddian Fiddian-Green *1920–1928*	Handsworth, Birmingham	22.12.1898	5. 9.1976
Ernest Frank Field *1897–1920*	Weethley Hamlet	23. 9.1874	25. 8.1934
Maxwell Nicholas Field *1974–1975*	Coventry	23. 3.1950	
Tom Silvester Fishwick *1896–1909*	Stone, Staffs	24. 7.1876	21. 2.1950
Kevin Frederick Flaherty *1969*	Birmingham	17. 9.1939	
Barry Elystan Fletcher *1956–1961*	Birmingham	7. 3.1935	
Barry John Flick *1969–1973*	Coventry	5. 3.1952	
Derrick Flint *1948–1949*	Creswell, Derbys	14. 6.1924	
Russell William Flower *1978*	Stone, Staffs	6.11.1942	
Thomas Forrester *1896–1899*	Clay Cross, Derbys	21. 9.1873	27.12.1927
Arthur Webster Foster *1914*	Deritend, Birmingham	12. 8.1894	9. 1.1954
Derek George Foster *1928–1934*	Sutton Coldfield	19.. 3.1907	13.10.1980
Frank Rowbotham Foster *1908–1914*	Deritend, Birmingham	31. 1.1889	3. 5.1958
John Fox *1922–1928*	Selly Park, Birmingham	7. 9.1904	15.11.1961
John George Fox *1959–1961*	Norton-on-Tees	22. 7.1929	
Reginald Carey Franklin *1900*	Radford Fields, Coventry	30. 4.1880	25. 6.1957
Fred Charles Gardner *1947–1961*	Bell Green, Coventry	4. 6.1922	13. 1.1979
Barry Keith Gardom *1973–1974*	Birmingham	31.12.1952	
Howard Charles Adie Gaunt *1919–1922*	Edgbaston, Birmingham	13.11.1902	1. 2.1983
William George *1901–1906*	Shrewsbury	29. 6.1874	4.12.1933
Lancelot Richard Gibbs *1967–1973*	Georgetown, B. Guiana	29. 9.1934	
Norman Gifford *1983–1988*	Ulverston, Lancs	30. 3.1940	
Albert Edward Gittins *1919*	Southport	12. 9.1897	6.10.1977
John Glassford *1969*	Sunderland	20. 7.1946	
Alfred Charles Stirrup Glover *1895–1909*	Stoke-on-Trent	19. 4.1872	22. 5.1949
Brian Thomas Glynn *1959–1961*	Birmingham	27. 4.1940	
Stanley Clarke Gobey *1946*	Stafford	18. 6.1916	
Cyril Clement Goodway *1937–1947*	Smethwick	10. 7.1909	
Harold James Goodwin *1907–1912*	Edgbaston, Birmingham	31. 1.1886	24. 4.1917
Alan Gordon *1966–1971*	Coventry	29. 3.1944	
Frederick Somerset Gough-Calthorpe *1919–1930*	Kensington, London	27. 5.1892	19.11.1935
Richard St. Leger Granville *1934*	Kingsworthy, Hants	24. 4.1907	8. 8.1972
John Denis Gray *1968–1969*	Meriden	9.10.1948	
Albert Victor Grayland *1922–1930*	Small Heath, Birmingham	24. 3.1900	3. 2.1963
John Herbert Green *1927*	Kenilworth	9. 5.1908	13. 9.1987

NAME AND EXTENT OF CAREER	BIRTHPLACE	DATE OF BIRTH	DATE OF DEATH
Simon James Green *1988–*	Bloxwich, Staffs	19. 3.1970	
Thomas Greening *1912*	Scotland	1883	25. 3.1956
Shirley Griffiths *1956–1958*	Bridgetown, Barbados	11. 7.1930	
Frederick Albert Gross *1934*	Southampton	17. 9.1902	11. 3.1975
Charles William Grove *1938–1953*	Birmingham	16.12.1912	15. 2.1982
John Bernard Guy *1950*	Ramsgate, Kent	16. 5.1916	
John Kenneth Hacking *1946*	Kenilworth	21. 3.1909	
William Hall *1905*	Bedworth	7. 4.1878	*c.* 1930
William Marcus Hampton *1922*	Bromsgrove	20. 1.1903	7. 4.1964
Barry Onslow Hands *1946–1947*	Moseley, Birmingham	26. 9.1916	1. 7.1984
William Cecil Hands *1909–1920*	Sparkhill, Birmingham	20.12.1886	31. 8.1974
Sam Hargreave *1899–1909*	Rusholme, Manchester	22. 9.1875	1. 1.1929
Archibald John Harris *1919*	Rugby	22.12.1892	10. 4.1955
Dennis Frank Harris *1946*	Birmingham	18. 4.1911	17.12.1959
Earlsdon Joseph Harris *1975*	Lodge Village, St. Kitts	3.11.1952	
William Henry Harris *1904–1919*	Rugby	13.12.1883	14.10.1967
Pater John Hartley *1982*	Keighley, Yorks	18. 4.1960	
William Henry Tomkins Harvey *1927*	Freemantle, Southampton	12. 4.1896	not known
Cyril Alexander Frederick Hastilow *1919*	Birmingham	31. 5.1895	30. 9.1975
Christopher George Hawkins *1957*	Slough	31. 8.1938	
Albert Hayhurst *1934–1935*	Birdwell, Yorks	17. 7.1905	
David Michael William Heath *1949–1953*	Birmingham	14.12.1931	
Michael Stephen Hellawell *1962*	Keighley, Yorks	30. 6.1938	
Edward Ernest Hemmings *1966–1978*	Leamington Spa	20. 2.1949	
Edward Pearson Hewetson *1919–1927*	Birmingham	27. 5.1902	26.12.1977
Eric Joseph Hewitt *1954*	Erdington, Birmingham	19.12.1935	
George Hickman *1929*	Burnopfield, Co. Durham	19. 1.1909	26. 8.1978
Thomas Arthur Hilditch *1907–1913*	Sandbach, Cheshire	10. 1.1885	7. 8.1957
Alfred John Bostock Hill *1920*	Olton, Solihull	8. 4.1887	20. 8.1959
Geoffrey Harold Hill *1958–1960*	Halesowen, Worcs	17. 9.1934	
Henry Barratt Grosvenor Hill *1894–1900*	Old Square, Birmingham	23. 7.1861	4. 6.1913
John Ernest Hill *1894–1898*	Birmingham	22. 9.1867	2.12.1963
William Aubrey Hill *1929–1948*	Carmarthen	27. 4.1910	
Raymond Edward Hitchcock *1949–1964*	Christchurch, N. Zealand	28.11.1929	
Dean Stewart Hoffman *1985*	Birmingham	13. 1.1966	
William Hogg *1981–1983*	Ulverston, Lancs	12. 7.1955	
William Hugh Holbech *1910*	Montreal, Canada	18. 8.1882	1.11.1914
Romilly Lisle Holdsworth *1919–1921*	Mysore, India	25. 2.1899	20. 6.1976
William Eric Hollies *1932–1957*	Old Hill, Staffs	5. 6.1912	16. 4.1981

NAME AND EXTENT OF CAREER	BIRTHPLACE	DATE OF BIRTH	DATE OF DEATH
Piran Christopher Laity Holloway *1988–*	Helston, Cornwall	1.10.1970	
David Charles Hopkins *1977–1981*	Birmingham	11. 2.1957	
Frank Jesse Hopkins *1898–1903*	King's Norton, Birmingham	30. 6.1875	16. 1.1930
Norman Frederick Horner *1951–1965*	Queensbury, Yorks	10. 5.1926	
John Johnson Hossell *1939–1947*	Birmingham	25. 5.1914	
William Eric Houghton *1946–1947*	Billingborough, Lincs	29. 6.1910	
Albert Louis Howell *1919–1922*	Ladywood, Birmingham	26. 7.1898	26. 7.1958
Henry Howell *1913–1928*	Hockley, Birmingham	29.12.1890	9. 7.1932
Geoffrey William Humpage *1974–*	Sparkhill, Birmingham	24. 4.1954	
Alfred Joseph Hyde *1905–1907*	unknown	*c.* 1884	unknown
Edward Arnold Illingworth *1920*	Dewsbury, Yorks	1896	2. 4.1924
Arnold Kenneth Jackson *1928–1931*	Edgbaston, Birmingham	21. 6.1903	31. 5.1971
John Alexander Jameson *1960–1976*	Bombay, India	30. 6.1941	
Thomas Edward Neville Jameson *1970*	Bombay, India	23. 7.1946	
Harold Harvey Jarrett *1932–1933*	Johannesburg, S. Africa	23. 9.1907	17. 3.1983
Percy Jeeves *1912–1914*	Earlsheaton, Yorks	5. 3.1888	22. 7.1916
George Adolphus Jennings *1923–1925*	The Friars, Exeter, Devon	14. 1.1895	7.1959
Alan Keith Colin Jones *1969–1973*	Solihull	20. 4.1951	
Richard Henry Cartwright Jones *1946*	Redditch, Worcs	3.11.1916	
Alvin Isaac Kallicharran *1971–*	Paidama, B. Guiana	21. 3.1949	
Rohan Bablal Kanhai *1968–1977*	Port Mourant, B. Guiana	26.12.1935	
Abdul Hafeez Kardar *1948–1950*	Lahore, India	17. 1.1925	
George Durant Kemp-Welch *1927–1935*	London	4. 8.1907	18. 6.1944
John Thomas Kendall *1948–1949*	Hawkesbury, Coventry	31. 3.1921	
John Maxwell Kennedy *1960–1962*	Manchester	15.12.1931	
Kenneth Gwynne Kent *1927–1931*	Moseley, Birmingham	10.12.1901	29.12.1974
Kevin John Kerr *1986*	Airdrie, Scotland	11. 9.1961	
Khalid Ibadulla *1954–1972*	Lahore, India	20.12.1935	
Norman Kilner *1924–1937*	Low Valley, Wombwell, Yorks	21. 7.1895	28. 4.1979
Edmund Hugh King *1928–1932*	Edgbaston, Birmingham	26. 3.1906	25.11.1981
Ian Metcalfe King *1952–1955*	Leeds	10.11.1931	
James Phillips Kingston *1894*	Northampton	8. 7.1857	14. 3.1929
Septimus Paul Kinneir *1898–1914*	Corsham, Wilts	13. 5.1871	16.10.1928
Edwin Kirk *1898*	Coventry	6. 5.1866	10. 3.1957

NAME AND EXTENT OF CAREER	BIRTHPLACE	DATE OF BIRTH	DATE OF DEATH
Harold Osborne Kirton *1925–1929*	London	4. 1.1894	9. 5.1974
Herbert John Knutton *1894*	St. Johns, Coventry	14. 6.1867	12.12.1946
Albert Frederick Lane *1919–1925*	Rowley Regis, Staffs	29. 8.1885	29. 1.1948
Colin Kendall Langley *1908–1914*	Narborough, Leics	11. 7.1888	26. 6.1948
Hubert Joseph Latham *1955–1959*	Winson Green, Birmingham	13.11.1932	
Alfred Law *1894–1899*	Birmingham	16.12.1862	10. 5.1919
Clive William Leach *1955–1958*	Bombay, India	4.12.1934	
Edric Leadbeater *1957–1958*	Huddersfield	15. 8.1927	
Edwin Legard *1962–1968*	Barnsley	23. 8.1935	
Christopher Lethbridge *1981–1985*	Castleford, Yorks	23. 6.1961	
Peter John Lewington *1970–1982*	Finchampstead, Berks	30. 1.1950	
Esmond Burman Lewis *1949–1958*	Shirley, Solihull	5. 1.1918	19.10.1983
Arthur Frederick Augustus Lilley *1894–1911*	Holloway Head, Birmingham	28.11.1866	17.11.1929
Timothy Andrew Lloyd *1977–*	Oswestry, Shropshire	5.11.1956	
Brian Lobb *1953*	Birmingham	11. 1.1931	
Gordon John Lord *1983–1986*	Edgbaston, Birmingham	25. 4.1961	
William Alsron Lord *1897–1899*	Washwood Heath, Birmingham	8. 8.1873	16. 6.1906
Frank Russell Loveitt *1898–1905*	Easenhall, Rugby	24. 4.1871	1. 9.1939
John Claude Malcolm Lowe *1907*	Coventry	21. 2.1888	27. 7.1970
Peter John Lowe *1964*	Sutton Coldfield	7. 1.1935	8.1988
Verner Valentine Luckin *1919*	Maybury Hill, Woking, Surrey	14. 2.1892	28.11.1931
John Lynes *1898–1905*	Coleshill	6. 6.1872	unknown
James Ian McDowall *1969–1973*	Sutton Coldfield	9.12.1947	
Brian Mervin McMillan *1986*	Welkom, OFS, S. Africa	22.12.1963	
Norman Michael McVicker *1969–1973*	Radcliffe, Lancs	4.11.1940	
Keith Robert Maguire *1982*	Marston Green	20. 3.1961	
Joseph Manton *1898*	West Bromwich, Staffs	4.12.1871	9.12.1958
Francis William Marshall *1922*	Rugby	30. 1.1888	24. 5.1955
Gordon Alex Marshall 1961–1963	Birmingham	12. 3.1935	
John Maurice Alex Marshall *1946–1950*	Kenilworth	26.10.1916	
Edward Matheson *1899*	Charlton, Kent	14. 6.1865	26. 2.1945
Ronald Harling Maudsley *1946–1951*	Lostock Gralam, Cheshire	8. 4.1918	29. 9.1981
Joseph Herbert Mayer *1926–1939*	Audley, Staffs	2. 3.1902	6. 9.1981
Christopher Maynard *1978–1981*	Haslemere, Surrey	8. 4.1958	
Richard Mead-Briggs *1946*	Sturry, Kent	25. 3.1902	15. 1.1956
William Waltrude Meldon *1909–1910*	Dublin	8. 4.1879	23. 5.1957
James Melville *1946*	Barrow-in-Furness	15. 3.1909	2. 8.1961
Michael David Mence *1962–1965*	Newbury, Berks	13. 4.1944	
Tyrone Anthony Merrick *1987–1989*	St. John's, Antigua	10. 6.1963	

NAME AND EXTENT OF CAREER	BIRTHPLACE	DATE OF BIRTH	DATE OF DEATH
James Brown Meunier *1920*	Poynton, Stockport	*c.* 1885	30. 9.1957
Edward Thomas Milburn *1987*	Nuneaton	15. 9.1967	
Harry Rayment Miller 1928	Gravesend, Kent	22. 2.1907	1. 9.1966
Roland Miller *1961–1968*	Philadelphia, Co. Durham	6. 1.1941	
John Michael Mills *1946*	Birmingham	27. 7.1921	
Frank Rollason Mitchell *1946–1948*	Goulborn, Australia	3. 6.1922	4. 4.1984
Andrew James Moles *1986–*	Solihull	12. 2.1961	
Steven Monkhouse *1985–1986*	Bury, Lancs	24.11.1962	
Fred Moorhouse *1900–1908*	Berry Brow, Yorks	25. 3.1880	7. 4.1933
Leonard John Morris *1925–1926*	Birmingham	26. 9.1898	9. 3.1984
Frank William Morter *1922*	High Elms Gardens, Down, Kent	14. 8.1897	20.12.1958
John Morton *1929–1930*	Drapers Field, Coventry	17. 8.1895	28. 5.1966
William Morton *1984–1985*	Stirling, Scotland	21. 4.1961	
Timothy Alan Munton *1985–*	Melton Mowbray, Leics	30. 7.1965	
Athol Leslie Murray *1922*	Mill Hill, Middlesex	29. 6.1901	10. 1.1981
Deryck Lance Murray *1972–1975*	Port-of-Spain, Trinidad	20. 5.1943	
Simon David Myles *1988*	Mansfield, Notts	2. 6.1966	
Alfred Leonard Nelson *1895*	Crackley Hill, Kenilworth	13.11.1871	2. 5.1927
Guy Montague Blyth Nelson *1921–1922*	Coten End, Warwick	28. 8.1900	13. 1.1969
Ernest Willmott Norton *1920*	Sparkhill, Birmingham	19. 6.1889	4.1972
Dennis Raymond Oakes 1965	Bedworth	10. 4.1946	
Alan Gerald Bernard Old *1969*	Middlesbrough, Yorks	23. 9.1945	
Christopher Middleton Old *1983–1985*	Middlesbrough, Yorks	22.12.1948	
Philip Robert Oliver *1975–1982*	West Bromwich, Staffs	9. 5.1956	
James Simpson Ord *1933–1953*	Backworth, Northumberland	12. 7.1912	
Christopher O'Rourke *1968*	Widnes, Lancs	13. 3.1945	
George Alfred Edward Paine *1929–1947*	Paddington, London	11. 6.1908	30. 3.1978
Henry James Pallett *1894–1998*	Birchfields, Birmingham	2. 1.1863	18. 6.1917
George Arthur Palmer *1928*	Hopsford Hale, Warwicks	5. 6.1897	1. 6.1962
Howard Roderick Parkes *1898*	Erdington, Birmingham	31. 5.1877	28. 5.1920

NAME AND EXTENT OF CAREER	BIRTHPLACE	DATE OF BIRTH	DATE OF DEATH
Matthew Croose Parry *1908–1910*	Birley, Herefordshire	12.12.1885	5. 2.1931
Gordon James Parsons *1986–1988*	Slough, Bucks	17.10.1959	
John Henry Parsons *1910–1934*	Oxford	30. 5.1890	2. 2.1981
Norman Ernest Partridge *1921–1937*	Great Barr, Staffs	10. 8.1900	10. 3.1982
Nigel Aldridge Paul *1954–1955*	Surbiton, Surrey	31. 3.1933	
William George Peare *1926*	Waterford, Ireland	25. 7.1905	16.11.1979
Godfrey Arnold Pell *1947*	Sunderland, Co. Durham	11. 3.1928	
Edward Thomas Pereira *1895–1896*	Wolseley Hall, Colwich, Staffs	26. 9.1866	25. 2.1939
Hubert George Perkins *1926–1927*	Attleborough, Nuneaton	18. 6.1907	4. 5.1935
Stephen Peter Perryman *1974–1981*	Yardley, Birmingham	22.10.1955	
Hugh Raymond Phillips *1951*	Kuala Lumpur, Malaya	8. 4.1929	
Joseph Herbert Phillips *1904–1911*	Ansley	2.12.1881	15. 1.1951
Adrian Roger Kirshaw Pierson 1985–	Enfield, Middlesex	21. 7.1963	
Keith John Piper *1989–*	Leicester	18.12.1969	
Wilfred Potter *1932*	Swincliffe Top, Felliscliffe, Yorks	2. 5.1910	
Reginald George Pridmore *1909–1912*	Edgbaston, Birmingham	29. 4.1886	13. 3.1918
Thomas Leslie Pritchard *1946–1955*	Kaupokonui, N. Zealand	10. 3.1917	
John Geoffrey Pugh *1922–1927*	Radford, Coventry	22. 1.1904	12. 2.1964
Bernard William Quaife *1920–1926*	Olton, Solihull	24.11.1899	27.11.1984
Walter Quaife *1894–1901*	Newhaven, Sussex	1. 3.1864	18. 1.1943
William Quaife *1894–1928*	Newhaven, Sussex	17. 3.1872	13.10.1951
David Philip Ratcliffe 1957–1968	Hall Green, Birmingham	11. 5.1939	
Jason David Ratcliffe *1988–*	Solihull	19. 6.1969	
Dermot Alexander Reeve *1988–*	Kowloon, Hong Kong	2. 4.1963	
James Rhodes *1895*	Aston, Birmingham	27. 7.1866	26. 8.1939
Thomas Basil Rhodes *1899*	Uttoxeter, Staffs	13. 8.1874	26. 5.1936
William Ignatius Rice *1920*	Birmingham	15. 3.1883	22. 4.1955
Walter Richards *1895–1896*	Balsall Heath, Birmingham	28. 9.1865	14.10.1917
Bryan Anthony Richardson 1963–1967	Kenilworth	24. 2.1944	
Stanley Hugh Richardson *1920*	Marston Green	2. 7.1890	24. 1.1958
Terence Michael Noel Riley *1961–1964*	Birmingham	25.12.1939	
Harley James Roberts *1932–1937*	Bearwood, Staffs	24. 5.1912	17. 2.1989
Harry Edmund Roberts *1949–1950*	Earlsdon, Coventry	5. 6.1924	
Derrick Harold Robins *1947*	Bexley Heath, Kent	27. 6.1914	
Maurice Robinson *1951–1952*	Lisburn, N. Ireland	17. 7.1921	

NAME AND EXTENT OF CAREER	BIRTHPLACE	DATE OF BIRTH	DATE OF DEATH
Thomas Lloyd Robinson *1946*	Swansea, S. Wales	21.12.1912	
Henry Roll *1927*	Alloa, Scotland	18. 3.1905	25. 5.1967
Gerard Alexander Rotherham *1919–1921*	Allesley, Coventry	28. 5.1899	31. 1.1985
Hugh Rotherham *1903*	Allesley, Coventry	16. 3.1861	24. 2.1939
Stephen John Rouse *1970–1981*	Merthyr Tydfil, S. Wales	20. 1.1949	
John Bernard Russell *1920*	Rushall, Walsall, Staffs	2.10.1883	18. 8.1965
Richard Sale *1939–1947*	Shrewsbury	4.10.1919	3. 2.1987
Wilfred Sanders *1028–1934*	Chilvers Coton, Nuneaton	4. 4.1910	22. 5.1965
Gerald Barry Sanderson *1901*	Toxteth Park, Liverpool	12. 5.1881	3.10.1964
Frederick Reginald Santall *1919–1939*	Acocks Green, Birmingham	12. 7.1903	3.11.1950
Sydney Santall *1894–1914*	Peterborough, Northants	10. 6.1873	19. 3.1957
Richard LeQuesne Savage *1976–1979*	Waterloo, London	10.12.1955	
Reginald Ivor Scorer *1921–1926*	Middlesbrough, Yorks	6. 1.1892	19. 3.1976
Norman Sharp *1923*	Derby	15. 4.1901	14. 7.1977
Dennis George Shaw *1949*	Salford, Lancs	16. 2.1931	
John Edward Shilton *1894–1895*	Horbury Junction, Yorks	2.10.1861	27. 9.1899
Norman Arthur Shortland *1938–1950*	Coventry	6. 7.1916	14. 3.1973
Sir Charles Gerald Stewkley Shuckburgh (Baronet) *1930*	Shuckburgh	28. 2.1911	4. 5.1988
Harry Lester Simms *1921–1922*	Adelaide, S. Australia	31. 1.1888	9. 6.1942
Gladstone Gleophas Small *1980–*	St George, Barbados	18.10.1961	
Cyril Cecil Smart *1920–1922*	Lacock, nr. Chippenham, Wilts	23. 7.1898	21. 5.1975
John Abbott Smart *1919–1936*	Forest Hill, Marlborough, Wilts	12. 4.1891	3.10.1979
Alan Christopher Smith *1958–1974*	Hall Green, Birmingham	25.10.1936	
David Martin Smith *1981–1983*	Coventry	21. 1.1962	
Ernest James Smith *1904–1930*	Highgate, Birmingham	6. 2.1886	31. 8.1979
Irving Wilmot Smith 1905	Harborne, Birmingham	5. 2.1884	21.10.1971
Kenneth David Smith *1973–1985*	Jesmond, Newcastle-on-Tyne	9. 7.1956	
Michael John Knight Smith *1956–1975*	Broughton Astley, Leics	30. 6.1933	

NAME AND EXTENT OF CAREER	BIRTHPLACE	DATE OF BIRTH	DATE OF DEATH
Neil Michael Knight Smith *1987–*	Birmingham	27. 7.1967	
Paul Andrew Smith *1982–*	Jesmond, Newcastle-on-Tyne	15. 4.1964	
William John Smith *1906*	Freasley, nr. Wood End	13. 5.1882	unknown
Andrew Watson Speed *1927–1928*	Glasgow	19. 1.1899	
Harry Norman Ernest Spencer *1930*	Shipston-on-Stour	1.10.1901	13. 8.1954
Richard Thompson Spooner *1948–1959*	Stockton-on-Tees, Co. Durham	30.12.1919	
Frank Garfield Stephens *1907–1912*	Edgbaston, Birmingham	26. 4.1889	9. 8.1970
George William Stephens *1907–1925*	Edgbaston, Birmingham	26. 4.1889	17. 3.1950
John Francis Stevenson *1919*	Handsworth, Birmingham	16. 3.1888	5.12.1951
William James Perver Stewart *1955–1969*	Llanelli, S. Wales	31. 8.1934	
Alastair Caleb Storie *1987–1988*	Bishopbriggs, Glasgow	25. 7.1965	
Lawrence Charles Street *1946*	Erdington, Birmingham	4. 2.1920	
Norman Kingsley Street *1908*	Birmingham	13. 8.1881	10. 8.1915
Ernest Suckling *1919*	Balsall Heath, Birmingham	27. 3.1890	24. 2.1962
Simon Paul Sutcliffe *1981–1983*	Watford, Herts	22. 5.1960	
Swaranjit Singh *1956–1958*	Amritsar, N. Punjab, India	18. 7.1932	
Cecil Frederick Tate *1931–1933*	Gillingham, Kent	1. 5.1908	
Frederick Ernest Tayler *1910*	Aston Blank, nr. Chedworth, Glos		
Albert Edward Taylor *1927*	Chilvers Coton, Nuneaton	14. 6.1894	19. 8.1960
Arthur Taylor *1913*	Maltby, Yorks	1880	13.11.1956
Charles James Taylor *1908—1909*	Bristol	8. 6.1881	8.1960
Chilton Richard Vernon Taylor *1970*	Birkenhead, Cheshire	3.10.1951	
Derief David Samuel Taylor *1948–1950*	Kingston, Jamaica	17.9.*c.* 1908	15. 3.1987
Donald Dougal Taylor *1949–1953*	Auckland, N. Zealand	2. 3.1923	5. 4.1980
Frederick Taylor *1939*	Leek, Staffs	29. 4.1916	
Kenneth Alexander Taylor *1946–1949*	Muswell Hill, London	29. 9.1916	
Geoffrey Alan Tedstone *1982–1988*	Southport, Lancs	19. 1.1961	
Peter Norie Tennant *1964*	Sutton Coldfield	17. 4.1942	
Gary Philip Thomas *1978–1981*	Birmingham	8.11.1958	
John Ross Thompson *1938–1954*	Berkhamsted, Herts	10. 5.1918	
Roland George Thompson *1949–1962*	Binley Village, Coventry	26. 9.1932	

NAME AND EXTENT OF CAREER	BIRTHPLACE	DATE OF BIRTH	DATE OF DEATH
David Anthony Thorne *1983–*	Coventry	12.12.1964	
Warwick Nigel Tidy *1970–1974*	Birmingham	10. 2.1953	
Bryan Stanley Valentine Timms *1969–1971*	Ropley, Hants	17.12.1940	
Alan Townsend *1948–1960*	Stockton-on-Tees, Co. Durham	26. 8.1921	
Richard Thornhill Tudor *1976*	Shrewsbury	27. 9.1948	
Roger Graham Twose *1989–*	Torquay, Devon	17. 4.1968	
Horace Venn *1919–1925*	Coventry	4. 7.1892	23.11.1953
Ernest Frederick Waddy *1919–1922*	Morpeth, New South Wales	5.10.1880	23. 9.1958
Gilbert Walker *1912*	Olton, Solihull	15. 2.1888	1938
Stephen Wall *1984–1985*	Ulverston, Lancs	10.12.1959	
Leslie Maynard Ward *1930*	Coventry	2. 5.1908	13. 1.1981
William Ward *1895–1904*	Smethwick, Staffs	24. 5.1874	28.12.1961
John Shaw Waring *1967*	Ripon, Yorks	1.10.1942	
Graham Sydney Warner *1966–1971*	Darlaston, Staffs	27.11.1945	
Albert Wassall *1923*	Aston, Birmingham	24. 6.1892	9.1975
Thomas Herman Watson *1904*	Water Orton	14.11.1880	15. 2.1944
Harry Watson Smith *1912*	Chesterfield, Derbys	30. 9.1886	24. 6.1955
Rudi Valentine Webster *1962–1966*	St. Philip, Barbados	10. 6.1939	
Raymond Thomas Weeks *1950–1957*	Camborne, Cornall	30. 4.1930	
George Weldrick *1906–1907*	Brighouse, Yorks	11. 1.1882	14. 4.1953
James William Welford *1896*	Barnard Castle, Co. Durham	27. 3.1869	17. 1.1945
Oswald Stephen Wheatley *1957–1960*	Low Fell, Gateshead, Co. Durham	28. 5.1935	
Allan Frederick Tinsdale White *1936–1937*	Coventry	5. 9.1915	
Henry Albert White *1923*	Watford, Herts	8. 8.1895	27.11.1972
Malcolm Frank White *1946*	Walsall, Staffs	15. 5.1924	
James George Whitehead *1902*	Cape Town, S. Africa	1877	23. 1.1940
Stephen James Whitehead *1894–1900*	Enfield, Middlesex	2. 9.1860	9. 6.1904
John Whitehouse *1971–1980*	Nuneaton	8. 4.1949	
Percy Gilbert Whitehouse *1926*	Edgbaston, Birmingham	1. 8.1893	24. 9.1959
Albert Edward Mark Whittle *1900–1906*	Bristol	16. 9.1877	18. 3.1917
Owen Leslie Williams *1967*	Cape Town, S. Africa	8. 4.1948	
Rowland Powell Williams *1897–1898*	Stratford-upon-Avon	9. 1.1872	16.12.1951
Robert George Dylan Willis *1972–1984*	Sunderland, Co. Durham	30. 5.1949	
Kilburn Wilmot *1931–1939*	Chilvers Coton, Nuneaton	3. 4.1911	
Ben Ambler Wilson *1951*	Harrogate, Yorks	22. 9.1921	

NAME AND EXTENT OF CAREER	BIRTHPLACE	DATE OF BIRTH	DATE OF DEATH
James Edwin Windridge *1909–1913*	Sparkbrook, Birmingham	21.10.1882	23. 9.1939
Albert Victor George Wolton *1947–1960*	Maidenhead, Berks	12. 6.1919	
Alfred Woodroffe *1947–1948*	Birmingham	1. 9.1918	23. 7.1964
Simon Howard Wootton *1981–1983*	Perivale, Middlesex	24. 2.1959	
Albert Wright *1960–1964*	Arley, near Nuneaton	25. 8.1941	
Robert Elliott Storey Wyatt *1923–1939*	Milford, Surrey	2. 5.1901	
Michael Youll *1956–1957*	Newcastle-on-Tyne	26. 4.1939	

CAREER RECORDS OF WARWICKSHIRE PLAYERS, 1894–1989

Name	*Inns*	*NO*	*Runs*	*HS*	*Avge*	*100s*	*Runs*	*Wkts*	*Avge*	*Best*	*5WI*
Abberley, R. N.	433	27	9825	117*	24.19	3	294	5	58.80	2/19	—
Abell, R. B.	—	—	—	—	—	—	112	4	28.00	3/64	—
Adderley, C. H.	8	2	27	12	4.50	—	255	4	63.75	1/19	—
Allan, J. M.	58	17	744	76*	18.14	—	2274	58	39.20	5/11	1
Amiss, D. L.	946	102	35146	232*	41.64	78	560	15	37.33	3/21	—
Asif Din, M.	255	38	6585	158*	30.34	5	3321	58	57.25	5/100	1
Austin, H.	6	2	45	13	11.25	—	234	2	117.00	1/47	—
Bainbridge, H. W.	186	16	4973	162	29.25	6	36	1	—	1/5	—
Baker, C. S.	355	42	9244	155*	29.53	10	1017	22	46.22	4/59	—
Banks, D. A.	16	4	343	61	28.58	—	13	0	—	—	—
Bannister, J. D.	448	120	3080	71	9.39	—	25918	1181	21.94	10/41	53
Barber, E. G.	3	0	31	13	10.33	—					
Barber, R. W.	214	11	5978	138	29.44	5	4854	197	24.63	6/74	4
Barber, W. H.	6	1	71	23	14.20	—	253	7	36.14	3/81	—
Barbery, A. E.	3	0	13	6	4.33	—	245	3	81.66	2/64	—
Barker, M. P.	9	2	55	17	7.85	—	378	16	23.62	7/68	1
Barnes, S. F.	6	2	38	18	9.50	—	199	3	66.33	2/95	—
Barnes, T. P.	1	0	7	7	—	—					
Barton, J.	4	0	38	16	9.50	—	165	7	23.57	5/73	1
Bates, L. T. A.	745	53	19326	211	27.92	21	471	9	52.33	2/16	—
Bates, S. H.	9	1	24	13	3.00	—	182	6	30.33	3/56	—
Bayley, M. G.	2	1	2	1*	—	—	125	3	41.66	2/54	—
Baynton, R. G.	19	1	212	36	11.77	—	479	14	34.21	4/56	—
Benjamin, H. L.	3	0	35	23	11.66	—	130	2	65.00	1/48	—
Benjamin, J. E.	4	1	25	8*	8.33	—	558	14	39.85	3/55	—
Benson, G. L.	5	2	102	46	34.00	—	32	2	16.00	2/25	—
Blenkiron, W.	137	30	1455	62	13.59	—	8094	287	28.20	5/45	7
Bourne, W. A.	76	13	1300	107	20.63	1	4074	126	32.33	6/47	2
Breeden, C. L.	8	1	80	27	11.42	—	29	0	—		
Brewster, V. C.	4	1	58	35*	19.33	—	175	10	17.50	7/58	1
Bridge, W. B.	131	33	1057	56*	10.78	—	7363	281	26.20	9/56	12
Brindle, R. G.	2	0	74	42	37.00	—					

Name	*Inns*	*NO*	*Runs*	*HS*	*Avge*	*100s*	*Runs*	*Wkts*	*Avge*	*Best*	*5WI*
Broberg, R. F.	1	0	4	4	—	—	16	0	—	—	—
Bromley, P. H.	66	11	1183	121*	21.50	1	1264	35	36.11	5/61	1
Brown, A.	1	1	1	1*	—	—	96	2	48.00	2/96	—
Brown, D. J.	370	99	3240	79	11.95	—	24078	1005	23.95	8/60	44
Brown, E.	29	9	134	19*	6.70	—	1877	56	33.51	8/35	3
Brown, J. D.	12	5	12	7	1.71	—	264	9	29.33	4/18	—
Buckingham, J.	142	23	2840	137*	23.86	3					
Burton, R. H. M.	1	0	47	47	—	—					
Busher, H. A.	2	1	15	15	—	—					
Byrne, G. R.	12	0	36	11	3.00	—	84	6	14.00	3/9	—
Byrne, J. F.	215	10	4720	222	23.02	4	2123	71	29.90	5/37	1
Canning, V. H. D.	77	25	745	61	14.32	—	2914	88	33.11	5/49	3
Carter, R. G.	109	20	635	37	7.13	—	6699	241	27.79	8/82	7
Cartwright, T. W.	558	70	10781	210	22.09	5	19838	1058	18.75	8/39	60
Charlesworth, C.	632	27	14289	216	23.61	15	8878	294	30.19	6/45	7
Clarkson, W.	4	0	59	41	14.75	—	52	2	26.00	2/34	—
Claughton, J. A.	30	5	545	108*	21.80	2					
Clifford, C. C.	33	12	171	26	8.14	—	4074	100	40.74	6/89	5
Clugston, D. L.	9	0	64	17	7.11	—	475	4	118.75	2/75	—
Collin, T.	75	7	1399	105*	20.57	1	1302	26	50.07	3/45	—
Cook, D. R.	13	5	108	28*	13.50	—	534	23	23.21	4/66	—
Cook, M. S.	4	0	110	52	27.50	—					
Cooke, R.	21	4	66	14	3.88	—	507	16	31.68	5/22	1
Cordner, J. P.	—	—	—	—	—	—	36	0	—	—	—
Cotton, R. H.	3	1	0	0*	0.00	—	128	2	64.00	2/42	—
Cowan, C. F. R.	49	2	735	78	15.63	—	9	0	—	—	
Cranmer, P.	268	13	5595	113	21.94	4	1098	22	49.90	3/31	—
Crawford, A. B.	10	3	140	40	20.00	—	310	13	23.84	6/36	1
Cresswell, J.	22	9	137	16	10.54	—	1144	42	27.23	6/69	1
Crichton, H. T.	3	0	26	26	8.66	—	30	2	15.00	2/21	—
Crockford, E. B.	35	0	394	55	11.26	—	199	2	99.50	1/7	—
Croom, A. J. W.	622	65	17662	211	31.70	24	6072	138	44.00	6/65	2
Croom, L. C. B.	8	0	73	26	9.12	—					
Cross, A. J.	2	0	38	20	19.00	—					
Cross, E. P.	12	4	61	12*	7.62	—					
Cumbes, J.	14	7	33	7*	4.71	—	993	21	47.29	4/47	—
Curle, A. C.	4	1	60	40	20.00	—					
Curle, G.	9	0	54	34	6.00	—	3	1	—	1/3	
Davies, C. S.	11	0	112	63	10.18	—	672	14	48.00	3/26	
Davies, R. J.	2	0	18	18	9.00	—					
Dempster, C. S.	5	0	69	40	13.80	—					
Devey, J. H. G.	251	20	6515	246	28.20	8	655	16	40.93	3/65	
Dickens, F.	32	6	172	35	6.61	—	1782	75	23.76	6/23	3
Diver, E. J.	186	8	4280	184	24.04	4	187	6	31.16	6/58	1
Dobson, F.	3	0	9	7	3.00	—	138	7	19.71	3/51	—
Dobson, K. W. C.	4	1	27	12*	9.00	—	24	0	—	—	—
Docker, L. C.	18	3	465	85*	31.00	—					
Dollery, H. E.	679	63	23457	212	38.07	49	32	0	—	—	—
Dollery, K. R.	94	21	927	41	12.69	—	5549	215	25.80	8/42	8
Donald, A. A.	42	12	400	40	13.33	—	2944	151	19.49	7/66	9
Donnelly, M. P.	30	0	988	120	32.93	1	35	2	17.50	2/20	—

Name	*Inns*	*NO*	*Runs*	*HS*	*Avge*	*100s*	*Runs*	*Wkts*	*Avge*	*Best*	*5WI*
Doshi, D. R.	45	19	179	35	6.88	—	4649	146	31.84	6/72	5
Dunkels, P. R.	1	0	0	0	—	—	91	0	—		
Durnell, T. W.	13	3	21	5	2.10	—	1190	42	28.33	7/29	3
Dyer, R. I. H. B.	116	11	2843	109*	27.07	3	41	0	—		
Edmonds, R. B.	100	31	1006	102*	14.57	1	3994	146	27.35	5/40	2
Elson, G.	2	1	7	4	—	—	116	1	—	1/99	—
Everitt, R. S.	5	0	57	38	11.40	—					
Fabling, A. H.	2	0	8	7	4.00	—					
Fantham, W. E.	103	12	1168	51	12.83	—	2907	64	45.42	5/55	2
Farren, G. C.	1	0	0	0	—	—					
Ferreira, A. M.	194	53	4088	112*	28.99	2	10891	335	32.51	6/70	6
Fiddian-Green, C. A. F.	106	24	2309	95	28.15	—	344	5	68.80	1/6	—
Field, E. F.	344	102	1867	39	7.71	—	22998	982	23.41	9/104	75
Field, M. N.	1	1	1	1*	—	—	114	0	—	—	—
Fishwick, T. S.	342	13	8644	140*	26.27	12	35	0	—	—	—
Flaherty, K. F.	—	—	—	—	—	—	107	4	26.75	3/38	—
Fletcher, B. E.	79	13	1511	102*	22.89	1	13	0	—		
Flick, B. J.	14	8	46	18	7.66	—					
Flint, D.	10	3	33	11	4.71	—	465	12	38.75	4/67	—
Flower, R. W.	8	4	23	10*	5.75	—	554	10	55.40	3/45	—
Forrester, T.	36	13	243	38	10.56	—	2229	77	28.94	7/56	2
Foster, A. W.	2	1	1	1*	—	—					
Foster, D. G.	75	6	728	70	10.55	—	3635	141	25.78	7/42	7
Foster, F. R.	215	14	5436	305*	27.04	5	12069	587	20.56	9/118	45
Fox, J.	50	19	469	27*	15.12	—	908	15	60.53	4/27	—
Fox, J. G.	54	6	515	52	10.72	—					
Franklin, R. C.	1	0	0	0	—	—					
Gardner, F. C.	593	66	17826	215*	33.82	29	99	0	—	—	
Gardom, B. K.	25	2	427	79*	18.56	—	700	17	41.17	6/139	1
Gaunt, H. C. A.	20	1	147	32	7.73	—	—	—	—		
George, W.	18	2	342	71	21.37	—					
Gibbs, L. R.	96	48	370	24	7.70	—	8281	338	24.50	8/37	18
Gifford, N.	134	53	741	39	9.14	—	9359	341	27.44	6/22	14
Gittins, A. E.	3	0	2	2	0.66	—	67	4	16.75	2/17	—
Glassford, J.	1	0	0	0	—	—	161	5	32.20	2/9	—
Glover, A. C. S.	226	28	5162	124	26.07	7	1578	49	32.20	5/21	1
Glynn, B. T.	3	1	13	7	6.50	—					
Gobey, S. C.	3	0	2	2	0.66	—	9	0	—		
Goodway, C. C.	66	12	434	37*	8.03	—					
Goodwin, H. J.	36	1	728	101	20.80	1	541	14	38.64	4/35	—
Gordon, A.	59	4	891	65	16.20	—	1	0	—		
Gough-Calthorpe, F. S.	362	28	8311	209	24.88	10	15299	514	29.76	5/20	13
Granville, R. st. L.	2	0	9	7	4.50	—					
Gray, J. D.	6	3	34	18	11.33	—	534	21	25.42	5/2	1
Grayland, A. V.	6	1	15	6*	3.00	—	204	2	102.00	1/23	—
Green, J. H.	1	1	0	0*	—	—	16	0	—		
Green, S. J.	5	0	47	28	9.40	—					
Greening, T.	2	1	26	14	—	—	91	1	—	1/35	—
Griffiths, S.	26	12	76	17*	5.42	—	1827	74	24.68	7/62	4
Gross, F. A.	1	1	0	0*	—	—	76	1	—	1/76	—
Grove, C. W.	288	36	2973	104*	11.79	1	15484	697	22.21	9/39	26

Name	*Inns*	*NO*	*Runs*	*HS*	*Avge*	*100s*	*Runs*	*Wkts*	*Avge*	*Best*	*5WI*
Guy, J. B.	3	0	24	18	8.00	—					
Hacking, J. K.	2	0	17	14	8.50	—					
Hall, W.	3	0	11	8	3.66	—	66	0	—		
Hampton, W. M.	1	0	34	34	—	—	13	0	—		
Hands, B. O.	2	0	13	9	6.50	—	137	4	34.25	3/76	—
Hands, W. C.	91	23	856	63	12.58	—	3509	142	24.71	5/10	3
Hargreave, S.	242	60	1811	45	9.95	—	18496	851	21.73	9/35	69
Harris, A. J.	2	0	18	14	9.00	—					
Harris, D. F.	1	0	2	2	—	—					
Harris, E. J.	5	2	26	16	8.66	—	295	9	32.77	3/66	—
Harris, W. H.	18	1	204	42	12.00	—					
Hartley, P. J.	4	1	31	16	10.33	—	215	2	107.50	2/456	—
Harvey, W. H. T.	1	0	24	24	—	—					
Hastilow, C. A. F.	3	0	26	14	8.66	—	72	2	36.00	2/56	—
Hawkins, C. G.	5	2	16	11*	5.33	—					
Hayhurst, A.	8	0	98	42	12.25	—	457	12	38.08	4/120	—
Heath, D. M. W.	23	1	376	54	17.09	—					
Hellawell, M. S.	2	2	59	30*	—	—	114	6	19.00	4/54	—
Hemmings, E. E.	256	59	4294	85	21.79	—	14056	441	31.87	7/33	19
Hewetson, E. P.	35	7	318	37*	11.35	—	1788	67	26.68	5/31	2
Hewitt, E. J.	2	0	41	40	20.50	—	60	1	—	1/20	—
Hickman, G.	4	0	19	17	4.75	—					
Hilditch, T. A.	11	1	42	17	4.20	—	319	9	35.44	3/41	—
Hill, A. J. B.	2	0	4	4	2.00	—	22	0	—		
Hill, G. H.	47	6	247	23	6.02	—	3156	107	29.49	8/70	3
Hill, H. B. G.	7	1	41	13	6.83	—	248	5	49.60	3/15	—
Hill, J. E.	34	4	665	139*	22.16	1	14	0	—		
Hill, W. A.	279	22	6423	147*	24.99	6	27	1	—	1/9	
Hitchcock, R. E.	511	70	12269	153*	27.82	13	5321	182	29.23	7/76	7
Hoffman, D. S.	15	4	39	13*	3.54	—	1160	29	40.00	4/100	—
Hogg, W.	49	12	274	31	7.40	—	3331	97	34.34	5/63	1
Holbech, W. H.	2	0	0	0	—	—					
Holdsworth, R. L.	54	1	1222	141	23.05	1	17	1	—	1/4	—
Hollies, W. E.	570	258	1544	47	4.94	—	45019	2201	20.45	10/49	173
Holloway, P. C. L.	5	0	40	16	8.00	—					
Hopkins, D. C.	44	12	332	34*	10.37	—	2021	53	38.13	6/67	1
Hopkins, F. J.	16	3	32	13	2.46	—	765	25	30.60	5/10	1
Horner, N. F.	647	33	18217	203*	29.66	25	78	0	—		
Hossell, J. J.	62	5	1217	83	21.35	—	370	7	52.85	3/24	—
Houghton, W. E.	11	0	165	41	15.00	—					
Howell, A. L.	57	16	249	26	6.07	—	1952	56	34.85	5/65	1
Howell, H.	292	94	1560	36	7.87	—	18089	899	20.12	10/51	72
Humpage, G. W.	541	69	17215	254	36.47	29	391	11	35.54	2/13	—
Hyde, A. J.	1	1	2	2*	—	—	121	2	60.50	1/22	—
Illingworth, E. A.	12	3	17	8*	1.88	—	312	8	39.00	2/18	—
Jackson, A. K.	3	2	5	3*	—	—	73	0	—		
Jameson, J. A.	581	43	18149	240*	33.73	31	3655	83	44.03	4/22	—
Jameson, T. E. N.	2	0	63	32	31.50	—	75	0	—		
Jarrett, H. H.	15	1	228	45	16.28	—	1605	47	34.14	8/187	2
Jeeves, P.	80	6	1193	86*	16.12	—	3919	194	20.20	7/34	12
Jennings, G. A.	27	5	243	41	11.04	—	916	23	39.82	5/92	1

Name	*Inns*	*NO*	*Runs*	*HS*	*Avge*	*100s*	*Runs*	*Wkts*	*Avge*	*Best*	*5WI*
Jones, A. K. C.	8	0	176	62	22.00	—					
Jones, R. H. C.	2	0	32	23	16.00	—	27	0	—		
Kallicharran, A. I.	461	55	17936	243*	44.17	52	2352	49	48.00	4/48	—
Kanhai, R. B.	272	47	11615	253	51.62	35	211	4	52.75	2/33	—
Kardar, A. H.	69	9	1372	112	22.86	1	3183	112	28.41	5/25	5
Kemp-Welch, G. D.	83	7	1419	123*	18.67	1	429	5	85.80	2/45	—
Kendall, J. T.	4	1	26	18*	8.66	—					
Kennedy, J. M.	55	9	1188	94	25.83	—	1	2	0.50	2/1	—
Kent, K. G.	10	1	40	23*	4.44	—	639	10	63.90	3/91	—
Kerr, K. J.	12	5	120	45*	17.14	—	955	24	39.79	5/47	1
Khalid Ibadulla	630	69	14766	171	26.32	17	12548	418	30.01	7/22	6
Kilner, N.	539	35	16075	228	31.89	23	166	2	83.00	1/19	—
King, E. H.	10	0	84	24	8.40	—	15	0	—		
King, I. M.	60	18	345	29*	8.21	—	2560	95	26.94	5/59	1
Kingston, J. P.	1	0	24	24	—	—					
Kinneir, S. P.	507	46	15040	268*	32.62	25	1451	48	30.22	3/13	—
Kirk, E.	1	0	0	0	—	—					
Kirton, H. O.	3	0	82	52	27.33	—					
Knutton, H. J.	1	0	4	4	—	—	61	0	—		
Lane, A. F.	21	3	259	58	14.38	—	674	23	29.30	4/56	—
Langley, C. K.	52	4	455	61*	9.47	—	1391	54	25.75	8/29	3
Latham, H. J.	13	2	129	26	11.72	—	751	27	27.81	6/49	1
Law, A.	81	5	1459	89	19.19	—					
Leach, C. W.	64	6	1025	67	17.67	—	657	26	25.26	3/19	—
Leadbeater, E.	35	5	456	116	15.20	1	1326	52	25.50	6/63	1
Legard, E.	24	11	144	21	11.07	—					
Lethbridge, C.	58	13	1033	87*	22.95	—	2996	77	38.90	5/68	1
Lewington, P. J.	70	19	376	34	7.37	—	5426	187	29.01	7/52	6
Lewis, E. B.	52	11	541	51	13.19	—					
Lilley, A. F. A.	497	29	12813	171	27.37	16	1439	40	35.97	6/46	1
Lloyd, T. A.	421	35	13764	208*	35.65	27	1253	16	78.31	3/62	—
Lobb, B.	—	—	—	—	—	—	31	2	15.50	2/31	—
Lord, G. J.	26	2	508	199	21.16	1	37	0	—		
Lord, W. A.	18	8	69	10*	6.90	—	811	26	31.19	5/73	1
Loveitt, F. R.	42	6	846	110	23.50	1					
Lowe, J. C. M.	2	0	8	8	4.00	—	42	1	—	1/29	—
Lowe, P. J.	—	—	—	—	—	—					
Luckin, V. V.	14	7	195	59*	27.85	—	332	11	30.18	3/19	—
Lynes, J.	8	0	79	26	9.87	—	576	15	38.40	3/54	—
McDowall, J. I.	21	3	365	89	20.27	—					
McMillan, B. M.	21	4	999	136	58.76	3	808	17	47.52	3/47	—
McVicker, N. M.	129	33	1701	65*	17.71	—	7732	300	25.77	7/29	14
Manton, J.	2	0	5	5	2.50	—	51	1	—	1/51	—
Marshall, F. W.	2	0	14	10	7.00	—					
Marshall, G. A.	5	3	24	18*	12.00	—	221	9	24.55	5/22	1
Marshall, J. M. A.	49	4	790	47	17.55	—	1581	47	33.63	5/65	2
Maguire, K. R.	3	0	3	2	1.00	—	123	1	—	1/32	—
Matheson, E.	2	0	14	9	7.00	—					
Maudsley, R. H.	74	3	1706	107	24.02	2	1173	39	30.07	6/54	1
Mayer, J. H.	408	115	2832	74*	9.66	—	25356	1142	22.20	8/62	71
Maynard, C.	28	5	550	85	23.91	—					

Name	Inns	NO	Runs	HS	Avge	100s	Runs	Wkts	Avge	Best	5WI
Mead-Briggs, R.	2	1	46	44*	—	—	96	1	—	1/44	—
Meldon, W. W.	9	0	122	44	13.55	—	149	4	37.25	3/27	—
Melville, J.	3	0	14	13	4.66	—	84	5	16.80	3/34	—
Mence, M. D.	43	8	467	53	13.34	—	1983	61	32.50	5/26	2
Merrick, T. A.	43	8	516	74*	14.74	—	3196	134	23.85	7/45	10
Meunier, J. B.	3	0	12	9	4.00	—	38	0	—		
Milburn, E. T.	4	2	37	24	18.50	—	128	2	64.00	1/26	—
Miller, H. R.	1	0	8	8	—	—	38	1	—	1/15	—
Miller, R.	166	34	1658	72	12.56	—	7289	241	30.24	6/28	6
Mills, J. M.	7	0	106	26	15.14	—	167	3	55.66	2/67	—
Mitchell, F. R.	29	2	224	43	8.29	—	856	22	38.90	4/69	—
Moles, A. J.	133	14	4275	151	35.92	9	847	18	47.05	3/21	—
Monkhouse, S.	3	1	7	5	3.50	—	95	2	47.50	1/34	—
Moorhouse, F.	154	37	1549	75	13.23	—	6232	260	23.96	7/53	8
Morris, L. J.	11	0	262	76	23.81	—	70	3	23.33	2/41	—
Morter, F. W.	5	2	13	8	4.33	—	138	3	46.00	2/5	—
Morton, J.	14	0	162	38	11.57	—					
Morton, W.	9	2	42	13*	6.00	—	708	16	44.25	4/85	—
Munton, T. A.	73	29	348	38	7.90	—	4517	176	25.66	6/21	7
Murray, A. L.	17	0	161	33	9.47	—	49	2	24.50	2/29	—
Murray, D. L.	87	12	1773	78	23.64	—	83	0	—		
Myles, S. D.	7	0	111	39	15.85	—	65	0	—		
Nelson, A. L.	2	0	0	0	0.00	—					
Nelson, G. M. B.	21	8	97	23	7.46	—	746	22	33.90	4/53	—
Norton, E. W.	1	1	26	26*	—	—	19	0	—	—	—
Oakes, D. R.	8	1	81	33	11.57	—	1	0	—		
Old, A. G. B.	1	0	34	34	—	—	93	1	—	1/64	—
Old, C. M.	53	10	911	70	21.18	—	3596	120	29.96	6/46	6
Oliver, P. R.	128	20	2679	171	24.80	2	2115	27	78.33	2/28	—
Ord, J. S.	459	35	11788	187*	27.80	16	244	2	122.00	1/0	—
O'Rourke, C.	1	1	23	23*	—	—					
Paine, G. A. E.	323	56	3234	79	12.11	—	21867	962	22.73	8/43	70
Pallett, H. J.	98	21	915	55*	11.88	—	6375	296	21.53	9/55	21
Palmer, G. A.	12	2	87	20	8.70	—	450	8	56.25	2/21	—
Parkes, H. R.	1	0	1	1	—	—					
Parry, M. C.	3	0	26	10	8.66	—	16	0	—		
Parsons, G. J.	56	11	918	67*	20.40	—	2961	94	31.50	7/16	4
Parsons, J. H.	494	48	15737	225	35.28	35	1916	55	34.83	4/13	—
Partridge, N. E.	144	17	2352	102	18.51	1	7900	347	22.76	7/66	16
Paul, N. A.	4	0	75	40	18.75	—	65	2	32.50	1/5	—
Peare, W. G.	9	7	17	12*	8.50	—	75	2	37.50	1/4	—
Pell, G. A.	2	1	24	16*	—	—	31	4	7.75	2/9	—
Pereira, E. J.	8	1	118	34	16.85	—	13	0	—		
Perkins, H. G.	5	2	10	6*	3.33	—	55	1	—	1/30	—
Perryman, S. P.	129	52	745	43	9.67	—	9371	309	30.32	7/49	16
Phillips, H. R.	1	0	3	3	—	—					
Phillips, J. H.	7	0	35	16	5.00	—	159	1	—	1/30	—
Pierson, A. R. K.	49	20	315	42*	10.86	—	2509	56	44.80	6/82	2
Piper, K. J.	15	2	208	41	16.00	—					
Potter, W.	2	0	0	0	0.00	—	31	1	—	1/19	—
Pridmore, R. G.	26	1	315	49	12.60	—					

Name	*Inns*	*NO*	*Runs*	*HS*	*Avge*	*100s*	*Runs*	*Wkts*	*Avge*	*Best*	*5WI*
Pritchard, T. L.	247	29	2853	81	13.08	—	16211	695	23.32	8/20	40
Pugh, J. G.	9	0	82	41	9.11	—	206	6	34.33	4/100	—
Quaife, B. W.	81	7	1096	99*	14.81	—	66	4	16.50	1/0	
Quaife, Walter	202	11	4935	144	25.83	7	204	7	29.14	2/5	—
Quaife, W. G.	1112	176	33862	255*	36.17	71	24779	900	27.53	7/76	31
Ratcliffe, D. P.	33	2	603	79	19.45	—					
Ratcliffe, J. D.	24	4	602	127*	30.10	1	82	1	—	1/15	—
Reeve, D. A.	40	7	1012	103	30.66	1	913	35	26.08	4/50	—
Rhodes, J.	6	0	89	64	14.83	—					
Rhodes, T. B.	7	1	105	55	17.50	—					
Rice, W. I.	4	0	15	9	3.75	—					
Richards, W.	11	1	112	61*	11.20	—					
Richardson, B. A.	72	4	1323	126	19.45	2	153	1	—	1/32	—
Richardson, S. H.	4	1	18	8*	6.00	—					
Riley, T. M. N.	23	2	440	84	20.95	—	15	0	—	—	
Roberts, H. E.	8	0	52	30	6.50	—					
Roberts, H. J.	27	4	348	61	15.13	—	407	9	45.22	3/6	—
Robins, D. H.	4	1	54	29*	18.00	—					
Robinson, M.	13	1	234	57	19.50	—	5	0	—		
Robinson, T. L.	7	1	27	13*	4.50	—	277	6	46.16	2/74	—
Roll, H.	1	0	0	0	—	—	40	0	—		
Rotherham, G. A.	75	4	1061	62	14.94	—	3678	130	28.29	7/69	6
Rotherham, H.	1	0	33	33	—	—					
Rouse, S. J.	152	33	1862	93	15.64	—	8043	266	30.23	6/34	5
Russell, J. B.	2	0	31	23	15.50	—					
Sale, R.	33	3	929	157	30.96	2					
Sanders, W.	100	18	706	64	8.60	—	4663	119	39.18	4/44	—
Sanderson, G. B.	1	0	0	0	—	—					
Santall, F. R.	789	84	17518	201*	24.84	21	12186	280	43.52	5/47	2
Santall, S.	534	117	6490	73	15.56	—	28923	1207	23.96	8/23	62
Savage, R. le Q.	23	14	67	15*	7.44	—	1924	54	35.62	7/50	1
Scorer, R. I.	52	8	718	113	16.31	1	659	18	36.61	3/1	—
Sharp, N.	1	0	3	3	—	—					
Shaw, D. G.	1	0	17	17	—	—	106	2	53.00	2/60	—
Shilton, J. E.	23	6	152	30	8.94	—	1300	56	23.21	7/75	3
Shortland, N. A.	40	5	487	70	13.91	—	50	0	—		
Shuckburgh, C. G. S.	1	0	0	0	—	—					
Simms, H. L.	10	0	133	38	13.30	—	216	5	43.20	2/8	—
Small, G. C.	227	51	2618	70	14.87	—	13922	513	27.13	7/15	20
Smart, C. C.	81	10	922	59	12.98	—	508	9	56.44	2/16	—
Smart, J. A.	340	43	3425	68*	11.53	—	1262	22	57.36	2/13	—
Smith, A. C.	499	74	8452	94	19.88	—	2894	118	24.52	5/47	1
Smith, D. M.	5	2	148	100*	49.33	1	201	2	100.50	1/44	—
Smith, E. J.	744	48	15911	177	22.86	20	81	1	—	1/18	—
Smith, I. W.	1	0	1	1	—	—	13	0	—		
Smith, K. D.	344	28	8718	140	27.58	9	3	0	—		
Smith, M. J. K.	741	99	27672	200*	43.10	48	112	3	37.33	1/0	—
Smith, N. M. K.	16	3	307	161	23.61	1	599	15	39.93	3/62	—
Smith, P. A.	239	28	6014	140	28.50	3	6326	163	38.80	5/82	1
Smith, W. J.	1	0	0	0	—	—	93	2	46.50	2/83	—
Speed, A. W.	7	3	29	11*	7.25	—	538	29	18.55	6/81	2

Name	*Inns*	*NO*	*Runs*	*HS*	*Avge*	*100s*	*Runs*	*Wkts*	*Avge*	*Best*	*5WI*
Spencer, H. N. E.	2	1	4	3*	—	—	146	1	—	1/44	—
Spooner, R. T.	506	59	12014	168	26.87	11	11	0	—		
Stephens, F. G.	50	7	1102	144*	25.62	1	205	3	68.33	2/24	—
Stephens, G. W.	203	13	3997	143	21.03	3	80	4	20.00	2/25	—
Stevenson, J. F.	2	0	18	18	9.00	—					
Stewart, W. J. P.	471	53	14249	182*	34.08	25	15	2	7.50	2/4	—
Storie, A. C.	43	10	665	68	20.15	—	20	0	—		
Street, L. C.	7	2	17	8*	3.40	—	146	3	48.66	2/15	—
Street, N. K.	9	0	43	14	4.77	—					
Suckling, E.	3	0	45	39	15.00	—	29	0	—		
Sutcliffe, S. P.	21	8	57	20	4.38	—	2475	46	53.80	5/151	1
Swaranjit Singh	43	10	872	68*	26.42	—	1248	42	29.71	5/132	1
Tate, C. F.	8	2	34	17	5.66	—	297	6	49.50	3/65	—
Tayler, F. E.	8	0	112	44	14.00	—	5	0	—		
Taylor, A.	11	2	83	17	9.22	—	137	4	34.25	2/10	—
Taylor, A. E.	1	0	0	0	—	—	7	0	—		
Taylor, C. J.	4	0	6	5	1.50	—	257	9	28.55	4/99	—
Taylor, C. R. V.	—	—	—	—	—	—					
Taylor, D. D. S.	23	7	519	121	32.43	1	607	15	40.46	3/41	
Taylor, D. D.	82	5	1624	90*	21.09	—	246	11	22.36	4/24	—
Taylor, F.	1	0	0	0	—	—	71	3	23.66	2/56	—
Taylor, K. A.	155	10	3145	102	21.68	1	33	1	—	1/18	—
Tedstone, G. A.	44	6	641	67*	16.86	—					
Tennant, P. N.	—	—	—	—	—	—					
Thomas, G. P.	15	1	277	52	19.78	—					
Thompson, J. R.	76	3	1922	103	26.32	2	13	0	—		
Thompson, R. G.	185	70	655	25*	5.69	—	10824	472	22.93	9/65	21
Thorne, D. A.	70	9	1074	76	17.60	—	465	3	155.00	1/21	—
Tidy, W. N.	34	14	70	12*	3.50	—	2775	81	34.25	5/24	3
Timms, B. S. V.	33	7	421	61	16.19	—					
Townsend, A.	549	69	11965	154	24.92	6	9238	323	28,60	7/84	7
Tudor, R. T.	1	0	6	6	—	—	42	0	—		
Twose, R. G.	9	3	139	37	23.16	—	143	1	—	1/54	—
Venn, H.	60	0	1047	151	17.45	2	28	0	—		
Waddy, E. F.	42	2	955	109*	23.87	1					
Walker, G.	2	0	13	13	6.50	—					
Wall, S.	25	9	175	28	10.93	—	1518	37	41.02	4/59	—
Ward, L. M.	1	0	5	5	—	—	29	1	—	1/29	—
Ward, W.	16	5	79	26	7.18	—	965	30	32.16	5/76	1
Waring, J. S.	2	0	15	15	7.50	—	129	2	64.50	1/30	—
Warner, G. S.	48	7	965	118*	23.53	2	14	0	—		
Wassall, A.	11	3	24	10	3.00	—	344	10	34.40	3/67	—
Watson, T. H.	3	0	18	12	6.00	—	137	—			
Watson Smith, H.	1	0	15	15	—	—					
Webster, R. V.	66	15	658	47	12.90	—	4532	234	19.36	8/19	12
Weeks, R. T.	139	35	1047	51	10.06	—	6004	228	26.33	7/70	8
Weldrick, G.	11	1	53	12	5.30	—					
Welford, J. W.	23	2	459	118	21.85	1	180	2	90.00	1/13	—
Wheatley, O. S.	76	34	207	17	4.92	—	5971	237	25.19	7/45	12
White, A. F. T.	15	2	311	55*	23.92	—					
White, H. A.	15	3	107	32	8.91	—	33	0	—		

Name	*Inns*	*NO*	*Runs*	*HS*	*Avge*	*100s*	*Runs*	*Wkts*	*Avge*	*Best*	*5WI*
White, M. F.	2	0	0	0	0.00	—					
Whitehead, J. G.	1	0	1	1	—	—	50	0	—		
Whitehead, S. J.	73	25	463	46*	9.64	—	4018	170	23.63	8/47	11
Whitehouse, J.	307	38	8689	197	32.30	15	471	6	78.50	2/55	—
Whitehouse, P. G.	6	3	41	13	13.66	—	122	8	15.25	4/23	—
Whittle, A. E. M.	80	10	1685	104	24.07	1	2011	56	35.91	5/28	2
Williams, O. L.	2	1	6	6*	—	—	60	1	—	1/32	—
Williams, R. P.	8	1	80	38	11.42	—	14	0	—		
Willis, R. G. D.	139	56	1389	72	16.73	—	8769	353	24.84	8/32	14
Wilmot, K.	101	25	871	54	11.46	—	5018	154	32.58	7/34	2
Wilson, B. A.	1	0	0	0	—	—	75	1	—	1/75	—
Windridge, J. E.	12	1	161	34*	14.63	—	13	1	—	1/13	—
Wolton, A. V. G.	477	61	12896	165	31.00	12	1226	37	33.13	4/15	—
Woodroffe, A.	7	0	77	41	11.00	—					
Wootton, S. H.	16	2	364	104	26.00	1	7	0	—		
Wright, A.	76	27	315	27	6.42	—	5953	236	25.22	6/58	11
Wyatt, R. E. S.	627	105	21687	232	41.55	51	21401	652	32.83	7/43	22
Youll, M.	2	0	15	9	7.50	—	302	14	21.57	5/99	1

RESULTS OF ALL INTER-COUNTY FIRST CLASS MATCHES 1894–1989

Year	*DY*	*EX*	*GM*	*GS*	*HT*	*KT*	*LA*	*LE*	*MX*	*NR*	*NT*	*SM*	*SY*	*SX*	*WO*	*YO*
1894	WL	WD		DD		WD		AW			DW		LW			DD
1895	DL	DW		WL	WW	DL	LW	DW					DL			DL
1896	DL	DL		DW	DW	WL	LD	DL					LL			DL
1897	DD	DL		WD	DD	DD	DD	WW					LL			LD
1898	DD	DL		LL	DD	DL	LW	DW					AL			DD
1899	DD	DD		DL	DW	WL	DL	DW					DD		DW	LL
1900	DD	DD		LD	DW		DL	WD					DD		DW	DD
1901	WD	WD		LL			WL	WL					WD		WW	DD
1902	WL	DD		DW	WW		DW	WD					DL		DL	LL
1903	DD	WD		DW	WD		LD	WD					DW		LL	DL
1904	DL	WW			WL		DL	LW		WW		DD	DD		DD	LW
1905	WL	WD			DW		DL	LD		WW		DD	DD	DD	DD	DL
1906	DW				DW		DL	DD		WW		WL	DL	WW	DD	DL
1907	WA				LW		DL	WD		WW		DL	DD	LD	DW	DL
1908	WW			LL	WD		LL	AL		WL		WL	DD	DD	LD	DL
1909	LD			WD	LL		DL	DD		LW			DL	WD	LD	DL
1910	WD			WW	LD		LD	WL		DL			LL	DL	DD	DL
1911	WW			WL	WD		WW	WW		WW			DL	WW	DL	LW
1912	WD			DW	DL		DA	LD	WL	WD			DL	WL	DW	DD
1913	WL			WL	WW	LL	WL	WL	LL	LD			DD	DL	WD	DL
1914	WW			WW	WL	LL	DW	WD	DL	DD			WL	DL	DW	LD
1919	LW			DL			DL	LD		DD			DL		DD	LL
1920	WW			WL	DL	LL	LL	DW	LL	DW		DL	DL	DL	WW	LL
1921	WD			LL	DL	LL	WL	LL	LL	WW		LL	LL	LL	DW	LL
1922	DW			WL	LL	LL	LD	WD	LL	WW	DL	LW	LD	LL	WW	LL
1923	LD			WW	LL	WW	LD	DD	LL	DD		WL	LD	LD	WL	LL
1924	DD		WW		DD	WD	DD	DL	LL	DD	AL	LW		WW	DW	DL
1925	DD		WD		WL	LL	DD	DW	DL	WL		WW	LL	WL	LW	LL
1926	DD		LL		DL	LL	LD	DD	DD	WD	DL	DD	DD	DL	WD	LD
1927	DL		WD		DL	DD	DL	DD	DD	WD	DL	DD	DD	DD	DD	DW
1928	DW		WD		DL	DL	DL	DL	DD	DL	DL	DD	DD	DW	DD	DD
1929	LD	LL	WW	DL	DL	WL	LL	LL	WD	DW	LL	DL	DL		DD	DL
1930	DD	DL	DL	DL	DW	LL	LD	DD	DL		DD	WL	DD		DD	LD
1931	DW		LW	DL	DD	DW	DD	DD	DD	WW	DD	LD	AL		DW	DL
1932	DL	WL	DD	AW		DL	DD	DD	DD	WW		DL	DD	LD	WD	DD
1933	WL	LW	DD	LW	WW	DL	DD	DW		DD		DD	WD	DD	WW	DL
1934	DL		WD	WW		DW		WD	WW	WL	LL		DD	DD	WD	DW
1935	WL		WW	DD		DD		DL	WW	WD	WD		DL	LW	LW	DL
1936	LL			LL		LD	DW	DL	DW	DD	DL		LW	DW	DD	DL
1937	DL		WD	WW	WL		DL	WD	DL	DW			DL	DL	LD	DL
1938	LW		DL	WD	WL		LD	DL	LL	WW			DW	DD	DD	LD
1939	WD		WL	WL	DD		WD	WW	DL	DD			LL	WL	DD	LL
1946	LD	WL	L–	–D	W–	LL	LL	WW	–L	DW	LL	W–	–W	DL	LL	LL
1947	LD	LW	–D	D–	–D	WL	DD	DL	L–	WW	DL	–W	L–	LW	LL	LL
1948	DW	W–	WL	DL	DW	D–	LD	WW	WL	–W	–L	DD	LL	–D	DD	W–

Year	*DY*	*EX*	*GM*	*GS*	*HT*	*KT*	*LA*	*LE*	*MX*	*NR*	*NT*	*SM*	*SY*	*SX*	*WO*	*YO*
1949	WD	–L	LD	WW	WD	–D	WD	DW	DD	W–	D–	WW	LW	W–	WL	–L
1950	LD	WD	DD	DD	–W	D–	LD	DW	WW	DD	LD	LW	L–	–W	LW	DD
1951	DD	DL	WD	WW	D–	–W	DL	WD	WW	WD	WW	WW	–D	W–	WD	WW
1952	DL	WD	D–	LD	DD	LW	LD	WW	–W	D–	WL	–L	WL	WT	LL	DL
1953	WD	DL	–L	DW	DW	LW	DD	DD	L–	–D	WD	D–	WL	DL	DD	DL
1954	DD	WW	WL	WD	–D	D–	DL	DW	DD	WL	DL	DW	–W	W–	LW	LD
1955	DW	LW	WL	LW	D–	–D	DL	DW	WL	DD	WL	DW	W–	–L	DW	LL
1956	WD	DL	D–	LW	DL	DW	WL	DD	–L	L–	DL	–D	DA	LW	DL	LL
1957	WD	DD	–W	WW	LD	DL	LL	WD	L–	–D	DL	W–	LL	WW	DD	DD
1958	LD	DD	DD	DD	–D	D–	LL	DD	DW	LD	DD	WL	–L	W–	DL	DD
1959	LW	WL	DL	WW	W–	–L	LD	WW	WL	DL	WL	WW	W–	–L	DW	DL
1960	LL	LD	WL	DL	LL	DD	DL	DD	WD	DW	DD	DD	DD	LL	DW	LL
1961	DL	DD	DW	WL	DL	LW	DW	WW	LL	WD	DL	WW	DD	LD	DL	DL
1962	DD	LD	WD	WW	DD	WL	DL	DW	DD	LD	WW	DD	DW	WW	DW	LW
1963	WW	DW	W–	WD	WA	LD	DW	DD	–D	D–	DW	DD	WD	WD	DD	LL
1964	LW	DD	–D	DW	WL	WD	WW	WW	D–	–L	WD	W–	WL	WW	LD	WD
1965	DW	DD	DD	DD	–D	L–	LD	DW	WD	LL	WD	WL	–D	D–	DD	DD
1966	LL	WL	WD	LD	L–	–D	DD	WD	AD	WD	DW	DW	L–	–D	LW	LW
1967	WD	DL	–W	WD	WD	AL	DA	DD	D–	–D	WD	D–	DD	DL	DD	DL
1968	DD	DW	L–	LA	DL	WL	LD	LD	–W	D–	DD	–D	WW	DW	LD	WL
1969	DL	–W	–D	DD	–D	W–	DD	WD	D–	DD	DL	DW	D–	W–	LW	–W
1970	LD	D–	W–	DD	L–	–W	WD	LW	–D	WW	WL	DD	–D	–L	DD	L–
1971	D–	WL	–W	L–	–W	W–	LD	–D	D–	DL	WL	–L	DL	WW	WL	WL
1972	D–	–D	W–	D–	–W	–W	WW	–D	W–	DD	WW	–D	W–	D–	DD	–D
1973	–W	D–	–D	–L	L–	D–	WW	W–	–L	LD	DD	D–	–L	–D	DW	D–
1974	D–	–L	D–	W–	–L	–D	DL	–L	W–	DD	WD	–W	D–	W–	LD	–D
1975	–L	D–	–L	–L	L–	D–	LL	L–	–L	LD	WD	W–	–W	–W	DD	L–
1976	D–	–L	DL	L–	–W	–W	WW	–L	W–	DL	–D	–L	L–	D–	DD	W–
1977	–L	L–	DD	–D	D–	L–	WD	W–	–W	WD	D–	LL	–L	–L	DL	DD
1978	DD	–L	DD	D–	–W	–D	DW	–D	W–	DD	–L	LL	D–	D–	DD	WL
1979	–D	L–	DW	–D	L–	W–	DD	D–	–D	LD	L–	DL	–L	–D	AW	DL
1980	D–	–D	DL	D–	–W	–L	DD	–D	D–	DD	–D	DW	D–	D–	LW	LD
1981	–D	L–	LL	–D	D–	W–	DD	L–	–L	DW	L–	LL	–D	–L	LL	DD
1982	D–	–D	DD	D–	–L	–D	DL	–D	L–	LD	–D	DL	D–	L–	DD	LL
1983	–L	W–	WW	DW	–L	DD	WW	D–	WL	DW	–D	–D	–D	W–	DD	WD
1984	–D	–L	LD	W–	WD	W–	DW	LL	–W	DD	DL	L–	D–	DL	DD	–W
1985	DL	DL	DD	–L	D–	–D	WD	–L	L–	LD	D–	DD	WL	–D	LD	D–
1986	D–	D–	DW	WD	–L	DL	DD	D–	LD	DW	–D	–D	–L	–D	LD	WD
1987	–L	–D	DD	L–	LD	W–	LL	DD	–D	DL	DL	D–	W–	DD	DD	–D
1988	–D	W–	LD	–D	W–	L–	LD	L–	–L	WL	W–	DD	–L	–L	DD	WW
1989	D–	–L	DW	W–	–W	–W	DL	–D	L–	DW	–D	DD	L–	D–	DD	DD

RESULTS OF ALL SUNDAY LEAGUE MATCHES 1969–1989

Year	*DY*	*EX*	*GM*	*GS*	*HT*	*KT*	*LA*	*LE*	*MX*	*NR*	*NT*	*SM*	*SY*	*SX*	*WO*	*YO*
1969	A	W	L	W	W	L	L	A	L	W	W	W	L	L	A	A
1970	L	W	W	A	L	L	A	L	W	L	W	L	W	W	W	W
1971	W	L	L	L	L	W	L	W	W	W	L	L	L	L	L	L
1972	L	L	L	A	L	L	L	L	W	W	L	W	W	W	W	W
1973	A	L	A	L	W	L	A	L	W	L	W	L	L	A	W	L
1974	W	L	W	W	L	L	W	L	W	L	L	L	L	W	W	A
1975	L	L	W	W	W	W	W	L	L	W	L	L	W	W	L	W
1976	W	L	W	W	W	W	L	L	W	L	W	L	L	W	L	W
1977	A	L	L	A	W	L	W	L	L	W	L	W	A	L	W	A
1978	W	W	L	L	L	L	L	L	L	W	A	L	L	W	L	L
1979	A	L	L	W	L	L	L	L	L	W	L	L	L	L	L	L
1980	L	W	W	W	W	T	W	W	W	W	L	L	W	W	L	W
1981	L	L	L	W	W	W	W	A	W	W	W	L	W	W	W	A
1982	L	W	L	L	L	L	L	L	L	W	L	L	L	A	A	W
1983	L	L	A	L	W	L	A	W	L	L	W	L	W	L	T	L
1984	L	L	W	W	L	L	W	A	L	A	W	L	W	W	A	W
1985	L	L	A	L	W	W	W	L	W	W	W	W	L	L	L	A
1986	W	L	L	W	L	A	W	W	T	L	W	L	A	L	L	T
1987	L	W	W	L	L	A	A	A	A	W	L	L	L	L	L	L
1988	W	W	L	A	W	L	L	W	L	L	W	W	A	L	L	L
1989	L	L	W	W	L	L	A	L	W	L	L	W	L	W	L	L

RESULTS IN BENSON AND HEDGES CUP COMPETITION 1972–1989

1972 Second in Group Midlands; *Q/Final*: beat Glamorgan; *S/Final*: lost to Leicestershire
1973 Third in Group Midlands
1974 Third in Group Midlands
1975 First in Group Midlands; *Q/Final*: beat Essex; *S/Final*: lost to Middlesex
1976 First in Group A; *Q/Final*: beat Lancashire; *S/Final*: lost to Worcestershire
1977 Second in Group B; *Q/Final*: lost to Northamptonshire
1978 Second in Group A: *Q/Final*: beat Glamorgan; *S/Final*: lost to Derbyshire
1979 First in Group B; *Q/Final*: lost to Essex
1980 Third in Group B
1981 Second in Group B; *Q/Final*: lost to Kent
1982 Third in Group B
1983 Second in Group B; *Q/Final*: lost to Essex
1984 First in Group A; *Q/Final*: beat Somerset; *S/Final*: beat Yorkshire; *Final*: lost to Lancashire
1985 Fourth in Group B
1986 Third in Group A
1987 Third in Group B
1988 Second in Group A; *Q/Final*: lost to Essex
1989 Fourth in Group D

RESULTS OF ALL NATWEST TROPHY/GILLETTE CUP MATCHES 1963–1989

1963 *1st Round*: lost to Northamptonshire
1964 *1st Round*:bye; *2nd Round*: beat Hampshire; *Q/Final*: beat Northamptonshire; *S/Final*: beat Lancashire; *Final*: lost to Sussex
1965 *1st Round*: beat Cambridgeshire; *2nd Round*: beat Lancashire; *Q/Final*: beat Hampshire; *S/Final*: lost to Yorkshire
1966 *1st Round*: bye; *2nd Round*: beat Glamorgan; *Q/Final*: beat Gloucestershire; *S/Final*: beat Somerset; *Final*: beat Worcestershire
1967 *1st Round*: bye; *2nd Round*: lost to Somerset
1968 *1st Round*: bye; *2nd Round*: beat Yorkshire; *Q/Final*: beat Hampshire; *S/Final*: beat Middlesex; *Final*: beat Sussex
1969 *1st Round*: bye; *2nd Round*: lost to Essex
1970 *1st Round*: lost to Nottinghamshire
1971 *1st Round*: bye; *2nd Round*: beat Lincolnshire; *Q/Final*: beat Hampshire; *S/Final*: lost to Kent

1972 *1st Round*: beat Yorkshire; *2nd Round*; beat Leicestershire; *Q/Final*: beat Glamorgan; *S/final*: beat Worcestershire; *Final*: lost to Lancashire
1973 *1st Round*: bye; *2nd Round*: lost to Worcestershire
1974 *1st Round*: bye; *2nd Round*: lost to Nottinghamshire
1975 *1st Round*: bye; *2nd Round*: lost to Middlesex
1976 *1st Round*: beat Glamorgan; *2nd Round*: beat Somerset; *Q/Final*: beat Sussex; *S/Final*: lost to Lancashire
1977 *1st Round*: lost to Middlesex
1978 *1st Round*: lost to Somerset
1979 *1st Round*: bye; *2nd Round*: lost to Nottinghamshire
1980 *1st Round*: beat Oxfordshire; *2nd Round*: beat Devon; *Q/Final*: lost to Sussex
1981 *1st Round*: bye; *2nd Round*: lost to Sussex
1982 *1st Round*: beat Cambridgeshire; *2nd Round*: beat Glamorgan; *Q/Final*: beat Somerset; *S/Final*: beat Yorkshire; *Final*: lost to Surrey
1983 *1st Round*: beat Oxfordshire; *2nd Round*: beat Surrey; *Q/Final*: lost to Kent
1984 *1st Round*: beat Oxfordshire; *2nd Round*: beat Shropshire *Q/Final*: beat Surrey; *S/Final*: lost to Kent
1985 *1st Round*: beat Devon; *2nd Round*: lost to Nottinghamshire
1986 *1st Round*: beat Durham; *2nd Round*: beat Essex; *Q/Final*: lost to Worcestershire
1987 *1st Round*: beat Staffordshire; *2nd Round*: beat Buckinghamshire; *Q/Final*: lost to Gloucestershire
1988 *1st Round*: beat Cambridgeshire; *2nd Round*: lost to Kent
1989 *1st Round*: beat Wiltshire; *2nd Round*: beat Kent; *Q/Final*: beat Northamptonshire; *S/Final*: beat Worcestershire; *Final*: beat Middlesex

GROUNDS USED BY WARWICKSHIRE IN FIRST-CLASS CRICKET 1894–1989

			FIRST-CLASS RECORD				
Ground	*First*	*Last*	*P*	*W*	*L*	*D*	*Tied*
Edgbaston, Birmingham	1894	1989	1038	276	234	528	—
Mitchell's & Butlers' Ground, Birmingham	1931	1961	13	4	1	8	—
Bull's Head Ground, Coventry	1903	1919*	13	7	2	4	—
Butts Ground, Coventry	1925	1930	10	—	2	8	—
Courtauld's Ground, Coventry	1946	1982	56	20	20	16	—
Morris Engineering Co.'s Ground, Coventry	1931	1932	2	1	—	1	—
Leamington C.C. Ground	1905	1910	4	1	1	2	—
Griff & Coton Ground, Nuneaton	1930	1989	27	6	6	15	—
Nuneaton C.C. Ground	1912	1914	3	1	1	1	—
Stratford-upon-Avon C.C. Ground	1951		1	—	—	1	—

**Bull's Head Ground has been reintroduced to the first-class circuit in 1990*

TEAM RECORDS

(1) HIGHEST AND LOWEST SCORE FOR WARWICKSHIRE AGAINST EACH COUNTY

Opponents	*Highest*	*Year*	*Lowest*	*Year*
Derbyshire	635 *at* Edgbaston	1900	28 *at* Derby	1937
Essex	614-8 dec *at* Edgbaston	1904	53 *at* Edgbaston	1957
Glamorgan	543-8 dex *at* Edgbaston	1927	61 *at* Neath	1959
Gloucestershire	518 *at* Gloucester	1937	62 *at* Edgbaston	1900
Hampshire	657-6 dec *at* Edgbaston	1899	36 *at* Portsmouth	1927
Kent	513 *at* Edgbaston	1928	16 *at* Tonbridge	1913
Lancashire	532-4 dec *at* Edgbaston	1901	49 *at* Edgbaston	1896
Leicestershire	605 *at* Leicester	1899	48 *at* Coventry (Bull's Head)	1919
Middlesex	507-6 dec *at* Lord's	1927	55 *at* Lord's	1956
Northamptonshire	565-8 dec *at* Northampton	1933	97 *at* Northampton	1923
Nottinghamshire	520 *at* Edgbaston	1930	49 *at* Edgbaston	1981
Somerset	494-5 dec *at* Edgbaston	1973	44 *at* Taunton	1906
Surrey	585-7 *at* The Oval	1905	45 *at* The Oval	1953
Sussex	517-9 dec *at* Leamington	1910	43 *at* Edgbaston	1982
Worcestershire	645-7 dec *at* Dudley	1914	66 *at* Edgbaston	1950
Yorkshire	536-7 dec *at* Edgbaston	1929	35 *at* Edgbaston	1963
			35 *at* Sheffield	1979

(2) HIGHEST AND LOWEST SCORE AGAINST WARWICKSHIRE BY EACH COUNTY

Opponents	*Highest*	*Year*	*Lowest*	*Year*
Derbyshire	561 *at* Derby	1902	39 *at* Edgbaston	1894
Essex	522-8 dec *at* Leyton	1930	47 *at* Leyton	1968
Glamorgan	524-9 dec *at* Edgbaston	1980	40 *at* Cardiff	1929
Gloucestershire	504 *at* Edgbaston	1898	56 *at* Bristol	1953
Hampshire	616-7 dec *at* Portsmouth	1920	15 *at* Edgbaston	1922
Kent	571 *at* Tonbridge	1898	42 *at* Edgbaston	1925
Lancashire	526 *at* Edgbaston	1920	70 *at* Old Trafford	1955
Leicestershire	438-3 *at* Edgbaston	1983	47 *at* Edgbaston	1900
Middlesex	543-7 dec *at* Lord's	1920	62 *at* Lord's	1932
Northamptonshire	419 *at* Edgbaston	1976	51 *at* Northampton	1989
Nottinghamshire	656-3 dec *at* Coventry (Bull's Head)	1928	34 *at* Nuneaton (G. & C.)	1964
Somerset	566-5 dec *at* Taunton	1985	50 *at* Edgbaston	1951
Surrey	634 *at* The Oval	1906	61 *at* The Oval	1962
Sussex	546-5 dec *at* Edgbaston	1937	23 *at* Worthing	1964
Worcestershire	633 *at* Worcester	1906	71 *at* Edgbaston	1903
			71 *at* Edgbaston	1949
Yorkshire	887 *at* Edgbaston	1896	49 *at* Huddersfield	1951

(3) HIGHEST AND LOWEST SCORES IN LIMITED-OVERS MATCHES

HIGHEST

Competition	*Score*	*Opponents and Venue*	*Year*
Sunday League	301-6 (39.3 overs)	Essex, Colchester	1982
Benson and Hedges Cup	308-4 (55 overs)	Scotland, Edgbaston	1988
Nat West/Gillette	392-5 (60 overs)	Oxfordshire, Edgbaston	1984

LOWEST

Competition	*Score*	*Opponents and Venue*	*Year*
Sunday League	65 (33.4 overs)	Kent, Maidstone	1979
Benson and Hedges Cup	96 (39.5 overs)	Leicestershire, Leicester	1972
Nat West/Gillette	109 (43 overs)	Kent, Canterbury	1971

INDIVIDUAL BATTING RECORDS

(1) DOUBLE CENTURIES IN FIRST-CLASS MATCHES

Score	*Batsman*	*Opponents*	*Venue*	*Year*
305*	F. R. Foster	Worcestershire	Dudley	1914
268*	S. P. Kinneir	Hampshire	Edgbaston	1911
255*	W. G. Quaife	Surrey	The Oval	1905
254	G. W. Humpage	Lancashire	Southport	1982
253	R. B. Kanhai	Nottinghamshire	Trent Bridge	1968
246	J. H. G. Devey	Derbyshire	Edgbaston	1900
243*	A. I. Kallicharran	Glamorgan	Edgbaston	1983
240*	J. A. Jameson	Gloucestershire	Edgbaston	1974
235	A. I. Kallicharran	Worcestershire	Worcester	1982
232*	D. L. Amiss	Gloucestershire	Bristol	1979
232	R. E. S. Wyatt	Derbyshire	Edgbaston	1937
231	J. A. Jameson	Indians	Edgbaston	1971
230*	R. B. Kanhai	Somerset	Edgbaston	1973
230*	A. I. Kallicharran	Lancashire	Southport	1982
228	N. Kilner	Worcestershire	Worcester	1935
225	J. H. Parsons	Glamorgan	Edgbaston	1927
223*	W. G. Quaife	Essex	Leyton	1900
222	J. F. Byrne	Lancashire	Edgbaston	1905
216	C. Charlesworth	Derbyshire	Blackwell Colliery	1910
215*	S. P. Kinneir	Lancashire	Edgbaston	1901
215*	F. C. Gardner	Somerset	Taunton	1950
213*	R. B. Kanhai	Gloucestershire	Edgbaston	1974

Score	Batsman	Opponents	Venue	Year
212	H. E. Dollery	Leicestershire	Edgbaston	1952
211	L. T. A. Bates	Gloucestershire	Gloucester	1932
211	A. J. W. Croom	Worcestershire	Edgbaston	1934
210	T. W. Cartwright	Middlesex	Nuneaton (G. & C.)	1962
210	A. I. Kallicharran	Leicestershire	Leicester	1982
209*	A. I. Kallicharran	Lancashire	Edgbaston	1983
209	F. S. Gough-Calthorpe	Hampshire	Edgbaston	1921
208*	T. A. Lloyd	Gloucestershire	Edgbaston	1983
207*	W. G. Quaife	Hampshire	Edgbaston	1899
206	C. Charlesworth	Yorkshire	Dewsbury	1914
205	G. W. Humpage	Derbyshire	Chesterfield	1984
203*	N. F. Horner	Surrey	The Oval	1960
201*	F. R. Santall	Northamptonshire	Northampton	1933
201*	R. E. S. Wyatt	Lancashire	Edgbaston	1937
200*	W. G. Quaife	Essex	Edgbaston	1904
200*	M. J. K. Smith	Worcestershire	Edgbaston	1959
200*	A. I. Kallicharran	Northamptonshire	Edgbaston	1984
200	F. R. Foster	Surrey	Edgbaston	1911
200	L. T. A. Bates	Worcestershire	Edgbaston	1928
200	H. E. Dollery	Gloucestershire	Gloucester	1949

(2) CENTURIES IN LIMITED-OVERS MATCHES

(a) Sunday League (John Player/Refuge Assurance)

Score	Batsman	Opponents	Venue	Year
123*	J. A. Jameson	Nottinghamshire	Trent Bridge	1973
120	R. B. Kanhai	Leicestershire	Edgbaston	1972
117*	D. L. Amiss	Sussex	Horsham	1981
112	R. B. Kanhai	Northamptonshire	Edgbaston	1971
111	J. A. Jameson	Lancashire	Edgbaston	1975
110	D. L. Amiss	Surrey	Edgbaston	1974
109*	G. W. Humpage	Gloucestershire	Edgbaston	1984
108*	G. W. Humpage	Middlesex	Edgbaston	1980
108	D. L. Amiss	Hampshire	Edgbaston	1981
108*	Asif Din	Essex	Chelmsford	1986
107*	D. L. Amiss	Nottinghamshire	Trent Bridge	1984
104	J. A. Jameson	Derbyshire	Buxton	1974
104	A. I. Kallicharran	Yorkshire	Headingly	1989
103	G. J. Lord	Derbyshire	Edgbaston	1985
102*	A. I. Kallicharran	Nottinghamshire	Edgbaston	1981
102	J. A. Jameson	Gloucestershire	Edgbaston	1976
102	R. B. Kanhai	Nottinghamshire	Edgbaston	1969
101*	A. I. Kallicharran	Derbyshire	Chesterfield	1972
101*	R. B. Kanhai	Kent	Edgbaston	1973
101	J. A. Jameson	Somerset	Edgbaston	1975
101	A. I. Kallicharran	Gloucestershire	Moreton-in-Marsh	1979
101	A. I. Kallicharran	Worcestershire	Edgbaston	1986
100	D. L. Amiss	Lancashire	Old Trafford	1974

(b) Benson and Hedges Cup

Score	*Batsman*	*Opponents*	*Venue*	*Year*
137*	T. A. Lloyd	Lancashire	Edgbaston	1985
122*	A. I. Kallicharran	Northamptonshire	Northampton	1984
119*	R. B. Kanhai	Northamptonshire	Northampton	1975
119*	A. I. Kallicharran	Derbyshire	Edgbaston	1983
115	D. L. Amiss	Leicestershire	Leicester	1984
113*	R. N. Abberley	Hampshire	Bournemouth	1976
109	A. I. Kallicharran	Gloucestershire	Bristol	1978
107	Asif Din	Scotland	Edgbaston	1988
105*	D. L. Amiss	Scotland	Edgbaston	1982
104	A. I. Kallicharran	Worcestershire	Worcester	1985
102*	R. Kanhai	Northamptonshire	Northampton	1974
100*	G. W. Humpage	Scotland	Edgbaston	1984

(c) NatWest Trophy/Gillette Cup

Score	*Batsman*	*Opponents*	*Venue*	*Year*
206	A. I. Kallicharran	Oxfordshire	Edgbaston	1984
141*	A. I. Kallicharran	Somerset	Taunton	1982
135	D. L. Amiss	Cambridgeshire	Edgbaston	1982
127	A. J. Moles	Buckinghamshire	Edgbaston	1987
126	R. B. Kanhai	Lincolnshire	Edgbaston	1971
121	T. A. Lloyd	Cambridgeshire	Edgbaston	1988
119	R. I. H. B. Dyer	Shropshire	Edgbaston	1984
114	R. W. Barber	Northamptonshire	Northampton	1964
113	D. L. Amiss	Glamorgan	Swansea	1966
113	R. W. Barber	Gloucestershire	Edgbaston	1966
113	K. D. Smith	Yorkshire	Edgbaston	1982
109	J. Whitehouse	Glamorgan	Edgbaston	1976
101	A. I. Kallicharran	Surrey	Edgbaston	1984
101	K. D. Smith	Oxfordshire	Edgbaston	1984
100*	J. A. Jameson	Hampshire	Edgbaston	1964

(3) CARRYING BAT THROUGH A COMPLETED FIRST-CLASS INNINGS

Batsman	*Score*	*Total*	*Opponents*	*Venue*	*Year*
H. W. Bainbridge	65*	(113)	Kent	Edgbaston	1894
W. G. Quaife	178*	(475)†	Hampshire	Southampton	1897
T. S. Fishwick	85*	(181)	Lancashire	Old Trafford	1907
S. P. Kinneir	70*	(239)	Leicestershire	Leicester	1907
S. P. Kinneir	69*	(166)	Leicestershire	Leicester	1907
(First and second innings of same match)					
S. P. Kinneir	65*	(164)	Somerset	Taunton	1908
J. H. Parsons	161*	(347)	Gloucestershire	Nuneaton (C.C.)	1913
L. T. A. Bates	96*	(207)	Surrey	The Oval	1921
L. T. A. Bates	50*	(125)††	Yorkshire	Huddersfield	1922
C. A. F. Fiddian-Green	60*	(123)††	Hampshire	Southampton	1922
N. Kilner	40*	(119)	Kent	Tunbridge Wells	1928
A. J. W. Croom	131*	(311)	Northamptonshire	Edgbaston	1929
A. J. W. Croom	58*	(120)	Gloucestershire	Cheltenham	1930
A. J. W. Croom	102*	(204)	Lancashire	Old Trafford	1931
A. J. W. Croom	69*	(133)	Leicestershire	Hinckley	1936
K. A. Taylor	81*	(222)	Yorkshire	Edgbaston	1948
F. C. Gardner	140*	(283)	Worcestershire	Edgbaston	1949
F. C. Gardner	73*	(133)	Glamorgan	Swansea	1950
F. C. Gardner	184*	(286)	Lancashire	Liverpool	1952
R. T. Spooner	98*	(210)	Worcestershire	Worcester	1952
F. C. Gardner	62*	(149)	Glamorgan	Edgbaston	1954
D. L. Amiss	160*	(315)†	West Indians	Edgbaston	1966
D. L. Amiss	122*	(273)	Essex	Colchester	1978
K. D. Smith	132*	(296)	Sussex	Edgbaston	1978
K. D. Smith	120*	(230)	Essex	Southend	1980
K. D. Smith	58*	(154)	Middlesex	Lord's	1981
T. A. Lloyd	124*	(230)	Surrey	The Oval	1983
A. J. Moles	67*	(107)††	Kent	Edgbaston	1988

†*Denotes 10 wickets in completed innings did not fall; one batsman retired or absent due to injury or illness*
††*Denotes two batsmen retired or absent due to injury or illness*

(4) CARRYING BAT THROUGH A COMPLETED LIMITED-OVERS INNINGS
(Full overs used)

(a) Sunday League

Batsman	*Score*	*Total*	*Opponents*	*Venue*	*Year*
G. W. Humpage	109*	215	Gloucestershire	Edgbaston	1984

(b) Benson and Hedges Cup

Batsman	*Score*	*Total*	*Opponents*	*Venue*	*Year*
R. N. Abberley	113*	245	Hampshire	Bournemouth	1976
T. A. Lloyd	137*	282	Lancashire	Edgbaston	1985

(5) CENTURY IN EACH INNINGS OF A FIRST-CLASS MATCH

Scores	*Batsman*	*Opponents*	*Venue*	*Year*
124 and 110	S. P. Kinneir	Sussex	Chichester	1911
124 and 109	W. G. Quaife	Surrey	The Oval	1913
100 and 101*	C. Charlesworth	Surrey	Edgbaston	1913
116 and 144	L. T. A. Bates	Kent	Coventry (Butts)	1927
107* and 101	J. S. Ord	Nottinghamshire	Trent Bridge	1948
113 and 101*	F. C. Gardner	Essex	Ilford	1950
155 and 125	W. J. Stewart	Lancashire	Blackpool	1959
126 and 105	B. A. Richardson	Cambridge University	Edgbaston	1967
155* and 112	D. L. Amiss	Worcestershire	Edgbaston	1978
109 and 127	D. L. Amiss	Derbyshire	Derby	1981
146 and 110	G. W. Humpage	Gloucestershire	Gloucester	1981
152 and 118*	A. I. Kallicharran	Sussex	Edgbaston	1983
200* and 117*	A. I. Kallicharran	Northamptonshire	Edgbaston	1984

(6) CENTURY ON FIRST-CLASS DEBUT FOR WARWICKSHIRE

Score	*Batsman*	*Opponents*	*Venue*	*Year*
139*	J. E. Hill	Nottinghamshire	Trent Bridge	1894
100	J. F. Byrne	Leicestershire	Edgbaston	1897
151	H. Venn	Worcestershire	Edgbaston	1919
173	J. Whitehouse	Oxford University	Oxford	1971
119	R. Kanhai	Cambridge University	Cambridge	1968

(Kanhai had previously appeared in much first-class and Test Cricket)

(7) 2,000 OR MORE FIRST-CLASS RUNS IN A SEASON FOR WARWICKSHIRE

Batsman	*Total*	*Year*	*Batsman*	*Total*	*Year*
M. J. K. Smith	2,417	1959	Khalid Ibadulla	2,098	1962
W. J. Stewart	2,318	1962	M. J. K. Smith	2,090	1962
A. I. Kallicharran	2,301	1984	H. E. Dollery	2,084	1949
D. L. Amiss	2,239	1984	R. E. S. Wyatt	2,075	1928
A. I. Kallicharran	2,120	1982	M. J. K. Smith	2,074	1957
N. Kilner	2,114	1933	H. E. Dollery	2,073	1952
M. J. K. Smith	2,099	1961	D. L. Amiss	2,030	1978

INDIVIDUAL BOWLING RECORDS

(1) HAT TRICKS IN FIRST-CLASS MATCHES

Bowler	*Opponents*	*Venue*	*Year*
E. F. Field	Hampshire	Edgbaston	1911
R. Cooke	Kent	Tunbridge Wells	1925
D. G. Foster	Hampshire	Edgbaston	1929
G. A. E. Paine	Middlesex	Lord's	1932
G. A. E. Paine	Glamorgan	Cardiff	1933
C. W. Grove	Somerset	Taunton	1947
T. L. Pritchard	Leicestershire	Edgbaston	1948
T. L. Pritchard	Kent	Maidstone	1949
T. L. Pritchard	Glamorgan	Edgbaston	1951
K. R. Dollery	Gloucestershire	Bristol	1953
J. D. Bannister	Yorkshire	Sheffield	1955
K. R. Dollery	Kent	Coventry (Courtaulds)	1956
R. G. Thompson	Sussex	Horsham	1956
R. W. Barber	Glamorgan	Edgbaston	1963
J. A. Jameson	Gloucestershire	Edgbaston	1965
A. C. Smith	Essex	Clacton	1965
T. W. Cartwright	Somerset	Edgbaston	1969
R. G. D. Willis	Derbyshire	Edgbaston	1972
R. G. D. Willis	West Indians	Edgbaston	1976
E. E. Hemmings	Worcestershire	Edgbaston	1977
T. A. Merrick	Derbyshire	Derby	1988
P. A. Smith	Northamptonshire	Northampton	1989

(2) NINE WICKETS PLUS IN AN INNINGS FOR WARWICKSHIRE

Analysis	*Bowler*	*Opponents*	*Venue*	*Year*
10-41	J. D. Bannister	Combined Services	Portland Road, B'ham	1959
10-49	W. E. Hollies	Nottinghamshire	Edgbaston	1946
10-51	H. Howell	Yorkshire	Edgbaston	1923
9-32	H. Howell	Hampshire	Edgbaston	1925
9-35	S. Hargreave	Surrey	The Oval	1903
9-35	H. Howell	Somerset	Taunton	1924
9-39	C. W. Grove	Sussex	Edgbaston	1952
9-35	J. D. Bannister	Yorkshire	Sheffield	1955
9-55	H. J. Pallett	Essex	Leyton	1894
9-56	W. E. Hollies	Northamptonshire	Edgbaston	1950
9-65	R. G. Thompson	Nottinghamshire	Edgbaston	1952
9-93	W. E. Hollies	Glamorgan	Edgbaston	1939
9-104	E. F. Field	Leicestershire	Leicester	1899
9-118	F. R. Foster	Yorkshire	Edgbaston	1911

(3) 15 WICKETS PLUS IN A MATCH FOR WARWICKSHIRE

Analysis	*Bowler*	*Opponents*	*Venue*	*Year*
15-76	S. Hargreave	Surrey	The Oval	1903
15-89	T. W. Cartwright	Glamorgan	Swansea	1967

(4) SIX WICKETS PLUS IN A LIMITED-OVERS MATCH

(a) Sunday League

Analysis	*Bowler*	*Opponents*	*Venue*	*Year*
6-20	N. Gifford	Northamptonshire	Edgbaston	1985

(b) Benson and Hedges Cup

Analysis	*Bowler*	*Opponents*	*Venue*	*Year*
7-32	R. G. D. Willis	Yorkshire	Edgbaston	1981

(c) NatWest/Gillette Cup

Analysis	*Bowler*	*Opponents*	*Venue*	*Year*
6-32	Khalid Ibadulla	Hampshire	Edgbaston	1965
6-32	A. I. Kallicharran	Oxfordshire	Edgbaston	1984

(5) 125 WICKETS IN A SEASON (100 since 1969)

Total	*Bowler*	*Year*	*Total*	*Bowler*	*Year*
128	S. Hargreave	1903	142	W. E. Hollies	1948
128	E. F. Field	1911	144	W. E. Hollies	1949
136	H. Howell	1920	126	W. E. Hollies	1950
152	H. Howell	1923	145	W. E. Hollies	1951
126	J. H. Mayer	1929	128	W. E. Hollies	1957
127	G. A. E. Paine	1931	131	J. D. Bannister	1961
136	G. A. E. Paine	1932	128	T. W. Cartwright	1964
155	G. A. E. Paine	1934	147	T. W. Cartwright	1967
127	W. E. Hollies	1935	131	L. R. Gibbs	1971
180	W. E. Hollies	1946	101	D. R. Doshi	1980
166	T. L. Pritchard	1948	104	N. Gifford	1983

RECORD WICKET PARTNERSHIPS

(1) IN FIRST-CLASS MATCHES

First Wicket (Qualification 250)

377*	N. F. Horner *and* Khalid Ibadulla *v* Surrey, The Oval	1960
333	J. F. Byrne *and* S. P. Kinneir *v* Lancashire, Edgbaston	1905
288	H. W. Bainbridge *and* W. G. Quaife *v* Hampshire, Southampton	1897
272	N. Kilner *and* A. J. W. Croom *v* Worcestershire, Edgbaston	1934
266	N. Kilner *and* E. J. Smith *v* Middlesex, Lord's	1927
257	J. A. Jameson *and* D. L. Amiss *v* Lancashire, Edgbaston	1973

Second Wicket (Qualification 250)

465*	J. A. Jameson *and* R. B. Kanhai *v* Gloucestershire, Edgbaston	1974
344	J. H. G. Devey *and* S. P. Kinneir *v* Derbyshire, Edgbaston	1900
318	D. L. Amiss *and* R. B. Kanhai *v* Lancashire, Edgbaston	1972
308	T. A. Lloyd *and* A. I. Kallicharran *v* Glamorgan, Edgbaston	1983
294	E. J. Smith *and* L. T. A. Bates *v* Kent, Coventry (Butts)	1927
293	T. A. Lloyd *and* A. I. Kallicharran *v* Lancashire, Edgbaston	1983
289	T. A. Lloyd *and* D. L. Amiss *v* Gloucestershire, Edgbaston	1983
263	D. L. Amiss *and* A. I. Kallicharran *v* Middlesex, Edgbaston	1974
255	D. L. Amiss *and* J. A. Jameson *v* Oxford University, Edgbaston	1964

Third Wicket (Qualification 250)

327	S. P. Kinneir *and* W. G. Quaife *v* Lancashire, Edgbaston	1901
287	W. A. Hill *and* R. E. S. Wyatt *v* Northamptonshire, Northampton	1939
282	J. Whitehouse *and* A. I. Kallicharran *v* Northamptonshire, Northampton	1979

Fourth wicket (Qualification 250)

470	A. I. Kallicharran *and* G. W. Humpage *v* Lancashire, Southport	1982
402	R. B. Kanhai *and* Khalid Ibadulla *v* Nottinghamshire, Trent Bridge	1968
319	R. E. S. Wyatt *and* H. E. Dollery *v* Lancashire, Edgbaston	1937
315	W. G. Quaife *and* J. H. Parsons *v* Glamorgan, Edgbaston	1927
279	A. J. Moles *and* G. W. Humpage *v* Glamorgan, Edgbaston	1989
275	F. C. Gardner *and* H. E. Dollery *v* Somerset, Coventry (Courtaulds)	1953
266*	J. Whitehouse *and* R. B. Kanhai *v* Yorkshire, Edgbaston	1976
262	D. L. Amiss *and* A. I. Kallicharran *v* Gloucestershire, Bristol	1979
253	R. E. S. Wyatt *and* H. E. Dollery *v* Derbyshire, Edgbaston	1937

Fifth Wicket (Qualification 200)

268	W. G. Quaife *and* Walter Quaife *v* Essex, Leyton	1900
266	R. E. S. Wyatt *and* A. J. W. Croom *v* Somerset, Edgbaston	1928
255*	J. A. Jameson *and* T. W. Cartwright *v* New Zealanders, Edgbaston	1965
228	C. S. Baker *and* A. F. A. Lilley *v* Worcestershire, Worcester	1907
224	A. I. Kallicharran *and* G. W. Humpage *v* Cambridge University, Cambridge	1986
219*	D. L. Amiss *and* R. B. Edmonds *v* Scotland, Edgbaston	1966
216	L. T. A. Bates *and* N. Kilner *v* Worcestershire, Edgbaston	1930
207	J. H. Parsons *and* A. J. W. Croom *v* West Indians, Edgbaston	1928
203	R. B. Kanhai *and* G. S. Warner *v* Northamptonshire, Peterborough	1969
203	A. I. Kallicharran *and* G. W. Humpage *v* Northamptonshire, Edgbaston	1984

Sixth Wicket (Qualification 200)

220 H. E. Dollery *and* J. Buckingham *v* Derbyshire, Derby 1938
204 W. G. Quaife *and* A. C. S. Glover *v* Worcestershire, Worcester 1908
204 H. E. Dollery *and* R. E. Hitchcock *v* Leicestershire, Edgbaston 1952

Seventh Wicket (Qualification 150)

250 H. E. Dollery *and* J. S. Ord *v* Kent, Maidstone 1953
244 T. W. Cartwright *and* A. C. Smith *v* Middlesex, Nuneaton (G. & C.) 1962
199 H. E. Dollery *and* T. Collins *v* Gloucestershire, Edgbaston 1935
194* W. G. Quaife *and* A. C. S. Glover *v* Hampshire, Edgbaston 1899
179 A. C. S. Glover *and* H. J. Goodwin *v* Sussex, Hove 1908
177 E. J. Diver *and* A. C. S. Glover *v* Leicestershire, Leicester 1897
175 A. M. Ferreira *and* R. G. D. Willis *v* Indians, Edgbaston 1982
170 T. W. Cartwright *and* A. C. Smith *v* Surrey, The Oval 1961
166 F. R. Foster *and* E. J. Smith *v* Worcestershire, Dudley 1914
165* W. G. Quaife *and* S. P. Kinneir *v* Hampshire, Edgbaston 1898
162 F. R. Santall *and* J. H. Parsons *v* Northamptonshire, Northampton 1933

Eighth Wicket (Qualification 150)

228 A. J. W. Croom *and* R. E. S. Wyatt *v* Worcestershire, Dudley 1925
203 G. W. Humpage *and* W. A. Bourne *v* Sussex, Edgbaston 1976
177 W. G. Quaife *and* A. E. M. Whittle *v* Essex, Edgbaston 1904
158 H. E. Dollery *and* K. Wilmot *v* Derbyshire, Edgbaston 1939
155 P. A. Smith *and* D. M. Smith *v* Oxford University, Edgbaston 1983

Ninth Wicket (Qualification 150)

154 A. J. W. Croom *and* G. W. Stephens *v* Derbyshire, Edgbaston 1925

Tenth Wicket (Qualification 100)

128 F. R. Santall *and* W. Sanders *v* Yorkshire, Edgbaston 1930
126 R. E. S. Wyatt *and* J. H. Mayer *v* Surrey, The Oval 1927
115 R. E. Hitchcock *and* R. B. Edmonds *v* Northamptonshire, Northampton 1964

(2) IN LIMITED OVERS MATCHES

(a) Sunday League

First Wicket (Qualification 150)

180* D. L. Amiss *and* J. A. Jameson *v* Nottinghamshire, Trent Bridge 1973
167 D. L. Amiss *and* J. A. Jameson *v* Derbyshire, Buxton 1974
158 D. L. Amiss *and* J. A. Jameson *v* Yorkshire, Edgbaston 1975
150 D. L. Amiss *and* A. I. Kallicharran *v* Gloucestershire, Moreton-in-Marsh 1979

Second Wicket (Qualification 150)

171 J. A. Jameson *and* J. Whitehouse *v* Worcestershire, Edgbaston 1973

Third Wicket (Qualifications 125)

163* A. I. Kallicharran *and* G. W. Humpage *v* Leicestershire, Leicester 1983
155 R. B. Kanhai *and* D. L. Amiss *v* Northamptonshire, Edgbaston 1971

Fourth Wicket (Qualification 125)

175★ M. J. K. Smith *and* D. L. Amiss *v* Yorkshire, Edgbaston 1970

Fifth Wicket (Qualification 100)

185★ Asif Din *and* B. M. McMillan *v* Essex, Chelmsford 1986
116★ D. A. Reeve *and* T. A. Lloyd *v* Glamorgan, Aberystwyth 1989

Sixth Wicket (Qualification 90)

91★ A. M. Ferreira *and* G. W. Humpage *v* Middlesex, Edgbaston 1980
90★ Asif Din *and* S. H. Wootton *v* Lancashire, Old Trafford 1982

Seventh Wicket

81★ A. M. Ferreira *and* P. A. Smith *v* Surrey, Edgbaston 1984

Eighth Wicket

83 W. Blenkiron *and* N. M. McVicker *v* Nottinghamshire, Edgbaston 1971

Ninth Wicket

48★ P. A. Smith *and* N. Gifford *v* Northamptonshire, Luton 1983

Tenth Wicket

50 A. C. Smith *and* D. J. Brown *v* Northamptonshire, Peterborough 1974

(b) Benson and Hedges Cup

First Wicket (Qualification 140)

141★ D. L. Amiss *and* K. D. Smith *v* Minor Counties West, Coventry (Courtaulds) 1977

Second Wicket

138 T. A. Lloyd *and* A. C. Storie *v* Yorkshire, Edgbaston 1987
138 T. A. Lloyd *and* Asif Din *v* Scotland, Edgbaston 1988

Third Wicket (Qualification 140)

147 Asif Din *and* A. I. Kallicharran *v* Scotland, Edgbaston 1988

Fourth Wicket (Qualification 150)

156 A. I. Kallicharran *and* G. W. Humpage *v* Worcestershire, Worcester 1985

Fifth Wicket (Qualification 100)

102 A. I. Kallicharran *and* P. A. Smith *v* Northamptonshire, Edgbaston 1989

Sixth Wicket (Qualification 100)

108★ R. B. Kanhai *and* P. R. Oliver *v* Worcestershire, Worcester 1977

Seventh Wicket

77★ T. A. Lloyd *and* S. J. Rouse *v* Glamorgan, Edgbaston 1978

Eighth Wicket

78 Asif Din *and* R. G. D. Willis *v* Nottinghamshire, Trent Bridge 1982

Ninth Wicket

24 D. J. Brown *and* R. G. D. Willis *v* Derbyshire, Ilkeston 1978
24 A. M. Ferreira *and* N. Gifford *v* Yorkshire, Edgbaston 1984

Tenth Wicket

42* W. A. Bourne *and* D. J. Brown *v* Northampton 1977

(c) NatWest Trophy/Gillette Cup

First Wicket (Qualification 140)

141 D. L. Amiss *and* T. A. Lloyd *v* Cambridgeshire, Edgbaston 1982

Second Wicket (Qualification 150)

197 K. D. Smith *and* A. I. Kallicharran *v* Oxfordshire, Edgbaston 1984
162 R. W. Barber *and* D. L. Amiss *v* Gloucestershire, Edgbaston 1966

Third Wicket (Qualification 150)

157 R. B. Kanhai *and* M. J. K. Smith *v* Lincolnshire, Edgbaston 1971
153 A. I. Kallicharran *and* D. L. Amiss *v* Somerset, Taunton 1982

Fourth Wicket (Qualification 150)

150 J. Whitehouse *and* G. W. Humpage *v* Somerset, Taunton 1978

Fifth Wicket (Qualification 120)

127 M. J. K. Smith *and* J. A. Jameson *v* Hampshire, Edgbaston 1964

Sixth Wicket

94 A. I. Kallicharran *and* N. M. McVicker *v* Glamorgan, Edgbaston 1972

Seventh Wicket

60* D. L. Amiss *and* A. C. Smith *v* Sussex, Lord's 1968

Eighth Wicket

69 S. J. Rouse *and* D. J. Brown *v* Middlesex, Lord's 1977

Ninth Wicket

62 Asif Din *and* G. C. Small *v* Surrey, Lord's 1982

Tenth Wicket

22 Asif Din *and* R. G. D. Willis *v* Surrey, Lord's 1982

WICKET-KEEPING RECORDS

(1) SIX DISMISSALS IN AN INNINGS

Keeper	*Total*	*Ct*	*St*	*Opponents and Venue*	*Year*
E. J. Smith	7	4	3	Derbyshire, Edgbaston	1926
A. F. A. Lilley	6	4	2	Worcestershire, Edgbaston	1906
J. Buckingham	6	5	1	Sussex, Edgbaston	1939
E. B. Lewis	6	6	0	Cambridge University, Cambridge	1956
R. T. Spooner	6	6	0	Nottinghamshire, Edgbaston	1957
A. C. Smith	6	6	0	Derbyshire, Derby	1970

(2) EIGHT DISMISSALS IN A MATCH

Keeper	*Total*	*Ct*	*St*	*Opponents and Venue*	*Year*
E. B. Lewis	9	8	1	Oxford University, Edgbaston	1949
A. F. A. Lilley	8	8	0	MCC, Lord's	1896
A. F. A. Lilley	8	8	0	Kent, Edgbaston	1897
E. J. Smith	8	5	3	Derbyshire, Edgbaston	1926
E. J. Smith	8	7	1	Worcestershire, Edgbaston	1930
R. T. Spooner	8	8	0	Leicestershire, Edgbaston	1959
G. W. Humpage	8	8	0	Lancashire, Edgbaston	1989

(3) 70 DISMISSALS IN A SEASON

Keeper	*Year*	*Total*	*Ct*	*St*	*Matches*
G. W. Humpage	1985	80	76	4	25
J. A. Smart	1932	79	56	23	28
A. C. Smith	1962	77	74	3	32
R. T. Spooner	1951	73	53	20	27
R. T. Spooner	1952	70	54	16	28

(4) 400 DISMISSALS IN A CAREER

Keeper	*Total*	*Ct*	*St*	*Career*
E. J. Smith	800	662	138	1904–1930
R. T. Spooner	682	527	155	1948–1959
G. W. Humpage	674	602	72	1974–1989
A. F. A. Lilley	632	500	132	1894–1911
A. C. Smith	596	557	39	1958–1974

(NB Every effort has been made to include only those catches taken while wicket-keeping)

FIELDING RECORDS

(1) FIVE CATCHES IN AN INNINGS

Fielder	*Opponents*	*Venue*	*Year*
M. J. K. Smith (6)	Leicestershire	Hinckley	1962
T. S. Fishwick	South Africans	Edgbaston	1904
M. J. K. Smith	Glamorgan	Swansea	1961
J. A. Jameson	Indians	Edgbaston	1971
J. Whitehouse	Oxford University	Oxford	1975
A. C. Storie	Leicestershire	Edgbaston	1988

(2) SEVEN CATCHES IN A MATCH

Fielder	*Opponents*	*Venue*	*Year*
H. E. Dollery	Hampshire	Portsmouth	1953
J. Whitehouse	Oxford University	Oxford	1975

(3) 40 CATCHES IN A SEASON

Fielder	*Total*	*Year*
M. J. K. Smith	52	1961
M. J. K. Smith	48	1962
R. Miller	44	1963
M. J. K. Smith	43	1959
Khalid Ibadulla		1964
A. Townsend	42	1953
A. Townsend	41	1951
Khalid Ibadulla		1962
T. S. Fishwick	40	1905

(4) THREE HUNDRED CATCHES FOR WARWICKSHIRE

Fielder	*Total*	*Career*
M. J. K. Smith	422	1956–1975
A. Townsend	409	1948–1960
D. L. Amiss	352	1960–1987
W. G. Quaife	332	1894–1928
Khalid Ibadulla	314	1954–1972

WARWICKSHIRE PLAYERS' TEST RECORDS

Name	*Country*	*Tests*	*M*	*Runs*	*Avge*	*Wkts*	*Avge*
D. L. Amiss	England	1966–77	50	3,612	46.30	—	—
R. W. Barber	England	1960–68	28	1,459	35.59	42	43.00
S. F. Barnes	England	1901/02–13/14	27	242	8.06	189	16.43
D. J. Brown	England	1965–69	26	342	11.79	79	28.31
T. W. Cartwright	England	1964–65	5	26	5.20	15	36.26
C. S. Dempster	N. Zealand	1929/30–32/33	10	723	65.72	0	—
H. E. Dollery	England	1947–50	4	72	10.28	—	—
M. P. Donnelly	N. Zealand	1937–49	7	582	52.90	0	—
D. R. Doshi	India	1979/80–83/84	33	129	4.60	114	30.71
F. R. Foster	England	1911/12–12	11	330	23.57	45	20.57
L. R. Gibbs	W. Indies	1957/58–75/76	79	488	6.97	309	29.09
N. Gifford	England	1964–73	15	179	16.27	33	31.09
F. S. Gough-Calthorpe	England	1929/30	4	129	18.42	1	91.00
E. E. Hemmings	England	1982–89	9	280	25.45	16	59.81
W. E. Hollies	England	1934/35–50	13	37	5.28	44	30.27
H. Howell	England	1920/21–24	5	15	7.50	7	79.85
J. A. Jameson	England	1971–73/74	4	214	26.75	1	17.00
A. I. Kallicharran	W. Indies	1971/72–80/81	66	4,399	44.43	4	39.50
R. B. Kanhai	W. Indies	1957–73/74	79	6,227	47.53	0	—
A. H. Kardar	India/Pakistan	1946–57/58	26	927	23.76	21	45.42
Khalid Ibadulla	Pakistan	1964/65–67	4	253	31.62	1	99.00
S. P. Kinneir	England	1911/12	1	52	26.00	—	—
E. Leadbeater	England	1951/52	2	40	20.00	2	109.00
A. F. A. Lilley	England	1896–1909	35	903	20.52	1	23.00
T. A. Lloyd	England	1984	1	10	—	—	
D. L. Murray	W. Indies	1963–80	62	1,993	22.90	—	—
C. M. Old	England	1972/73–81	46	845	14.82	143	28.11
G. A. E. Paine	England	1934/35	4	97	16.16	17	27.47
W. G. Quaife	England	1899–1900/01	7	228	19.00	0	—
G. C. Small	England	1986–89	6	120	24.00	24	27.16
A. C. Smith	England	1962/63	6	118	29.50	—	—
E. J. Smith	England	1911/12–13/14	11	113	8.69	—	—
M. J. K. Smith	England	1958–72	50	2,278	31.63	1	128.00
R. T. Spooner	England	1951/52–55	7	354	27.23	—	—
D. D. Taylor	N. Zealand	1946/47–55/56	3	159	31.80	—	—
R. G. D. Willis	England	1970/71–84	90	840	11.50	325	25.20
R. E. S. Wyatt	England	1927/28–36/37	40	1,839	31.70	18	35.66

WARWICKSHIRE'S OFFICIAL CAPTAINS

1894–date	
1894–1901	H. W. Bainbridge
1902	H. W. Bainbridge and T. S. Fishwick
1903–1906	J. F. Byrne
1907	J. F. Byrne and T. S. Fishwick
1908–1909	A. C. S. Glover
1910	H. J. Goodwin
1911–1914	F. R. Foster
1919	G. W. Stephens
1920–1929	Hon. F. S. Gough-Calthorpe
1930–1937	R. E. S. Wyatt
1938–1947	P. Cranmer
1948	R. H. Maudsley and H. E. Dollery
1949–1955	H. E. Dollery
1956	W. E. Hollies
1957–1967	M. J. K. Smith
1968–1974	A. C. Smith
1975–1977	D. J. Brown
1978–1979	J. Whitehouse
1980–1984	R. G. D. Willis
1985–1987	N. Gifford
1988–	T. A. Lloyd

WARWICKSHIRE CRICKETERS TO BE AWARDED A BLUE

AT OXFORD

J. M. Allan 1953, 1954, 1955, 1956
J. A. Claughton 1976, 1977, 1978, 1979
M. P. Donnelly 1946, 1947
E. P. Hewetson 1923, 1924, 1925
R. L. Holdsworth 1919, 1920, 1921, 1922
A. K. C. Jones 1971, 1972, 1973
A. H. Kardar 1947, 1948, 1949
J. C. M. Lowe 1907, 1908, 1909
R. H. Maudsley 1946, 1947
R. Sale 1939, 1946
R. le Q. Savage 1976, 1977, 1978
A. C. Smith 1958, 1959, 1960
M. J. K. Smith 1954, 1955, 1956
S. P. Sutcliffe 1980, 1981
D. A. Thorne 1984, 1985, 1986

AT CAMBRIDGE

H. W. Bainbridge 1884, 1885, 1886
R. W. Barber 1956, 1957
C. A. F. Fiddian-Green 1921, 1922
M. N. Field 1974
H. J. Goodwin 1907, 1908
F. S. Gough-Calthorpe 1912, 1913, 1914, 1919
T. E. N. Jameson 1970
G. D. Kemp-Welch 1929, 1930, 1931
J. I. McDowall 1969
J. M. Mills 1946, 1947, 1948
D. L. Murray 1965, 1966
N. E. Partridge 1920
G. A. Rotherham 1919
Swaranjit Singh 1955, 1956
C. R. V. Taylor 1971, 1972, 1973
J. R. Thompson 1938, 1939
O. S. Wheatley 1957, 1958
A. F. T. White 1936

BROTHERS WHO HAVE REPRESENTED WARWICKSHIRE

L. T. A. Bates, S. H. Bates
D. R. Cook, M. S. Cook
A. C. Curle, G. Curle
A. W. Foster, F. R. Foster
A. J. Harris, W. H. Harris
H. B. G. Hill, J. E. Hill
A. L. Howell, H. Howell
J. A. Jameson, T. E. N. Jameson
A. G. B. Old, C. M. Old
W. Quaife, W. G. Quaife
C. C. Smart, J. A. Smart
K. D. Smith, P. A. Smith
F. G. Stephens, G. W. Stephens

FATHERS AND SONS WHO HAVE REPRESENTED WARWICKSHIRE

Father *Son*
A. J. W. Croom—L. C. B. Croom
W. G. Quaife—B. W. Quaife
D. P. Ratcliffe—J. D. Ratcliffe
S. Santall—F. R. Santall
M. J. K. Smith—N. M. K. Smith
C. J. Taylor—F. Taylor

SELECT BIBLIOGRAPHY

Robert Brooke and David Goodyear: *A Who's Who of Warwickshire County Cricket Club* (Robert Hale Ltd, 1989)

Tom Duckworth: *The Story of Warwickshire Cricket* (Stanley Paul & Co. Ltd, 1974)

Barry Griffiths: *A Warwickshire Cricket Chronicle* (The Book Guild Ltd, 1988)

Ken Kelly: *Cricket Reflections* (David & Charles, Inc., 1985)

Warwickshire County Cricket Club *Annual Reports*

ACKNOWLEDGEMENTS

The author would like to thank Warwickshire CCC for their co-operation in giving access to their Annual Reports.

Thanks are also due to Robert Brooke, who compiled the Statistical Section.

INDEX

Abberley, R. Neal 4, 192–3, 196, 200, 206, 219, 227, 231, 234–5
Adderley, Charles H. 111, 114–15
Amiss, Dennis L.
as batsman 201, 219, 223, 227, 243, 249–50, 256, 265
debut 176–7, 181, 185, 234
final season 261, 262–5, 270–2
Packer affaii 226–31
in Test matches 199–200, 216
1000 runs 190, 195, 198, 206, 212, 232, 240, 244, 246, 248, 253
Ansell, William 33, 72
club status 20, 23–4, 29, 46, 47, 65
cricket ground 15–18, 148, 191
formation of club 9–11, 13–14
resignation of 47–8, 50
as secretary 26–8, 36, 43
and Shilton 30–1
Asif Din, M. 240, 243–4, 267, 270, 272, 275
Austin, George 146, 186

Bainbridge, H. W. 18–20, 25–6, 30, 33, 104
as batsman 36–7, 39, 53, 94
as captain 34–5, 40, 42–3
as chairman 91, 97, 99, 102
and club status 24, 28–9
debut 22–3
as secretary 50, 58
Baker, Chrles S. 51, 62, 65, 70, 72, 74
Barber, Robert W. 4, 6–7, 179, 192, 199
as bowler 185, 187–8
debut 176, 184–5
as part-time cricketer 193, 198, 209, 235
in Test matches 190–1, 199–200
Barnes, Dr Stanley 157–8
Bates, Leonard T. A. 67, 98, 209
as batsman 71, 81, 84–5, 87–8, 90–1
as captain 94, 96
Bates, John 22, 35, 66
Bedser, Alec 150, 180, 200
Bennett, Lord 161, 169
Blakemore, David 148, 272
Blenkiron, William 5, 198, 206–7, 210, 219–20
Botham, Ian T. 69, 238, 241, 243, 260, 265
Breedon, Frank 17, 22
Bridge, W. Basil 3–4, 159, 173, 176, 179, 183, 187
Bromley, P. H. 119, 123, 128–9, 146, 148, 157
Brown, David J. 2, 4–7, 72, 192,
benefit match 218
as bowler 186–7, 193, 197, 201, 206, 212, 216, 219, 243
as captain 210, 220, 222–4, 226–7
debut 176–, 179, 183
in dispute 252, 261, 263–5, 267
injury 184, 205, 207
as manager 232, 234–5, 239–40, 244–6, 255, 257, 260, 262, 269
in Test matches 190–1, 199–200
Buchanan, David 9, 12–18, 26, 42
Buckingham, John 96, 104–5, 111, 267
Byrne, J. F. 49–52, 54, 60

Cannings, Victor H. D. 115, 117, 121, 128
Carter, Raymond G. 2, 129, 143, 153, 167, 171
Cartland, George H. 17–18, 47–8, 52, 58, 65, 91
Cartwright, Thomas W. 3–5, 7, 157, 201
as batsman 171, 173, 176, 178, 184
benefit match 198–9
as bowler 148–9, 163, 168, 183, 186–7, 193, 195–7, 203, 206, 234
contract 143, 180, 202, 204
in Test matches 190, 200
Charlesworth, Crowther 41, 43–5, 50, 65, 70, 74–5
as batsman 57, 59, 63, 67, 85, 98, 229
benefit match 73, 122
Claughton, John A. 237–9
Close Brian 36, 143, 159, 195–6
Copson, Bill 101, 104
Cottam, Bob 265–9
Cowan, C. F. R. 58, 113, 127, 172
Cranmer, Perer 49, 96, 102–3, 105, 124
as captain 111, 113, 117–18, 162, 206
Crook, Winifred 148, 271
Croom, A. J. W. 87–8, 92, 100, 103, 111, 117
Cumbes, James 259–64

Deakins, Leslie Thomas 36, 93, 108, 222, 275
as administrator 105, 107–9, 139–41, 147–8, 158, 170, 225–6, 247
Dempster, C. S. 106, 111, 113
Devey, J. H. G. 43, 52–3
Diver, Edwin J. 27, 30, 94, 164
Docker, Ludford C. 19, 21, 25–6, 30, 32–3, 72, 84, 91, 170
Dollery, H. E. 'Tom' 3, 92–3, 136, 138, 142, 172, 267
as batsman 96, 98–101, 103–5, 111, 113–14, 116–18, 159–60
benefit match 123
as captain 63, 119, 121, 124–5, 127, 130–2, 140–1, 144–6, 149–53, 157–8, 161
on Grove 155–6
on Hollies 169
retirement 168, 204
Dollery, Keith R. 134, 148, 150, 159, 163, 175, 183
Donald, Allan A. 267, 270, 274, 275
Donnelly, Martin P. 119, 121, 123
Doshi, Dilip R. 4, 236–8, 240–1
Dyer, Robin I. H. B. 248, 253, 258

Edgell, George 78, 87
Evans, R. F. 252, 261, 264, 269

Fantham, William E. 101, 111, 123
Ferreira, Anthonie M. 232, 237–8, 240–1, 243, 245, 247–9, 253, 257–8
Field, E. Frank 38, 65, 74
as bowler 37, 41–5, 50–1, 54, 57, 60–1, 63–4, 67–70
injury 52, 62
Fishwick, Tom S. 37, 41, 43, 51–3, 94, 133, 164, 258
Flack, Bernard 158, 191
Foster, Derek G. 88, 90, 92, 239
Foster, Frank R. 38, 41, 44, 69–70, 72, 172
as bowler 53–7, 60–1, 63–4, 66–7, 83, 181
as captain 58–9, 62, 65, 68, 74

Gardner, Fred C. 1–3, 119, 138, 142, 233
as batsman 100, 117, 120, 126, 131, 135, 140, 150–1, 156, 159, 166
benefit match 171
as bowler 144–6
injury 162, 176–7
retirement 178, 180
Gibbs, Lancelot R. 4–5, 197–8, 201, 206–8, 210–11, 215–18
Gifford, Norman 4, 7, 244–7, 249–50, 253–7, 259–62, 264, 269–70
Glover, A. C. S. 39, 41, 45, 54, 56–7, 94, 133
Goodway, Cyril C. 106, 111, 113–14, 116, 147, 172, 191, 196
as chairman 215, 230–1, 233, 247
Goodwin, Harold J. 57, 70, 162
Gough-Calthorpe, Lord F. H. A. 17, 52
Gough-Calthorpe, Hon. F. S. G. 71–3, 75–7, 79–82, 85, 87–9
Gough-Calthorpe, Brig. Sir R.A. 223, 232
Grace, W. G. 12, 14–15, 19, 22, 37, 70, 86–7, 265
Grove, Charles W. 1, 111, 121, 130–1, 144–6, 153–5, 245
benefit match 138–9
as bowler 105–6, 115–17, 120, 125, 130, 132, 135–6, 140
Hollies and 149–50

Hammond, Walter 71, 93, 97, 106, 114, 172, 265
Hampton, Ted 153, 215, 239
Hargreave, Sam 41–5, 49–50, 52–4, 56, 89, 196
Hassett, Lindsay 151–2, 188
Hastilow, C. Alexander F. 102, 111–12, 119, 122, 191, 222–3
as chairman 123, 143, 147, 153–5, 172, 183–4
Hayward, Tom 27, 32, 46, 54, 86,
Heath, David M. W. 129, 132, 149, 252, 259–64
Hemmings, Edward E. 5, 219, 222, 224–5, 227, 231
Hiley, Edgar 136–7, 147, 155, 233
Hill, Geoffrey H. 4, 171, 176, 178
Hill, J. Ernest 32, 43, 172, 186
Hill, W. Aubrey 105, 115, 117, 123, 159, 179
Hitchcock, Raymond E. 4, 129, 132, 135, 138, 142, 149, 169
as batsman 139–41, 144, 150, 156, 159, 162, 258
retirement 186, 189–90, 204
1000 runs 176, 178, 181, 185
Hobbs, J. 64, 69, 79, 265
Hoffman, Dean S. 238, 252, 254
Hogg, William 239, 243, 248
Hollies, W. Eric 1, 3–4, 142, 144–5, 172
as batsman 101, 111
benefit match 73, 119, 122
as bowler 33, 97–8, 104, 113–18, 120, 126, 129–30, 134–40, 151, 156–7, 199, 234
as captain 162–4
and club 204, 233
contract 92–4
final season 167–9
and Grove 149–50
100 wickets 42, 105–6, 132, 146
injury 148–9
in Test matches 96, 121
on Wyatt 99–100
Horner, Norman F 1–2, 98, 148, 169, 177
benefit match 185–6
century 146, 150, 164
retirement 189–90
1000 runs 149, 156, 159, 162, 163, 167, 171, 173, 176, 178, 181, 187
Howell Henry 38, 68, 71, 73, 76–9, 81–4, 90, 114, 120
Humpage, Geoffrey W. 1, 237, 267
as allrounder 218–19, 223
as batsman 231, 236, 243–4, 246, 265, 273, 275
century 235, 249–50, 259
1000 runs 224, 227, 236, 238, 240, 243–4, 259
as wicket keeper 91, 232, 236, 253–4, 271
Hyde, Sir Charles 91, 98, 102, 106

Jameson, John A. 4, 6, 191–2, 218, 220
as batsman 195, 212, 219, 223
debut 176, 181, 185
final season 224–5
1000 runs 187, 190, 196, 198, 206–7, 216
Jeeves, Percy 67–70, 74
Jervis, Col W. Swynfen 9, 14–15
Jessop, Gilbert L. 39, 46, 65

Kallicharran, Alvin I. 5–6, 210
as batsman 218, 236–8, 243–4, 250
century 239, 242, 246, 274
injury 231, 271
as overseas players 212, 215–16, 240, 257–9, 267
Packer affair 226–7
1000 runs 219, 223, 232, 248
Kanhai, Rohan B. 5, 210, 220
as batsman 101, 197–8, 205–6, 218–19, 224, 227–8, 244
as overseas player 215–16
1000 runs 201, 207, 212, 222
Kardar, Abdul H. 119, 122, 125, 132, 134
Kemp-Welch, G. D. 91–2, 96
Khalid Ibadulla 4, 7, 192, 202
as batsman 98, 167, 171, 176–7, 179, 198, 258
retirement 215
1000 runs 181, 187, 196

Kilner, Norman 83–4, 87–8, 94, 101, 103, 233
King, Edmund H. 183, 191, 202, 215, 241–2
King, Ian M. 143, 157, 159, 161–2, 179
Kinneir, Septimus P. 64–6, 74
as batsman 37, 39–40, 42–4, 51–3, 59–63, 67, 85
retirement 70, 100

Langley, Colin K. 70, 109, 112, 115, 122
Leese, Lt-General Sir Oliver 191, 223, 231
Lewington, Peter J. 5, 218, 222
Lewis, Esmond B. 129, 160, 168, 171,
Lilley, A. F. A. 'Dick' 21–2, 33, 43, 89
as batsman 27, 52, 56–7, 59
benefit match 44, 54
contract 40, 50
injury 24–5, 53
retirement 62, 65
in Test Match 41, 46
as wicket keeper 23, 37, 45
Lloyd, T. Andrew 231–2, 234, 236–8, 240, 243–4, 246–9, 253, 259, 267–70, 274

McDowall, James I. 147, 216, 233, 252
McMillan, Brian M. 255, 257–9
McVicker, Norman M. 5, 201, 207, 210–11, 213, 217
Martineua, Sir Thomas 16–17
Maudsley, Ronald H. 118–20, 241–2
Maul, H. C. 17, 22
Mayer. J. H. 111, 241–2
benefit match 91, 94, 100
as bowler 83, 87–8, 90, 92, 96, 101–2, 105, 234
Mead, Phil 60, 64, 76–7, 86, 265
Merrick, T. Anthony 267, 270, 274
Miller, Roland 4, 179, 183, 185, 187, 191, 193
Moles, Andrew J. 259, 265, 267, 270, 273, 274
Mordaunt, Revd Osbert 13–14
Munton, Timothy A. 258, 270, 275
Muray, Deryck L. 5, 210, 212, 215–19, 237

Oakman, Alan 204, 234, 269
Old, Christopher M. 228, 244–8, 253
Oliver, Phillip R. 223, 237–40
Ord, James S. 111, 132, 138, 142, 161–2
as batsman 98, 105, 116, 118, 120–1, 125–6, 140–1, 144–5

Paine, George A. E. 88, 90, 92–4, 96–8, 100, 105, 231
Pallett, H. J. 37
as bowler 21, 27–8, 32–3, 35–6, 39
and Shilton 15, 19, 23, 25, 70
Parks, Jim 175, 179, 248
Parsons, John H. 59, 65, 74, 88
as batsman 60, 67–8, 70–1, 79, 81–7, 90, 137
as captain 91, 96, 97
contract 72, 78
Partridge, Norman E. 78, 84, 89, 96, 245
Perryman, Stephen P. 5, 222, 227, 231–2, 238
Pritchard, Thomas L. 1–2, 111, 126, 142, 146, 163
as batsman 117, 125, 130–2, 139
as bowler 115–16, 120, 135, 138, 144–5, 149, 153
retirement 157, 161–2

Quaife, Walter G. 24, 27, 30, 33, 39–41, 43, 45, 52–3
Quaife, Willis G. 24, 30, 33, 74, 78, 86–7, 141
as batsman 27, 32, 37–40, 42, 51, 56, 59, 61–7, 79, 81, 84–5
as bowler 43–4, 70, 73
contract 50, 72
in dispute 52–3, 76
games for club 83, 91, 102
records, cricketing 149, 156, 246
in Test Matches 45–6, 191

Reeve, Dermot A. 270, 272, 275
Rhodes, Wilfred 39, 46–7, 64, 83, 86, 265
Richards, Walter 24, 50–1
Rotherham, Hugh 14–16, 19, 21
Rouse, Stephen J. 5, 210, 219, 222, 224, 227, 232, 238, 241

Ryder, R. V.
as administrator 36–7, 40, 47–8, 56, 71, 93, 105, 107, 128
contract 50
and finances 52, 58
on Foster 69–70
on Pallett and Shilton 19
presentation to 66, 80, 97
on Willis Quaife 86
and Test Matches 45–6
and Wyatt 91, 99, 101

Santall, F. Reginald 97, 111, 133
as batsman 77, 81, 83, 88, 90, 94, 103, 105, 164
Santall, Sydney 30, 41–2, 54, 65, 74, 91, 170
as batsman 45, 56
as bowler 33–5, 39, 53, 57, 61, 70, 234
contract 25, 50–1
Scorer, Lt-Col 'Rusty' 105–7, 109
Shilton, John E. 30–1, 122
as bowler 17–18, 22, 27–8, 32–3, 35
and Pallett 15, 19, 23, 25, 70
Shrewsbury, Arthur 21, 25, 27, 49, 58
Small, Gladstone G. 237–8, 243, 245, 248, 253, 255, 261, 267, 270–1, 275
Smart, John A. 92, 253
Smith, Alan C. 4–5, 7, 192, 199, 201, 217
as batsman 181–2, 184
as captain 190, 197–8, 203, 207, 209–10, 214, 216, 218
retirement 220–1
as secretary 222, 247, 254–5, 259–60, 269
as wicket keeper 177–9
Smith, David M. 224, 231–2, 238, 240, 242–4, 246
Smith, E. J. 'Tiger' 50, 65, 70, 73–4, 85, 146, 163, 172, 233
as batsman 60–1, 63, 81–2, 87–8, 90, 94
as coach 111, 115, 118, 129, 192
contract 72, 91
in Test matches 64, 66–8
as wicket keeper 54, 56–7, 59, 77, 84, 271

Smith Michael J. K. 112, 166, 169, 179, 192, 210, 246, 260, 265
as captain 102, 165, 172, 184, 186–7, 194–5
comeback 203, 206, 208, 216
contract 162, 164
final season 222–3, 227
retirement 190, 197
in Test Matches 171, 175–7, 180, 191
1000 runs 181, 212, 248
Smith, Paul A. 246, 252, 259, 267, 270, 275
Snow, John 7, 201, 236, 238
Spofforth, F. R. 14–16
Spooner, Richard T. 1, 136, 138, 142
as batsman 130, 137, 140–1, 144–6, 258
final season 171, 173–4
injury 157, 167–8
1000 runs 132, 135, 149, 156, 159
as wicket keeper 119, 121, 126, 164
Stephens, Frank G. 61–2, 65
Stephens, G. W. 65, 71–3, 133, 162
Steven, Tony 248, 253, 260–2, 264, 268
Stewart, W. James P. 4, 157, 163, 174, 197
as batsman 167, 177–8, 187, 190, 193, 229
injury 184–5
retirement 201–2, 204
1000 runs 173, 176, 181, 198
Sutcliffe, Herbert 79, 83, 90, 106, 239, 265
Taylor, Derief D. S. 3, 127, 223, 225, 267
Taylor, Donald D. 130–1, 135, 142, 144, 239
Taylor, Kenneth A. 111, 116, 120, 128
Thompson, John R. 111, 113, 117, 121, 126, 132, 258
Thompson Roland G. 2, 123, 128, 142–3, 153, 183
as bowler 135, 140–1, 144–6, 159, 163, 173, 176, 179
Thwaite, Dr Harold 91–2, 96–7, 102, 170
as chairman 104–5
as president 106, 109, 123, 127–8, 134–5, 140, 142, 154, 158
Tidy, Warwick N. 5, 159, 206–7, 210
Townsend, Alan 1, 119, 125–6, 136, 138, 142, 160, 169, 180–1
as batsman 132, 140, 150, 159, 176–8
as bowler 120–1, 135, 145–6
1000 runs 149, 156, 167, 173
Tyldesley, Johhny T. 37–8, 46, 59, 86, 265

Waddy, Revd E. F. 71, 73, 172
Warner, Pelham, F. 39, 57, 64, 66–7, 69, 106, 141
Warwick, Earl of 12, 50, 52, 65, 142, 170
Webster, Rudi V. 3, 184, 192–3
Weeks, Raymond T. 1, 129, 134–5, 138–9, 145–6, 159, 179
Wheatley, Oswald S. 3, 169, 173, 176–9, 183
Whitehead, S. J. 27–8, 30, 32–3, 35, 50–1
Whitehouse, John 4, 6, 206–7, 210, 218, 259
as batsman 212, 223–4, 227, 236
as captain 228, 231–2
final season 238–9
Willis, Robert G. D. 5, 8, 210, 213, 239, 260
as bowler 212, 215, 217, 219, 222, 232, 237–8, 246
as captain 234–5, 241, 243, 250–1
in dispute 252, 262–4, 269
injury 224, 248
Packer affair 226–8, 231, 245
Willoughbly de Broke, Lord 9, 17, 19, 45, 141
Wolton, Albert V. G. 1, 142, 178
as batsman 117, 121, 130, 132, 139, 163–4, 176
as bowler 144–5, 151
retirement 180–1
1000 runs 135, 149, 156, 159, 162, 171, 173
Woodroffe, A. 119, 123
Wright, Albert 3–4, 182–4
Wyatt, R. E. S. 78, 81, 105–6, 109, 118, 265
as batsman 84, 87–8, 137, 149, 156, 176, 244
as bowler 79, 83, 85
as captain 89–98
dismissal of 99–102, 107, 111–12